Diesel & El LOCu REGISTER

FOURTH EDITION

Andy Chard

Published by Platform 5 Publishing Ltd,
52 Broadfield Road, Sheffield, S8 0XJ, England.

Printed in England by The Lavenham Press Ltd, Lavenham, Suffolk.

ISBN 978 1 909431 67 6

▲ D182 was delivered new to Gateshead depot in 1962, later renumbered 46045 under TOPS and subsequently 97404 while in departmental use. The locomotive is now preserved and has reverted to its original number. On 21 May 2016 a token exchange is about to take place as D182 approaches Arley with the 0955 Kidderminster–Bridgnorth during the Severn Valley Railway Diesel Festival, one of its many appearances at heritage railways in recent years. **Andy Chard**

CONTENTS

Front Cover Photograph (top): Looking impressive at the head of a full rake of National Express stock, 90003 "Raedwald of East Anglia" heads south past Mellis with the 09.30 Norwich–London Liverpool Street on 4 March 2008.   **John Chalcraft/Rail Photoprints**

Front Cover Photograph (bottom): 31105 is one of a small number of locomotives operated by national infrastructure operator, Network Rail. On 4 May 2015, wearing NR's conspicuous yellow livery, it stands at Derby at the head of a short rake of departmental coaching stock with another Class 31 at the rear.   **Rail Photoprints Collection**

Back Cover Photograph: Class 27/0 27056 is seen stabled at Falkland Junction, Ayr on 4 August 1984. This locomotives had previously been classified as Class 27/1 whilst fitted with push-pull equipment for operation between Edinburgh and Glasgow.   **Richard Priestley/Rail Photoprints**

PREFACE

There has been a massive amount of change on Britain's railways since the third edition of Diesel and Electric Loco Register was published in 1994, with vast differences to diesel and electric locomotive duties, locations and the number of locomotives in existence. In 1994 locomotives on the national rail network were all operated by British Rail (BR), with plenty of passenger services still being locomotive-hauled. There were very few preserved diesel and electric locomotives. Since then both of these situations have reversed; BR has been privatised and although many new passenger trains have been introduced in the decades since, most have been multiple units, leading to a second great wave of locomotive withdrawals. Over the same period the preservation and heritage railway movements have exploded, with railways, preservation groups and individuals operating and restoring many ex-BR locomotives. In more recent years, there has been a largely unforeseen return of locomotives back onto the main line, with a number of Class 37s and 73s for example being sold or hired by preservation groups to commercial operators for short or medium term use on the national network. There is further transience in the form of commercial freight operators sending their locomotives to operate at special events at heritage railways, or to reside on them for longer periods. In addition, commercial hire firms provide shunting locomotives to main line maintenance depots and a variety of industrial sites.

All this gives a much more complex situation, where it is difficult to clearly segregate main line, preserved and industrial locomotives, the latter two no longer necessarily being static for the long term in one location. This book lists all diesel and electric locomotives that have operated on Britain's rail network, as operated by BR, its predecessors and its successors, listing locomotives by their current status, which gives a complete and up to date list of scrapped and extant locomotives.

Whilst this book shares the name and publisher of the third edition, it is effectively a new work, the contents all a result of new, original research. It can be used as a reference source listing the status of diesel and electric locomotives in 2018 and has also been written with the rail enthusiast in mind, who along with many locomotives now, travels between the national network and heritage railways.

Andy Chard
Manchester, April 2018

▲ Formerly classified EM1, 76030 and 76041 stand face to face at Wath on 18 June 1978. The pipes protruding from the front of each locomotive reveal that 76030 is fitted with air and vacuum brake equipment, while 76041 is vacuum only. **Pete Berry/Rail Photoprints**

INTRODUCTION

This book lists every standard gauge (4' 8½") diesel and electric locomotive that is, or has been capable of working on the main line railway network. Locomotives used solely in workshops are excluded, as are those solely built for export. Industrial locomotives are excluded, as they are mainly smaller locomotives whose working lives have generally been spent on private localised sites. Most of the small number of purpose built departmental locomotives are also excluded, as they too are small, low power locomotives akin to their industrial relatives, generally unsuitable for the main line and many of these were scrapped before the TOPS era. A small number of purpose-built departmental locomotives are included, as they did see limited use on the main line.

The information in this book comes from a multitude of different sources, including the traditional reference tools of railway books and magazines, as well as many on-line sources, such as the websites and social media outlets of heritage railways, preservation groups and enthusiasts' and my own observations and records. Of particular use in clarifying some details are the multitude of dated railway photographs that can be found on the website Flickr.com.

Everything has been cross-referenced across many different information sources, so that the information is as accurate as possible. The information is updated to 16th April 2018 and has been thoroughly checked but the author would be pleased to hear from any reader with information about any inaccuracies or suggestion for enhancements in future editions. Please send any comments to the publisher's address on the title page of this book, or by email to: updates@platform5.com.

LAYOUT OF INFORMATION

Locomotives are listed in three sections, Experimental Locomotives that were purpose built as prototypes, followed by Diesel Locomotives and then Electric Locomotives. These three sections are sub-divided into locomotive types, which are listed alpha-numerically for experimental locomotives and in class number order for BR pre-TOPS classes and TOPS classes. Classes are further sub-divided by sub-class order where there are sub-classes. Finally, each class or sub-class lists individual locomotives numerically, with the latest number carried shown first. The latest number is one of a TOPS number, a BR 1957 scheme number or a BR 1948 scheme number.

Most locomotives listed have a TOPS class number, which is derived from the classification system first introduced by BR in 1968 and has been used by BR and its successors since. A number of locomotive types were not given TOPS classification or numbers as they no longer existed by the time TOPS was introduced. These are listed by their BR 1955 classification, which is the most commonly used of a number of previous classification systems which BR and its predecessors had prior to the introduction of TOPS.

For some classes, not all the individual locomotives survived until the class was renumbered when a new numbering system was introduced (either the BR 1957 or TOPS numbers). For clarity and to give the most logical listings, some locomotives are listed in the position they would have occupied had they survived long enough to be allocated a 1957 or TOPS number. For example, the first four members of Class 03 did not survive long enough to be given a TOPS number and are therefore listed under their latest carried numbers D2000/01/02/03, whereas the fifth and sixth members of the class were given a TOPS number and D2004 and D2005 are shown in the Previous Number 1 column. Similarly, the Class 47s that did not survive long enough to receive a TOPS number are listed in the position they would be found had they received a TOPS number, e.g. D1671 is listed after 47085 which has the previously carried 1957 number D1670.

Previous editions of this book have listed diesel and electric locomotives in their 1957 number order. As the TOPS classes and numbers have been in use for around 50 years now and an increasing number of classes never had a 1957 number or pre-TOPS classification, it is logical to list locomotive classes and individual numbers in TOPS class order. The vast majority of diesel and electric locomotives have a TOPS class and of the nearly 7,000 locos listed in this book, less than 300 do not have a TOPS class and most of these have a 1955 BR pre-TOPS class, which leaves a very small number of unclassified and experimental locomotives.

NUMBERING AND CLASSIFICATION SYSTEMS

Under the first universal diesel and electric locomotive numbering scheme adopted by British Railways in 1948, numbers consisted of five digits, with locomotives assigned to one of the five bands below according to their type. Note that locomotives were not numbered consecutively in these bands and fewer than 800 locos in total were given a BR 1948 number, which is considerably less than the number ranges allow for.

10000–10999	Main Line Diesel Locomotives
11000–17999	Shunting and Trip Diesel Locomotives
18000–19999	Gas Turbine Locomotives
20000–25999	Electric DC Third Rail Locomotives
26000–29999	Electric DC Overhead Locomotives

In 1955 a new classification system was introduced with locomotive classes allocated in the Dx/yy format, consisting of a letter (D in most cases), followed by two sets of numbers.

In 1957 British Railways introduced a new numbering system which applied to all diesel locomotives except those built to pre-nationalisation designs. Each locomotive was allocated a number of up to four digits prefixed with a "D" for diesel locomotives or "E" for electric locomotives. Diesel electric shunters already built numbered in the 13xxx series had the "1" replaced by a "D". Diesel mechanical shunters already built numbered in the 11xxx series were allocated numbers in the D2xxx series.

When all steam locomotives had been withdrawn, the prefix letter was officially eliminated from the number of diesel locomotives, although it continued to be carried on many of them. For this reason, no attempt is made to distinguish between those locomotives which did or did not have the "D" prefix removed. Similarly, in preservation, no distinction is made between locomotives which do or do not carry a "D" prefix at present.

British Railways also introduced a new classification system for diesel & electric locomotives. Each main line diesel locomotive class was designated a "Type", based on engine horsepower. This broadly took the following form:

Type	Engine Horsepower (hp)	Number Range	TOPS Classification
1	800–1000	D 8000–D 8999	15–20
2	1001–1499	D 5000–D 6499/D7500–D7999	21–31
3	1500–1999	D 6500–D 7499	33–37
4	2000–2999	D 1 –D 1999	40–53
5	3000+	D 9000–D 9499	55–70
Shunting	150/300	D 2000–D 2999	01–07
Shunting	350/400	D 3000–D 4999	08–13
Shunting/trip	650	D 9500–D 9999	14
AC Electric		E 1000–E 4999	81–92
DC Electric		E 5000–E 6999	71–77

In 1968 British Railways introduced a new classification scheme with two-digit numerical class codes for diesel and electric locomotives (01, 02 etc). Sub-classifications were used to identify variants within classes (27/1, 27/1 etc). The numbering of locomotives remained unaltered until the advent of computerised (TOPS) communications in 1972 when a new numbering scheme was introduced. Each locomotive was allocated a new five-digit number comprising the two-digit class number followed by a three-digit serial number. These TOPS numbers have now been in use for over 45 years.

LOCOMOTIVE CLASS HEADINGS

Each locomotive class heading has technical details.

WHEEL ARRANGEMENT

This is shown on the right hand side of the title. For smaller shunting locomotives, the Whyte Notation is used, where the number of leading (non-driving) wheels is given first, followed by the number of driving wheels and then the number of trailing (non-driving) wheels.

For main line locomotives, the number of driven axles is given by a letter (A = 1, B = 2, C = 3), followed by a number which states the number of non-powered axles. When a letter o is used, this indicates that each axle is individually powered.

BUILT

The year(s) that locomotives in the class were built and details of the builder and location.

ENGINE

Details of the engine installed and the power rating. Any programmes where locos were re-engined within the class are also given.

TRANSMISSION TYPE

Details of the transmission type for locomotives in the class.

MAXIMUM SPEED

Maximum design speed for locomotives in the class as built.

TRAIN HEATING/SUPPLY

Details of train heating fitted to locomotives when built. There was a general evolution from steam heating to electric train supply (for heating and air-conditioning) and by the late 1980s steam heating was no longer used. Changes to train heating/supply are not given for individual locomotives, such as when steam heating generators were isolated or removed. Where batch changes to heating type were subsequently made as part of a conversion programme, details are listed in the newly created sub-class heading if applicable, such as for Class 37/4s when this batch were fitted with electric train supply.

TRAIN BRAKES

Details of train brakes fitted to locomotives when built. As with train heating, there was a general evolution from vacuum braking to air braking during the lives of many locomotives resulting in many examples being fitted with dual-brakes. Details of the many changes to individual locomotive braking arrangements made since they were built are not listed.

LOCOMOTIVE SUB-CLASS HEADINGS

Where locomotive classes have been divided into sub-classes, often as a result of a batch of locomotive modifications and renumbering to reflect this, the listings for the class are split into corresponding batches, in numerical sub-class order. For example, Class 37 listings start with the 37/0 sub-class, listing these in numerical order (starting with 37003, being the lowest numbered 37/0 not renumbered), followed by the 37/3 sub-class, then 37/4 sub-class etc. Listing locos this way reflects the long standing situation where locos are listed in their TOPS number order, rather than the order in which they were built, as sub-classes such as 31/4 and 37/4 were renumbered well over three decades ago.

Sub-classes are only listed where they currently exist, or did so at the end of the life of locomotives. Historic sub-classes such as 50/1, 86/3 etc. are not listed as the locomotives within these sub-classes were later renumbered, rendering the sub-class defunct. Details of the numbers carried in these historic sub-classes are shown in the previous numbers carried columns and Appendix 2.

Each sub-class heading lists the differences that distinguish the locos in the sub-class and any other relevant information. For locos that were converted by way of a major change, such as a new engine and new classification, these are given the status of "converted" and details of the newly created loco are given in the class heading for the new locomotive.

Where locomotives have carried more than one number and the reader wishes to establish which class particular locomotives are listed under (e.g. it's not obvious that 12052 is a Class 11, or D9500 is a class 14), the appendices can be used to identify the other numbers carried and where each locomotive can be found in this book.

INDIVIDUAL LOCOMOTIVE LISTINGS

Column headings for the locomotive listings are arranged in five sections.

NUMBERS CARRIED

All official numbers carried while in service are listed, starting with the most recent TOPS number, followed by previous numbers carried in reverse chronological order. The three main series' of numbering cover the vast majority of numbers listed and these are TOPS numbers, the preceding BR 1957 Series numbers and prior BR 1948 Series numbers. For the very small number of diesel and electric locos that existed before the creation of BR in 1948, the pre-BR numbers carried are also listed.

There are a very small number of numbers that were carried by more than one locomotive, although not simultaneously (such as D2956, 27103, 20301–20307, 37271–37274 and 5 x class 76s). To distinguish these, in each case the second loco to carry the particular number has been given a suffix of [2].

Unofficial numbers or those carried during periods of industrial service are not included, unless they are still currently carried.

Departmental locomotive numbers are listed as a renumbering, as there are more instances where the departmental renumbering is a reflection of a change in use of the locomotive, rather than a conversion. Where the departmental number is the latest number carried, this is the first number listed, followed by previously carried numbers, consistent with all locomotive listings.

Where locos have been de-registered from TOPS and subsequently re-registered and given a new TOPS number in the 89xxx series, such as preserved locomotives that have been restored, the 89xxx number is not listed, as these are administrative numbers and not carried or visible externally on locomotives.

The appendices can be used to find other numbers carried, including departmental numbers.

YEAR ENTERED SERVICE

This is the year the locomotive first entered service, from the early twentieth century North Eastern Railway electric locomotives, through to the most recent Colas operated Class 70s and Direct Rail Services Class 68s and Class 88s, which entered service in 2017. Where a locomotive has been converted, such as in the case of Class 57s and 73/9s, the date given is the year the subsequently converted locomotive entered service, irrespective of when the previous incarnation entered service. There are two entries marked as not applicable (n/a) for Year Entered Service, being D5910 which at the start of 2018 is an incomplete conversion and 70012 which never entered service, as it was returned to USA in 2011 due to damage in transit.

YEAR WITHDRAWN

The year the locomotive was withdrawn from active service from British Rail, or one of its predecessor or successor companies. Where locomotives were reinstated and subsequently withdrawn again, the last known withdrawal date is given. In many cases locos are put into storage as the first stage of their demise, especially in the post-BR era and this may lead to withdrawal, or reinstatement in some cases. When a loco enters storage in one year and is formally withdrawn in a subsequent year (it's not uncommon for this to be many years later), the year that the loco entered the episode of storage which led to its withdrawal is given, rather than the year it was formally withdrawn or de-registered from TOPS, which is years after it has been scrapped in some cases. This is a particularly difficult area to quantify and verify, however multiple sources have been checked to give the most accurate information possible.

For locomotives that currently remain in active service, or are in long term storage under the ownership of commercial operators, no withdrawal date is given, as withdrawal has not taken place.

In some cases locomotives have been purchased directly from a commercial operator and entered preservation in operational condition, as 37688 did for example when it changed hands in 2017. In such instances, the withdrawal date has been left blank, as withdrawal did not take place.

CURRENT STATUS

Every diesel and electric locomotive is listed under one of the following six status categories. For those commercially operated or owned, the name of the commercial firm is given. No distinction is made between operational or stored locos, as they can move in and out of storage, both in preservation and commercial service. This includes locomotives being used as a spare parts donor, which are not expected to be restored or run again.

Scrapped
Locomotives that have been scrapped and no longer exist. These are shaded in grey to easily distinguish locomotives that exist and those that don't. In some cases one or both cabs remain and this is stated in the notes. No details of when or where diesel and electric locomotives were scrapped are given, partly because this would increase the size of the book and also because it has come to light in recent years that some previously published locomotive disposal information may not be correct and research into this is ongoing.

Exported
Locomotives that have been exported to another country. Diesel locomotives were exported as long ago as the 1940s and others have been exported for a variety of uses abroad through to recent years. For exported locomotives, a date when the locomotive was withdrawn from service in the UK has been given, with the exception of Class 66s and 92s, as these were exported relatively recently, directly into service abroad, not being withdrawn from service in the UK as most other locomotives were. Also, as the remainder of these two classes are still operational in the UK, the exported examples could potentially return to UK service, unlike locomotives from other classes that have been exported.

Awaiting Disposal
Locomotives that have already been moved to the site of a scrapping firm and their disposal is likely to be soon. Locomotives that are in poor condition, or are being stripped of parts and are expected to be scrapped have not been given this status, as their scrapping may not be inevitable.

Converted
Locomotives that no longer exist in their original condition, having been converted to a new locomotive, reflected by being given a new classification and number. For these locomotives, the withdrawal date is given with a brief explanation in the notes column, with the exception of 37372 which is currently part way through a long term conversion. As these locomotives no longer exist in this form, they are shaded grey in the same way as scrapped locomotives are.

Preserved
Locomotives owned by a heritage railway, preservation group or privately, which are no longer in commercial ownership or operation. This excludes locomotives in industrial use and those operated by a Train Operating Company (TOC), including preserved locos on hire to a TOC. Preserved locomotives can be permanently based at a particular heritage railway, on short or long term loan from one heritage railway or base to another. Preserved locomotives can be operational, under restoration or a spare parts donor.

Commercial Owners and Operators
Locomotives in this category are listed by current commercial owner or operating company. This includes passenger and freight train operators which own, lease or hire locomotives, as well as those that aren't train operators but own or operate locomotives at a variety of sites across the UK. Some locomotives are based in a location for long term industrial use and are not approved for operation on the national rail network, such as at quarries, cement and steel works. Others may be owned by spot hire firms which send locomotives to a variety of locations, usually for shorter periods, such as Railway Support Services, RMS Locotec and HNRC. Where a locomotive is on hire to a TOC, it is listed by the current hiring operating company, irrespective of whether it is being hired from a preservation group, or another commercial operator. Commercially owned or operated locomotives are given the status of one of the following companies:

Aggregate Industries
Alstom
Arlington Fleet Services
Arriva Traincare
AV Dawson
Bombardier Transportation
Class 20189

Colas Rail
Cross Country
DB Cargo
Direct Rail Services
East Midlands Trains
Europhoenix
Eurostar International

Freightliner
GB Railfreight
Great Western Railway
Greater Anglia
Hanson UK
Harry Needle Railroad Company (HNRC)
Hunslet Engine Company
Knorr-Bremse Rail UK
Locomotive Services
London Overground
Loram UK
Mendip Rail
Nemesis Rail
Network Rail
Rail Operations Group
Railway Support Services

Riviera Trains
RMS Locotec
Russell Logistics
Scotrail
SembCorp Utilities UK
South Western Railway
Southern
Transmart Trains
UK Rail Leasing
Victoria Group
Vintage Trains
Virgin Trains East Coast
Wabtec
West Coast Railway Company
West Midlands Trains

NOTES

This section gives details of anything unusual, of interest or exceptions to the definitions described above. Items noted in this section include:

- Locomotives that have undergone, or are currently part way through a conversion to another locomotive.
- Instances when two locomotives carried the same numbers, the note stating whether it was the first or second locomotive to carry the number. The second locomotive to carry a duplicate number has a superscript 2 after the duplicate locomotive number to distinguish it from the first locomotive that carried the number.
- Locomotives of one status that are temporarily listed as a different status, due to their current use.
- Anything unusual, such as locomotives that have sustained damage after an accident, had a cab removed, or were not completely disposed of when scrapped.

APPENDICES

At the end of the book, there are five Appendices, with reference information and tables, for locomotives where it may not be obvious where they are listed in this book.

APPENDIX 1: LOCOMOTIVE CLASSES

A summary of all locomotives by classification, in the order that they are listed in this book, showing the total number produced and the number ranges for each locomotive classification.

APPENDIX 2: MULTIPLE TOPS NUMBERS

Of the more than 5,200 locomotives which have carried a TOPS number, over 800 have carried more than one TOPS number, due to being renumbered. This Appendix lists all previously carried TOPS numbers and shows the locomotive class and latest TOPS number under which the locomotive is listed in this book. Where a locomotive has two or more previously carried TOPS numbers, there are multiple entries for such locomotives. For example 47780 has previously carried three different TOPS numbers (47030, 47618 and 47836), therefore each of these three previously carried numbers are listed, each entry referring to 47780 where the locomotive is found in this book. Locomotives that have only carried one TOPS number are not included in Appendix 2.

APPENDIX 3: BR 1948 AND 1957 NUMBERS

This lists locomotives that carried a 1948 BR Number or 1957 BR Number and were subsequently given a different number, under which they are listed in this book. The 1948 numbers are listed numerically, showing the corresponding 1957 number (where the locomotive was not given a

TOPS number) or TOPS number, under which it can be found in this book. Locomotives that only carried one 1948 or one 1957 number throughout their lives are not listed in this Appendix, as they are listed under that one number.

There are a small number of locomotives where the "Number Loco is listed by" is not the latest number carried, but a previously carried number, to which it is more logical to refer, such as for some industrial or departmental renumberings. For example, for D5061 the table refers to 24061 to find the locomotive, rather than its last carried departmental number RDB968007 and for D8066, it refers to 20066 rather than the last carried number 82.

APPENDIX 4: DEPARTMENTAL NUMBERS

This lists all locomotives that were renumbered for Departmental use. It therefore does not include locomotives that were assigned a Departmental number which was not actually carried, or Departmental locomotives that were not given a separate Departmental number, such as D5901 or the Network Rail HSTs (43013, 43014 and 43062). In each case, the Departmental number is shown, along with the corresponding locomotive class and the number by which it is listed in this book.

APPENDIX 5: LOCOMOTIVE NAMES

A list of all official locomotive names carried during main line service with BR or its successors. Names given during preservation are not included. The name listings are case sensitive as carried on locos and where a locomotive has carried more than one name, they are listed chronologically, in the order they were carried.

Names are listed adjacent to the locomotive number carried in the period when the name was also carried. In the case of subsequently renumbered locomotives, this is not the number under which the locomotive's entry can be found in this book. Please refer to Appendices 2 and 3 as necessary to locate where the locomotive's details can be found in this book.

Unofficial names are not included and in cases where it is not clear whether a name is official, names on cast nameplates are included and names painted on to the sides of locos have been excluded. Where a crest or plaque is mounted separately and this also includes text, this is not listed. For example, 31602 had a separate "19B" plaque under the "DRIVER DAVE GREEN" nameplate and only the text on the nameplate is included.

ABBREVIATIONS

The following general abbreviation s are used in this book:

AC	Alternating Current
BR	British Railways, later British Rail
BREL	British Rail Engineering Limited
DC	Direct Current
GWR	Great Western Railway
hp	Horsepower
kW	Kilowatts
LMS	London Midland & Scottish Railway
LNER	London & North Eastern Railway
mph	Miles per hour
SR	Southern Railway
TOPS	Total Operations Processing System
V	Volts

1. EXPERIMENTAL LOCOMOTIVES

1.1. EXPERIMENTAL SHUNTING LOCOMOTIVES

EXPERIMENTAL ENGLISH ELECTRIC SHUNTER   0-6-0

Built: 1957 by English Electric, Vulcan Foundry, Newton-le-Willows.
Engine: English Electric 6RKT of 373 kW (500 hp) at 750 rpm.
Transmission: D0226 Electric and D0227 Hydraulic.
Maximum Speed: 35 mph.

Latest Number Carried	Previous Number 1	Year Entered Service	Year Withdrawn	Current Status	Notes
D226	D0226	1957	1960	Preserved	
D227	D0227	1957	1959	Scrapped	

EXPERIMENTAL BRUSH SHUNTER   0-4-0

Built: 1961 by Brush Electrical Engineering Company Ltd, Loughborough.
Engine: Petter McLaren of 200 hp.
Transmission: Electric.
Maximum Speed: 18 mph.

Latest Number Carried	Previous Number 1	Year Entered Service	Year Withdrawn	Current Status	Notes
D9998		1961	1962	Exported	

EXPERIMENTAL YORKSHIRE ENGINE CO. SHUNTER   0-6-0

Built: 1956 (JANUS) and 1961 (TAURUS) by Yorkshire Engine Company, Sheffield.
Engine: Two Rolls Royce C6 of 300 kW (400 hp) for JANUS and two Rolls Royce C8 of 450 kW (600 hp) for TAURUS.
Transmission: Electric (JANUS) and Hydraulic (TAURUS).
Maximum Speed: 23 mph (JANUS) and 36 mph (TAURUS).

Latest Number Carried	Previous Number 1	Year Entered Service	Year Withdrawn	Current Status	Notes
JANUS		1956	1956	Scrapped	
TAURUS		1961	1964	Scrapped	

EXPERIMENTAL NORTH BRITISH SHUNTER   0-4-0

Built: 1954 by North British Locomotive Company, Glasgow.
Engine: Paxman 6 VRPHXL of 160 kW (225 hp) at 1250 rpm.
Transmission: Hydraulic.
Maximum Speed: 12 mph.

Latest Number Carried	Previous Number 1	Year Entered Service	Year Withdrawn	Current Status	Notes
TOM	27414	1954		Preserved	
TIGER		1954		Preserved	

1.2. EXPERIMENTAL MAIN LINE DIESEL LOCOMOTIVES

EXPERIMENTAL ENGLISH ELECTRIC TYPE 3   Co-Co

Built: 1947 (10000) and 1948 (10001) by English Electric, Vulcan Foundry, Newton-le-Willows.
Engine: English Electric 16SVT of 1200 kW (1600 hp) at 750 rpm.
Transmission: Electric.
Maximum Speed: 93 mph.
Train Heating/Supply: Steam.
Train Brakes: Vacuum.

Latest Number Carried	Previous Number 1	Year Entered Service	Year Withdrawn	Current Status	Notes
10000		1947	1963	Scrapped	
10001		1948	1966	Scrapped	

EXPERIMENTAL BRITISH RAILWAYS TYPE 4   2-D-2

Built: 1952 by British Railways, Derby Works.
Engine: Four Paxman 12RPH of 1500 kW (2040 hp) at 750 rpm.
Transmission: Mechanical.
Maximum Speed: 84 mph.
Train Heating/Supply: Steam.
Train Brakes: Vacuum.

Latest Number Carried	Previous Number 1	Year Entered Service	Year Withdrawn	Current Status	Notes
10100		1950	1958	Scrapped	

▲ The second of the two experimental Co-Co diesel-electrics built in 1947–48 by English Electric, 10001 sits on shed at Willesden, together with an English Electric Type 1 Bo-Bo (later Class 20) on 3 May 1964. Sister locomotive 10000 had already been withdrawn the previous December, but 10001 survived until March 1966. It was sold for scrap to Cox & Danks and cut up in North Acton in February 1968.   **Geoff Plumb Collection**

EXPERIMENTAL ENGLISH ELECTRIC TYPE 3/TYPE 4   1Co-Co1

Built: 1950–54 by British Railways, Ashford Works and Brighton Works.
Engine: English Electric 16SVT of 1300 kW (1750 hp) for 10201 & 10202 and 1500 kW (2000 hp) for 10203.
Transmission: Electric.
Maximum Speed: 90 mph.
Train Heating/Supply: Steam.
Train Brakes: Vacuum.

Latest Number Carried	Previous Number 1	Year Entered Service	Year Withdrawn	Current Status	Notes
10201		1950	1963	Scrapped	
10202		1951	1963	Scrapped	
10203		1954	1963	Scrapped	

EXPERIMENTAL NORTH BRITISH TYPE 1   Bo-Bo

Built: 1950 by North British Locomotive Company, Glasgow.
Engine: Paxman 16PHXL of 617 kW (827 hp), later re-engined with Maybach MD655 of 1000 kW (1400 hp).
Transmission: Electric.
Maximum Speed: 70 mph.
Train Heating/Supply: Steam.
Train Brakes: Vacuum.

Latest Number Carried	Previous Number 1	Year Entered Service	Year Withdrawn	Current Status	Notes
10800		1950	1959	Scrapped	

▲ Experimental English Electric Type 3 10202 leaves Southampton Central with the "down" Bournemouth Belle on 17 May 1958.   **Dave Cobbe Collection/Rail Photoprints**

EXPERIMENTAL BRCW/SULZER TYPE 4   Co-Co

Built: 1962 by Birmingham Railway Carriage and Wagon Company.
Engine: Sulzer 12LDA 28C of 2050 kW (2750 hp).
Transmission: Electric.
Maximum Speed: 100 mph.
Train Heating/Supply: Steam.
Train Brakes: Vacuum.

Latest Number Carried	Previous Number 1	Year Entered Service	Year Withdrawn	Current Status	Notes
D0260		1962	1963	Scrapped	

CLASS 53   Co-Co

Built: 1961 by Brush Electrical Engineering Company Ltd, Loughborough.
Engine: Two Bristol Siddeley Maybach MD655 of 1075 kW (1400 hp) at 1500 rpm.
Transmission: Hydraulic.
Maximum Speed: 100mph.
Train Heating/Supply: Steam.
Train Brakes: Vacuum.

Latest Number Carried	Previous Number 1	Year Entered Service	Year Withdrawn	Current Status	Notes
D1200	D0280	1961	1975	Scrapped	

EXPERIMENTAL ENGLISH ELECTRIC TYPE 5   Co-Co

Built: 1955 by English Electric, Vulcan Foundry, Newton-le-Willows.
Engine: Two Napier Deltic D18-25 of 1230 kW (1650 hp) at 1500 rpm.
Transmission: Electric.
Maximum Speed: 105 mph.
Train Heating/Supply: Steam.

Latest Number Carried	Previous Number 1	Year Entered Service	Year Withdrawn	Current Status	Notes
DELTIC		1955	1961	Preserved	

EXPERIMENTAL CLAYTON TYPE 3   Bo-Bo

Built: 1962–63 by Clayton Equipment Company, Derbyshire.
Engine: Four Rolls Royce C8TFL of 1120 kW (1500 hp).
Transmission: Hydraulic.
Maximum Speed: 90 mph.
Train Heating/Supply: Steam.
Train Brakes: Vacuum.

Latest Number Carried	Previous Number 1	Year Entered Service	Year Withdrawn	Current Status	Notes
DHP1		1963	1964	Scrapped	

EXPERIMENTAL ENGLISH ELECTRIC TYPE 4   Co-Co

Built: 1962 by English Electric, Vulcan Foundry, Newton-le-Willows.
Engine: English Electric 16CSVT of 2000 kW (2700 hp).
Transmission: Electric.
Maximum Speed: 90 mph.
Train Heating/Supply: Steam.
Train Brakes: Dual braked (vacuum and air).

Latest Number Carried	Previous Number 1	Year Entered Service	Year Withdrawn	Current Status	Notes
DP2		1962	1967	Scrapped	

▲ Brush's "FALCON" was the only experimental main line diesel locomotive to survive into the TOPS era, becoming designated Class 53 although it never actually carried a TOPS number. In April 1967, carrying the number D0280, "FALCON" waits to leave Bristol Temple Meads with 1A22 for London Paddington. **Mike Jefferies/Rail Photoprints**

▼ The prototype "DELTIC" was for many years a prime exhibit at the Science Museum in London. Following its transfer to the National Railway Museum in York, it is seen here in rather less illustrious surroundings on 26 May 2004. **Rail Photoprints Collection**

EXPERIMENTAL BRUSH TYPE 5 Co-Co

Built: 1968 by Brush Electrical Engineering Company Ltd, Loughborough.
Engine: Sulzer 16LVA24 of 2983 kW (4000 hp) at 1100 rpm.
Transmission: Electric.
Maximum Speed: 110 mph.
Train Heating/Supply: Electric.
Train Brakes: Dual braked (vacuum and air).

Latest Number Carried	Previous Number 1	Year Entered Service	Year Withdrawn	Current Status	Notes
HS4000		1968	1971	Exported	

1.3. EXPERIMENTAL GAS TURBINE LOCOMOTIVES

EXPERIMENTAL BROWN BOVERI GAS TURBINE A1A-A1A

Built: 1950 by Brown Boveri, Switzerland.
Engine: Brown Boveri gas turbine of 1828 kW (2500 hp).
Transmission: Electric.
Maximum Speed: 90 mph.
Train Heating/Supply: Steam.

Latest Number Carried	Previous Number 1	Year Entered Service	Year Withdrawn	Current Status	Notes
18000		1950	1960	Preserved	

EXPERIMENTAL METROPOLITAN VICKERS GAS TURBINE
Co-Co

Built: 1951 by Metropolitan Vickers, Manchester.
Engine: Gas turbine of 2240 kW (3000 hp).
Transmission: Electric.
Maximum Speed: 90 mph.
Train Heating/Supply: Steam.
Train Brakes: Vacuum.
In 1958 18100 was converted to experimental electric Class 80 and renumbered E1000 (see below).

Latest Number Carried	Previous Number 1	Year Entered Service	Year Withdrawn	Current Status	Notes
18100		1952	1958	Converted	Converted to E1000 in 1958

EXPERIMENTAL ENGLISH ELECTRIC GAS TURBINE 4-6-0

Built: 1958–61 by English Electric, Vulcan Foundry, Newton-le-Willows.
Engine: EM27L of 2050 kW (2750 hp) at 9000 rpm.
Transmission: Mechanical.
Maximum Speed: 90mph.
Train Heating/Supply: Steam.

Latest Number Carried	Previous Number 1	Year Entered Service	Year Withdrawn	Current Status	Notes
GT3		1961	1962	Scrapped	

▲ Another English Electric prototype, DP2, is seen waiting to depart with an express from London Kings Cross in August 1963. This locomotive was damaged beyond repair in a serious accident at Thirsk on 31 July 1967.   **Colin Whitfield/Rail Photoprints**

▼ HS4000 "KESTREL" was the most powerful of all British Railways' experimental main line diesel locomotives. Following three years of test operation, the locomotive was sold to the Soviet Union in 1971. On 19 April 1970 it was stabled at Hull Dairycoates.   **Norman Preedy/Rail Photoprints**

1.4. EXPERIMENTAL MAIN LINE ELECTRIC LOCOMOTIVES

CLASS 80 A1A-A1A

Built: 1951 by Metropolitan Vickers, Manchester (see 18100) and converted to E1000 in 1958.
Electric Supply System: 25 kV AC overhead.
Power Output: 2500 kW (625 hp).
Maximum Speed: 90 mph.
Train Heating/Supply: Electric.
Train Brakes: Vacuum.

Latest Number Carried	Previous Number 1	Year Entered Service	Year Withdrawn	Current Status	Notes
E2001	E1000	1958	1968	Scrapped	Converted from 18100

2. DIESEL LOCOMOTIVES

2.1. PURPOSE-BUILT DEPARTMENTAL LOCOMOTIVES

RUSTON & HORNSBY 0-4-0 SHUNTER 0-4-0

Built: 1955 by Ruston & Hornsby, Lincoln.
Engine: Ruston & Hornsby Mark 4V of 88 hp.
Transmission: Mechanical.
Train Brakes: None.

Latest Number Carried	Previous Number 1	Year Entered Service	Year Withdrawn	Current Status	Notes
56		1955	1970	Scrapped	

RUSTON & HORNSBY 0-4-0 SHUNTER 0-4-0

Built: 1958–61 by Ruston & Hornsby, Lincoln.
Engine: Ruston & Hornsby of 150 hp.
Transmission: Mechanical.
Train Brakes: None.

Latest Number Carried	Previous Number 1	Year Entered Service	Year Withdrawn	Current Status	Notes
82		1958	1970	Scrapped	
83		1959	1970	Scrapped	
84		1959	1970	Scrapped	
85		1959	1970	Scrapped	
86		1961	1970	Scrapped	
87		1961	1970	Scrapped	

▲ In appearance not unlike a steam tender locomotive, brand new experimental gas turbine locomotive GT3 is seen at Whitchurch in the company of "Peak" (later Class 44) D10 in January 1961. British Railways decided not to pursue this form of power and the locomotive was returned to English Electric in 1962. **Hugh Ballantyne Collection/Rail Photoprints**

▼ Ruston & Hornsby 0-4-0 shunter, 20, lurks in its "shed" at Reading Signal Works (the bridge was effectively used as its shed!) on 2 September 1978. This locomotive's forays onto the main line consisted almost exclusively of trips from the signal works to Reading MPD for the purpose of servicing and maintenance. **Graham Smith/Rail Photoprints**

CLASS 97 RUSTON & HORNSBY 0-4-0 SHUNTER | 0-4-0

Built: 1957 by Ruston & Hornsby, Lincoln.
Engine: Ruston 4 Cylinder of 66 kW (88 hp).
Transmission: Mechanical.

Latest Number Carried	Previous Number 1	Year Entered Service	Year Withdrawn	Current Status	Notes
97020	20	1957	1981	Scrapped	

CLASS 97 RUSTON & HORNSBY 0-6-0 SHUNTER | 0-6-0

Built: 1953–59 by Ruston & Hornsby, Lincoln.
Engine: Ruston 6VPH of 123 kW (165 hp).
Transmission: Electric.
Maximum Speed: 20 mph.
Train Heating/Supply: None.
Train Brakes: Vacuum.

Latest Number Carried	Previous Number 1	Year Entered Service	Year Withdrawn	Current Status	Notes
97650	PWM650	1953	1987	Preserved	
97651	PWM651	1959	1998	Preserved	
97652	PWM652	1959	1987	Scrapped	
97653	PWM653	1959	1992	Scrapped	
97654	PWM654	1959	1997	Preserved	

RUSTON & HORNSBY 0-4-0 SHUNTER | 0-4-0

Built: 1948 by Ruston & Hornsby, Lincoln.
Engine: Ruston of 48 hp.
Transmission: Mechanical.
Train Brakes: None.

Latest Number Carried	Previous Number 1	Year Entered Service	Year Withdrawn	Current Status	Notes
DS1169		1948	1972	Scrapped	

FOWLER 0-4-0 SHUNTER | 0-4-0

Built: 1935 by John Fowler & Co., Leeds.
Engine: Ruston & Hornsby VQ of 88 hp.
Transmission: Mechanical.
Maximum Speed: 15 mph.
Train Brakes: None.

Latest Number Carried	Previous Number 1	Year Entered Service	Year Withdrawn	Current Status	Notes
ED1	2	1935	1962	Scrapped	

FOWLER 0-4-0 SHUNTER 0-4-0

Built: 1949 by John Fowler & Co., Leeds.
Engine: Fowler 4C of 88 hp.
Transmission: Mechanical.
Maximum Speed: 15 mph.
Train Brakes: None.

Latest Number Carried	Previous Number 1	Year Entered Service	Year Withdrawn	Current Status	Notes
ED2		1949	1965	Scrapped	
ED3		1949	1967	Scrapped	
ED4		1949	1964	Scrapped	
ED5		1949	1965	Scrapped	
ED6		1949	1967	Scrapped	

▲ Purpose-built departmental shunter PWM650 stands outside Gloucester shed in the company of 08826 and 37206 on 8 August 1979. **Gordon Edgar/Rail Photoprints**

FOWLER 0-4-0 SHUNTER
0-4-0

Built: 1940 by John Fowler & Co., Leeds.
Engine: Fowler Type C of 150 hp.
Transmission: Mechanical.
Maximum Speed: 15 mph.
Train Brakes: None.

Latest Number Carried	Previous Number 1	Year Entered Service	Year Withdrawn	Current Status	Notes
ED7		1955	1964	Scrapped	

2.2. UNCLASSIFIED DIESEL SHUNTING LOCOMOTIVES

LMS PAXMAN 400HP SHUNTER
0-6-0

Built: 1934 by London Midland and Scottish Railway, Derby Works.
Engine: Paxman 4 Stroke of 298 kW (400 hp) at 750 rpm.
Transmission: Hydraulic.
Maximum Speed: 25 mph.
Train Brakes: Vacuum.

Latest Number Carried	Previous Number 1	Year Entered Service	Year Withdrawn	Current Status	Notes
1831		1934	1939	Scrapped	

LMS ALLAN 160HP SHUNTER
0-4-0

Built: 1934 by English Electric at Preston works for Drewry Car company.
Engine: W H Allan 8RS18 of 119 kW (160 hp) at 1200 rpm, subsequently fitted with Gardner 6L3 of 114 kW (153 hp).
Transmission: Mechanical.
Maximum Speed: 12 mph.

Latest Number Carried	Previous Number 1	Year Entered Service	Year Withdrawn	Current Status	Notes
7050	7400	1934	1943	Preserved	

LMS HUNSLET 150HP SHUNTER
0-6-0

Built: 1933 by Hunslet Engine Company, Leeds.
Engine: MAN WV16/22 of 112 kW (150 hp) at 900 rpm. Later McLaren Ricardo MR6 of 98kW (132 hp).
Transmission: Mechanical.
Maximum Speed: 30 mph.
Train Brakes: None.

Latest Number Carried	Previous Number 1	Year Entered Service	Year Withdrawn	Current Status	Notes
7051	7401	1933	1945	Preserved	

LMS HUNSLET 150HP SHUNTER   0-6-0

Built: 1934 by Hunslet Engine Company, Leeds.
Engine: McLaren-Benz 8MDB of 112 kW (150 hp) at 1000 rpm.
Transmission: Mechanical.
Maximum Speed: 8 mph.
Train Brakes: None.

Latest Number Carried	Previous Number 1	Year Entered Service	Year Withdrawn	Current Status	Notes
7052	7402	1934	1943	Scrapped	

LMS HUNSLET 150HP SHUNTER   0-6-0

Built: 1934 by Hunslet Engine Company, Leeds.
Engine: Brotherhood-Ricardo RZ5 of 112 kW (150 hp) at 1200 rpm.
Transmission: Mechanical.
Maximum Speed: 14 mph.
Train Brakes: None.

Latest Number Carried	Previous Number 1	Year Entered Service	Year Withdrawn	Current Status	Notes
7053	7403	1934	1942	Scrapped	

LMS HUNSLET 180HP SHUNTER   0-6-0

Built: 1934 by Hunslet Engine Company, Leeds.
Engine: Davey Paxman 6VZS of 134 kW (180 hp) at 900 rpm.
Transmission: Mechanical.
Maximum Speed: 13 mph.
Train Brakes: None.

Latest Number Carried	Previous Number 1	Year Entered Service	Year Withdrawn	Current Status	Notes
7054		1934	1943	Scrapped	

LMS HUDSWELL CLARKE 150HP SHUNTER   0-6-0

Built: 1934–35 by Hudswell-Clarke & Company, Leeds.
Engine: Mirrlees Ricardo of 112 kW (150 hp).
Transmission: Mechanical.
Maximum Speed: 19 mph.
Train Brakes: None.

Latest Number Carried	Previous Number 1	Year Entered Service	Year Withdrawn	Current Status	Notes
7055		1934	1963	Scrapped	
7056		1935	1955	Scrapped	

LMS HARLAND & WOLFF 175HP SHUNTER   0-6-0

Built: 1935 by Harland and Wolff.
Engine: Harland & Wolff TR of 1300 kW (175 hp) at 1100 rpm.
Transmission: Mechanical.
Maximum Speed: 10 mph.
Train Brakes: None.

Latest Number Carried	Previous Number 1	Year Entered Service	Year Withdrawn	Current Status	Notes
7057		1935	1944	Exported	

LMS ARMSTONG WHITWORTH 250HP SHUNTER   0-6-0

Built: 1934 by Armstrong Whitworth.
Engine: Armstrong Whitworth 6LV22 of 186 kW (250 hp) at 775 rpm.
Transmission: Electric.
Maximum Speed: 30 mph.
Train Brakes: None.

Latest Number Carried	Previous Number 1	Year Entered Service	Year Withdrawn	Current Status	Notes
7058	7408	1934	1949	Scrapped	

LMS ARMSTONG WHITWORTH 350HP SHUNTER   0-6-0

Built: 1934 by Armstrong Whitworth.
Engine: Armstrong Whitworth 6LV22 of 186 kW (350 hp) at 775 rpm.
Transmission: Electric.
Maximum Speed: 30 mph.
Train Brakes: None.

Latest Number Carried	Previous Number 1	Year Entered Service	Year Withdrawn	Current Status	Notes
7059		1936	1944	Exported	
7060		1936	1942	Exported	
7061		1936	1944	Exported	
7062		1936	1944	Exported	
7063		1936	1944	Scrapped	
7064		1936	1944	Exported	
7065		1936	1942	Exported	
7066		1936	1942	Exported	
7067		1936	1944	Exported	
7068		1936	1942	Exported	

▲ Unclassified Bullied-designed diesel shunter 11001 is pictured at Derby in 1955. On the right is Brand new Hudswell Clarke Class D2/7 11117 which has not yet been accepted into service.

R. S. Wilkins/Rail Photoprints

BR BULLEID SHUNTER   0-6-0

Built: 1950 by British Railways, Ashford Works.
Engine: Paxman Ricardo of 373 kW (500 hp) at 1250 rpm.
Transmission: Mechanical.
Maximum Speed: 44 mph.
Train Brakes: None.

Latest Number Carried	Previous Number 1	Year Entered Service	Year Withdrawn	Current Status	Notes
11001		1950	1959	Scrapped	

BR HIBBERD 52HP SHUNTER   0-4-0

Built: 1950 by F C Hibberd & Co Ltd.
Engine: English National DA4 of 39 kW (52 hp) at 1250 rpm.
Transmission: Mechanical.
Maximum Speed: 15 mph.
Train Brakes: None.

Latest Number Carried	Previous Number 1	Year Entered Service	Year Withdrawn	Current Status	Notes
11104	52	1950	1967	Scrapped	

BR PETTER BRUSH 360HP SHUNTER   0-6-0

Built: 1949 by Brush Electrical Engineering Company, Loughborough.
Engine: Petter SS4 of 268 kW (360 hp).
Transmission: Electric.
Maximum Speed: 20 mph.
Train Brakes: None.

Latest Number Carried	Previous Number 1	Year Entered Service	Year Withdrawn	Current Status	Notes
15107		1949	1958	Scrapped	

2.3. DIESEL SHUNTING LOCOMOTIVES WITH PRE-TOPS CLASSIFICATION

CLASS D1/1 HUNSLET SHUNTER   0-4-0

Built: 1954–55 by Hunslet Engine Company, Leeds.
Engine: Gardner 6L3 of 114 kW (153 hp) at 1200 rpm.
Transmission: Mechanical.
Maximum Speed: 14 mph.
Train Brakes: None.

Latest Number Carried	Previous Number 1	Year Entered Service	Year Withdrawn	Current Status	Notes
D2950	11500	1954	1967	Scrapped	
D2951	11501	1954	1967	Scrapped	
D2952	11502	1955	1966	Scrapped	

▲ Built by BR at Swindon in 1949, 15107 was an 0-6-0 diesel shunter fitted with a 360 hp Petter diesel engine and two Brush traction motors. It spent its whole life allocated to Bristol St. Philip's Marsh depot before being withdrawn in June 1958 and finally broken up at its Swindon birthplace.
Rail Photoprints Collection

▼ Hunslet Engine Company Class D1/1 0-4-0 diesel mechanical shunter D2952 crosses one of the swing bridges in Ipswich Docks with a trip working in 1962. **Martyn Hunt/Rail Photoprints**

CLASS D1/3 RUSTON & HORNSBY SHUNTER   0-4-0

Built: 1956 by Ruston & Hornsby, Lincoln.
Engine: Ruston 6VPHL of 123 kW (165 hp).
Transmission: Mechanical.
Maximum Speed: 15 mph.
Train Brakes: None.

Latest Number Carried	Previous Number 1	Year Entered Service	Year Withdrawn	Current Status	Notes
D2957	11507	1956	1967	Scrapped	
D2958	11508	1956	1968	Scrapped	

CLASS D2/1 NORTH BRITISH SHUNTER   0-4-0

Built: 1953–56 by North British Locomotive Company, Glasgow.
Engine: Paxman 6PR of 149 kW (200 hp).
Transmission: Hydraulic.
Maximum Speed: 14 mph (D2700–D2702) and 12 mph (D2703–D2707).
Train Brakes: None.

Latest Number Carried	Previous Number 1	Year Entered Service	Year Withdrawn	Current Status	Notes
D2700	11700	1953	1963	Scrapped	
D2701	11701	1953	1967	Scrapped	
D2702	11702	1954	1967	Scrapped	
D2703	11703	1955	1968	Scrapped	
D2704	11704	1955	1967	Scrapped	
D2705	11705	1955	1967	Scrapped	
D2706	11706	1955	1967	Scrapped	
D2707	11707	1956	1967	Scrapped	

CLASS D2/5 ANDREW BARCLAY SHUNTER   0-6-0

Note that Class D2/5 locomotives differ from Class 05; some sources incorrectly classify Class D2/5 locomotives as Class 05.
Built: 1956–57 by Andrew Barclay, Kilmarnock.
Engine: Gardner 8L3 of 152 kW (204 hp).
Transmission: Mechanical.
Maximum Speed: 17.75 mph.
Train Brakes: None.

Latest Number Carried	Previous Number 1	Year Entered Service	Year Withdrawn	Current Status	Notes
D2400	11177	1956	1967	Scrapped	
D2401	11178	1956	1968	Scrapped	
D2402	11179	1956	1967	Scrapped	
D2403	11180	1956	1969	Scrapped	
D2404	11181	1956	1969	Scrapped	
D2405	11182	1956	1968	Scrapped	
D2406	11183	1956	1967	Scrapped	
D2407	11184	1957	1969	Scrapped	
D2408	11185	1957	1967	Scrapped	
D2409	11186	1957	1968	Scrapped	

▲ One of Stratford's "pet" locomotives, Class D1/3 Ruston & Hornsby 165 hp diesel mechanical shunter D2957 is seen at its home shed in 1963.	**Colin Whitfield/Rail Photoprints**

▼ It's the end of the line for Class D2/10 North British diesel hydraulic shunter D2718 and 204 hp Hunslet shunter (later Class 05) D2584 as they sit in the sidings at the rear of Dundee shed on 19 August 1967. D2584 was cannibalised for spares but both locomotives were destined to be scrapped shortly after this photo was taken.	**R. Collen-Jones/Rail Photoprints**

CLASS D2/7 HUDSWELL CLARKE SHUNTER   0-6-0

Built: 1955–56 by Hudswell-Clarke & Company, Leeds.
Engine: Gardner 8L3 of 152 kW (204 hp).
Transmission: Mechanical.
Maximum Speed: 14 mph.
Train Brakes: None.

Latest Number Carried	Previous Number 1	Year Entered Service	Year Withdrawn	Current Status	Notes
D2500	11116	1955	1967	Scrapped	
D2501	11117	1956	1967	Scrapped	
D2502	11118	1956	1967	Scrapped	
D2503	11119	1956	1967	Scrapped	
D2504	11120	1956	1967	Scrapped	
D2505	11144	1956	1967	Scrapped	
D2506	11145	1956	1967	Scrapped	
D2507	11146	1956	1967	Scrapped	
D2508	11147	1956	1967	Scrapped	
D2509	11148	1956	1967	Scrapped	

CLASS D2/10 NORTH BRITISH SHUNTER   0-4-0

Built: 1957–61 by North British Locomotive Company, Glasgow.
Engine: MAN W6V of 168 kW (225 hp) at 1100 rpm.
Transmission: Hydraulic.
Maximum Speed: 15 mph.

Latest Number Carried	Previous Number 1	Year Entered Service	Year Withdrawn	Current Status	Notes
D2708	11708	1957	1967	Scrapped	
D2709	11709	1957	1967	Scrapped	
D2710	11710	1957	1967	Scrapped	
D2711	11711	1957	1967	Scrapped	
D2712	11712	1957	1967	Scrapped	
D2713	11713	1957	1967	Scrapped	
D2714	11714	1957	1967	Scrapped	
D2715	11715	1957	1967	Scrapped	
D2716	11716	1957	1967	Scrapped	
D2717	11717	1957	1967	Scrapped	
D2718	11718	1957	1967	Scrapped	
D2719	11719	1957	1967	Scrapped	
D2720		1958	1967	Scrapped	
D2721		1958	1967	Scrapped	
D2722		1958	1967	Scrapped	
D2723		1958	1967	Scrapped	
D2724		1958	1967	Scrapped	
D2725		1958	1967	Scrapped	
D2726		1958	1967	Scrapped	
D2727		1958	1967	Scrapped	
D2728		1958	1967	Scrapped	
D2729		1958	1967	Scrapped	
D2730		1958	1967	Scrapped	
D2731		1958	1967	Scrapped	
D2732		1958	1967	Scrapped	
D2733		1958	1967	Scrapped	
D2734		1958	1967	Scrapped	
D2735		1958	1967	Scrapped	
D2736		1958	1967	Scrapped	
D2737		1958	1967	Scrapped	
D2738		1958	1967	Scrapped	

D2739	1958	1967	Scrapped
D2740	1958	1967	Scrapped
D2741	1959	1967	Scrapped
D2742	1959	1967	Scrapped
D2743	1959	1967	Scrapped
D2744	1959	1967	Scrapped
D2745	1960	1967	Scrapped
D2746	1960	1967	Scrapped
D2747	1960	1967	Scrapped
D2748	1960	1967	Scrapped
D2749	1960	1967	Scrapped
D2750	1960	1967	Scrapped
D2751	1960	1967	Scrapped
D2752	1960	1967	Scrapped
D2753	1960	1967	Scrapped
D2754	1960	1967	Scrapped
D2755	1960	1967	Scrapped
D2756	1960	1968	Scrapped
D2757	1960	1967	Scrapped
D2758	1960	1968	Scrapped
D2759	1960	1967	Scrapped
D2760	1960	1968	Scrapped
D2761	1960	1967	Scrapped
D2762	1960	1967	Scrapped
D2763	1960	1967	Scrapped
D2764	1960	1968	Scrapped
D2765	1960	1967	Scrapped
D2766	1960	1967	Scrapped
D2767	1960	1967	Preserved
D2768	1960	1968	Scrapped
D2769	1960	1968	Scrapped
D2770	1960	1968	Scrapped
D2771	1960	1967	Scrapped
D2772	1960	1967	Scrapped
D2773	1960	1968	Scrapped
D2774	1960	1967	Preserved
D2775	1960	1968	Scrapped
D2776	1960	1967	Scrapped
D2777	1960	1967	Scrapped
D2778	1960	1967	Scrapped
D2779	1961	1968	Scrapped
D2780	1961	1968	Scrapped

CLASS D2/11 BEYER PEACOCK/BRUSH SHUNTER   0-4-0

Built: 1960 by Brush Electrical Engineering Company Ltd, Loughborough and Beyer Peacock &
Co., Gorton, Manchester
Engine: National M4AAV6 of 149 kW (200 hp).
Transmission: Electric.
Maximum Speed: 18 mph.
Train Brakes: None.

Latest Number Carried	Previous Number 1	Year Entered Service	Year Withdrawn	Current Status	Notes
D2999		1960	1967	Scrapped	

CLASS D2/12 HUSWELL CLARKE SHUNTER — 0-6-0

Built: 1961 by Hudswell-Clarke & Company, Leeds.
Engine: Gardner 8L3 of 152 kW (204 hp) at 1200 rpm.
Transmission: Mechanical.
Maximum Speed: 25 mph.

Latest Number Carried	Previous Number 1	Year Entered Service	Year Withdrawn	Current Status	Notes
D2510		1961	1967	Scrapped	
D2511		1961	1967	Preserved	
D2512		1961	1967	Scrapped	
D2513		1961	1967	Scrapped	
D2514		1961	1967	Scrapped	
D2515		1961	1967	Scrapped	
D2516		1961	1967	Scrapped	
D2517		1961	1967	Scrapped	
D2518		1961	1967	Scrapped	
D2519		1961	1967	Scrapped	

CLASS D3/1 NORTH BRITISH SHUNTER — 0-4-0

Built: 1958–59 North British Locomotive Company, Glasgow.
Engine: NBL MAN W6V of 246 kW (330 hp).
Transmission: Hydraulic.
Maximum Speed: 20 mph.

Latest Number Carried	Previous Number 1	Year Entered Service	Year Withdrawn	Current Status	Notes
D2900		1958	1967	Scrapped	
D2901		1958	1967	Scrapped	
D2902		1958	1967	Scrapped	
D2903		1958	1967	Scrapped	
D2904		1958	1967	Scrapped	
D2905		1958	1967	Scrapped	
D2906		1958	1967	Scrapped	
D2907		1958	1967	Scrapped	
D2908		1958	1967	Scrapped	
D2909		1958	1967	Scrapped	
D2910		1958	1967	Scrapped	
D2911		1959	1967	Scrapped	
D2912		1959	1967	Scrapped	
D2913		1959	1967	Scrapped	

CLASS D3/3 BR SHUNTER — 0-6-0

Built: 1955–57 by British Railways, Derby Works.
Engine: Crossley ESNT6 of 261 kW (350 hp).
Transmission: Electric.
Maximum Speed: 20 mph.
Train Brakes: Vacuum.

Latest Number Carried	Previous Number 1	Year Entered Service	Year Withdrawn	Current Status	Notes
D3117	13117	1955	1967	Scrapped	
D3118	13118	1955	1967	Scrapped	
D3119	13119	1955	1967	Scrapped	
D3120	13120	1955	1967	Scrapped	
D3121	13121	1955	1967	Scrapped	
D3122	13122	1955	1966	Scrapped	
D3123	13123	1955	1966	Scrapped	
D3124	13124	1955	1966	Scrapped	
D3125	13125	1957	1967	Scrapped	
D3126	13126	1957	1966	Scrapped	

▲ Class D2/12 was the second generation of Hudswell Clarke 204 hp diesel mechanical shunters, of which D2510 was the first built. It is seen at an unknown location, circa 1965.

Rail Photoprints Collection

▼ A rare image showing early diesel days at Crewe South in March 1937. In the centre is Class D3/6 LMS 0-6-0 shunter 7079, and on the right unclassified Armstrong Whitworth 0-6-0 350 hp shunter 7063. The locomotive on the left is Sentinel vertical-boilered steam loco 7192.

Rail Photoprints Collection

CLASS D3/5 BR SHUNTER   0-6-0

Built: 1955 by British Railways, Darlington Works.
Engine: Lister Blackstone ERT6 of 261 kW (350 hp).
Transmission: Electric.
Maximum Speed: 20 mph.
Train Brakes: Vacuum.

Latest Number Carried	Previous Number 1	Year Entered Service	Year Withdrawn	Current Status	Notes
D3152	13152	1955	1967	Scrapped	
D3153	13153	1955	1967	Scrapped	
D3154	13154	1955	1967	Scrapped	
D3155	13155	1955	1967	Scrapped	
D3156	13156	1955	1967	Scrapped	
D3157	13157	1955	1967	Scrapped	
D3158	13158	1955	1967	Scrapped	
D3159	13159	1955	1967	Scrapped	
D3160	13160	1955	1967	Scrapped	
D3161	13161	1955	1967	Scrapped	
D3162	13162	1955	1967	Scrapped	
D3163	13163	1955	1967	Scrapped	
D3164	13164	1955	1967	Scrapped	
D3165	13165	1955	1967	Scrapped	
D3166	13166	1955	1967	Scrapped	

CLASS D3/6 LMS SHUNTER   0-6-0

Built: 1934–36 by London Midland and Scottish Railway.
Engine: English Electric 6K of 261 kW (350 hp) at 675 rpm.
Transmission: Electric.
Maximum Speed: 12 mph.

Latest Number Carried	Previous Number 1	Year Entered Service	Year Withdrawn	Current Status	Notes
7069			1936	1940	Preserved
7070			1936	1940	Exported
7071			1936	1940	Exported
7072			1936	1940	Exported
7073			1936	1940	Exported
12000	7074		1936	1961	Scrapped
7075			1936	1940	Exported
12001	7076		1936	1962	Scrapped
7077			1936	1940	Exported
7078			1936	1940	Exported
12002	7079		1934	1956	Scrapped

CLASS D3/7 LMS SHUNTER   0-6-0

Built: 1939–42 by London Midland and Scottish Railway, Derby.
Engine: English Electric 6KT of 261 kW (350 hp) at 680 rpm.
Transmission: Electric.
Maximum Speed: 20 mph.

Latest Number Carried	Previous Number 1	Year Entered Service	Year Withdrawn	Current Status	Notes
12003	7080	1939	1967	Scrapped	
12004	7081	1939	1967	Scrapped	
12005	7082	1939	1967	Scrapped	
12006	7083	1939	1967	Scrapped	
12007	7084	1939	1967	Scrapped	
12008	7085	1939	1967	Scrapped	

12009	7086	1939	1967	Scrapped
12010	7087	1939	1967	Scrapped
12011	7088	1939	1966	Scrapped
12012	7089	1939	1967	Scrapped
12013	7090	1940	1967	Scrapped
12014	7091	1940	1967	Scrapped
12015	7092	1940	1967	Scrapped
12016	7093	1940	1967	Scrapped
12017	7094	1940	1967	Scrapped
12018	7095	1940	1967	Scrapped
12019	7096	1940	1967	Scrapped
12020	7097	1940	1967	Scrapped
12021	7098	1940	1967	Scrapped
12022	7099	1940	1966	Scrapped
7100		1940	1942	Exported
7101		1941	1942	Exported
7102		1941	1942	Exported
7103		1941	1942	Exported
7104		1941	1942	Exported
7105		1941	1942	Exported
7106		1941	1942	Exported
7107		1941	1942	Exported
7108		1941	1942	Exported
7109		1941	1942	Exported
12023	7110	1942	1967	Scrapped
12024	7111	1942	1967	Scrapped
12025	7112	1942	1967	Scrapped
12026	7113	1942	1967	Scrapped
12027	7114	1942	1967	Scrapped
12028	7115	1942	1967	Scrapped
12029	7116	1942	1966	Scrapped
12030	7117	1942	1964	Scrapped
12031	7118	1942	1967	Scrapped
12032	7119	1942	1967	Scrapped

CLASS D3/9 LNER SHUNTER 0-6-0

Built: 1944–45 by London and North Eastern Railway, Doncaster Works.
Engine: English Electric 6KT of 261 kW (350 hp).
Transmission: Electric.
Maximum Speed: 20 mph.
Train Brakes: Vacuum.

Latest Number Carried	Previous Number 1	Year Entered Service	Year Withdrawn	Current Status	Notes
15000	8000	1944	1967	Scrapped	
15001	8001	1944	1967	Scrapped	
15002	8002	1944	1967	Scrapped	
15003	8003	1945	1967	Scrapped	

CLASS D3/10 GWR SHUNTER

Built: 1936 by English Electric at Hawthorn Leslie.
Engine: English Electric 6K of 261 kW (350 hp).
Transmission: Electric.
Maximum Speed: 19 mph.
Train Brakes: None.

Latest Number Carried	Previous Number 1	Year Entered Service	Year Withdrawn	Current Status	Notes
15100	2	1936	1965	Scrapped	

CLASS D3/11 ENGLISH ELECTRIC SHUNTER   0-6-0

Built: 1948 by British Railways, Swindon Works.
Engine: English Electric 6KT of 260 kW (350 hp).
Transmission: Electric.
Maximum Speed: 20 mph.
Train Brakes: None.

Latest Number Carried	Previous Number 1	Year Entered Service	Year Withdrawn	Current Status	Notes
15101		1948	1967	Scrapped	
15102		1948	1967	Scrapped	
15103		1948	1967	Scrapped	
15104		1948	1967	Scrapped	
15105		1948	1967	Scrapped	
15106		1948	1967	Scrapped	

CLASS D3/12 SR SHUNTER   0-6-0

Built: 1937 by Southern Railway, Ashford Works.
Engine: English Electric 6K of 260 kW (350 hp).
Transmission: Electric.
Maximum Speed: 30 mph.
Train Brakes: None.

Latest Number Carried	Previous Number 1	Year Entered Service	Year Withdrawn	Current Status	Notes
15201	1	1937	1964	Scrapped	
15202	2	1937	1964	Scrapped	
15203	3	1937	1964	Scrapped	

CLASS D3/14 LNER/BRUSH SHUNTER   0-6-0

Built: 1949 by London and North Eastern Railway, Doncaster Works.
Engine: Brush Petter SS of 270 kW (360 hp).
Transmission: Electric.
Maximum Speed: 22 mph.
Train Brakes: Vacuum.

Latest Number Carried	Previous Number 1	Year Entered Service	Year Withdrawn	Current Status	Notes
15004		1949	1962	Scrapped	

2.4. DIESEL LOCOMOTIVES WITH TOPS CLASSIFICATION

CLASS 01   0-4-0

Built: 1956/58 by Andrew Barclay, Kilmarnock.
Engine: Gardner 6L3 of 114 kW (153 hp) at 1200 rpm.
Transmission: Mechanical.
Maximum Speed: 14 mph.
Train Brakes: None.

Latest Number Carried	Previous Number 1	Previous Number 2	Year Entered Service	Year Withdrawn	Current Status	Notes
D2953	11503		1956	1966	Preserved	
01001	D2954	11504	1956	1979	Scrapped	
01002	D2955	11505	1956	1981	Scrapped	
D2956	11506		1956	1966	Preserved	First of 2 locomotives to be numbered D2956
D2956[2]	81		1958	1967	Scrapped	Second of 2 locomotives to be numbered D2956. Numbered D2956 in 1967 after the first D2956 was withdrawn.

▲ Departmental 0-4-0 diesel mechanical shunter 81 is seen at Doncaster in June 1966. This locomotive subsequently received the number D2956, thus becoming the second loco to carry that number following the withdrawal of the first D2956. This type of Andrew Barclay shunter was later designated Class 01, although D2956 was itself withdrawn from service long before TOPS numbers began to be applied. **Charlie Cross/Gordon Edgar Collection/Rail Photoprints**

CLASS 02   0-4-0

Built: 1960/61 by Yorkshire Engine Company, Sheffield.
Engine: Rolls Royce C6NFL of 127 kW (170 hp) at 1800 rpm.
Transmission: Hydraulic.
Maximum Speed: 19.5 mph.
Train Brakes: Vacuum.

Latest Number Carried	Previous Number 1	Year Entered Service	Year Withdrawn	Current Status	Notes
D2850		1960	1970	Scrapped	
02001	D2851	1960	1975	Scrapped	
D2852		1960	1973	Scrapped	
02003	D2853	1960	1975	Preserved	
D2854		1960	1970	Preserved	
D2855		1960	1970	Scrapped	
02004	D2856	1960	1975	Scrapped	
D2857		1960	1971	Scrapped	
D2858		1960	1970	Preserved	
D2859		1960	1970	Scrapped	
D2860		1961	1970	Preserved	
D2861		1961	1969	Scrapped	
D2862		1961	1969	Scrapped	
D2863		1961	1969	Scrapped	
D2864		1961	1970	Scrapped	
D2865		1961	1970	Scrapped	
D2866		1961	1970	Preserved	
D2867		1961	1970	Preserved	
D2868		1961	1969	Preserved	
D2869		1961	1969	Scrapped	

CLASS 03   0-6-0

Built: 1957–62 by British Railways, Doncaster & Swindon.
Engine: Gardner 8L3 of 152 kW (204 hp) at 1200 rpm.
Transmission: Mechanical.
Maximum Speed: 28 mph.
Train Brakes: Vacuum. Some were later dual-braked (air & vacuum).

Latest Number Carried	Previous Number 1	Previous Number 2	Year Entered Service	Year Withdrawn	Current Status	Notes
D2000	11187		1957	1969	Scrapped	
D2001	11188		1957	1969	Scrapped	
D2002	11189		1957	1969	Scrapped	
D2003	11190		1957	1969	Scrapped	
03004	D2004	11191	1958	1976	Scrapped	
03005	D2005	11192	1958	1976	Scrapped	
D2006	11193		1958	1972	Scrapped	
03007	D2007	11194	1958	1976	Scrapped	
03008	D2008	11195	1958	1978	Scrapped	
03009	D2009	11196	1958	1976	Scrapped	
03010	D2010	11197	1958	1974	Scrapped	Locomotive exported and subsequently scrapped
D2011	11198		1958	1972	Scrapped	
03012	D2012	11199	1958	1975	Scrapped	
03013	D2013	11200	1958	1976	Scrapped	
03014	D2014	11201	1958	1974	Scrapped	
D2015	11202		1958	1971	Scrapped	
03016	D2016	11203	1958	1978	Scrapped	
03017	D2017	11204	1958	1982	Scrapped	
03018	D2018	11205	1958	1975	Preserved	
D2019	11206		1958	1971	Scrapped	Locomotive exported and subsequently scrapped

03020	D2020	11207	1958	1975	Preserved	
03021	D2021	11208	1958	1982	Scrapped	
03022	D2022	11209	1958	1982	Preserved	
D2023	11210		1958	1971	Preserved	
D2024	11211		1958	1971	Preserved	
03025	D2025		1958	1977	Scrapped	
03026	D2026		1958	1983	Scrapped	
03027	D2027		1958	1976	Preserved	
D2028			1958	1969	Scrapped	
03029	D2029		1958	1979	Scrapped	
D2030			1958	1969	Scrapped	
D2031			1958	1969	Scrapped	
D2032			1958	1971	Scrapped	Locomotive exported and subsequently scrapped
D2033			1958	1971	Scrapped	Locomotive exported and subsequently scrapped
03034	D2034		1959	1983	Scrapped	
03035	D2035		1959	1976	Scrapped	
D2036			1959	1971	Scrapped	Locomotive exported and subsequently scrapped
03037	D2037		1959	1976	Preserved	
D2038			1959	1972	Scrapped	
D2039			1959	1972	Scrapped	
D2040			1959	1969	Scrapped	
D2041			1959	1970	Preserved	
D2042			1959	1969	Scrapped	
D2043			1959	1971	Scrapped	
03044	D2044		1958	1976	Scrapped	
03045	D2045		1958	1979	Scrapped	
D2046			1958	1971	Preserved	
03047	D2047		1958	1979	Scrapped	
D2048			1958	1972	Scrapped	
D2049			1958	1971	Scrapped	
03050	D2050		1959	1978	Scrapped	
D2051			1959	1972	Preserved	
D2052			1959	1972	Scrapped	
D2053			1959	1972	Scrapped	
D2054			1959	1972	Scrapped	
03055	D2055		1959	1974	Scrapped	
03056	D2056		1959	1980	Scrapped	
D2057			1959	1971	Scrapped	
03058	D2058		1959	1975	Scrapped	
03059	D2059		1959	1987	Preserved	
03060	D2060		1959	1982	Scrapped	
03061	D2061		1959	1980	Scrapped	
03062	D2062		1959	1980	Preserved	
03063	D2063		1959	1987	Preserved	
03064	D2064		1959	1981	Scrapped	
D2065			1959	1972	Scrapped	
03066	D2066		1959	1988	Preserved	
03067	D2067		1959	1981	Scrapped	
03068	D2068		1959	1976	Scrapped	
03069	D2069		1959	1983	Preserved	
D2070			1959	1971	Scrapped	
D2071			1959	1972	Scrapped	
03072	D2072		1959	1981	Preserved	
03073	D2073		1959	1989	Preserved	
D2074			1959	1972	Scrapped	
03075	D2075		1959	1976	Scrapped	
03076	D2076		1959	1976	Scrapped	
D2077			1959	1972	Scrapped	
03078	D2078		1959	1988	Preserved	
03079	D2079		1960	1996	Preserved	
03080	D2080		1960	1980	Scrapped	

▲ Yorkshire Engine Company Class 02 diesel hydraulic shunter D2858 is pictured at an unknown location in 1962. **Rail Photoprints Collection**

▼ Class 03 03382 stands at Lawrence Hill, Bristol on 12 July 1979. **John Chalcraft/Rail Photoprints**

03081	D2081		1960	1980	Preserved
D2082			1959	1969	Scrapped
D2083			1959	1969	Scrapped
03084	D2084		1959	1987	Preserved
D2085			1959	1969	Scrapped
03086	D2086		1959	1983	Scrapped
D2087			1959	1971	Scrapped
D2088			1959	1972	Scrapped
03089	D2089		1960	1987	Preserved
03090	D2090		1960	1976	Preserved
03091	D2091		1960	1974	Scrapped
03092	D2092		1960	1977	Scrapped
D2093			1960	1971	Scrapped
03094	D2094		1960	1988	Preserved
03095	D2095		1960	1975	Scrapped
03096	D2096		1960	1976	Scrapped
03097	D2097		1960	1976	Scrapped
03098	D2098		1960	1975	Scrapped	Locomotive exported and subsequently scrapped
03099	D2099		1960	1976	Preserved
D2100			1960	1971	Scrapped
D2101			1960	1971	Scrapped
03102	D2102		1960	1976	Scrapped
03103	D2103		1960	1979	Scrapped
03104	D2104		1960	1975	Scrapped
03105	D2105		1960	1976	Scrapped
03106	D2106		1960	1975	Scrapped
03107	D2107		1960	1981	Scrapped
03108	D2108		1960	1976	Scrapped
03109	D2109		1960	1975	Scrapped
03110	D2110		1960	1976	Scrapped
03111	D2111		1960	1980	Scrapped
03112	D2112		1960	1987	Preserved
03113	D2113		1960	1975	Preserved
D2114			1959	1968	Scrapped
D2115			1959	1968	Scrapped
D2116			1959	1971	Scrapped
D2117			1959	1971	Preserved
03118	D2118		1959	1972	Preserved
03119	D2119		1959	1986	Preserved
03120	D2120		1959	1986	Preserved
03121	D2121		1959	1981	Scrapped
D2122			1959	1972	Scrapped
D2123			1959	1968	Scrapped
D2124			1959	1970	Scrapped
D2125			1959	1968	Scrapped
D2126			1959	1971	Scrapped
D2127			1959	1968	Scrapped
03128	03901	D2128	1960	1976	Preserved
03129	D2129		1960	1981	Scrapped
D2130			1960	1972	Scrapped
D2131			1960	1968	Scrapped
D2132			1960	1969	Scrapped
D2133			1960	1969	Preserved
03134	D2134		1960	1976	Preserved
03135	D2135		1960	1976	Scrapped
D2136			1960	1972	Scrapped
03137	D2137		1960	1976	Scrapped
D2138			1960	1969	Preserved
D2139			1960	1968	Preserved
D2140			1960	1970	Scrapped
03141	D2141		1960	1985	Preserved
03142	D2142		1960	1983	Scrapped
D2143			1961	1968	Scrapped

03144	D2144		1961	1986	Preserved	
03145	D2145		1961	1985	Preserved	
D2146			1961	1968	Scrapped	
03147	D2147		1960	1975	Scrapped	
D2148			1960	1972	Preserved	
03149	D2149		1960	1982	Scrapped	
D2150			1960	1972	Scrapped	
03151	D2151		1960	1985	Scrapped	
03152	D2152		1960	1983	Preserved	
03153	D2153		1960	1975	Scrapped	Locomotive exported and subsequently scrapped
03154	D2154		1960	1983	Scrapped	
03155	D2155		1960	1975	Scrapped	
03156	D2156		1960	1975	Exported	
03157	D2157		1960	1975	Scrapped	Locomotive exported and subsequently scrapped
03158	D2158		1960	1987	Preserved	
03159	D2159		1960	1977	Scrapped	
03160	D2160		1960	1981	Scrapped	
03161	D2161		1960	1981	Scrapped	
03162	D2162		1960	1989	Preserved	
03163	D2163		1960	1976	Scrapped	
03164	D2164		1960	1976	Scrapped	Locomotive exported and subsequently scrapped
03165	D2165		1960	1975	Scrapped	
03166	D2166		1960	1975	Scrapped	
03167	D2167		1960	1975	Scrapped	
03168	D2168		1960	1981	Scrapped	
03169	D2169		1960	1975	Scrapped	
03170	D2170		1960	1989	Preserved	
03171	D2171		1960	1977	Scrapped	
03172	D2172		1960	1976	Scrapped	
D2173			1960	1973	Scrapped	
03174	D2174		1960	1975	Scrapped	
03175	D2175		1961	1983	Scrapped	
D2176			1961	1968	Scrapped	
D2177			1961	1968	Scrapped	
D2178			1962	1969	Preserved	
03179	D2179		1962		Preserved	
03180	D2180		1962	1984	Preserved	
D2181			1962	1968	Scrapped	
D2182			1962	1968	Preserved	
D2183			1962	1968	Scrapped	
D2184			1962	1968	Preserved	
D2185			1962	1968	Scrapped	
D2186			1962	1969	Scrapped	
D2187			1961	1968	Scrapped	
D2188			1961	1968	Scrapped	
03189	D2189		1961	1986	Preserved	
D2190			1961	1968	Scrapped	
D2191			1961	1968	Scrapped	
D2192			1961	1969	Preserved	
D2193			1961	1969	Scrapped	
D2194			1961	1968	Scrapped	
D2195			1961	1968	Scrapped	
03196	D2196		1961		West Coast Railway Co	
03197	D2197		1961	1987	Preserved	
D2198			1961	1970	Scrapped	
D2199			1961	1972	Preserved	
03370	D2370	91	1958	1982	Scrapped	
03371	D2371	92	1958	1987	Preserved	
D2372			1961	1970	Scrapped	
D2373			1961	1968	Scrapped	
D2374			1961	1968	Scrapped	

D2375		1961	1968	Scrapped
D2376		1961	1968	Scrapped
D2377		1961	1968	Scrapped
D2378		1961	1971	Scrapped
D2379		1961	1968	Scrapped
D2380		1961	1968	Scrapped
D2381		1961		West Coast Railway Co
03382	D2382	1961	1983	Scrapped
D2383		1961	1971	Scrapped
D2384		1961	1968	Scrapped
D2385		1961	1970	Scrapped
03386	D2386	1961	1976	Scrapped
D2387		1961	1972	Scrapped
D2388		1961	1972	Scrapped
03389	D2389	1961	1983	Scrapped
D2390		1961	1968	Scrapped
D2391		1961	1970	Scrapped
D2392		1961	1971	Scrapped
D2393		1961	1969	Scrapped
D2394		1961	1968	Scrapped
D2395		1961	1968	Scrapped
D2396		1961	1968	Scrapped
03397	D2397	1961	1987	Scrapped
D2398		1961	1971	Scrapped
03399	D2399	1961	1987	Preserved

CLASS 04   0-6-0

Built: 1948–62 to Drewry design at Vulcan Foundry, Newton-le-Willows and Robert Stephenson & Hawthorns, Darlington.
Engine: Gardner 8L3 of 152 kW (204 hp) at 1200 rpm.
Transmission: Mechanical.
Maximum Speed: D2200–14/D2341 25 mph; D2215–73/D2296–2340 25.8 mph; D2274–95 27.5 mph.
Train Brakes: Vacuum.

Latest Number Carried	Previous Number 1	Year Entered Service	Year Withdrawn	Current Status	Notes
D2200	11100	1952	1968	Scrapped	
D2201	11101	1952	1968	Scrapped	
D2202	11102	1952	1968	Scrapped	
D2203	11103	1952	1967	Preserved	
D2204	11105	1953	1969	Scrapped	
D2205	11106	1953	1969	Preserved	
D2206	11107	1953	1969	Scrapped	
D2207	11108	1953	1967	Preserved	
D2208	11109	1953	1968	Scrapped	
D2209	11110	1953	1968	Scrapped	
D2210	11111	1954	1970	Scrapped	
D2211	11112	1954	1970	Scrapped	
D2212	11113	1954	1970	Scrapped	
D2213	11114	1954	1968	Scrapped	
D2214	11115	1954	1968	Scrapped	
D2215	11121	1955	1969	Scrapped	
D2216	11122	1955	1971	Scrapped	Locomotive exported and subsequently scrapped
D2217	11123	1955	1972	Scrapped	
D2218	11124	1955	1968	Scrapped	
D2219	11125	1955	1968	Scrapped	
D2220	11126	1955	1968	Scrapped	
D2221	11127	1955	1968	Scrapped	
D2222	11128	1955	1968	Scrapped	
D2223	11129	1955	1971	Scrapped	
D2224	11130	1955	1968	Scrapped	

D2225	11131	1955	1969	Scrapped
D2226	11132	1955	1968	Scrapped
D2227	11133	1955	1968	Scrapped
D2228	11134	1955	1968	Scrapped
D2229	11135	1955	1969	Preserved
D2230	11149	1956	1968	Scrapped
D2231	11150	1956	1969	Scrapped
D2232	11151	1956	1968	Scrapped
D2233	11152	1956	1968	Scrapped
D2234	11153	1956	1968	Scrapped
D2235	11154	1956	1968	Scrapped
D2236	11155	1956	1968	Scrapped
D2237	11156	1956	1969	Scrapped
D2238	11157	1956	1968	Scrapped
D2239	11158	1956	1971	Scrapped
D2240	11159	1956	1968	Scrapped
D2241	11160	1956	1971	Scrapped
D2242	11212	1956	1969	Scrapped
D2243	11213	1956	1969	Scrapped
D2244	11214	1956	1970	Scrapped
D2245	11215	1956	1968	Preserved
D2246	11216	1956	1968	Preserved
D2247	11217	1956	1969	Scrapped
D2248	11218	1957	1970	Scrapped
D2249	11219	1957	1970	Scrapped
D2250	11220	1957	1968	Scrapped
D2251	11221	1957	1968	Scrapped
D2252	11222	1957	1968	Scrapped

▲ After a British Rail career in the North of England, followed by use by the National Coal Board, Class 04 D2246 entered preservation and is now owned by the Devon Diesel Society and based at the South Devon Railway. The loco is shown stabled in Buckfastleigh Yard on 25 August 2017.

Andy Chard

D2253	11223	1957	1969	Scrapped	
D2254	11224	1957	1967	Scrapped	
D2255	11225	1957	1968	Scrapped	
D2256	11226	1957	1968	Scrapped	
D2257	11227	1957	1968	Scrapped	
D2258	11228	1957	1970	Scrapped	
D2259	11229	1957	1968	Scrapped	
D2260		1957	1970	Scrapped	
D2261		1957	1970	Scrapped	
D2262		1957	1968	Scrapped	
D2263		1957	1967	Scrapped	
D2264		1957	1969	Scrapped	
D2265		1957	1970	Scrapped	
D2266		1958	1967	Scrapped	
D2267		1958	1969	Scrapped	
D2268		1958	1968	Scrapped	
D2269		1958	1968	Scrapped	
D2270		1958	1968	Scrapped	
D2271		1958	1969	Preserved	
D2272		1958	1970	Preserved	
D2273		1958	1967	Scrapped	
D2274		1959	1969	Scrapped	
D2275		1959	1967	Scrapped	
D2276		1959	1969	Scrapped	
D2277		1959	1969	Scrapped	
D2278		1959	1970	Scrapped	
D2279		1960	1971	Preserved	
D2280		1960	1971	Preserved	
D2281		1960	1968	Scrapped	
D2282		1960	1970	Scrapped	
D2283		1960	1969	Scrapped	
D2284		1960	1971	Preserved	
D2285		1960	1969	Scrapped	
D2286		1960	1968	Scrapped	
D2287		1960	1968	Scrapped	
D2288		1960	1967	Scrapped	
D2289		1960	1971	Exported	
D2290		1960	1967	Scrapped	
D2291		1960	1967	Scrapped	
D2292		1960	1967	Scrapped	
D2293		1960	1971	Scrapped	
D2294		1960	1971	Scrapped	
D2295		1960	1971	Scrapped	Locomotive exported and subsequently scrapped
D2296		1960	1969	Scrapped	
D2297		1960	1970	Scrapped	
D2298		1960	1968	Preserved	
D2299		1960	1970	Scrapped	
D2300		1960	1969	Scrapped	
D2301		1960	1968	Scrapped	
D2302		1960	1969	Preserved	
D2303		1960	1967	Scrapped	
D2304		1960	1968	Scrapped	
D2305		1960	1968	Scrapped	
D2306		1960	1968	Scrapped	
D2307		1960	1968	Scrapped	
D2308		1960	1968	Scrapped	
D2309		1960	1968	Scrapped	
04110	D2310	1960	1969	Preserved	
D2311		1960	1968	Scrapped	
D2312		1961	1968	Scrapped	
D2313		1961	1968	Scrapped	
D2314		1961	1968	Scrapped	
D2315		1961	1968	Scrapped	
D2316		1961	1968	Scrapped	

D2317	1961	1969	Scrapped
D2318	1961	1968	Scrapped
D2319	1961	1968	Scrapped
D2320	1961	1968	Scrapped
D2321	1961	1968	Scrapped
D2322	1961	1968	Scrapped
D2323	1961	1968	Scrapped
D2324	1961	1968	Preserved
D2325	1961	1968	Preserved
D2326	1961	1968	Scrapped
D2327	1961	1968	Scrapped
D2328	1961	1968	Scrapped
D2329	1961	1968	Scrapped
D2330	1961	1969	Scrapped
D2331	1961	1968	Scrapped
D2332	1961	1969	Scrapped
D2333	1961	1969	Scrapped
D2334	1961	1968	Preserved
D2335	1961	1968	Scrapped
D2336	1961	1968	Scrapped
D2337	1961	1968	Preserved
D2338	1961	1968	Scrapped
D2339	1961	1967	Scrapped
D2340		1962	1968	Scrapped
D2341	DS1173	1948	1968	Scrapped

CLASS 05   0-6-0

Built: 1955–61 by Hunslet Engine Company, Leeds.
Engine: Gardner 8L3 of 152 kW (204 hp) at 1200 rpm.
Transmission: Mechanical.
Maximum Speed: 18 mph.
Train Brakes: Vacuum.

Latest Number Carried	Previous Number 1	Previous Number 2	Previous Number 3	Previous Number 4	Year Entered Service	Year Withdrawn	Current Status	Notes
D2550	11136				1955	1966	Scrapped	
D2551	11137				1955	1968	Scrapped	
D2552	11138				1956	1967	Scrapped	
D2553	11139				1956	1968	Scrapped	
D2554	97803	05001	D2554	11140	1956	1983	Preserved	
D2555	11141				1956	1968	Scrapped	
D2556	11142				1956	1967	Scrapped	
D2557	11143				1956	1967	Scrapped	
D2558	11161				1956	1967	Scrapped	
D2559	11162				1956	1967	Scrapped	
D2560	11163				1957	1967	Scrapped	
D2561	11164				1957	1967	Scrapped	
D2562	11165				1957	1968	Scrapped	
D2563	11166				1957	1967	Scrapped	
D2564	11167				1957	1967	Scrapped	
D2565	11168				1957	1967	Scrapped	
D2566	11169				1957	1968	Scrapped	
D2567	11170				1957	1967	Scrapped	
D2568	11171				1957	1967	Scrapped	
D2569	11172				1957	1967	Scrapped	
D2570	11173				1957	1967	Scrapped	
D2571	11174				1957	1968	Scrapped	
D2572	11175				1957	1967	Scrapped	
D2573	11176				1958	1968	Scrapped	
D2574					1958	1968	Scrapped	
D2575					1958	1968	Scrapped	
D2576					1958	1968	Scrapped	

D2577	1958	1967	Scrapped
D2578	1958	1967	Preserved
D2579	1958	1968	Scrapped
D2580	1958	1968	Scrapped
D2581	1958	1968	Scrapped
D2582	1959	1968	Scrapped
D2583	1959	1968	Scrapped
D2584	1959	1967	Scrapped
D2585	1959	1968	Scrapped
D2586	1959	1967	Scrapped
D2587	1959	1967	Preserved
D2588	1959	1967	Scrapped
D2589	1959	1967	Scrapped
D2590	1959	1968	Scrapped
D2591	1959	1967	Scrapped
D2592	1959	1968	Scrapped
D2593	1959	1967	Scrapped
D2594	1960	1967	Scrapped
D2595	1960	1968	Preserved
D2596	1960	1968	Scrapped
D2597	1960	1967	Scrapped
D2598	1960	1967	Scrapped
D2599	1960	1967	Scrapped
D2600	1960	1967	Scrapped
D2601	1960	1967	Scrapped
D2602	1960	1967	Scrapped
D2603	1960	1967	Scrapped

▲ A "Nottingham Railway Enthusiasts" brake van special reaches the end of track at Epworth on the Isle of Axholme Light Railway, a Lancashire & Yorkshire Railway & North Eastern Railway Joint Line. The five brake vans, hauled by Hunslet Class 05 0-6-0 D2611, stand in the remains of the long disused passenger station on 14 September 1963. Passenger services had ceased in July 1933 and the remaining lines were closed in April 1965. **Geoff Plumb Collection**

D2604				1960	1967	Scrapped
D2605				1960	1967	Scrapped
D2606				1960	1967	Scrapped
D2607				1960	1967	Scrapped
D2608				1960	1967	Scrapped
D2609				1960	1967	Scrapped
D2610				1960	1967	Scrapped
D2611				1961	1967	Scrapped
88	D2612			1961	1967	Scrapped
D2613				1961	1967	Scrapped
D2614				1961	1967	Scrapped
89	D2615			1961	1967	Scrapped
D2616				1961	1967	Scrapped
D2617				1961	1967	Scrapped
D2618				1961	1968	Scrapped

CLASS 06   0-4-0

Built: 1958–60 by Andrew Barclay, Kilmarnock.
Engine: Gardner 8L3 of 152 kW (204 hp) at 1200 rpm.
Transmission: Mechanical.
Maximum Speed: 22.75 mph.
Train Brakes: Vacuum.

Latest Number Carried	Previous Number 1	Previous Number 2	Previous Number 3	Year Entered Service	Year Withdrawn	Current Status	Notes
D2410				1958	1969	Scrapped	
D2411				1958	1968	Scrapped	
D2412				1958	1968	Scrapped	
06001	D2413			1958	1976	Scrapped	
06002	D2414			1958	1981	Scrapped	
D2415				1958	1968	Scrapped	
D2416				1958	1972	Scrapped	
D2417				1958	1968	Scrapped	
D2418				1959	1968	Scrapped	
D2419				1959	1969	Scrapped	
06003	97804	06003	D2420	1959	1984	Preserved	
06004	D2421			1959	1979	Scrapped	
06005	D2422			1959	1980	Scrapped	
06006	D2423			1959	1980	Scrapped	
D2424				1959	1972	Scrapped	
D2425				1959	1968	Scrapped	
06007	D2426			1959	1977	Scrapped	
D2427				1959	1969	Scrapped	
D2428				1959	1968	Scrapped	
D2429				1960	1969	Scrapped	
D2430				1960	1968	Scrapped	
D2431				1960	1971	Scrapped	
D2432				1960	1968	Scrapped	Locomotive exported and subsequently scrapped
D2433				1960	1972	Scrapped	
D2434				1960	1969	Scrapped	
D2435				1960	1971	Scrapped	
D2436				1960	1971	Scrapped	
06008	D2437			1960	1980	Scrapped	
D2438				1960	1972	Scrapped	
D2439				1960	1971	Scrapped	
06009	D2440			1960	1975	Scrapped	
D2441				1960	1967	Scrapped	
D2442				1960	1972	Scrapped	
D2443				1960	1972	Scrapped	
06010	D2444			1960	1975	Scrapped	

▲ Class 06 locomotives are particularly associated with Scotland, having been built at Andrew Barclay in Kilmarnock and having spent most of their working lives north of the border. 06007 is seen at Polmadie depot, Glasgow on 9 April 1977. **Rail Photoprints Collection**

▼ Ruston & Hornsby Class 07 shunters 2996 and 2987 stand at Southampton Western Docks on 12 July 1970. **Gordon Edgar/Rail Photoprints**

CLASS 07   0-6-0

Built: 1962 by Ruston & Hornsby, Lincoln.
Engine: Paxman 6RPHL of 205 kW (275 hp) at 1360 rpm.
Transmission: Electric.
Maximum Speed: 20 mph.
Train Brakes: Vacuum. Some were later dual-braked (air & vacuum).

Latest Number Carried	Previous Number 1	Previous Number 2	Year Entered Service	Year Withdrawn	Current Status	Notes
07001	D2985		1962	2013	Preserved	
07002	D2986		1962	1977	Scrapped	
07003	D2987		1962	1976	Scrapped	
D2988			1962	1973	Scrapped	
07005	D2989		1962	1977	Preserved	
07006	D2990		1962	1977	Scrapped	
07007	D2991		1962		Arlington Fleet Services	
D2992			1962	1973	Scrapped	
07009	D2993		1962	1976	Scrapped	Locomotive exported and subsequently scrapped
07010	D2994		1962	1976	Preserved	
07011	D2995		1962	1977	Preserved	
07012	D2996		1962	1977	Preserved	
07013	D2997		1962	1977	Preserved	
D2998			1962	1973	Scrapped	

CLASS 08   0-6-0

Built: 1952–62 by British Railways, Derby, Darlington, Crewe, Horwich & Doncaster.
Engine: English Electric 6KT of 298 kW (400 hp) at 680 rpm.
Transmission: Electric.
Maximum Speed: 15 mph.
Train Brakes: Vacuum; except D3092–D3101 which did not have train brakes. Some were later dual-braked (air & vacuum).

Latest Number Carried	Previous Number 1	Previous Number 2	Previous Number 3	Year Entered Service	Year Withdrawn	Current Status	Notes
D3000	13000			1952	1972	Preserved	
D3001	13001			1952	1972	Scrapped	
D3002	13002			1952	1972	Preserved	
D3003	13003			1952	1972	Scrapped	
08001	D3004	13004		1952	1978	Scrapped	
08002	D3005	13005		1952	1977	Scrapped	
ADB966507	D3006	13006		1952	1979	Scrapped	Locomotive was not self-propelled whilst in departmental use.
08003	D3007	13007		1952	1977	Scrapped	
08004	D3008	13008		1952	1983	Scrapped	
08005	D3009	13009		1952	1978	Scrapped	
08006	D3010	13010		1952	1980	Scrapped	
D3011	13011			1952	1972	Scrapped	
08007	D3012	13012		1952	1973	Scrapped	
D3013	13013			1952	1972	Scrapped	
D3014	13014			1952	1972	Preserved	
08008	D3015	13015		1953	1983	Scrapped	
08009	D3016	13016		1953	1975	Scrapped	
08010	D3017	13017		1953	1977	Scrapped	
08011	D3018	13018		1953	1991	Preserved	
08012	D3019	13019		1953	1973	Preserved	
08013	D3020	13020		1953	1973	Scrapped	
08014	D3021	13021		1953	1980	Scrapped	
08015	D3022	13022		1953	1980	Preserved	

08016	D3023	13023		1953	1980	Preserved	
08017	D3024	13024		1953	1973	Scrapped	
08018	D3025	13025		1953	1983	Scrapped	
D3026	13026			1953	1972	Scrapped	
08019	D3027	13027		1953	1983	Scrapped	
08020	D3028	13028		1953	1973	Scrapped	
08021	D3029	13029		1953	1986	Preserved	
08022	D3030	13030		1953	1985	Preserved	
08023	D3031	13031		1953	1983	Scrapped	
08024	D3032	13032		1953	1982	Scrapped	
08025	D3033	13033		1953	1977	Scrapped	
D3034	13034			1953	1972	Scrapped	
ADB966508	D3035	13035		1953	1979	Scrapped	Locomotive was not self-propelled whilst in departmental use.
08026	D3036	13036		1953	1982	Scrapped	
ADB966510	D3037	13037		1953	1978	Scrapped	Locomotive was not self-propelled whilst in departmental use.
D3038	13038			1953	1972	Scrapped	
08027	D3039	13039		1953	1980	Scrapped	
08028	D3040	13040		1954	1981	Scrapped	
08029	D3041	13041		1954	1978	Scrapped	
08030	D3042	13042		1954	1982	Scrapped	
08031	D3043	13043		1954	1982	Scrapped	
08032	D3044	13044		1954	1974	Preserved	
D3045	13045			1954	1972	Scrapped	
08033	D3046	13046		1954	1985	Scrapped	
08034	D3047	13047		1954	1973	Exported	
08035	D3048	13048		1954	1979	Scrapped	
08036	D3049	13049		1954	1981	Scrapped	
08037	D3050	13050		1954	1980	Scrapped	
08038	D3051	13051		1954	1973	Scrapped	
08039	D3052	13052		1954	1973	Scrapped	
08040	D3053	13053		1954	1973	Scrapped	
08041	D3054	13054		1954	1978	Scrapped	
08042	D3055	13055		1954	1979	Scrapped	
08043	D3056	13056		1954	1977	Scrapped	
08044	D3057	13057		1954	1978	Scrapped	
08045	D3058	13058		1954	1982	Scrapped	
08046	D3059	13059		1954	1980	Preserved	
08047	D3060	13060		1953	1979	Scrapped	
08048	D3061	13061		1953	1977	Scrapped	
08049	D3062	13062		1953	1981	Scrapped	
08050	D3063	13063		1953	1981	Scrapped	
08051	D3064	13064		1953	1982	Scrapped	
08052	D3065	13065		1953	1981	Scrapped	
08053	D3066	13066		1953	1981	Scrapped	
08054	D3067	13067		1953	1980	Preserved	
08055	D3068	13068		1953	1980	Scrapped	
ADB966509	D3069	13069		1953	1979	Scrapped	Locomotive was not self-propelled whilst in departmental use.
08056	D3070	13070		1953	1986	Scrapped	
08057	D3071	13071		1953	1976	Scrapped	
08058	D3072	13072		1953	1982	Scrapped	
08059	D3073	13073		1953	1980	Scrapped	
08060	D3074	13074		1953	1984	Preserved	
08061	D3075	13075		1953	1984	Scrapped	
08062	D3076	13076		1954	1984	Scrapped	
08063	D3077	13077		1954	1984	Scrapped	

ADB966506	D3078	13078	1954	1978	Scrapped	Locomotive was not self-propelled whilst in departmental use.
08064	D3079	13079	1954	1984	Preserved	
08065	D3080	13080	1954	1977	Scrapped	
08066	D3081	13081	1954	1977	Scrapped	
08067	D3082	13082	1954	1983	Scrapped	
08068	D3083	13083	1954	1983	Scrapped	
08069	D3084	13084	1954	1983	Scrapped	
08070	D3085	13085	1954	1977	Scrapped	
08071	D3086	13086	1954	1978	Scrapped	
08072	D3087	13087	1954	1973	Scrapped	
08073	D3088	13088	1954	1973	Scrapped	
08074	D3089	13089	1954	1973	Scrapped	
08075	D3090	13090	1954	1981	Scrapped	
08076	D3091	13091	1954	1980	Scrapped	
D3092	13092		1954	1972	Exported	
D3093	13093		1954	1972	Scrapped	
D3094	13094		1954	1972	Exported	
D3095	13095		1954	1972	Scrapped	
D3096	13096		1954	1972	Scrapped	
D3097	13097		1955	1972	Scrapped	
D3098	13098		1955	1972	Exported	
D3099	13099		1955	1972	Scrapped	
D3100	13100		1955	1972	Exported	
D3101	13101		1955	1972	Preserved	
08077	D3102	13102	1955	1977	Scrapped	
08078	D3103	13103	1955	1983	Scrapped	
08079	D3104	13104	1955	1983	Scrapped	
08080	D3105	13105	1955	1980	Scrapped	
08081	D3106	13106	1955	1980	Scrapped	
08082	D3107	13107	1955	1980	Scrapped	
08083	D3108	13108	1955	1984	Scrapped	
08084	D3109	13109	1955	1980	Scrapped	
08085	D3110	13110	1955	1986	Scrapped	
08086	D3111	13111	1955	1980	Scrapped	
08087	D3112	13112	1955	1979	Scrapped	
08088	D3113	13113	1955	1983	Scrapped	
08089	D3114	13114	1955	1980	Scrapped	
08090	D3115	13115	1955	1977	Scrapped	
08091	D3116	13116	1955	1982	Scrapped	
08092	D3127	13127	1954	1978	Scrapped	
08093	D3128	13128	1954	1981	Scrapped	
08094	D3129	13129	1954	1983	Scrapped	
08095	D3130	13130	1954	1983	Scrapped	
08096	D3131	13131	1954	1984	Scrapped	
08097	D3132	13132	1954	1981	Scrapped	
08098	D3133	13133	1954	1980	Scrapped	
08099	D3134	13134	1954	1982	Scrapped	
08100	D3135	13135	1954	1982	Scrapped	
08101	D3136	13136	1954	1983	Scrapped	
08102	D3167	13167	1955	1988	Preserved	
08103	D3168	13168	1955	1983	Scrapped	
08104	D3169	13169	1955	1982	Scrapped	
08105	D3170	13170	1955	1983	Scrapped	
08106	D3171	13171	1955	1982	Scrapped	
D3172	13172		1955	1972	Scrapped	
08107	D3173	13173	1955	1982	Scrapped	
08108	D3174	13174	1955	1984	Preserved	
08109	D3175	13175	1955	1981	Scrapped	
08110	D3176	13176	1955	1979	Scrapped	

ADB968012	ADB966512	08111	D3177	1955	1979	Scrapped	Locomotive was not self-propelled whilst in departmental use. Also carried previous number 4: 13177
08112	D3178	13178		1955	1982	Scrapped	
08113	D3179	13179		1955	1984	Scrapped	
08114	D3180	13180		1955	1983	Preserved	
08115	D3181	13181		1955	1984	Scrapped	
08116	D3182	13182		1955	1982	Scrapped	
D3183	13183			1955	1972	Scrapped	
ADB968010	ADB968013	ADB966513	08117	1955	1979	Scrapped	Locomotive was not self-propelled whilst in departmental use. Also carried previous number 4: D3184 and previous number 5: 13184
08118	D3185	13185		1955	1980	Scrapped	
ADB968011	ADB966511	08119	D3186	1955	1979	Scrapped	Locomotive was not self-propelled whilst in departmental use. Also carried previous number 4: 13186
08120	D3187	13187		1955	1981	Scrapped	
08121	D3188	13188		1955	1984	Scrapped	
08122	D3189	13189		1955	1977	Scrapped	
08123	D3190	13190		1955	1984	Preserved	
08124	D3191	13191		1955	1981	Scrapped	
08125	D3192	13192		1955	1981	Scrapped	
D3193	13193			1955	1967	Scrapped	
08126	D3194	13194		1955	1980	Scrapped	
08127	D3195	13195		1955	1980	Scrapped	
08128	D3196	13196		1955	1980	Scrapped	
08129	D3197	13197		1955	1983	Scrapped	
08130	D3198	13198		1955	1982	Scrapped	
08131	D3199	13199		1955	1981	Scrapped	
08132	D3200	13200		1955	1986	Scrapped	
08133	D3201	13201		1955	1980	Preserved	
08134	D3202	13202		1955	1981	Scrapped	
08135	D3203	13203		1955	1977	Scrapped	
08136	D3204	13204		1955	1983	Scrapped	
08137	D3205	13205		1955	1982	Scrapped	
08138	D3206	13206		1955	1978	Scrapped	
08139	D3207	13207		1956	1980	Scrapped	
08140	D3208	13208		1956	1977	Scrapped	
08141	D3209	13209		1956	1988	Scrapped	
08142	D3210	13210		1956	1983	Scrapped	
08143	D3211	13211		1956	1976	Scrapped	
08144	D3212	13212		1956	1977	Scrapped	
08145	D3213	13213		1956	1977	Scrapped	
08146	D3214	13214		1956	1980	Scrapped	
08147	D3215	13215		1956	1983	Scrapped	
08148	D3216	13216		1956	1984	Scrapped	
08149	D3217	13217		1955	1981	Scrapped	
08150	D3218	13218		1955	1984	Scrapped	
08151	D3219	13219		1955	1979	Scrapped	
08152	D3220	13220		1955	1980	Scrapped	
08153	D3221	13221		1955	1982	Scrapped	
08154	D3222	13222		1955	1979	Scrapped	
08155	D3223	13223		1955	1979	Scrapped	
08156	D3224	13224		1955	1979	Scrapped	
08157	D3225	13225		1955	1977	Scrapped	
08158	D3226	13226		1955	1979	Scrapped	

				Built	Withdrawn	Status	Notes
08159	D3227	13227		1955	1985	Scrapped	
08160	D3228	13228		1955	1985	Scrapped	
08161	D3229	13229		1955	1985	Scrapped	
08162	D3230	13230		1955	1980	Scrapped	
08163	D3231	13231		1955	1982	Scrapped	
08164	D3232	13232		1956	1986	Preserved	
08165	D3233	13233		1956	1980	Scrapped	
08166	D3234	13234		1956	1982	Scrapped	
08167	D3235	13235		1956	1977	Scrapped	
08168	D3236	13236		1956		Nemesis Rail	
08169	D3237	13237		1956	1981	Scrapped	
08170	D3238	13238		1956	1986	Scrapped	
08171	D3239	13239		1956	1983	Scrapped	
08172	D3240	13240		1956	1985	Scrapped	
PO1[2]	08173	D3241	13241	1956	1978	Scrapped	Second of two locomotives to be numbered PO1
08174	D3242	13242		1956	1981	Scrapped	
08175	D3243	13243		1956	1978	Scrapped	
08176	D3244	13244		1956	1985	Scrapped	
08177	D3245	13245		1956	1988	Scrapped	
08178	D3246	13246		1956	1982	Scrapped	
08179	D3247	13247		1956	1975	Scrapped	
08180	D3248	13248		1956	1981	Scrapped	
08181	D3249	13249		1956	1982	Scrapped	
08182	D3250	13250		1956	1981	Scrapped	
08183	D3251	13251		1956	1984	Scrapped	
08184	D3252	13252		1956	1981	Scrapped	
08185	D3253	13253		1956	1982	Scrapped	
08186	D3254	13254		1956	1985	Scrapped	
D3255	13255			1956	1972	Preserved	
08187	D3256	13256		1956	1983	Scrapped	
08188	D3257	13257		1956	1983	Scrapped	
08189	D3258	13258		1956	1981	Scrapped	
08190	D3259	13259		1956	1980	Scrapped	
08191	D3260	13260		1956	1988	Scrapped	
D3261	13261			1956	1972	Preserved	
08192	D3262	13262		1956	1982	Scrapped	
08193	D3263	13263		1956	1983	Scrapped	
08194	D3264	13264		1956	1980	Scrapped	
08195	D3265	13265		1956	1983	Preserved	
08196	D3266	13266		1956	1983	Scrapped	
08197	D3267	13267		1956	1982	Scrapped	
08198	D3268	13268		1956	1980	Scrapped	
08199	D3269	13269		1956	1983	Scrapped	
08200	D3270	13270		1956	1986	Scrapped	
08201	D3271	13271		1956	1982	Scrapped	
08202	D3272	13272		1956	1989	Preserved	
08204	D3274	13274		1956	1983	Scrapped	
08205	D3275	13275		1956	1983	Scrapped	
08206	D3276	13276		1956	1988	Scrapped	
08207	D3277	13277		1956	1980	Scrapped	
08208	D3278	13278		1956	1984	Scrapped	
08209	D3279	13279		1956	1983	Scrapped	
08210	D3280	13280		1956	1988	Scrapped	
08211	D3281	13281		1956	1985	Scrapped	
08212	D3282	13282		1956	1981	Scrapped	
08213	D3283	13283		1956	1980	Scrapped	
08214	D3284	13284		1956	1984	Scrapped	
08215	D3285	13285		1956	1982	Scrapped	
08216	D3286	13286		1956	1980	Scrapped	
08217	D3287	13287		1956	1982	Scrapped	
08218	D3288	13288		1956	1980	Scrapped	
08219	D3289	13289		1956	1983	Scrapped	

08220	D3290	13290		1956		Preserved	Preserved locomotive on hire to EMD Longport
08221	D3291	13291		1956	1981	Scrapped	
08222	D3292	13292		1956	1984	Scrapped	
08223	D3293	13293		1956	1979	Scrapped	
08224	D3294	13294		1956	1988	Scrapped	
08225	D3295	13295		1957	1985	Scrapped	
08226	D3296	13296		1957	1985	Scrapped	
08227	D3297	13297		1957	1983	Scrapped	
08228	D3298	13298		1956	1985	Scrapped	
08229	D3299	13299		1956	1977	Scrapped	
08230	D3300	13300		1956	1980	Scrapped	
08231	D3301	13301		1956	1981	Scrapped	
08232	D3302	13302		1956	1982	Scrapped	
08233	D3303	13303		1956	1981	Scrapped	
08234	D3304	13304		1956	1982	Scrapped	
08235	D3305	13305		1956	1983	Scrapped	
08236	D3306	13306		1956	1975	Scrapped	
08237	D3307	13307		1956	1984	Scrapped	
08238	D3308	13308		1956	1984	Preserved	
08239	D3309	13309		1956	1984	Scrapped	
08240	D3310	13310		1956	1982	Scrapped	
08241	D3311	13311		1956	1981	Scrapped	
08242	D3312	13312		1956	1986	Scrapped	
08243	D3313	13313		1956	1985	Scrapped	
08244	D3314	13314		1956	1986	Scrapped	
08245	D3315	13315		1956	1984	Scrapped	
08246	D3316	13316		1956	1982	Scrapped	
PO1	08247	D3317	13317	1956	1981	Scrapped	First of two locomotives to be numbered PO1
08248	D3318	13318		1956	1984	Scrapped	
08249	D3319	13319		1956	1985	Scrapped	
08250	D3320	13320		1956	1988	Scrapped	
08251	D3321	13321		1956	1980	Scrapped	
08252	D3322	13322		1956	1981	Scrapped	
08253	D3323	13323		1956	1987	Scrapped	
08254	D3324	13324		1956	1986	Scrapped	
08255	D3325	13325		1956	1984	Scrapped	
08256	D3326	13326		1956	1984	Scrapped	
08257	D3327	13327		1956	1985	Scrapped	
08258	D3328	13328		1956	1988	Scrapped	
08260	D3330	13330		1956	1983	Scrapped	
08261	D3331	13331		1956	1983	Scrapped	
08262	D3332	13332		1957	1984	Scrapped	
08263	D3333	13333		1957	1984	Scrapped	
08264	D3334	13334		1957	1984	Scrapped	
08265	D3335	13335		1957	1981	Scrapped	
08266	D3336	13336		1957	1985	Preserved	
97801	RDB968020	08267	D3337	1957	1981	Scrapped	Also carried previous number 4: 13337
08268	D3338	13338		1957	1985	Scrapped	
08269	D3339	13339		1957	1984	Scrapped	
08270	D3340	13340		1957	1982	Scrapped	
08271	D3341	13341		1957	1981	Scrapped	
08272	D3342	13342		1957	1987	Scrapped	
08273	D3343	13343		1957	1982	Scrapped	
08274	D3344	13344		1957	1984	Scrapped	
08275	D3345	13345		1957	1983	Scrapped	
08276	D3346	13346		1957	1977	Scrapped	
08277	D3347	13347		1957	1981	Scrapped	
08278	D3348	13348		1957	1977	Scrapped	
08279	D3349	13349		1957	1981	Scrapped	

08280	D3350	13350		1957	1980	Scrapped	
08281	D3351	13351		1957	1980	Scrapped	
08282	D3352	13352		1957	1980	Scrapped	
08283	D3353	13353		1957	1986	Scrapped	
08284	D3354	13354		1957	1985	Scrapped	
08285	D3355	13355		1957	1988	Scrapped	
08286	D3356	13356		1957	1982	Scrapped	
08287	D3357	13357		1957	1983	Scrapped	
08288	D3358			1957	1983	Preserved	
08289	D3359			1957	1985	Scrapped	
08290	D3360			1957	1982	Scrapped	
08291	D3361			1957	1983	Scrapped	
08292	D3362			1957	1984	Scrapped	
08293	D3363	13363		1957	1985	Scrapped	
08294	D3364	13364		1957	1980	Scrapped	
08295	D3365	13365		1957	1988	Scrapped	
08787[2]	08296	D3366	13366	1957	1991	Scrapped	Second locomotive to carry 08787, renumbered shortly before scrapping
08297	D3367			1957	1988	Scrapped	
08298	D3368			1957	1981	Scrapped	
08299	D3369			1957	1981	Scrapped	
08300	D3370			1957	1983	Scrapped	
08301	D3371			1957	1981	Scrapped	
08302	D3372			1957	1981	Scrapped	
08303	D3373			1957	1981	Scrapped	
08304	D3374			1957	1985	Scrapped	
08305	D3375			1957	1988	Scrapped	
08306	D3376			1957	1977	Scrapped	
08307	D3377			1957	1977	Scrapped	
08308	D3378			1957		RMS Locotec	
08309	D3379			1957	1992	Scrapped	
08310	D3380			1957	1977	Scrapped	
08311	D3381			1957	1982	Scrapped	
08312	D3382			1957	1983	Scrapped	
08313	D3383			1957	1982	Scrapped	
08314	D3384			1957	1981	Scrapped	
08315	D3385			1957	1979	Scrapped	
08316	D3386			1957	1976	Scrapped	
08317	D3387			1957	1982	Scrapped	
08318	D3388			1957	1976	Scrapped	
08319	D3389			1957	1983	Scrapped	
08320	D3390			1957	1982	Scrapped	
08321	D3391			1957	1984	Scrapped	
08322	D3392			1957	1983	Scrapped	
08323	D3393			1957	1981	Scrapped	
08324	D3394			1957	1984	Scrapped	
08325	D3395			1957	1984	Scrapped	
08326	D3396			1957	1983	Scrapped	
08327	D3397			1957	1983	Scrapped	
08328	D3398			1957	1981	Scrapped	
08329	D3399			1957	1984	Scrapped	
08330	D3400			1957	1984	Scrapped	
08331	D3401			1957		Class 20189	
08332	D3402			1957	1984	Scrapped	
08333	D3403			1957	1982	Scrapped	
08334	D3404			1957	1986	Scrapped	
08335	D3405			1957	1987	Scrapped	
08336	D3406			1957	1981	Scrapped	
08337	D3407			1957	1987	Scrapped	
08338	D3408			1958	1985	Scrapped	
08339	D3409			1958	1984	Scrapped	
08340	D3410			1958	1981	Scrapped	

08341	D3411		1958	1983	Scrapped
08342	D3412		1958	1982	Scrapped
08343	D3413		1958	1983	Scrapped
08344	D3414		1958	1984	Scrapped
08345	D3415		1958	1983	Scrapped
08346	D3416		1958	1984	Scrapped
08347	D3417		1958	1983	Scrapped
08348	D3418		1958	1982	Scrapped
08349	D3419		1957	1983	Scrapped
08350	D3420		1957	1984	Scrapped
08351	D3421		1957	1984	Scrapped
08352	D3422		1957	1983	Scrapped
08353	D3423		1958	1981	Scrapped
08354	D3424		1958	1986	Scrapped
08355	D3425		1958	1983	Scrapped
08356	D3426		1958	1982	Scrapped
08357	D3427		1958	1977	Scrapped
08358	D3428		1958	1977	Scrapped
08359	D3429		1958	1984	Preserved
08360	D3430		1958	1983	Scrapped
08361	D3431		1958	1988	Scrapped
08362	D3432		1958	1982	Scrapped
08363	D3433		1958	1982	Scrapped
08364	D3434		1958	1983	Scrapped
08365	D3435		1958	1980	Scrapped
08366	D3436		1958	1980	Scrapped
08367	D3437		1958	1988	Scrapped
08368	D3438		1958	1980	Scrapped
08369	D3454		1957	1985	Scrapped
08370	D3455		1957	1984	Scrapped
08371	D3456		1957	1983	Scrapped
08372	D3457		1957	1984	Scrapped
08373	D3458		1957	1985	Scrapped
08374	D3459		1957	1982	Scrapped
21	08375	D3460	1957		RMS Locotec
08376	D3461		1957	1983	Scrapped
08377	D3462		1957	1983	Preserved
08378	D3463		1957	1981	Scrapped
08379	D3464		1957	1980	Scrapped
08380	D3465		1957	1982	Scrapped
08381	D3466		1957	1982	Scrapped
08382	D3467		1957	1985	Scrapped
08383	D3468		1957	1985	Scrapped
08384	D3469		1957	1986	Scrapped
08385	D3470		1957	1988	Scrapped
08386	D3471		1957	1987	Scrapped
08387	D3472		1957	1982	Scrapped
08388	D3503		1958	1996	Scrapped
08389	CELSA 1	D3504	1958		Harry Needle Railroad Co
08390	D3505		1958	1993	Scrapped
08391	D3506		1958	1985	Scrapped
08392	D3507		1958	1984	Scrapped
08393	D3508		1958	2011	Scrapped
08394	D3509		1958	1987	Scrapped
08395	D3510		1958	1988	Scrapped
08396	D3511		1958	1986	Scrapped
08397	D3512		1958	2004	Scrapped
08398	D3513		1958	1985	Scrapped
08399	D3514		1958	1992	Scrapped
08400	D3515		1958	1987	Scrapped
08401	D3516		1958		Hunslet Engine Co
08402	D3517		1958	2004	Scrapped
08403	D3518		1958	1981	Scrapped
08404	D3519		1958	1978	Scrapped

			Built	Withdrawn	Status	Notes
08405	D3520		1958		East Midlands Trains	RSS locomotive on hire to EMT
08406	D3521		1958	1988	Scrapped	
08407	D3522		1958	1993	Scrapped	
08408	D3523		1958	1988	Scrapped	
08409	D3524		1958	1986	Scrapped	
08410	D3525		1958		Great Western Railway	
08411	D3526		1958		Railway Support Services	
08412	D3527		1958	1985	Scrapped	
08413	D3528		1958	1999	Scrapped	
08414	D3529		1958	1999	Scrapped	
08415	D3530		1958	1996	Scrapped	
08416	D3531		1958	1992	Scrapped	
08417	D3532		1958		Network Rail	
08418	D3533		1958		West Coast Railway Co	
08419	D3534		1958	1993	Scrapped	
08420	D3535		1958	1988	Scrapped	
08421	D3536		1958	1992	Converted	Converted to 09201 in 1992
08422	D3537		1958	1985	Scrapped	
14	08423	D3538	1958		RMS Locotec	
08424	D3539		1958	1985	Scrapped	
08425	D3540		1958	1985	Scrapped	
08426	D3541		1958	1976	Scrapped	
08427	D3542		1958	1986	Scrapped	
08428	D3543		1958		Harry Needle Railroad Co	
08429	D3544		1958	1983	Scrapped	
08430	D3545		1958	1985	Scrapped	
08431	D3546		1958	1985	Scrapped	
08432	D3547		1958	1983	Scrapped	
08433	D3548		1958	1986	Scrapped	
08434	D3549		1958	1992	Scrapped	

▲ Great Western Railway's **08822** "Dave Mills", resplendent in BR InterCity livery complete with Swallow logo, is seen on display at Bristol St Philip's Marsh depot open day on 2 May 2016.

Robert Pritchard

08435	D3550	1958	1980	Scrapped
08436	D3551	1958	1992	Preserved
08437	D3552	1958	1984	Scrapped
08438	D3553	1958	1986	Scrapped
08439	D3554	1958	1988	Scrapped
08440	D3555	1958	1990	Scrapped
08441	D3556	1958		Virgin Trains East Coast
08442	D3557	1958		Arriva Traincare
08443	D3558	1958	1985	Preserved
08444	D3559	1958	1986	Preserved
08445	D3560	1958		Hunslet Engine Co
08446	D3561	1958	1985	Scrapped
08447	D3562	1958		Russell Logistics
08448	D3563	1958	1994	Scrapped
08449	D3564	1958	1996	Scrapped
08450	D3565	1958	1986	Scrapped
08451	D3566	1958		Alstom
08452	D3567	1958	1985	Scrapped
08453	D3568	1958	1980	Scrapped
08454	D3569	1958		Alstom
08455	D3570	1958	1981	Scrapped
08456	D3571	1959	1988	Scrapped
08457	D3572	1959	1981	Scrapped
08458	D3573	1958	1988	Scrapped
08459	D3574	1958	1988	Scrapped
08460	D3575	1958		Railway Support Services
08461	D3576	1958	1988	Scrapped
08463	D3578	1958	1989	Scrapped
08464	D3579	1958	1981	Scrapped
08465	D3580	1958	1985	Scrapped
08466	D3581	1958	2009	Scrapped
08467	D3582	1958	1981	Scrapped
08468	D3583	1958	1988	Scrapped
08469	D3584	1958	1981	Scrapped
08470	D3585	1958	1986	Scrapped
08471	D3586	1958	1985	Preserved
08472	D3587	1958		Wabtec
08473	D3588	1958	1986	Preserved
08474	D3589	1958	1986	Scrapped
08475	D3590	1958	1987	Scrapped
08476	D3591	1958	1985	Preserved
08477	D3592	1958	1986	Scrapped
08478	D3593	1958	1988	Scrapped
08479	D3594	1958	1991	Preserved
08480	D3595	1958		Railway Support Services
08481	D3596	1958	2005	Scrapped
08482	D3597	1958	2010	Scrapped
08483	D3598	1958		Great Western Railway
08484	D3599	1958		Railway Support Services
08485	D3600	1958		West Coast Railway Co
08486	D3601	1958	1986	Scrapped
08487	D3602	1958	1988	Scrapped
08488	D3603	1958	1986	Scrapped
08489	D3604	1958	2004	Scrapped
08490	D3605	1958	1985	Preserved
08491	D3606	1958	1985	Scrapped
08492	D3607	1958	2000	Scrapped
08493	D3608	1958	1999	Scrapped
08494	D3609	1958	1988	Scrapped
08495	D3610	1958		Preserved
08496	D3611	1958	1990	Scrapped
08497	D3652	1958	1985	Scrapped
08498	D3653	1958	1994	Scrapped
08499	D3654	1958		Colas Rail

08500	D3655		1958		Harry Needle Railroad Co
08501	D3656		1958	1985	Scrapped
08502	D3657		1958		Harry Needle Railroad Co
08503	D3658		1958		Harry Needle Railroad Co
08504	D3659		1958	1988	Scrapped
08505	D3660		1958	1981	Scrapped
08506	D3661		1958	2004	Scrapped
08507	D3662		1958		Riviera Trains
08508	D3663		1958	1991	Scrapped
08509	D3664		1958	1999	Scrapped
08510	D3672		1958	2004	Scrapped
08511	D3673		1958		Railway Support Services
08512	D3674		1958	2008	Scrapped
08513	D3675		1958	1978	Scrapped
08514	D3676		1958	2008	Scrapped
08515	D3677		1958	1992	Scrapped
08516	D3678		1958		Arriva Traincare
08517	D3679		1958	1999	Scrapped
08518	D3680		1958	1986	Scrapped
08519	D3681		1958	1999	Scrapped
08520	D3682		1958	1986	Scrapped
08521	D3683		1958	1993	Scrapped
08522	D3684		1958	1985	Scrapped
08523	D3685		1958		RMS Locotec
08524	D3686		1958	1986	Scrapped
08525	D3687		1959		East Midlands Trains
08526	D3688		1959	2006	Scrapped
08527	D3689		1959		Harry Needle Railroad Co
08528	D3690		1959	2005	Preserved
08529	D3691		1959	1999	Scrapped
08530	D3692		1959		Freightliner
08531	D3693		1959		Freightliner
08532	D3694		1959	1993	Scrapped
08533	D3695		1959	1992	Scrapped
08534	D3696		1959	2002	Scrapped
D3697			1959	1965	Converted	Converted to D4502 (slave) in 1965
D3698			1959	1965	Converted	Converted to D4500 (slave) in 1965
08535	D3699		1959	2000	Scrapped
08536	D3700		1959		Loram UK
08537	D3701		1959	1992	Scrapped
08538	D3702		1959	2009	Scrapped
08539	D3703		1959	1992	Scrapped
08540	D3704		1959	2004	Scrapped
08541	D3705		1959	1999	Scrapped
08542	D3706		1959	2000	Scrapped
08543	D3707		1959	2004	Scrapped
08544	D3708		1959	1992	Scrapped
08545	D3709		1959	1980	Scrapped
08546	D3710		1959	1985	Scrapped
08547	D3711		1959	1981	Scrapped
08548	D3712		1959	1982	Scrapped
08549	D3713		1959	1985	Scrapped
08550	D3714		1959	1983	Scrapped
08551	D3715		1959	1982	Scrapped
08552	D3716		1959	1982	Scrapped
08553	D3717		1959	1981	Scrapped
08554	D3718		1959	1982	Scrapped
08555	D3722		1959	1982	Scrapped
08556	D3723		1959	1990	Preserved
08557	D3724		1959	1982	Scrapped
08558	D3725		1959	1986	Scrapped
08559	D3726		1959	1981	Scrapped

08560	D3727		1959	1981	Scrapped	
08561	D3728		1959	2005	Scrapped	
08562	D3729		1959	1994	Scrapped	
08563	D3730		1959	1982	Scrapped	
08564	D3731		1959	1985	Scrapped	
08565	D3732		1959	1993	Scrapped	
08566	D3733		1959	1975	Scrapped	
08567	D3734		1959		Arlington Fleet Services	
08568	D3735		1959		Railway Support Services	
08569	D3736		1959	2004	Scrapped	
08570	D3737		1959	1992	Scrapped	
08571	D3738		1959		Wabtec	
08731[2]	08572	D3739	1959	1995	Scrapped	Second locomotive to carry 08731, renumbered during repairs in 1983
08573	D3740		1959		RMS Locotec	
08574	D3741		1959	1981	Scrapped	
08575	D3742		1959		Freightliner	
08576	D3743		1959	2006	Scrapped	
08577	D3744		1959	2004	Scrapped	
08578	D3745		1959		Harry Needle Railroad Co	
08579	D3746		1959	1988	Scrapped	
08580	D3747		1959		Railway Support Services	
08581	D3748		1959	1995	Scrapped	
08582	D3749		1959	2004	Scrapped	
08583	D3750		1959	1993	Scrapped	
08584	D3751		1959	1991	Scrapped	
08585	D3752		1959		Freightliner	
08586	D3753		1959	1999	Scrapped	
08587	D3754		1959	2006	Scrapped	
08588	D3755		1959		RMS Locotec	
08589	D3756		1959	1992	Scrapped	
08590	D3757		1959	1993	Preserved	
08591	D3758		1959	1993	Scrapped	
08593	D3760		1959		Railway Support Services	
08594	D3761		1959	1999	Scrapped	
08595	D3762		1959	1993	Scrapped	
08596	D3763		1959		Wabtec	
08597	D3764		1959	2004	Scrapped	
08598	D3765		1959		AV Dawson	
08599	D3766		1959	2004	Scrapped	
08600	97800	D3767	1959		AV Dawson	
08601	D3768		1959	1999	Scrapped	
004	08602	D3769	1959		Bombardier Transportation	
08603	D3770		1959	1994	Scrapped	
08604	D3771		1959	1993	Preserved	
08605	D3772		1959		Riviera Trains	
08606	D3773		1959	1988	Scrapped	
08607	D3774		1959	1996	Scrapped	
08608	D3775		1959	1988	Scrapped	
08609	D3776		1959	1993	Scrapped	
08610	D3777		1959	1994	Scrapped	
08611	D3778		1959		Alstom	
08612	D3779		1959	1990	Scrapped	
08613	D3780		1959		RMS Locotec	
08614	D3781		1959	1993	Scrapped	
08615	D3782		1959		Wabtec	
08616	D3783		1959		West Midlands Trains	
08617	D3784		1959		Alstom	
08618	D3785		1959	1990	Scrapped	
08619	D3786		1959	1998	Scrapped	
08620	D3787		1959	1992	Converted	Converted to 09205 in 1992

08621	D3788		1959	1988	Scrapped
08622	D3789		1959		RMS Locotec
08623	D3790		1959		Harry Needle Railroad Co
08624	D3791		1959		Freightliner
08625	D3792		1959	1997	Scrapped
08626	D3793		1959	1988	Scrapped
08627	D3794		1959	1994	Scrapped
08628	D3795		1959	1999	Scrapped
08629	D3796		1959		Knorr-Bremse Rail UK
08630	CELSA 3	D3797	1959		Harry Needle Railroad Co
08631	D3798		1959		Locomotive Services
08632	D3799		1959		Railway Support Services
08633	D3800		1959	2014	Preserved
08634	D3801		1959	1993	Scrapped
08635	D3802		1959	2004	Preserved
08636	D3803		1958	1980	Scrapped
08637	D3804		1958	1991	Scrapped
08638	D3805		1958	1992	Scrapped
08639	D3806		1958	1988	Scrapped
08640	D3807		1958	1988	Scrapped
08641	D3808		1959		Great Western Railway
08642	D3809		1959	2006	Scrapped
08643	D3810		1959		Mendip Rail
08644	D3811		1959		Great Western Railway
08645	D3812		1959		Great Western Railway
08646	D3813		1959	2009	Scrapped
08647	D3814		1959	1993	Scrapped
08648	D3815		1959		RMS Locotec
08649	D3816		1959		Knorr-Bremse Rail UK
08650	D3817		1959		Mendip Rail
08651	D3818		1959	2004	Scrapped
08652	D3819		1959		Mendip Rail
08653	D3820		1959		Harry Needle Railroad Co
08654	D3821		1959	1991	Scrapped
08655	D3822		1959	2004	Scrapped
08656	D3823		1959	1993	Scrapped
08657	D3824		1959	1991	Scrapped
08658	D3825		1959	1993	Scrapped
08659	D3826		1959	1991	Scrapped
08660	D3827		1959	1991	Scrapped
08661	D3828		1959	2003	Scrapped
08662	D3829		1959	2011	Scrapped
08663	D3830		1959		Great Western Railway
08664	D3831		1959	2008	Scrapped
08665	D3832		1960	2004	Scrapped
08666	D3833		1960	1994	Scrapped
08667	D3834		1960	1992	Scrapped
08668	D3835		1960	1997	Scrapped
08669	D3836		1960		Wabtec
08670	D3837		1960		Railway Support Services
08671	D3838		1960	1988	Scrapped
08672	D3839		1960	1992	Scrapped
08673	D3840		1960	1995	Scrapped
08674	D3841		1960	1981	Scrapped
08675	D3842		1959	1999	Scrapped
08676	D3843		1959		Harry Needle Railroad Co
08677	D3844		1959	1999	Scrapped
08678	D3845		1959		West Coast Railway Co
08679	D3846		1959	1976	Scrapped
08680	D3847		1959	1992	Scrapped
08681	D3848		1959	1985	Scrapped
08682	D3849		1959		Bombardier Transportation
08683	D3850		1959		Railway Support Services
08684	D3851		1959	1986	Scrapped

08685	D3852		1959		Harry Needle Railroad Co	
08686	D3853		1959	1991	Scrapped	
08688	D3855		1959	1991	Scrapped	
08689	D3856		1959	2007	Scrapped	
08690	D3857		1959		East Midlands Trains	
08691	D3858		1959		Freightliner	
08692	D3859		1959	1994	Scrapped	
08693	D3860		1959	1999	Scrapped	
08694	D3861		1959	2004	Preserved	
08695	D3862		1959	2004	Scrapped	
08696	D3863		1959		Alstom	
08697	D3864		1959	2014	Scrapped	
08698	D3865		1959	2005	Scrapped	
08699	D3866		1960	1993	Scrapped	
08700	D3867		1960		Harry Needle Railroad Co	
08701	D3868		1960		Harry Needle Railroad Co	
08702	D3869		1960	1998	Scrapped	
08703	D3870		1960		Railway Support Services	
08704	D3871		1960		Riviera Trains	
08705	D3872		1960	1994	Scrapped	
08706	D3873		1960		Harry Needle Railroad Co	
08707	D3874		1960	1993	Scrapped	
08708	D3875		1960	1992	Scrapped	
08709	D3876		1960		Railway Support Services	
08710	D3877		1960	1993	Scrapped	
08711	D3878		1960		Harry Needle Railroad Co	
08712	D3879		1960	1992	Scrapped	
08713	D3880		1960	1998	Scrapped	
08714	D3881		1960		Harry Needle Railroad Co	
08715	D3882		1960	1998	Scrapped	
08716	D3883		1960	1988	Scrapped	
08717	D3884		1960	1992	Converted	Converted to 09204 in 1992
D3885			1960	1972	Scrapped	
08718	D3886		1960	1999	Scrapped	
08719	D3887		1960	1991	Scrapped	
08720	D3888		1960	2002	Scrapped	
08721	D3889		1960		Alstom	
08722	D3890		1960	1987	Scrapped	
08723	D3891		1960	1995	Scrapped	
08724	D3892		1960		Wabtec	
08725	D3893		1960	1992	Scrapped	
08726	D3894		1960	1987	Scrapped	
08727	D3895		1960	1993	Scrapped	
08728	D3896		1960	1987	Scrapped	
08729	D3897		1960	1990	Scrapped	
08730	D3898		1960		Knorr-Bremse Rail UK	
08572[2]	08731	D3899	1960	1981	Scrapped	Second locomotive to carry 08572, renumbered shortly before scrapping
08732	D3900		1960	1992	Converted	Converted to 09202 in 1992
08733	D3901		1960	1993	Scrapped	
08734	D3902		1960	1999	Scrapped	
08735	D3903		1960		DB Cargo	
08736	D3904		1960	1987	Scrapped	
08737	D3905		1960		Locomotive Services	
08738	D3906		1960		Railway Support Services	
08739	D3907		1960	1997	Scrapped	
08740	D3908		1960	1997	Scrapped	
08741	D3909		1960	1991	Scrapped	
08742	D3910		1960		Harry Needle Railroad Co	
08743	D3911		1960		SembCorp Utilities UK	

08744	D3912		1960	1992	Scrapped	
08745	D3913		1960	2012	Scrapped	
08746	D3914		1960	1999	Scrapped	
08747	D3915		1960	1990	Scrapped	
08748	D3916		1960	1994	Scrapped	
08749	D3917		1960	1993	Converted	Converted to 09104 in 1993
08750	D3918		1960		RMS Locotec	
08751	D3919		1960	1997	Scrapped	
08752	D3920		1960		Railway Support Services	
08753	D3921		1960	1993	Scrapped	
08754	D3922		1961		RMS Locotec	
08755	D3923		1961	1993	Scrapped	
08756	D3924		1961		RMS Locotec	
08757	D3925		1961	2012	Preserved	
08758	D3926		1961	1997	Scrapped	
08759	D3927		1961	1993	Converted	Converted to 09106 in 1993
08760	D3928		1961	1992	Scrapped	
08761	D3929		1961	1992	Scrapped	
08762	D3930		1961		RMS Locotec	
08763	D3931		1961	1989	Scrapped	
08764	D3932		1961		Alstom	
08765	D3933		1961		Harry Needle Railroad Co	
08766	D3934		1961	1992	Converted	Converted to 09103 in 1992
08767	D3935		1961	1994	Preserved	
08768	D3936		1961	2000	Scrapped	
08769	D3937		1960	1989	Preserved	
08770	D3938		1960	2008	Scrapped	
08771	D3939		1960	1992	Scrapped	
08772	D3940		1960	1994	Preserved	
08773	D3941		1960	1999	Preserved	
08774	D3942		1960		AV Dawson	
08775	D3943		1960	2008	Scrapped	
08776	D3944		1960	2008	Scrapped	
08777	D3945		1960	1991	Scrapped	
08778	D3946		1960	1992	Scrapped	
08779	D3947		1960	1988	Scrapped	
08780	D3948		1960	2005	Preserved	
08781	D3949		1960	1992	Converted	Converted to 09203 in 1992
08782	D3950		1960		Harry Needle Railroad Co	
08783	D3951		1960		Awaiting Disposal	At EMR Kingsbury
08784	D3952		1960	2011	Preserved	
08785	D3953		1960		Freightliner	
08786	D3954		1960		Harry Needle Railroad Co	
08296[2]	08787	D3955	1960		Hanson UK	Second locomotive to carry 08296, renumbered in 1992
08788	D3956		1960		RMS Locotec	
08789	D3957		1960	1993	Scrapped	
08790	D3958		1960		Alstom	
08791	D3959		1960	1992	Scrapped	
08792	D3960		1960	2004	Scrapped	
08793	D3961		1960	1993	Scrapped	
08794	D3962		1960	1992	Scrapped	
08795	D3963		1960		Great Western Railway	
08796	D3964		1960	1990	Scrapped	
08797	D3965		1960	1990	Scrapped	
08798	D3966		1960		Awaiting Disposal	At EMR Attercliffe
08799	D3967		1960		Harry Needle Railroad Co	
08800	D3968		1960	1993	Scrapped	

08801	D3969		1960	2000	Scrapped	
08802	D3970		1960		Harry Needle Railroad Co	
08803	D3971		1960	1992	Scrapped	
08804	D3972		1960		Harry Needle Railroad Co	
08805	D3973		1960		West Midlands Trains	
08806	D3974		1960	2001	Scrapped	
08807	D3975		1960	2004	Scrapped	
08808	D3976		1960	1990	Scrapped	
08809	D3977		1960		RMS Locotec	
08810	D3978		1960		Arriva Traincare	
08811	D3979		1960	1997	Scrapped	
08812	D3980		1960	1978	Scrapped	
08813	D3981		1960	2005	Scrapped	
08814	D3982		1960	1992	Scrapped	
08815	D3983		1960	1996	Scrapped	
08816	D3984		1960	1986	Scrapped	
08817	D3985		1960	1999	Scrapped	
08818	D3986		1960		Harry Needle Railroad Co	
08819	D3987		1960	1999	Scrapped	
08820	D3988		1960	1990	Scrapped	
08821	D3989		1960	1992	Scrapped	
08822	D3990		1960		Great Western Railway	
08823	D3991		1960		Hunslet Engine Co	
08824	IEMD 01	D3992	1960		Harry Needle Railroad Co	
08825	D3993		1960	1999	Preserved	
08826	D3994		1960	1999	Scrapped	
08827	D3995		1960	2000	Scrapped	
08828	D3996		1960	2004	Scrapped	
08829	D3997		1960	1993	Scrapped	
08830	D3998		1960	2006	Preserved	
08831	D3999		1960	1993	Scrapped	
08832	D4000		1960	1992	Converted	Converted to 09102 in 1992
08833	D4001		1960	1992	Converted	Converted to 09101 in 1992
08834	D4002		1960		Harry Needle Railroad Co	
08835	D4003		1960	1993	Converted	Converted to 09105 in 1993
08836	D4004		1960		Great Western Railway	
08837	D4005		1960	2000	Scrapped	
08838	D4006		1960	1990	Scrapped	
08839	D4007		1960	1992	Scrapped	
08840	D4008		1960	1991	Scrapped	
08841	D4009		1960	1990	Scrapped	
08842	D4010		1960	2008	Scrapped	
08843	D4011		1961	1990	Scrapped	
08844	D4012		1961	2009	Scrapped	
08845	D4013		1961	1993	Converted	Converted to 09107 in 1993
003	08846	D4014	1961		Bombardier Transportation	
08847	D4015		1961		RMS Locotec	
08848	D4016		1961	1992	Scrapped	
08849	D4017		1961	1993	Scrapped	
08850	D4018		1961	1992	Preserved	
08851	D4019		1961	1990	Scrapped	
08852	D4020		1961	1988	Scrapped	
08853	D4021		1961		Wabtec	
08854	D4022		1961	2008	Scrapped	
08855	D4023		1961	1993	Scrapped	
08856	D4024		1961	2004	Scrapped	
08857	D4025		1961	1991	Scrapped	
08858	D4026		1961	1992	Scrapped	
08859	D4027		1961	1992	Scrapped	
08860	D4028		1960	1981	Scrapped	

08861	D4029		1960	1981	Scrapped	
08862	D4030		1960	1980	Scrapped	
08863	D4031		1960	1980	Scrapped	
08864	D4032		1960	1981	Scrapped	
08865	D4033		1960		Harry Needle Railroad Co	
08866	D4034		1960	2008	Scrapped	
08867	D4035		1960	1999	Scrapped	
08868	D4036		1960		Arriva Traincare	
08869	D4037		1960	1997	Scrapped	
H024	08870	D4038	1960		RMS Locotec	
08871	H074	D4039	1960		RMS Locotec	
08872	D4040		1960		Awaiting Disposal	At EMR Attercliffe
08873	D4041		1960		Freightliner	
08874	D4042		1960		RMS Locotec	
08875	D4043		1960	1991	Scrapped	
08876	D4044		1960	1991	Scrapped	
08877	D4045		1960		Harry Needle Railroad Co	
08878	D4046		1960	1997	Scrapped	
08879	D4047		1960		Arlington Fleet Services	HNRC locomotive on hire to Arlington Fleet Services
08880	D4048		1960	1996	Scrapped	
08881	D4095		1961	2004	Preserved	
08882	D4096		1961	2001	Scrapped	
08883	D4097		1961	2004	Scrapped	
08884	D4098		1961	2004	Scrapped	
08885	H042	D4115	1962		RMS Locotec	
08886	D4116		1962	2012	Scrapped	
08887	D4117		1962		Alstom	
08888	D4118		1962	2016	Preserved	
08889	D4119		1962	1992	Scrapped	
08890	D4120		1962	2004	Scrapped	
08891	D4121		1962		Freightliner	
08892	D4122		1962		Harry Needle Railroad Co	
08893	D4123		1962	1994	Scrapped	
08894	D4124		1962	1998	Scrapped	
08895	D4125		1962	1993	Scrapped	
08896	D4126		1962	2004	Preserved	
08897	D4127		1962	2009	Scrapped	
08898	D4128		1962	1988	Scrapped	
08899	D4129		1962		East Midlands Trains	
08900	D4130		1962	2005	Scrapped	
08901	D4131		1962	1993	Scrapped	
08902	D4132		1962	1996	Scrapped	
08903	D4133		1962		SembCorp Utilities UK	
08904	D4134		1962		Harry Needle Railroad Co	
08905	D4135		1962		Harry Needle Railroad Co	
08906	D4136		1962	1998	Scrapped	
08907	D4137		1962	2014	Preserved	
08908	D4138		1962		East Midlands Trains	
08909	D4139		1962	2011	Scrapped	
08910	D4140		1962	2002	Scrapped	
08911	D4141		1962	2004	Preserved	
08912	D4142		1962		AV Dawson	
08913	D4143		1962		Awaiting Disposal	At EMR Kingsbury
08914	D4144		1962	1997	Scrapped	
08915	D4145		1962	2004	Preserved	
08916	D4146		1962	1992	Scrapped	
08917	D4147		1962	1991	Scrapped	
08918	D4148		1962		Harry Needle Railroad Co	
08919	D4149		1962	2004	Scrapped	
08920	D4150		1962	2004	Scrapped	
08921	D4151		1962		Railway Support Services	
08922	D4152		1962	2011	Preserved	

				Year Entered Service	Year Withdrawn	Current Status	Notes
08923	D4153			1962	1993	Scrapped	
CELSA2	08924	D4154		1962		Harry Needle Railroad Co	
08925	D4155			1962		GB Railfreight	
08926	D4156			1962	1996	Scrapped	
08927	D4157			1962		Railway Support Services	
08928	D4158			1962	2001	Scrapped	
08929	D4159			1962	1991	Scrapped	
08930	D4160			1962	1990	Scrapped	
08931	D4161			1962	1995	Scrapped	
08932	D4162			1962	1999	Scrapped	
08933	D4163			1962		Mendip Rail	
08934	D4164			1962		GB Railfreight	
08935	D4165			1962	1993	Scrapped	
08936	D4166			1962		RMS Locotec	
08937	D4167			1962		RMS Locotec	
08938	D4168			1962	1999	Scrapped	
08939	D4169			1962		Railway Support Services	
08940	D4170			1962	2003	Scrapped	
08941	D4171			1962	2008	Scrapped	
08942	D4172			1962	1998	Scrapped	
08943	D4173			1962		Harry Needle Railroad Co	
08944	D4174			1962	1999	Preserved	
08945	D4175			1962	1993	Scrapped	
08946	D4176			1962	2002	Scrapped	
08947	D4177			1962		Mendip Rail	
08948	D4178			1962		Eurostar International	
08949	D4179			1962	1993	Scrapped	
08950	D4180			1962		East Midlands Trains	
08951	D4181			1962	2011	Scrapped	
08952	D4182			1962	1999	Scrapped	
08953	D4183			1962	2006	Scrapped	
08954	D4184			1962		Alstom	HNRC loco on hire to Alstom
08955	D4185			1962	2000	Scrapped	
08956	D4186			1962		LORAM UK	
D4187				1962	1965	Converted	Converted to D4502 (master) in 1965
D4188				1962	1965	Converted	Converted to D4500 (master) in 1965
D4189				1962	1965	Converted	Converted to D4501 (master) in 1965
D4190				1962	1965	Converted	Converted to D4501 (slave) in 1965
08957	D4191			1962	2001	Scrapped	
08958	D4192			1962	2001	Scrapped	

Class 08/9
Cabs cut down to reduce height.
Details as Class 08.

Latest Number Carried	Previous Number 1	Previous Number 2	Previous Number 3	Year Entered Service	Year Withdrawn	Current Status	Notes
08991	08203	D3273	13273	1956	1987	Scrapped	
08992	08259	D3329	13329	1956	1987	Scrapped	
08993	08592	D3759		1959	2015	Preserved	
08994	08462	D3577		1958		Harry Needle Railroad Co	
08995	08687	D3854		1959	2013	Preserved	

CLASS 09

0-6-0

Built: 1959–62 by British Railways, Darlington & Horwich.
Engine: English Electric 6KT of 298 kW (400 hp) at 680 rpm.
Transmission: Electric.
Maximum Speed: 27 mph.
Train Brakes: Vacuum. All were later dual-braked (air & vacuum)

Class 09/0

Latest Number Carried	Previous Number 1	Previous Number 2	Year Entered Service	Year Withdrawn	Current Status	Notes
09001	D3665		1959	2009	Preserved	
09002	D3666		1959		GB Railfreight	
09003	D3667		1959	2008	Scrapped	
09004	D3668		1959	1999	Preserved	
09005	D3669		1959	2009	Scrapped	
09006	D3670		1959		Harry Needle Railroad Co	
09007	D3671		1959		London Overground	
09008	D3719		1959	2004	Scrapped	
09009	D3720		1959		GB Railfreight	
09010	D3721		1959	2010	Preserved	
09011	D4099		1961	2005	Scrapped	
09012	D4100		1961	2004	Preserved	
09013	D4101		1961	2008	Scrapped	
09014	D4102		1961		Harry Needle Railroad Co	
09015	D4103		1961		Railway Support Services	
09016	D4104		1961	2004	Scrapped	
09017	97806	D4105	1961	2010	Preserved	

▲ 09105 passes East Usk Junction on 27 August 1998 with a trip freight from Alexandra Dock Junction to Llanwern. Class 09 locomotives are ideally suited to trip working, given their higher maximum speed than comparable Class 08s. Note the headlight attached to the front of the locomotive.   **Rail Photoprints Collection**

09018	D4106		1961	2013	Preserved	HNRC loco on long term loan to Bluebell Railway
09019	D4107		1961	2013	Preserved	
09020	D4108		1961	2011	Scrapped	
09021	D4109		1961	2004	Scrapped	
09022	D4110		1961		Victoria Group	
09023	D4111		1961		Awaiting Disposal	At EMR Attercliffe
09024	D4112		1961	2008	Preserved	
09025	D4113		1962	2005	Preserved	
09026	D4114		1962	2016	Preserved	

Class 09/1
Converted from Class 08. 110V electrical equipment.
Details as Class 09/0.

Latest Number Carried	Previous Number 1	Previous Number 2	Year Entered Service	Year Withdrawn	Current Status	Notes
09101	08833	D4001	1992	2008	Scrapped	
09102	08832	D4000	1992	2005	Scrapped	
09103	08766	D3934	1992	2008	Scrapped	
09104	08749	D3917	1993	2002	Scrapped	
09105	08835	D4003	1993	2009	Scrapped	
09106	08759	D3927	1993		Harry Needle Railroad Co	
09107	08845	D4013	1993	2010	Preserved	

Class 09/2
Converted from Class 08. 90V electrical equipment.
Details as Class 09/0.

Latest Number Carried	Previous Number 1	Previous Number 2	Year Entered Service	Year Withdrawn	Current Status	Notes
09201	08421	D3536	1992		Harry Needle Railroad Co	
09202	08732	D3900	1992	2006	Scrapped	
09203	08781	D3949	1992	2005	Scrapped	
09204	08717	D3884	1992		Arriva Traincare	
09205	08620	D3787	1992	2008	Scrapped	

CLASS 10 0-6-0

Built: 1952–62 by British Railways, Darlington & Doncaster.
Engine: Blackstone ERT6 of 261 kW (350 hp) at 750 rpm.
Transmission: Electric.
Maximum Speed: 20 mph.
Train Brakes: Vacuum.

Latest Number Carried	Previous Number 1	Year Entered Service	Year Withdrawn	Current Status	Notes
D3137	13137	1955	1970	Scrapped	
D3138	13138	1955	1972	Scrapped	
D3139	13139	1955	1968	Scrapped	
D3140	13140	1955	1968	Scrapped	
D3141	13141	1955	1971	Scrapped	
D3142	13142	1955	1968	Scrapped	
D3143	13143	1955	1969	Scrapped	
D3144	13144	1955	1969	Scrapped	
D3145	13145	1955	1972	Scrapped	
D3146	13146	1955	1968	Scrapped	
D3147	13147	1955	1968	Scrapped	
D3148	13148	1955	1968	Scrapped	
D3149	13149	1955	1970	Scrapped	
D3150	13150	1955	1968	Scrapped	
D3151	13151	1955	1967	Scrapped	
D3439		1957	1968	Scrapped	
D3440		1957	1968	Scrapped	
D3441		1957	1968	Scrapped	

D3442	1957	1968	Scrapped
D3443	1957	1968	Scrapped
D3444	1957	1968	Scrapped
D3445	1957	1968	Scrapped
D3446	1957	1968	Scrapped
D3447	1957	1968	Scrapped
D3448	1957	1968	Scrapped
D3449	1957	1967	Scrapped
D3450	1957	1968	Scrapped
D3451	1957	1968	Scrapped
D3452	1957	1968	Preserved
D3453	1957	1968	Scrapped
D3473	1957	1968	Scrapped
D3474	1957	1968	Scrapped
D3475	1957	1968	Scrapped
D3476	1957	1968	Scrapped
D3477	1957	1968	Scrapped
D3478	1958	1968	Scrapped
D3479	1958	1969	Scrapped
D3480	1958	1968	Scrapped
D3481	1958	1968	Scrapped
D3482	1958	1968	Scrapped
D3483	1958	1969	Scrapped
D3484	1958	1968	Scrapped
D3485	1958	1968	Scrapped
D3486	1958	1970	Scrapped
D3487	1958	1968	Scrapped
D3488	1958	1968	Scrapped
D3489	1958	1968	Preserved
D3490	1958	1968	Scrapped
D3491	1958	1968	Scrapped
D3492	1958	1969	Scrapped
D3493	1958	1968	Scrapped
D3494	1958	1968	Scrapped
D3495	1958	1968	Scrapped
D3496	1958	1967	Scrapped
D3497	1957	1968	Scrapped
D3498	1957	1968	Scrapped
D3499	1957	1968	Scrapped
D3500	1958	1968	Scrapped
D3501	1958	1968	Scrapped
D3502	1958	1968	Scrapped
D3612	1958	1969	Scrapped
D3613	1958	1969	Scrapped
D3614	1958	1969	Scrapped
D3615	1958	1968	Scrapped
D3616	1958	1969	Scrapped
D3617	1958	1969	Scrapped
D3618	1958	1969	Scrapped
D3619	1958	1969	Scrapped
D3620	1958	1967	Scrapped
D3621	1958	1969	Scrapped
D3622	1958	1969	Scrapped
D3623	1958	1969	Scrapped
D3624	1958	1968	Scrapped
D3625	1958	1968	Scrapped
D3626	1958	1968	Scrapped
D3627	1958	1968	Scrapped
D3628	1958	1967	Scrapped
D3629	1958	1969	Scrapped
D3630	1958	1968	Scrapped
D3631	1958	1967	Scrapped
D3632	1958	1968	Scrapped
D3633	1958	1968	Scrapped

D3634		1958	1971	Scrapped	
D3635		1958	1968	Scrapped	
D3636		1958	1968	Scrapped	
D3637		1958	1968	Scrapped	
D3638		1958	1970	Scrapped	
D3639		1958	1969	Scrapped	
D3640		1958	1968	Scrapped	
D3641		1958	1971	Scrapped	
D3642		1958	1969	Scrapped	
D3643		1958	1968	Scrapped	
D3644		1958	1970	Scrapped	
D3645		1958	1969	Scrapped	
D3646		1958	1971	Scrapped	
D3647		1958	1970	Scrapped	
D3648		1959	1971	Scrapped	
D3649		1959	1969	Scrapped	
D3650		1959	1971	Scrapped	
D3651		1959	1971	Scrapped	
D4049		1961	1972	Scrapped	
D4050		1961	1971	Scrapped	
D4051		1961	1971	Scrapped	
D4052		1961	1970	Scrapped	
D4053		1961	1971	Scrapped	
D4054		1961	1972	Scrapped	
D4055		1961	1971	Scrapped	
D4056		1961	1972	Scrapped	
D4057		1961	1972	Scrapped	
D4058		1961	1972	Scrapped	
D4059		1961	1971	Scrapped	
D4060		1961	1971	Scrapped	
D4061		1961	1972	Scrapped	
D4062		1961	1972	Scrapped	
D4063		1961	1972	Scrapped	
D4064		1961	1968	Scrapped	
D4065		1961	1971	Scrapped	
D4066		1961	1972	Scrapped	
10119	D4067	1961	1970	Preserved	Number 10119 carried during preservation only
D4068		1961	1972	Scrapped	
D4069		1961	1972	Scrapped	
D4070		1961	1972	Scrapped	
D4071		1961	1968	Scrapped	
D4072		1961	1972	Scrapped	
D4073		1961	1972	Scrapped	
D4074		1961	1972	Scrapped	
D4075		1961	1972	Scrapped	
D4076		1961	1968	Scrapped	
D4077		1961	1970	Scrapped	
D4078		1961	1972	Scrapped	
D4079		1961	1972	Scrapped	
D4080		1961	1968	Scrapped	
D4081		1962	1968	Scrapped	
D4082		1962	1968	Scrapped	
D4083		1962	1968	Scrapped	
D4084		1962	1968	Scrapped	
D4085		1962	1968	Scrapped	
D4086		1962	1968	Scrapped	
D4087		1962	1968	Scrapped	
D4088		1962	1968	Scrapped	
D4089		1962	1968	Scrapped	
D4090		1962	1968	Scrapped	
D4091		1962	1968	Scrapped	
D4092		1962	1968	Preserved	
D4093		1962	1968	Scrapped	
D4094		1962	1968	Scrapped	

CLASS 11 0-6-0

Built: 1945–52 by LMS/British Railways Derby & Darlington.
Engine: English Electric 6KT of 261 kW (350 hp) at 750 rpm.
Transmission: Electric.
Maximum Speed: 20mph.
Train Brakes: None when built.

Latest Number Carried	Previous Number 1	Year Entered Service	Year Withdrawn	Current Status	Notes
12033	7120	1945	1969	Scrapped	
12034	7121	1945	1968	Scrapped	
12035	7122	1945	1968	Scrapped	
12036	7123	1945	1968	Scrapped	
12037	7124	1945	1968	Scrapped	
12038	7125	1945	1969	Scrapped	
12039	7126	1947	1968	Scrapped	
12040	7127	1947	1968	Scrapped	
12041	7128	1947	1968	Scrapped	
12042	7129	1947	1968	Scrapped	
12043	7130	1948	1968	Scrapped	
12044	7131	1948	1968	Scrapped	
12045		1948	1969	Scrapped	
12046		1948	1969	Scrapped	
12047		1948	1969	Scrapped	
12048		1948	1969	Scrapped	
12049		1949	1971	Scrapped	First of 2 locomotives to be numbered 12049
12050		1949	1970	Scrapped	
12051		1949	1971	Scrapped	
12052		1949	1971	Preserved	
12053		1949	1971	Scrapped	
12054		1949	1970	Scrapped	
12055		1949	1971	Scrapped	
12056		1949	1971	Scrapped	
12057		1949	1969	Scrapped	
12058		1949	1971	Scrapped	
12059		1949	1969	Scrapped	
12060		1949	1971	Scrapped	
12061		1949	1971	Scrapped	
12062		1949	1970	Scrapped	
12063		1949	1972	Scrapped	
12064		1949	1969	Scrapped	
12065		1949	1971	Scrapped	
12066		1949	1969	Scrapped	
12067		1950	1969	Scrapped	
12068		1950	1967	Scrapped	
12069		1950	1971	Scrapped	
12070		1950	1969	Scrapped	
12071		1950	1971	Scrapped	
12072		1950	1968	Scrapped	
12073		1950	1971	Scrapped	
12074		1950	1972	Scrapped	
12075		1950	1971	Scrapped	
12076		1950	1971	Scrapped	
12077		1950	1971	Preserved	
12078		1950	1971	Scrapped	
12079		1950	1971	Scrapped	
12080		1950	1971	Scrapped	
12081		1950	1970	Scrapped	
12049[2]	12082	1950	1971	Preserved	Second of 2 locomotives to be numbered 12049 (only in Preservation)
12083		1950	1971	Preserved	
12084		1950	1971	Scrapped	

12085	1950	1971	Scrapped
12086	1950	1969	Scrapped
12087	1950	1971	Scrapped
12088	1951	1971	Preserved
12089	1951	1970	Scrapped
12090	1951	1971	Scrapped
12091	1951	1970	Scrapped
12092	1951	1969	Scrapped
12093	1951	1971	Preserved
12094	1951	1971	Scrapped
12095	1951	1969	Scrapped
12096	1951	1969	Scrapped
12097	1951	1971	Scrapped
12098	1952	1971	Scrapped
12099	1952	1971	Preserved
12100	1952	1969	Scrapped
12101	1952	1970	Scrapped
12102	1952	1971	Scrapped
12103	1952	1971	Scrapped
12104	1952	1967	Scrapped
12105	1952	1971	Scrapped
12106	1952	1970	Scrapped
12107	1952	1967	Scrapped
12108	1952	1971	Scrapped
12109	1952	1972	Scrapped
12110	1952	1972	Scrapped
12111	1952	1971	Scrapped
12112	1952	1969	Scrapped
12113	1952	1971	Scrapped
12114	1952	1970	Scrapped
12115	1952	1970	Scrapped
12116	1952	1969	Scrapped
12117	1952	1969	Scrapped
12118	1952	1971	Scrapped
12119	1952	1968	Scrapped
12120	1952	1969	Scrapped
12121	1952	1971	Scrapped
12122	1952	1971	Scrapped
12123	1952	1967	Scrapped
12124	1952	1968	Scrapped
12125	1952	1969	Scrapped
12126	1952	1968	Scrapped
12127	1952	1972	Scrapped
12128	1952	1970	Scrapped
12129	1952	1967	Scrapped
12130	1952	1972	Scrapped
12131	1952	1969	Preserved
12132	1952	1972	Scrapped
12133	1952	1969	Scrapped
12134	1952	1972	Scrapped
12135	1952	1969	Scrapped
12136	1952	1971	Scrapped
12137	1952	1968	Scrapped
12138	1952	1968	Scrapped

CLASS 12 {#class-12}   0-6-0

Built: 1949–52 by British Railways, Ashford Works.
Engine: English Electric 6KT of 261 kW (350hp) at 750 rpm.
Transmission: Electric.
Maximum Speed: 27.5 mph.
Train Brakes: None when built.

Latest Number Carried	Previous Number 1	Year Entered Service	Year Withdrawn	Current Status	Notes
15211		1949	1971	Scrapped	
15212		1949	1971	Scrapped	
15213		1949	1968	Scrapped	
15214		1949	1971	Scrapped	
15215		1949	1968	Scrapped	
15216		1949	1969	Scrapped	
15217		1949	1970	Scrapped	
15218		1949	1970	Scrapped	
15219		1949	1971	Scrapped	
15220		1949	1971	Scrapped	
15221		1949	1971	Scrapped	
15222		1949	1971	Scrapped	
15223		1949	1969	Scrapped	
15224		1949	1971	Preserved	
15225		1949	1971	Scrapped	
15226		1950	1969	Scrapped	
15227		1951	1970	Scrapped	
15228		1951	1969	Scrapped	
15229		1951	1971	Scrapped	
15230		1951	1971	Scrapped	
15231		1951	1971	Scrapped	
15232		1951	1971	Scrapped	
15233		1951	1969	Scrapped	
15234		1951	1968	Scrapped	
15235		1951	1971	Scrapped	
15236		1952	1968	Scrapped	

CLASS 13 {#class-13}   0-6-0 + 0-6-0

Each shunting locomotive was formed from two former Class 08s, one master and one slave for hump shunting in Tinsley Yard, Sheffield.

Conversions Completed: 1965
Engine: Two English Electric 6KT.
Horsepower: 700hp.
Transmission: Electric.
Maximum Speed: 20 mph.
Train Brakes: Vacuum.

Latest Number Carried	Previous Number 1	Year Entered Service	Year Withdrawn	Current Status	Notes
13001	D4501	1965	1985	Scrapped	
13002	D4502	1965	1981	Scrapped	
13003	D4500	1965	1985	Scrapped	

▲ In 1965 six Class 08 shunters were converted to three Class 13s, each consisting of a master and slave unit, for hump shunting at the newly-opened Tinsley Marshalling Yard in Sheffield. Here, 13003 is seen atop the hump on 8 January 1978, with the fuelling and minor servicing depot to the left and the vast marshalling yard extending into the distance. **Rail Photoprints Collection**

▼ Class 14 D9527 is the filling in a Class 47 sandwich at Severn Tunnel Junction on 16 February 1969. The Class 14 would be withdrawn from service before the end of the year. **Rail Photoprints Collection**

CLASS 14 0-6-0

Built: 1964–65 by British Railways, Swindon Works.
Engine: Paxman Ventura 6YJXL of 485 kW (650 hp) at 680 rpm.
Transmission: Hydraulic.
Maximum Speed: 40 mph.
Train Heating/Supply: None.
Train Brakes: Vacuum.

Latest Number Carried	Previous Number 1	Year Entered Service	Year Withdrawn	Current Status	Notes
D9500		1964	1969	Preserved	
D9501		1964	1968	Scrapped	
D9502		1964	1969	Preserved	
D9503		1964	1968	Scrapped	
D9504		1964	1968	Preserved	
D9505		1964	1968	Scrapped	Locomotive exported and subsequently scrapped
D9506		1964	1968	Scrapped	
D9507		1964	1968	Scrapped	
D9508		1964	1968	Scrapped	
D9509		1964	1968	Scrapped	
D9510		1964	1968	Scrapped	
D9511		1964	1968	Scrapped	
D9512		1964	1968	Scrapped	
38	D9513	1964	1968	Preserved	
D9514		1964	1969	Scrapped	
D9515		1964	1968	Scrapped	Locomotive exported and subsequently scrapped
D9516		1964	1968	Preserved	
D9517		1964	1968	Scrapped	
D9518		1964	1969	Preserved	
D9519		1964	1968	Scrapped	
D9520		1964	1968	Preserved	
D9521		1964	1969	Preserved	
D9522		1964	1967	Scrapped	
D9523		1964	1968	Preserved	
14901	D9524	1964	1969	Preserved	
D9525		1965	1968	Preserved	
D9526		1965	1968	Preserved	
D9527		1965	1969	Scrapped	
D9528		1965	1969	Scrapped	
D9529		1965	1968	Preserved	
D9530		1965	1968	Scrapped	
D9531		1965	1967	Preserved	
D9532		1965	1968	Scrapped	
D9533		1965	1968	Scrapped	
D9534		1965	1968	Scrapped	Locomotive exported and subsequently scrapped
D9535		1965	1968	Scrapped	
D9536		1965	1969	Scrapped	
D9537		1965	1968	Preserved	
D9538		1965	1969	Scrapped	
D9539		1965	1968	Preserved	
D9540		1965	1968	Scrapped	
D9541		1965	1968	Scrapped	
D9542		1965	1968	Scrapped	
D9543		1965	1968	Scrapped	
D9544		1965	1968	Scrapped	
D9545		1965	1968	Scrapped	
D9546		1965	1968	Scrapped	
D9547		1965	1968	Scrapped	
D9548		1965	1968	Scrapped	Locomotive exported and subsequently scrapped
D9549		1965	1968	Scrapped	Locomotive exported and subsequently scrapped
D9550		1965	1968	Scrapped	
D9551		1965	1968	Preserved	

D9552	1965	1968	Scrapped
D9553	1965	1968	Preserved
D9554	1965	1968	Scrapped
D9555	1965	1969	Preserved

CLASS 15   Bo-Bo

Built: 1957–61 by Yorkshire Engine Company, Sheffield and BTH/Clayton Equipment Company, Derbyshire.
Engine: Paxman 16YHXL of 485 kW (800 hp) at 1500 rpm.
Transmission: Electric.
Maximum Speed: 60 mph.
Train Heating/Supply: None.
Train Brakes: Vacuum.

Latest Number Carried	Previous Number 1	Year Entered Service	Year Withdrawn	Current Status	Notes
D8200		1957	1971	Scrapped	
D8201		1958	1971	Scrapped	
D8202		1958	1968	Scrapped	
ADB968003	D8203	1958	1981	Scrapped	Locomotive was not self-propelled whilst in departmental use
D8204		1958	1971	Scrapped	
D8205		1958	1968	Scrapped	
D8206		1958	1968	Scrapped	
D8207		1958	1971	Scrapped	
D8208		1958	1968	Scrapped	
D8209		1958	1971	Scrapped	
D8210		1959	1971	Scrapped	
D8211		1959	1971	Scrapped	
D8212		1959	1968	Scrapped	
D8213		1959	1968	Scrapped	
D8214		1959	1970	Scrapped	
D8215		1959	1970	Scrapped	
D8216		1959	1971	Scrapped	
D8217		1960	1968	Scrapped	
D8218		1960	1971	Scrapped	
D8219		1960	1968	Scrapped	
D8220		1960	1971	Scrapped	
D8221		1960	1971	Scrapped	
D8222		1960	1971	Scrapped	
D8223		1960	1968	Scrapped	
D8224		1960	1971	Scrapped	
D8225		1960	1971	Scrapped	
D8226		1960	1971	Scrapped	
D8227		1960	1968	Scrapped	
D8228		1960	1971	Scrapped	
D8229		1960	1971	Scrapped	
D8230		1960	1971	Scrapped	
D8231		1960	1971	Scrapped	
D8232		1960	1971	Scrapped	
ADB968001	D8233	1960	1982	Preserved	Locomotive was not self-propelled whilst in departmental use
D8234		1960	1971	Scrapped	
D8235		1960	1968	Scrapped	
D8236		1960	1968	Scrapped	
ADB968002	D8237	1960	1982	Scrapped	Locomotive was not self-propelled whilst in departmental use
D8238		1960	1968	Scrapped	
D8239		1961	1971	Scrapped	
D8240		1961	1968	Scrapped	
D8241		1961	1968	Scrapped	
D8242		1961	1971	Scrapped	
ADB968000	D8243	1961	1987	Scrapped	Locomotive was not self-propelled whilst in departmental use

CLASS 16   Bo-Bo

Built: 1958 by North British Locomotive Company, Glasgow.
Engine: Paxman 16YHXL of 597 kW (800 hp) at 1250 rpm.
Transmission: Electric.
Maximum Speed: 60 mph.
Train Heating/Supply: None.
Train Brakes: Vacuum.

Latest Number Carried	Previous Number 1	Year Entered Service	Year Withdrawn	Current Status	Notes
D8400		1958	1968	Scrapped	
D8401		1958	1968	Scrapped	
D8402		1958	1968	Scrapped	
D8403		1958	1968	Scrapped	
D8404		1958	1968	Scrapped	
D8405		1958	1968	Scrapped	
D8406		1958	1968	Scrapped	
D8407		1958	1968	Scrapped	
D8408		1958	1968	Scrapped	
D8409		1958	1968	Scrapped	

CLASS 17   Bo-Bo

Built: 1962–65 by Clayton Equipment Company, Derbyshire and Beyer Peacock & Co, Manchester.
Engine: Paxman 2 x 6ZHXL of 336 kW (450 hp) at 1500 rpm (except D8586 & D8587 which had 2 x Rolls Royce D Series engines).
Transmission: Electric.
Maximum Speed: 60mph.
Train Heating/Supply: None.
Train Brakes: Vacuum.

Latest Number Carried	Previous Number 1	Year Entered Service	Year Withdrawn	Current Status	Notes
D8500		1962	1971	Scrapped	
D8501		1962	1968	Scrapped	
D8502		1962	1971	Scrapped	
D8503		1962	1971	Scrapped	
D8504		1962	1971	Scrapped	
D8505		1962	1971	Scrapped	
D8506		1962	1971	Scrapped	
D8507		1962	1971	Scrapped	
D8508		1962	1971	Scrapped	
D8509		1962	1968	Scrapped	
D8510		1962	1971	Scrapped	
D8511		1962	1968	Scrapped	
D8512		1962	1968	Scrapped	
D8513		1962	1971	Scrapped	
D8514		1963	1968	Scrapped	
D8515		1963	1971	Scrapped	
D8516		1963	1971	Scrapped	
D8517		1963	1968	Scrapped	
D8518		1963	1968	Scrapped	
D8519		1963	1968	Scrapped	
D8520		1963	1968	Scrapped	
S18521	D8521	1963	1978	Scrapped	Locomotive was not self-propelled whilst in departmental use
D8522		1963	1968	Scrapped	
D8523		1963	1968	Scrapped	
D8524		1963	1968	Scrapped	
D8525		1963	1971	Scrapped	
D8526		1963	1968	Scrapped	
D8527		1963	1968	Scrapped	

▲ North British Class 16 D8408 stands at Stratford depot in April 1967 in the company of locomotives from Classes 31 and 37. **Rail Photoprints Collection**

▼ The last day of the Waverley Route, 5 January 1969, finds Class 17 Clayton D8606 stabled at Hawick. Concerns about possible public protests meant the loco was scheduled to run in front of the last service train as far as Newcastleton to ensure the line was free from obstruction.
Rail Photoprints Collection

D8528	1963	1971	Scrapped
D8529	1963	1971	Scrapped
D8530	1963	1971	Scrapped
D8531	1963	1971	Scrapped
D8532	1963	1968	Scrapped
D8533	1963	1968	Scrapped
D8534	1963	1968	Scrapped
D8535	1963	1971	Scrapped
D8536	1963	1971	Scrapped
D8537	1963	1968	Scrapped
D8538	1963	1971	Scrapped
D8539	1963	1971	Scrapped
D8540	1963	1971	Scrapped
D8541	1963	1971	Scrapped
D8542	1963	1971	Scrapped
D8543	1963	1971	Scrapped
D8544	1963	1969	Scrapped
D8545	1963	1971	Scrapped
D8546	1963	1971	Scrapped
D8547	1963	1969	Scrapped
D8548	1963	1971	Scrapped
D8549	1963	1971	Scrapped
D8550	1963	1971	Scrapped
D8551	1963	1971	Scrapped
D8552	1963	1971	Scrapped
D8553	1963	1968	Scrapped
D8554	1963	1969	Scrapped
D8555	1963	1971	Scrapped
D8556	1963	1969	Scrapped
D8557	1963	1971	Scrapped
D8558	1963	1971	Scrapped
D8559	1963	1971	Scrapped
D8560	1963	1969	Scrapped
D8561	1963	1971	Scrapped
D8562	1963	1971	Scrapped
D8563	1963	1971	Scrapped
D8564	1963	1969	Scrapped
D8565	1963	1971	Scrapped
D8566	1963	1968	Scrapped
D8567	1964	1971	Scrapped
D8568	1964	1971	Preserved
D8569	1964	1968	Scrapped
D8570	1964	1968	Scrapped
D8571	1964	1969	Scrapped
D8572	1964	1969	Scrapped
D8573	1964	1971	Scrapped
D8574	1964	1971	Scrapped
D8575	1964	1968	Scrapped
D8576	1964	1969	Scrapped
D8577	1964	1969	Scrapped
D8578	1964	1969	Scrapped
D8579	1964	1971	Scrapped
D8580	1964	1971	Scrapped
D8581	1964	1971	Scrapped
D8582	1964	1969	Scrapped
D8583	1964	1971	Scrapped
D8584	1964	1968	Scrapped
D8585	1964	1968	Scrapped
D8586	1964	1971	Scrapped
D8587	1965	1971	Scrapped
D8588	1964	1971	Scrapped
D8589	1964	1970	Scrapped
D8590	1964	1971	Scrapped
D8591	1964	1968	Scrapped

D8592	1964	1971	Scrapped
D8593	1964	1971	Scrapped
D8594	1964	1971	Scrapped
D8595	1964	1968	Scrapped
D8596	1964	1968	Scrapped
D8597	1964	1971	Scrapped
D8598	1964	1971	Scrapped
D8599	1964	1971	Scrapped
D8600	1964	1971	Scrapped
D8601	1964	1971	Scrapped
D8602	1964	1971	Scrapped
D8603	1964	1971	Scrapped
D8604	1964	1971	Scrapped
D8605	1964	1968	Scrapped
D8606	1964	1971	Scrapped
D8607	1964	1971	Scrapped
D8608	1964	1971	Scrapped
D8609	1964	1968	Scrapped
D8610	1964	1971	Scrapped
D8611	1964	1968	Scrapped
D8612	1965	1971	Scrapped
D8613	1965	1971	Scrapped
D8614	1965	1971	Scrapped
D8615	1965	1971	Scrapped
D8616	1965	1971	Scrapped

CLASS 20 Bo-Bo

Built: 1957–68 by English Electric, Vulcan Foundry, Newton-le-Willows and Robert Stephenson & Hawthorns, Darlington.
Engine: English Electric 8SVT of 746 kW (1000 hp) at 850 rpm.
Transmission: Electric.
Maximum Speed: 75 mph.
Train Heating/Supply: None.
Train Brakes: Built vacuum, most later dual braked (air & vacuum).

Class 20/0

Latest Number Carried	Previous Number 1	Previous Number 2	Previous Number 3	Year Entered Service	Year Withdrawn	Current Status	Notes
20001	D8001			1957	1988	Preserved	
20002	D8002			1957	1988	Scrapped	
20003	D8003			1957	1982	Scrapped	
20004	D8004			1957	1990	Scrapped	
20005	D8005			1957	1989	Scrapped	
20006	D8006			1957	1990	Scrapped	
20007	D8007			1957		Class 20189	
20008	D8008			1957	1989	Scrapped	
20009	D8009			1957	1989	Scrapped	
20010	D8010			1957	1991	Scrapped	
20011	D8011			1957	1987	Scrapped	
20012	D8012			1957	1976	Scrapped	
20013	D8013			1957	1991	Scrapped	
20014	D8014			1957	1976	Scrapped	
20015	D8015			1957	1987	Scrapped	
20016	D8016			1958		Harry Needle Railroad Co	
20017	D8017			1958	1982	Scrapped	
20018	D8018			1958	1976	Scrapped	
20019	D8019			1958	1991	Scrapped	
20020	D8020			1959	1990	Preserved	
20021	D8021			1959	1991	Scrapped	
20022	D8022			1959	1988	Scrapped	

82

20023	20301	D8023	1959	1991	Scrapped	First of 2 locomotives to be numbered 20301
20024	D8024		1959	1977	Scrapped	
20025	D8025		1959	1991	Scrapped	
20026	D8026		1959	1990	Scrapped	
20027	D8027		1959	1982	Scrapped	
20028	D8028		1959	1992	Scrapped	
20029	D8029		1959	1991	Scrapped	
20030	D8030		1959	1990	Scrapped	
20031	D8031		1960	1990	Preserved	
20032	D8032		1960	1993	Scrapped	
20033	D8033		1960	1977	Scrapped	
20034	D8034		1960	1990	Scrapped	
2001	20035	D8035	1959	1991	Preserved	
20036	D8036		1959	1984	Scrapped	
20037	D8037		1959	1987	Scrapped	
20038	D8038		1959	1976	Scrapped	
20039	D8039		1959	1986	Scrapped	
20040	D8040		1959	1991	Scrapped	
20043	D8043		1959	1991	Scrapped	
20044	D8044		1959	1989	Scrapped	
20045	D8045		1959	1990	Scrapped	
20046	D8046		1959	1993	Scrapped	
20048	D8048		1959	1990	Preserved	
20049	D8049		1959	1987	Scrapped	
20050	D8000		1957	1980	Preserved	
20051	D8051		1961	1991	Scrapped	
20052	D8052		1961	1990	Scrapped	
20053	D8053		1961	1990	Scrapped	
20054	D8054		1961	1989	Scrapped	
20055	D8055		1961	1993	Scrapped	
81	20056	D8056	1961		Harry Needle Railroad Co	
20057	D8057		1961	1994	Preserved	
20058	D8058		1961	1992	Scrapped	
20059	20302	D8059	1961	1993	Preserved	
20061	D8061		1961	1991	Scrapped	
20062	D8062		1961	1976	Scrapped	
2002	20063	D8063	1961	1991	Preserved	
20064	D8064		1961	1990	Scrapped	
20065	D8065		1961	1991	Scrapped	
82	20066	D8066	1961		Harry Needle Railroad Co	
20067	D8067		1961	1987	Scrapped	
20068	D8068		1961	1987	Scrapped	
20069	D8069		1961	1991	Harry Needle Railroad Co	HNRC locomotive stored on Mid Norfolk Railway
20070	D8070		1961	1991	Scrapped	
20071	D8071		1961	1993	Scrapped	
20072	D8072		1961	1992	Scrapped	
20073	D8073		1961	1992	Scrapped	
20074	D8074		1961	1976	Scrapped	
20076	D8076		1961	1988	Scrapped	
20077	D8077		1961	1988	Scrapped	
20078	D8078		1961	1992	Scrapped	
20079	D8079		1961	1977	Scrapped	
20080	D8080		1961	1990	Scrapped	
20081	D8081		1961		Harry Needle Railroad Co	
20082	D8082		1961	1993	Scrapped	
20085	D8085		1961	1991	Scrapped	
20086	D8086		1961	1988	Scrapped	
20087	D8087		1961	1995	Harry Needle Railroad Co	
20088	D8088		1961		Harry Needle Railroad Co	
20089	D8089		1961	1987	Scrapped	
20090	D8090		1961	1993	Scrapped	
20091	D8091		1961	1978	Scrapped	

20092	D8092	1961	1994	Scrapped	
20093	D8093	1961	1991	Scrapped	
20094	D8094	1961	1993	Scrapped	
20096	D8096	1961		GB Railfreight	HRNC locomotive on hire to GBRf
20097	D8097	1961	1989	Scrapped	
20098	D8098	1961	1991	Preserved	
20099	D8099	1961	1991	Scrapped	
20100	D8100	1961	1989	Scrapped	
20103	D8103	1961	1991	Scrapped	
20105	D8105	1961	1991	Scrapped	
20106	D8106	1961	1993	Scrapped	
20107	D8107	1961		GB Railfreight	HRNC locomotive on hire to GBRf
20108	D8108	1961	1991	Scrapped	
20109	D8109	1961	1982	Scrapped	
20110	D8110	1962	1990	Harry Needle Railroad Co	
20111	D8111	1962	1987	Scrapped	
20112	D8112	1962	1991	Scrapped	
20113	D8113	1962	1991	Scrapped	
20114	D8114	1962	1990	Scrapped	
20115	D8115	1962	1987	Scrapped	
20116	D8116	1962	1987	Scrapped	
20118	D8118	1962		GB Railfreight	HRNC locomotive on hire to GBRf
20119	D8119	1962	1992	Scrapped	
20121	D8121	1962		Harry Needle Railroad Co	
20122	D8122	1962	1991	Scrapped	
20123	D8123	1962	1987	Scrapped	
20124	D8124	1962	1991	Scrapped	
20125	D8125	1962	1986	Scrapped	
20126	D8126	1962	1989	Scrapped	
20129	D8129	1966	1990	Scrapped	

▲ Class 20 20010 sits outside Derby works, resplendent in a new coat of BR Railfreight Grey livery, with yellow cab, red lower body stripe and large BR logo. **Richard Priestley/Rail Photoprints**

20130	D8130			1966	1990	Scrapped	
20132	D8132			1966		GB Railfreight	HRNC locomotive on hire to GBRf
20133	D8133			1966	1991	Scrapped	
20134	20303	D8134		1966	1989	Scrapped	First of 2 locomotives to be numbered 20303
20135	D8135			1966	1993	Scrapped	
20136	D8136			1966	1990	Scrapped	
20137	D8137			1966	1992	Preserved	
20138	D8138			1966	1995	Scrapped	
20139	D8139			1966	1991	Scrapped	
20140	D8140			1966	1993	Scrapped	
20141	D8141			1966	1991	Scrapped	
20142	D8142			1966		Class 20189	
20143	D8143			1966	1992	Scrapped	
20144	D8144			1966	1990	Scrapped	
20145	D8145			1966	1991	Scrapped	
20146	D8146			1966	1988	Scrapped	
20147	D8147			1966	1989	Scrapped	
20148	D8148			1966	1991	Scrapped	
20149	D8149			1966	1987	Scrapped	
20150	D8150			1966	1987	Scrapped	
20151	D8151			1966	1993	Scrapped	
20152	D8152			1966	1988	Scrapped	
20153	D8153			1966	1987	Scrapped	
20154	D8154			1966	1993	Preserved	
20155	D8155			1966	1987	Scrapped	
20156	D8156			1966	1991	Scrapped	
20157	D8157			1966	1990	Scrapped	
20158	D8158			1966	1989	Scrapped	
20159	D8159			1966	1991	Scrapped	
20160	D8160			1966	1990	Scrapped	
20161	D8161			1966	1988	Scrapped	
20162	D8162			1966	1987	Scrapped	
20163	D8163			1966	1992	Scrapped	
20164	D8164			1966	1987	Scrapped	
20165	D8165			1966	1995	Scrapped	
20166	D8166			1966		Harry Needle Railroad Co	HNRC locomotive on long term loan to Wensleydale Railway
20167	D8167			1966	1987	Scrapped	
2	20168	20304	D8168	1966		Harry Needle Railroad Co	First of 2 locomotives to be numbered 20304.
20169	D8169			1966	2001	Preserved	
20170	D8170			1966	1991	Scrapped	
20171	D8171			1966	1989	Scrapped	
20172	20305	D8172		1966	1990	Scrapped	First of 2 locomotives to be numbered 20305
20173	20306	D8173		1966	1991	Scrapped	First of 2 locomotives to be numbered 20306
20174	D8174			1966	1988	Scrapped	
20175	D8175			1966	1991	Scrapped	
20176	D8176			1966	1991	Scrapped	
20177	D8177			1966	1993	Scrapped	The cab remains
20178	D8178			1966	1989	Scrapped	
20179	D8179			1966	1989	Scrapped	
20180	D8180			1966	1988	Scrapped	
20181	D8181			1966	1987	Scrapped	
20182	D8182			1966	1991	Scrapped	
20183	D8183			1966	1990	Scrapped	
20184	D8184			1966	1986	Scrapped	
20185	D8185			1967	1992	Scrapped	
20186	D8186			1967	1993	Scrapped	
20188	D8188			1967	1990	Preserved	
20189	D8189			1967		Class 20189	
20191	D8191			1967	1987	Scrapped	

20192	D8192		1967	1989	Scrapped	
20193	D8193		1967	1989	Scrapped	
20195	D8195		1967	1993	Scrapped	
20196	20308	D8196	1967	1993	Scrapped	First of 2 locomotives to be numbered 20308
20197	D8197		1967	1991	Scrapped	
20198	D8198		1967	1991	Scrapped	
20199	D8199		1967	1990	Scrapped	
20200	D8300		1967	1979	Scrapped	
20201	D8301		1967	1988	Scrapped	
20202	D8302		1967	1989	Scrapped	
20203	D8303		1967	1988	Scrapped	
20204	D8304		1967	1989	Scrapped	
20205	D8305		1967		Preserved	
20206	D8306		1967	1991	Scrapped	
20207	D8307		1967	1983	Scrapped	
20208	D8308		1967	1991	Scrapped	
20209	D8309		1967	1989	Scrapped	
20210	D8310		1967	1993	Scrapped	
20211	D8311		1967	1991	Scrapped	
20212	D8312		1967	1991	Scrapped	
20213	D8313		1967	1991	Scrapped	
20214	D8314		1967	1993	Preserved	
20215	D8315		1967	1991	Scrapped	
20216	D8316		1967	1987	Scrapped	
20217	D8317		1967	1989	Scrapped	
20218	D8318		1967	1989	Scrapped	
20220	D8320		1967	1987	Scrapped	
20221	D8321		1967	1987	Scrapped	
20222	D8322		1967	1987	Scrapped	
20223	D8323		1967	1987	Scrapped	
20224	D8324		1967	1990	Scrapped	
20226	D8326		1968	1988	Scrapped	
20227	D8327		1968		Preserved	
2004	20228	D8128	1966	1991	Preserved	

Class 20/3 First Batch
In 1986 eight Class 20s were fitted with Slow Speed Control for Peak Forest aggregate workings and renumbered 20301–20308. All locos reverted to their original Class 20/0 numberings before the end of 1986 and are therefore listed with Class 20/0s.

Class 20/3 Second Batch
Refurbished locos with extra fuel tanks and air brakes.
Details as Class 20/0 except:
Maximum Speed: 60 mph (some locos 75 mph).

Latest Number Carried	Previous Number 1	Previous Number 2	Previous Number 3	Year Entered Service	Year Withdrawn	Current Status	Notes
20301[2]	20047	D8047		1959		Direct Rail Services	Second of 2 locomotives to be numbered 20301
20302[2]	20084	D8084		1961		Direct Rail Services	Second of 2 locomotives to be numbered 20302
20303[2]	20127	D8127		1962		Direct Rail Services	Second of 2 locomotives to be numbered 20303
20304[2]	20120	D8120		1962		Direct Rail Services	Second of 2 locomotives to be numbered 20304
20305[2]	20095	D8095		1961		Direct Rail Services	Second of 2 locomotives to be numbered 20305
20306[2]	20131	D8131		1966	2009	Scrapped	Second of 2 locomotives to be numbered 20306
20307[2]	20128	D8050		1961	2013	Scrapped	Second of 2 locomotives to be numbered 20307
20308	20187	D8187		1967		Direct Rail Services	
20309	20075	D8075		1961		Direct Rail Services	
20310	20190	D8190		1967	2008	Scrapped	

20311	20102	D8102		1961		GB Railfreight	HRNC locomotive on hire to GBRf
20312	20042	D8042		1959		Direct Rail Services	
20313	20194	20307	D8194	1967	2008	Scrapped	
20314	20117	D8117		1962		GB Railfreight	HRNC locomotive on hire to GBRf
20315	20104	D8104		1961	2008	Scrapped	

Class 20/9
Refurbished locos with air brakes.

Latest Number Carried	Previous Number 1	Previous Number 2	Previous Number 3	Year Entered Service	Year Withdrawn	Current Status	Notes
20901	20101	D8101		1961		GB Railfreight	HRNC locomotive on hire to GBRf
20902	20060	D8060		1961	2003	Scrapped	
20903	20083	D8083		1961		Harry Needle Railroad Co	
20904	20041	D8041		1959		Harry Needle Railroad Co	
20905	20225	D8325		1967		GB Railfreight	HRNC locomotive on hire to GBRf
3	20906	20219	D8319	1968		Harry Needle Railroad Co	

CLASS 21 Bo-Bo

Built: 1958–60 by North British Locomotive Company, Glasgow.
Engine D6100–D6109: MAN L12V18 of 746 kW (1000 hp) at 1445 rpm.
D6110–D6157: MAN L12V21 of 820 kW (1100 hp) at 1530 rpm.
Transmission: Electric.
Maximum Speed: 75 mph.
Train Heating/Supply: Steam heating.
Train Brakes: Vacuum.

Latest Number Carried	Year Entered Service	Year Withdrawn	Current Status	Notes
D6100	1958	1967	Converted	Re-engined 1967 with Paxman Ventura engine and reclassified as Class 29
D6101	1958	1965	Converted	Re-engined 1965 with Paxman Ventura engine and reclassified as Class 29
D6102	1958	1965	Converted	Re-engined 1965 with Paxman Ventura engine and reclassified as Class 29
D6103	1959	1965	Converted	Re-engined 1965 with Paxman Ventura engine and reclassified as Class 29
D6104	1959	1967	Scrapped	
D6105	1959	1968	Scrapped	
D6106	1959	1965	Converted	Re-engined 1965 with Paxman Ventura engine and reclassified as Class 29
D6107	1959	1967	Converted	Re-engined 1967 with Paxman Ventura engine and reclassified as Class 29
D6108	1959	1967	Converted	Re-engined 1967 with Paxman Ventura engine and reclassified as Class 29
D6109	1959	1968	Scrapped	
D6110	1959	1968	Scrapped	
D6111	1959	1968	Scrapped	
D6112	1959	1966	Converted	Re-engined 1966 with Paxman Ventura engine and reclassified as Class 29
D6113	1959	1966	Converted	Re-engined 1966 with Paxman Ventura engine and reclassified as Class 29
D6114	1959	1966	Converted	Re-engined 1966 with Paxman Ventura engine and reclassified as Class 29
D6115	1959	1968	Scrapped	
D6116	1959	1966	Converted	Re-engined 1966 with Paxman Ventura engine and reclassified as Class 29
D6117	1959	1968	Scrapped	
D6118	1959	1967	Scrapped	
D6119	1959	1967	Converted	Re-engined 1967 with Paxman Ventura engine and reclassified as Class 29
D6120	1959	1967	Scrapped	
D6121	1959	1966	Converted	Re-engined 1966 with Paxman Ventura engine and reclassified as Class 29
D6122	1959	1967	Scrapped	
D6123	1959	1963	Converted	Re-engined 1963 with Paxman Ventura engine and reclassified as Class 29
D6124	1959	1967	Converted	Re-engined 1967 with Paxman Ventura engine and reclassified as Class 29
D6125	1959	1967	Scrapped	
D6126	1959	1968	Scrapped	
D6127	1959	1967	Scrapped	
D6128	1959	1967	Scrapped	
D6129	1959	1967	Converted	Re-engined 1967 with Paxman Ventura engine and reclassified as Class 29
D6130	1959	1966	Converted	Re-engined 1966 with Paxman Ventura engine and reclassified as Class 29
D6131	1959	1967	Scrapped	
D6132	1959	1966	Converted	Re-engined 1966 with Paxman Ventura engine and reclassified as Class 29

D6133	1959	1966	Converted	Re-engined 1966 with Paxman Ventura engine and reclassified as Class 29
D6134	1959	1967	Scrapped	
D6135	1959	1967	Scrapped	
D6136	1959	1967	Scrapped	
D6137	1959	1967	Converted	Re-engined 1967 with Paxman Ventura engine and reclassified as Class 29
D6138	1960	1967	Scrapped	
D6139	1960	1967	Scrapped	
D6140	1960	1967	Scrapped	
D6141	1960	1967	Scrapped	
D6142	1960	1967	Scrapped	
D6143	1960	1967	Scrapped	
D6144	1960	1967	Scrapped	
D6145	1960	1967	Scrapped	
D6146	1960	1967	Scrapped	
D6147	1960	1967	Scrapped	
D6148	1960	1967	Scrapped	
D6149	1960	1967	Scrapped	
D6150	1960	1967	Scrapped	
D6151	1960	1967	Scrapped	
D6152	1960	1968	Scrapped	
D6153	1960	1967	Scrapped	
D6154	1960	1967	Scrapped	
D6155	1960	1967	Scrapped	
D6156	1960	1967	Scrapped	
D6157	1960	1967	Scrapped	

▲ North British Class 21 D6150 stands at the entrance to Keith Shed on 17 April 1965.

Dave Cobbe Collection/Rail Photoprints

CLASS 22

B-B

Built: 1959–62 by North British Locomotive Company, Glasgow.
Engine D6300–D6305: MAN L12V18 of 750 kW (1000 hp) at 1445 rpm.
D6306–D6359: MAN L12V21 of 820 kW (1100 hp) at 1530 rpm.
Transmission: Hydraulic.
Maximum Speed: 75 mph.
Train Heating/Supply: Steam heating.
Train Brakes: Vacuum.

Latest Number Carried	Previous Number 1	Year Entered Service	Year Withdrawn	Current Status	Notes
D6300		1959	1968	Scrapped	
D6301		1959	1967	Scrapped	
D6302		1959	1968	Scrapped	
D6303		1959	1968	Scrapped	
D6304		1959	1968	Scrapped	
D6305		1960	1968	Scrapped	
D6306		1959	1968	Scrapped	
D6307		1959	1971	Scrapped	
D6308		1960	1971	Scrapped	
D6309		1960	1971	Scrapped	
D6310		1960	1971	Scrapped	
D6311		1960	1968	Scrapped	
D6312		1960	1971	Scrapped	
D6313		1960	1968	Scrapped	
D6314		1960	1969	Scrapped	
D6315		1960	1971	Scrapped	
D6316		1960	1968	Scrapped	
D6317		1960	1968	Scrapped	
D6318		1960	1971	Scrapped	
D6319		1960	1971	Scrapped	
D6320		1960	1971	Scrapped	
D6321		1960	1968	Scrapped	
D6322		1960	1971	Scrapped	
D6323		1960	1971	Scrapped	
D6324		1960	1968	Scrapped	
D6325		1960	1968	Scrapped	
D6326		1960	1971	Scrapped	
D6327		1960	1971	Scrapped	
D6328		1960	1971	Scrapped	
D6329		1960	1968	Scrapped	
D6330		1960	1971	Scrapped	
D6331		1960	1971	Scrapped	
D6332		1960	1971	Scrapped	
D6333		1960	1972	Scrapped	
D6334		1960	1971	Scrapped	
D6335		1961	1968	Scrapped	
D6336		1961	1972	Scrapped	
D6337		1962	1971	Scrapped	
D6338		1962	1972	Scrapped	
D6339		1962	1972	Scrapped	
D6340		1962	1971	Scrapped	
D6341		1962	1968	Scrapped	
D6342		1962	1968	Scrapped	
D6343		1962	1971	Scrapped	
D6344		1962	1968	Scrapped	
D6345		1962	1968	Scrapped	
D6346		1962	1969	Scrapped	
D6347		1962	1968	Scrapped	
D6348		1962	1971	Scrapped	
D6349		1962	1968	Scrapped	
D6350		1962	1968	Scrapped	

▲ North British Class 22 D6303 leads GWR 4900 Class 4914 "CRANMORE HALL" up Dainton Bank with the 12.20 Cardiff–Newquay service on 30 July 1960. **Hugh Ballantyne/Rail Photoprints**

▼ Refurbished but still set for an early demise, "Baby Deltic" (Class 23) D5905 basks in the April sun at Finsbury Park on 20 April 1969. Although none of this class survived into preservation, a new locomotive is being created using the body of Class 37 37372 and Class 20 bogies.
Dave Cobbe Collection/Rail Photoprints

D6351	1962	1968	Scrapped
D6352	1962	1971	Scrapped
D6353	1962	1968	Scrapped
D6354	1962	1971	Scrapped
D6355	1962	1968	Scrapped
D6356	1962	1971	Scrapped
D6357	1962	1968	Scrapped

CLASS 23   Bo-Bo

Built: 1959 by English Electric, Vulcan Foundry, Newton-le-Willows.
Engine: Deltic T9-29 of 820 kW (1100 hp) at 1600 rpm.
Transmission: Electric.
Maximum Speed: 75 mph.
Train Heating/Supply: Steam heating.
Train Brakes: Vacuum.

Latest Number Carried	Previous Number 1	Year Entered Service	Year Withdrawn	Current Status	Notes
D5900		1959	1968	Scrapped	
D5901		1959	1969	Scrapped	
D5902		1959	1969	Scrapped	
D5903		1959	1968	Scrapped	
D5904		1959	1969	Scrapped	
D5905		1959	1971	Scrapped	
D5906		1959	1968	Scrapped	
D5907		1959	1968	Scrapped	
D5908		1959	1969	Scrapped	
D5909		1959	1971	Scrapped	
D5910		N/A		Preserved	Created from body of 37372 on Class 20 bogies

CLASS 24   Bo-Bo

Class 24 locomotives were divided into two sub classes, 24/0 (24001–24049) and 24/1 (24050–24150) which had small differences in electrical equipment, weight and fuel capacity.

Built: 1958–61 by British Rail Derby, Crewe and Darlington.
Engine: Sulzer 6LDA28 of 870 kW (1160 hp) at 750 rpm.
Transmission: Electric.
Maximum Speed: 75mph.
Train Heating/Supply: Steam heating.
Train Brakes: Vacuum.

Class 24/0

Latest Number Carried	Previous Number 1	Previous Number 2	Previous Number 3	Year Entered Service	Year Withdrawn	Current Status	Notes
24001	D5001			1958	1975	Scrapped	
24002	D5002			1958	1975	Scrapped	
24003	D5003			1958	1975	Scrapped	
24004	D5004			1958	1975	Scrapped	
D5005				1959	1969	Scrapped	Body shell transferred to D5025 in 1969
24005	D5000			1958	1976	Scrapped	
24006	D5006			1959	1975	Scrapped	
24007	D5007			1959	1975	Scrapped	
24008	D5008			1959	1975	Scrapped	
24009	D5009			1959	1976	Scrapped	
24010	D5010			1959	1975	Scrapped	

24011	D5011			1959	1975	Scrapped	
24012	D5012			1959	1975	Scrapped	
24013	D5013			1959	1975	Scrapped	
24014	D5014			1959	1975	Scrapped	
24015	D5015			1959	1975	Scrapped	
24016	D5016			1959	1975	Scrapped	
24017	D5017			1959	1975	Scrapped	
24018	D5018			1959	1975	Scrapped	
24019	D5019			1959	1975	Scrapped	
24020	D5020			1959	1975	Scrapped	
24021	D5021			1959	1975	Scrapped	
24022	D5022			1959	1976	Scrapped	
24023	D5023			1959	1978	Scrapped	
24024	D5024			1959	1975	Scrapped	
24025	D5025			1959	1976	Scrapped	Received body shell of D5005 during repairs in 1969
24026	D5026			1959	1975	Scrapped	
24027	D5027			1959	1976	Scrapped	
D5028				1959	1972	Scrapped	
24029	D5029			1959	1975	Scrapped	
24030	D5030			1959	1976	Scrapped	
24031	D5031			1959	1975	Scrapped	
24032	D5032			1959	1976	Preserved	
24033	D5033			1959	1975	Scrapped	
24034	D5034			1959	1976	Scrapped	
24035	D5035			1959	1978	Scrapped	
24036	D5036			1959	1977	Scrapped	
24037	D5037			1959	1976	Scrapped	
24038	D5038			1959	1976	Scrapped	
24039	D5039			1959	1976	Scrapped	
24040	D5040			1959	1976	Scrapped	
24041	D5041			1959	1976	Scrapped	
24042	D5042			1959	1975	Scrapped	
D5043				1959	1969	Scrapped	
24044	D5044			1959	1976	Scrapped	
24045	D5045			1959	1975	Scrapped	
24046	D5046			1959	1976	Scrapped	
24047	D5047			1959	1978	Scrapped	
24048	D5048			1959	1975	Scrapped	
24049	D5049			1959	1976	Scrapped	

Class 24/1

24050	D5050				1959	1975	Scrapped	
D5051					1959	1967	Scrapped	
24052	D5052				1959	1976	Scrapped	
24053	D5053				1959	1976	Scrapped	
D5054	ADB968008	24054	D5054	1959	1982	Preserved	Locomotive was not self-propelled whilst in departmental use
24055	D5055				1959	1975	Scrapped	
24056	D5056				1959	1975	Scrapped	
24057	D5057				1959	1978	Scrapped	
24058	D5058				1960	1975	Scrapped	
24059	D5059				1959	1975	Scrapped	
24060	D5060				1960	1975	Scrapped	
D5061	97201	RDB968007	24061	1988	1988	Preserved	Also carried previous number 4: D5061
24062	D5062				1960	1975	Scrapped	
24063	D5063				1960	1979	Scrapped	
24064	D5064				1960	1976	Scrapped	
24065	D5065				1960	1976	Scrapped	
24066	D5066				1959	1976	Scrapped	
D5067					1959	1972	Scrapped	

D5068		1959	1972	Scrapped
24069	D5069	1960	1976	Scrapped
24070	D5070	1960	1976	Scrapped
24071	D5071	1960	1975	Scrapped
24072	D5072	1960	1975	Scrapped
24073	D5073	1960	1978	Scrapped
24074	D5074	1960	1975	Scrapped
24075	D5075	1960	1976	Scrapped
24076	D5076	1960	1975	Scrapped
24077	D5077	1960	1976	Scrapped
24078	D5078	1960	1976	Scrapped
24079	D5079	1960	1976	Scrapped
24080	D5080	1960	1976	Scrapped
24081	D5081	1960	1980	Preserved
24082	D5082	1960	1979	Scrapped
24083	D5083	1960	1976	Scrapped
24084	D5084	1960	1976	Scrapped
24085	D5085	1960	1976	Scrapped
24086	D5086	1960	1976	Scrapped
24087	D5087	1960	1978	Scrapped
D5088		1960	1970	Scrapped
24089	D5089	1960	1976	Scrapped
24090	D5090	1960	1976	Scrapped
24091	D5091	1960	1977	Scrapped
24092	D5092	1960	1975	Scrapped
D5093		1960	1969	Scrapped

▲ Class 24 24107 stands outside Motherwell depot with Class 25 25011 in August 1976. 24107 was withdrawn from service later that year, whilst 25011 soldiered on for another four years, finally succumbing in 1980. **Rail Photoprints Collection**

24094	D5094		1960	1976	Scrapped
24095	D5095		1960	1975	Scrapped
24096	D5096		1960	1975	Scrapped
24097	D5097		1960	1976	Scrapped
24098	D5098		1960	1975	Scrapped
24099	D5099		1960	1976	Scrapped
24100	D5100		1960	1976	Scrapped
24101	D5101		1960	1976	Scrapped
24102	D5102		1960	1976	Scrapped
24103	D5103		1960	1976	Scrapped
24104	D5104		1960	1976	Scrapped
24105	D5105		1960	1975	Scrapped
24106	D5106		1960	1976	Scrapped
24107	D5107		1960	1976	Scrapped
24108	D5108		1960	1976	Scrapped
24109	D5109		1960	1976	Scrapped
24110	D5110		1960	1976	Scrapped
24111	D5111		1960	1976	Scrapped
24112	D5112		1960	1976	Scrapped
24113	D5113		1961	1976	Scrapped
D5114			1960	1972	Scrapped
24115	D5115		1960	1976	Scrapped
24116	D5116		1960	1976	Scrapped
24117	D5117		1960	1976	Scrapped
24118	D5118		1960	1976	Scrapped
24119	D5119		1960	1976	Scrapped
24120	D5120		1960	1976	Scrapped
24121	D5121		1960	1976	Scrapped
D5122			1960	1968	Scrapped
24123	D5123		1960	1976	Scrapped
24124	D5124		1960	1976	Scrapped
24125	D5125		1960	1976	Scrapped
24126	D5126		1960	1976	Scrapped
24127	D5127		1960	1976	Scrapped
24128	D5128		1960	1976	Scrapped
24129	D5129		1960	1976	Scrapped
24130	D5130		1960	1976	Scrapped
D5131			1960	1971	Scrapped
24132	D5132		1960	1976	Scrapped
24133	D5133		1960	1978	Scrapped
24134	D5134		1960	1976	Scrapped
24135	D5135		1960	1976	Scrapped
24136	D5136		1960	1975	Scrapped
24137	D5137		1960	1976	Scrapped
D5138			1960	1969	Scrapped
D5139			1960	1969	Scrapped
24140	D5140		1960	1976	Scrapped
24141	D5141		1960	1976	Scrapped
ADB968009	24142	D5142	1960	1982	Scrapped	Locomotive was not self-propelled whilst in departmental use.
24143	D5143		1960	1976	Scrapped
24144	D5144		1960	1976	Scrapped
24145	D5145		1960	1976	Scrapped
24146	D5146		1960	1976	Scrapped
24147	D5147		1960	1976	Scrapped
24148	D5148		1960	1975	Scrapped
D5149			1961	1972	Scrapped
24150	D5150		1961	1976	Scrapped

CLASS 25 Bo-Bo

Class 25 locomotives were initially divided into four sub-classes, 25/0 (25001–25025), 25/1 (25026–25082), 25/2 (25083–25247) and 25/3 (25248–25327), mainly due to differences in electrical equipment. 25/9 sub-class was created when a number of locomotives were renumbered.

Built: 1961–67 by British Railways Darlington, Derby and Beyer Peacock & Co, Manchester.
Engine: Sulzer 6LDA28B of 930 kW (1250 hp) at 750 rpm.
Transmission: Electric.
Maximum Speed: 90 mph.
Train Heating/Supply: D5176–78, D5183–5237 and D7568–97 were built with steam heating generators.
Train Brakes: 25308–25319 were built with dual brakes (air & vacuum); other locomotives were built with vacuum brakes only and from 1968 air brakes were fitted so that many of the class were dual braked.

Class 25/0

Latest Number Carried	Previous Number 1	Previous Number 2	Year Entered Service	Year Withdrawn	Current Status	Notes
25001	D5151		1961	1980	Scrapped	
25002	D5152		1961	1980	Scrapped	
25003	D5153		1961	1976	Scrapped	
25004	D5154		1961	1976	Scrapped	
25005	D5155		1961	1980	Scrapped	
25006	D5156		1961	1980	Scrapped	
25007	D5157		1961	1980	Scrapped	
25008	D5158		1961	1980	Scrapped	
25009	D5159		1961	1980	Scrapped	
25010	D5160		1961	1980	Scrapped	
25011	D5161		1961	1980	Scrapped	
25012	D5162		1961	1977	Scrapped	
25013	D5163		1961	1980	Scrapped	
25014	D5164		1961	1977	Scrapped	
25015	D5165		1961	1975	Scrapped	
25016	D5166		1961	1976	Scrapped	
25017	D5167		1961	1976	Scrapped	
25018	D5168		1961	1976	Scrapped	
25019	D5169		1961	1980	Scrapped	
25020	D5170		1961	1976	Scrapped	
25021	D5171		1962	1980	Scrapped	
25022	D5172		1962	1976	Scrapped	
25023	D5173		1962	1980	Scrapped	
25024	D5174		1962	1976	Scrapped	
25025	D5175		1962	1977	Scrapped	

Class 25/1

Latest Number Carried	Previous Number 1	Previous Number 2	Year Entered Service	Year Withdrawn	Current Status	Notes
25026	D5176		1963	1980	Scrapped	
25027	D5177		1963	1983	Scrapped	
25028	D5178		1963	1980	Scrapped	
25029	D5179		1963	1977	Scrapped	
25030	D5180		1963	1976	Scrapped	
25031	D5181		1963	1977	Scrapped	
25032	D5182		1963	1986	Scrapped	
25033	D5183		1963	1983	Scrapped	
25034	D5184		1963	1986	Scrapped	
25035	D5185		1963	1987	Preserved	
25036	D5186		1963	1982	Scrapped	
25037	D5187		1963	1987	Scrapped	
25038	D5188		1963	1981	Scrapped	
25039	D5189		1963	1981	Scrapped	
25040	D5190		1963	1980	Scrapped	
25041	D5191		1963	1981	Scrapped	

25042	D5192	1963	1986	Scrapped
25043	D5193	1963	1981	Scrapped
25044	D5194	1963	1985	Scrapped
25045	D5195	1963	1975	Scrapped
25046	D5196	1963	1981	Scrapped
25047	D5197	1963	1980	Scrapped
25048	D5198	1963	1986	Scrapped
25049	D5199	1963	1984	Scrapped
25050	D5200	1963	1983	Scrapped
25051	D5201	1963	1985	Scrapped
25052	D5202	1963	1980	Scrapped
25053	D5203	1963	1980	Scrapped
25054	D5204	1963	1985	Scrapped
25055	D5205	1963	1980	Scrapped
25056	D5206	1963	1982	Scrapped
25057	D5207	1963	1987	Preserved
25058	D5208	1963	1987	Scrapped
25059	D5209	1963	1987	Preserved
25060	D5210	1963	1985	Scrapped
25061	D5211	1963	1980	Scrapped
25062	D5212	1963	1982	Scrapped
25063	D5213	1963	1980	Scrapped
25064	D5214	1963	1985	Scrapped
25065	D5215	1963	1981	Scrapped
25066	D5216	1963	1981	Scrapped
25067	D5217	1963	1982	Preserved
25068	D5218	1963	1980	Scrapped
25069	D5219	1963	1983	Scrapped
25070	D5220	1963	1980	Scrapped
25071	D5221	1963	1981	Scrapped
25072	D5222	1963	1985	Preserved
25073	D5223	1963	1981	Scrapped
25074	D5224	1963	1980	Scrapped
25075	D5225	1963	1983	Scrapped
25076	D5226	1963	1984	Scrapped
25077	D5227	1963	1978	Scrapped
25078	D5228	1963	1985	Scrapped
25079	D5229	1963	1983	Scrapped
25080	D5230	1963	1985	Scrapped
25081	D5231	1963	1982	Scrapped
25082	D5232	1963	1981	Scrapped

Class 25/2

25083	D5233	1963	1984	Preserved
25084	D5234	1963	1983	Scrapped
25085	D5235	1963	1982	Scrapped
25086	D5236	1963	1983	Scrapped
25087	D5237	1963	1980	Scrapped
25088	D5238	1963	1981	Scrapped
25089	D5239	1963	1986	Scrapped
25090	D5240	1964	1983	Scrapped
25091	D5241	1964	1978	Scrapped
25092	D5242	1964	1980	Scrapped
25093	D5243	1964	1982	Scrapped
25094	D5244	1964	1981	Scrapped
25095	D5245	1964	1986	Scrapped
25096	D5246	1964	1977	Scrapped
25097	D5247	1964	1983	Scrapped
25098	D5248	1964	1978	Scrapped
25099	D5249	1964	1980	Scrapped
25100	D5250	1964	1981	Scrapped
25101	D5251	1964	1983	Scrapped
25102	D5252	1964	1980	Scrapped
25103	D5253	1964	1980	Scrapped

25104	D5254	1964	1982	Scrapped
25105	D5255	1964	1982	Scrapped
25106	D5256	1964	1983	Scrapped
25107	D5257	1964	1981	Scrapped
25108	D5258	1964	1980	Scrapped
25109	D5259	1964	1987	Scrapped
25110	D5260	1964	1980	Scrapped
25111	D5261	1964	1980	Scrapped
25112	D5262	1964	1980	Scrapped
25113	D5263	1964	1983	Scrapped
25114	D5264	1964	1981	Scrapped
25115	D5265	1964	1983	Scrapped
25116	D5266	1964	1980	Scrapped
25117	D5267	1964	1984	Scrapped
25118	D5268	1964	1981	Scrapped
25119	D5269	1964	1985	Scrapped
25120	D5270	1964	1983	Scrapped
25121	D5271	1964	1980	Scrapped
25122	D5272	1964	1980	Scrapped
25123	D5273	1964	1983	Scrapped
25124	D5274	1964	1983	Scrapped
25125	D5275	1964	1981	Scrapped
25126	D5276	1964	1982	Scrapped
25127	D5277	1964	1980	Scrapped
D5278		1964	1971	Scrapped
25129	D5279	1964	1982	Scrapped

▲ Class 25/1 25035 passes Leek Brook Junction with a stone train from Cauldon Low bound for Witton on 27 May 1986. The line to Cauldon Low was mothballed in 1988 but since 2011 has been used for heritage operations by the Churnet Valley Railway. **Brian Robbins/Rail Photoprints**

25130	D5280		1964	1982	Scrapped
97202	25131	D5281	1964	1984	Scrapped
25132	D5282		1964	1982	Scrapped
25133	D5283		1964	1983	Scrapped
25134	D5284		1964	1982	Scrapped
25135	D5285		1964	1983	Scrapped
25136	D5286		1964	1983	Scrapped
25137	D5287		1964	1980	Scrapped
25138	D5288		1964	1983	Scrapped
25139	D5289		1964	1982	Scrapped
25140	D5290		1964	1983	Scrapped
25141	D5291		1964	1982	Scrapped
25142	D5292		1964	1981	Scrapped
25143	D5293		1964	1982	Scrapped
25144	D5294		1964	1983	Scrapped
25145	D5295		1964	1986	Scrapped
25146	D5296		1964	1983	Scrapped
25147	D5297		1964	1980	Scrapped
25148	D5298		1964	1981	Scrapped
25149	D5299		1965	1982	Scrapped
25150	D7500		1964	1982	Scrapped
25151	D7501		1964	1982	Scrapped
25152	D7502		1964	1984	Scrapped
25153	D7503		1964	1983	Scrapped
25154	D7504		1964	1985	Scrapped
25155	D7505		1964	1980	Scrapped
25156	D7506		1964	1981	Scrapped
25157	D7507		1964	1982	Scrapped
25158	D7508		1964	1983	Scrapped
25159	D7509		1964	1980	Scrapped
25160	D7510		1964	1982	Scrapped
25161	D7511		1964	1984	Scrapped
25162	D7512		1964	1981	Scrapped
25163	D7513		1964	1980	Scrapped
25164	D7514		1964	1983	Scrapped
25165	D7515		1964	1978	Scrapped
25166	D7516		1964	1980	Scrapped
25167	D7517		1964	1983	Scrapped
25168	D7518		1964	1983	Scrapped
25169	D7519		1965	1981	Scrapped
25170	D7520		1964	1982	Scrapped
25171	D7521		1965	1978	Scrapped
25172	D7522		1965	1981	Scrapped
25173	D7523		1965	1987	Preserved
25174	D7524		1965	1976	Scrapped
25175	D7525		1965	1985	Scrapped
25176	D7526		1965	1987	Scrapped
25177	D7527		1965	1982	Scrapped
25178	D7528		1965	1985	Scrapped
25179	D7529		1965	1982	Scrapped
25180	D7530		1965	1982	Scrapped
25181	D7531		1965	1986	Scrapped
25182	D7532		1965	1985	Scrapped
25183	D7533		1965	1980	Scrapped
25184	D7534		1965	1983	Scrapped
25185	D7535		1965	1984	Preserved
25186	D7536		1965	1982	Scrapped
25187	D7537		1965	1982	Scrapped
25188	D7538		1965	1982	Scrapped
25189	D7539		1965	1985	Scrapped
25190	D7540		1965	1987	Scrapped
25191	D7541		1965	1987	Preserved
25192	D7542		1965	1986	Scrapped
25193	D7543		1965	1984	Scrapped

25194	D7544	1965	1985	Scrapped
25195	D7545	1965	1985	Scrapped
25196	D7546	1965	1986	Scrapped
25197	D7547	1965	1980	Scrapped
25198	D7548	1965	1986	Scrapped
25199	D7549	1965	1987	Scrapped
25200	D7550	1965	1986	Scrapped
25201	D7551	1965	1987	Scrapped
25202	D7552	1965	1986	Scrapped
25203	D7553	1965	1980	Scrapped
25204	D7554	1965	1980	Scrapped
25205	D7555	1965	1986	Scrapped
25206	D7556	1965	1986	Scrapped
25207	D7557	1965	1984	Scrapped
25208	D7558	1965	1984	Scrapped
25209	D7559	1965	1985	Scrapped
25210	D7560	1965	1985	Scrapped
25211	D7561	1965	1986	Scrapped
25212	D7562	1965	1985	Scrapped
25213	D7563	1965	1987	Scrapped
25214	D7564	1965	1982	Scrapped
25215	D7565	1965	1983	Scrapped
25216	D7566	1966	1980	Scrapped
25217	D7567	1966	1981	Scrapped
25218	D7568	1963	1985	Scrapped
25219	D7569	1963	1983	Scrapped
25220	D7570	1963	1982	Scrapped
25221	D7571	1963	1984	Scrapped
25222	D7572	1963	1980	Scrapped
25223	D7573	1963	1980	Scrapped
25224	D7574	1963	1986	Scrapped
25225	D7575	1963	1980	Scrapped
25226	D7576	1963	1985	Scrapped
25227	D7577	1963	1983	Scrapped
25228	D7578	1963	1984	Scrapped
25229	D7579	1963	1985	Scrapped
25230	D7580	1963	1986	Scrapped
25231	D7581	1963	1985	Scrapped
25232	D7582	1964	1980	Scrapped
25233	D7583	1964	1983	Scrapped
25234	D7584	1964	1985	Scrapped
25235	D7585	1964	1985	Preserved
25236	D7586	1964	1984	Scrapped
25237	D7587	1964	1985	Scrapped
25238	D7588	1964	1980	Scrapped
25239	D7589	1964	1984	Scrapped
25240	D7590	1964	1983	Scrapped
25241	D7591	1964	1981	Scrapped
25242	D7592	1964	1984	Scrapped
25243	D7593	1964	1983	Scrapped
25244	D7594	1964	1986	Preserved
25245	D7595	1964	1985	Scrapped
25246	D7596	1964	1981	Scrapped
25247	D7597	1964	1983	Scrapped

Class 25/3

25248	D7598	1966	1982	Scrapped
25249	D7599	1966	1987	Scrapped
25250	D7600	1966	1984	Scrapped
25251	D7601	1966	1985	Scrapped
25252	D7602	1966	1980	Scrapped
25253	D7603	1966	1983	Scrapped
25254	D7604	1966	1986	Scrapped
D7605		1966	1972	Scrapped

25256	D7606		1966	1985	Scrapped	
25257	D7607		1966	1985	Scrapped	
25258	D7608		1966	1984	Scrapped	
25259	D7609		1966	1986	Scrapped	
25260	D7610		1966	1982	Scrapped	
25261	D7611		1966	1981	Scrapped	
25263	D7613		1966	1980	Scrapped	
25264	D7614		1966	1980	Scrapped	
25265	D7615		1966	1987	Preserved	
25266	D7616		1966	1986	Scrapped	
25267	D7617		1966	1981	Scrapped	
25269	D7619		1966	1986	Scrapped	
25270	D7620		1966	1982	Scrapped	
25271	D7621		1966	1981	Scrapped	
25272	D7622		1966	1981	Scrapped	
25273	D7623		1966	1981	Scrapped	
25274	D7624		1965	1982	Scrapped	
25275	D7625		1965	1982	Scrapped	
25277	D7627		1965	1984	Scrapped	
25278	D7628		1965	1987	Preserved	
25279	D7629		1965	1987	Preserved	
25280	D7630		1965	1981	Scrapped	
25281	D7631		1965	1981	Scrapped	
25282	D7632		1965	1986	Scrapped	
25284	D7634		1965	1985	Scrapped	
25285	D7635		1965	1986	Scrapped	
25287	D7637		1965	1985	Scrapped	
25288	D7638		1965	1987	Scrapped	
25289	D7639		1965	1984	Scrapped	
25290	D7640		1965	1981	Scrapped	
25291	D7641		1966	1981	Scrapped	
25292	D7642		1966	1981	Scrapped	
25293	D7643		1966	1981	Scrapped	
25294	D7644		1966	1982	Scrapped	
25295	D7645		1966	1978	Scrapped	
25298	D7648		1966	1985	Scrapped	
25299	D7649		1966	1981	Scrapped	
25300	D7650		1966	1985	Scrapped	
25301	D7651		1966	1983	Scrapped	
25302	D7652		1966	1985	Scrapped	
25303	D7653		1966	1986	Scrapped	
25304	D7654		1966	1982	Scrapped	
97251	25305	D7655	1966	1993	Scrapped	Locomotive was not self-propelled whilst in departmental use. The cab remains
25306	D7656		1966	1985	Scrapped	
25308	D7658		1966	1983	Scrapped	
97250	25310	D7660	1966	1993	Scrapped	Locomotive was not self-propelled whilst in departmental use.
25311	D7661		1966	1986	Scrapped	
25312	D7662		1966	1982	Scrapped	
25313	D7663		1966	1987	Preserved	
97252	25314	D7664	1966	1993	Scrapped	Locomotive was not self-propelled whilst in departmental use.
25317	D7667		1967	1983	Scrapped	
25318	D7668		1967	1982	Scrapped	
25319	D7669		1967	1983	Scrapped	
25320	D7670		1967	1983	Scrapped	
25321	D7671		1967	1986	Preserved	
25323	D7673		1967	1987	Scrapped	
25324	D7674		1967	1985	Scrapped	
25325	D7675		1967	1985	Scrapped	
25326	D7676		1967	1985	Scrapped	
25327	D7677		1967	1984	Scrapped	

Class 25/9
Class 25s assigned to industrial mineral railfreight in the North West in 1985.
Details as Class 25/0:

Latest Number Carried	Previous Number 1	Previous Number 2	Year Entered Service	Year Withdrawn	Current Status	Notes
25901	25262	D7612	1966	1987	Preserved	
25902	25268	D7618	1966	1987	Scrapped	
25903	25276	D7626	1965	1987	Scrapped	
25904	25283	D7633	1965	1987	Preserved	
25905	25286	D7636	1965	1986	Scrapped	
25906	25296	D7646	1966	1986	Scrapped	
25907	25297	D7647	1966	1986	Scrapped	
25908	25307	D7657	1966	1986	Scrapped	
25909	25309	D7659	1966	1986	Preserved	
25910	25315	D7665	1966	1987	Scrapped	
25911	25316	D7666	1966	1986	Scrapped	
25912	25322	D7672	1967	1991	Preserved	

CLASS 26   Bo-Bo

Built: 1958–59 by Birmingham Railway Carriage and Wagon Company.
Engine: Sulzer 6LDA28A of 870 kW (1160 hp) at 750 rpm.
Transmission: Electric.
Maximum Speed: 75 mph.
Train Heating/Supply: Steam heating.
Train Brakes: Built with vacuum brakes; most were later dual-braked (air & vacuum).

Class 26/0

Latest Number Carried	Previous Number 1	Year Entered Service	Year Withdrawn	Current Status	Notes
26001	D5301	1958	1993	Preserved	
26002	D5302	1958	1992	Preserved	
26003	D5303	1958	1993	Scrapped	
26004	D5304	1958	1992	Preserved	
26005	D5305	1958	1993	Scrapped	
26006	D5306	1958	1993	Scrapped	
26007	D5300	1958	1993	Preserved	
26008	D5308	1958	1993	Scrapped	
26009	D5309	1958	1977	Scrapped	
26010	D5310	1959	1992	Preserved	
26011	D5311	1959	1992	Preserved	
26012	D5312	1959	1982	Scrapped	
26013	D5313	1959	1985	Scrapped	
26014	D5314	1959	1992	Preserved	
26015	D5315	1959	1991	Scrapped	
26016	D5316	1959	1975	Scrapped	
26017	D5317	1959	1977	Scrapped	
26018	D5318	1959	1982	Scrapped	
26019	D5319	1959	1985	Scrapped	
26020	D5307	1958	1977	Scrapped	

Class 26/1

26021	D5321	1959	1991	Scrapped	
26022	D5322	1959	1981	Scrapped	
26023	D5323	1959	1990	Scrapped	
26024	D5324	1959	1992	Preserved	
26025	D5325	1959	1993	Preserved	
26026	D5326	1959	1992	Scrapped	
26027	D5327	1959	1991	Scrapped	
26028	D5320	1959	1991	Scrapped	
D5328		1959	1972	Scrapped	
26029	D5329	1959	1988	Scrapped	

26030	D5330	1959	1985	Scrapped
26031	D5331	1959	1989	Scrapped
26032	D5332	1959	1993	Scrapped
26033	D5333	1959	1985	Scrapped
26034	D5334	1959	1989	Scrapped
26035	D5335	1959	1992	Preserved
26036	D5336	1959	1993	Scrapped
26037	D5337	1959	1993	Scrapped
26038	D5338	1959	1992	Preserved
26039	D5339	1959	1990	Scrapped
26040	D5340	1959	1992	Preserved
26041	D5341	1959	1992	Scrapped
26042	D5342	1959	1992	Scrapped
26043	D5343	1959	1993	Preserved
26044	D5344	1959	1984	Scrapped
26045	D5345	1959	1983	Scrapped
26046	D5346	1959	1991	Scrapped

▲ BR Railfreight grey-liveried Class 26 26006 joins the East Coast Main Line at Prestonpans on 9 March 1987, with a train of loaded MGR coal hoppers from Blindwells Opencast Colliery to Cockenzie Power Station. A London-bound HST passes in the background.

John Chalcraft/Rail Photoprints

CLASS 27   Bo-Bo

Built: 1961–62 by Birmingham Railway Carriage and Wagon Company.
Engine: Sulzer 6LDA28B of 930 kW (1250 hp) at 750 rpm.
Transmission: Electric.
Maximum Speed: 90 mph.
Train Heating/Supply: D5347–69 and D5379–5415 were built with steam heating generators. D5374 subsequently fitted.
Train Brakes: Built with vacuum brakes; some were later dual-braked (air & vacuum).

Class 27/0

Latest Number Carried	Previous Number 1	Previous Number 2	Previous Number 3	Year Entered Service	Year Withdrawn	Current Status	Notes
27001	D5347			1961	1987	Preserved	
27002	D5348			1961	1986	Scrapped	
27003	D5349			1961	1987	Scrapped	
27004	D5350			1961	1986	Scrapped	
27005	D5351			1961	1987	Preserved	
27006	D5352			1961	1976	Scrapped	
27007	D5353			1961	1985	Preserved	Assigned for conversion to a Class 21
27008	D5354			1961	1987	Scrapped	
27009	D5355			1961	1980	Scrapped	
27010	D5356			1961	1986	Scrapped	
27011	D5357			1961	1981	Scrapped	
27012	D5358			1961	1986	Scrapped	
27013	D5359			1961	1976	Scrapped	
27014	D5360			1961	1986	Scrapped	
27015	D5361			1961	1977	Scrapped	
27016	D5362			1961	1984	Scrapped	
27017	D5363			1961	1986	Scrapped	
27018	D5364			1961	1986	Scrapped	
27019	D5365			1961	1984	Scrapped	
27020	D5366			1962	1986	Scrapped	
27021	D5367			1962	1985	Scrapped	
27022	D5368			1962	1985	Scrapped	
27023	D5369			1962	1986	Scrapped	
ADB968028	27024	D5370		1962	1989	Preserved	
27025	D5371			1962	1987	Scrapped	
27026	D5372			1962	1987	Scrapped	
27027	D5373			1962	1983	Scrapped	
27028	D5375			1962	1984	Scrapped	
27029	D5376			1962	1986	Scrapped	
27030	D5377			1962	1986	Scrapped	
27031	D5378			1962	1978	Scrapped	
27032	D5379			1962	1985	Scrapped	
27033	D5381			1962	1986	Scrapped	
27034	D5382			1962	1984	Preserved	
D5383				1962	1966	Scrapped	
27035	D5384			1962	1976	Scrapped	
27036	D5385			1962	1986	Scrapped	
27037	D5389			1962	1986	Scrapped	
27038	D5390			1962	1987	Scrapped	
27039	D5398			1962	1975	Scrapped	
27040	D5402			1962	1986	Scrapped	
27041	D5405			1962	1986	Scrapped	
27042	D5406			1962	1987	Scrapped	
27043	D5414			1962	1980	Scrapped	Disposed of in landfill site
27044	D5415			1962	1980	Scrapped	
27045	27101	D5374		1962	1986	Scrapped	
27046	27102	D5380		1962	1987	Scrapped	
27047	27103[2]	27118	D5413	1962	1986	Scrapped	Second locomotive to be numbered 27103

27048	27104	D5387		1962	1986	Scrapped	
27049	27105	D5388		1962	1987	Scrapped	
27050	27106	D5394		1962	1987	Preserved	
27051	27107	D5395		1962	1987	Scrapped	
27052	27108	D5396		1962	1987	Scrapped	
27053	27109	D5397		1962	1987	Scrapped	
27054	27110	D5399		1962	1987	Scrapped	
27055	27111	D5400		1962	1987	Scrapped	
27056	27112	D5401		1962	1987	Preserved	
27058	27204	27122	D5403	1962	1986	Scrapped	
27059	27205	27123	D5410	1962	1987	Preserved	
27063	27209	27115	D5408	1962	1987	Scrapped	
27064	27210	27116	D5409	1962	1986	Scrapped	
27065	27211	27117	D5411	1962	1986	Scrapped	
27066	27212	27103	D5386	1962	1987	Preserved	First of 2 locomotives to be numbered 27103

Class 27/1
24 Class 27s were converted for push-pull operation between Glasgow and Edinburgh. Locomotives 27101-118 were steam heat only and 27119–124 were electric supply only. All Class 27/1 were subsequently renumbered back to Class 27/0 after removal of push-pull equipment or converted to Class 27/2.

Class 27/2
Modified for push-pull operation between Glasgow and Edinburgh; locomotives were fitted with electric train supply and some reverted back to Class 27/0 numbers after removal of push-pull equipment.

Details as Class 27/0 except:
Train Heating/Supply: Electric.

27201	27119	D5391		1962	1979	Scrapped	
27202	27120	D5392		1962	1980	Scrapped	
27203	27121	D5393		1962	1983	Scrapped	
27206	27124	D5412		1962	1986	Scrapped	
ADB968025	27207	27113	D5404	1962	1987	Scrapped	
27208	27114	D5407		1962	1986	Scrapped	

CLASS 28   Co-Bo

Built: 1958–59 by Metropolitan Vickers, Manchester and Bowesfield Works, Stockton.
Engine: Crossley HST V8 of 896 kW (1200 hp) at 625 rpm.
Transmission: Electric.
Maximum Speed: 75 mph.
Train Heating/Supply: Steam heating.
Train Brakes: Vacuum.

Latest Number Carried	Previous Number 1	Previous Number 2	Previous Number 3	Year Entered Service	Year Withdrawn	Current Status	Notes
D5700				1958	1967	Scrapped	
D5701				1958	1968	Scrapped	
D5702				1958	1968	Scrapped	
D5703				1958	1967	Scrapped	
D5704				1958	1967	Scrapped	
D5705	TDB968006	S15705	D5705	1958	1977	Preserved	Locomotive was not self-propelled whilst in departmental use.
D5706				1958	1968	Scrapped	
D5707				1958	1968	Scrapped	
D5708				1959	1968	Scrapped	
D5709				1959	1967	Scrapped	
D5710				1959	1967	Scrapped	
D5711				1959	1968	Scrapped	
D5712				1959	1968	Scrapped	
D5713				1959	1967	Scrapped	
D5714				1959	1968	Scrapped	

▲ D5705 is the sole remaining example of Class 28, having a unique wheel arrangement of one 6-wheel bogie and one 4-wheel bogie. After a short service life with BR starting in 1958, its survival was only secured after several years of further departmental use. It is now preserved and based at the East Lancashire Railway where it is being meticulously restored. It is seen here at Bury Bolton Street station on 9 July 2016. **Andy Chard**

▼ The classic view of Oban station, overlooked by McCaig's Tower, with North British Class 29 Bo-Bo D6119 about to depart with a train for Glasgow on 21 August 1968. These locomotives were built between 1958 and 1960 and became Class 21, but 20 examples were re-engined with a more powerful Paxman power unit and were re-classified as Class 29. The class was not a success and all had been withdrawn by 1972. **Geoff Plumb Collection**

D5715		1959	1968	Scrapped
D5716		1959	1968	Scrapped
D5717		1959	1968	Scrapped
D5718		1959	1968	Scrapped
D5719		1959	1968	Scrapped

CLASS 29   Bo-Bo

20 Locomotives were converted from Class 21 Locomotives. No change in number when reclassified as Class 29. Technical details were the same as Class 21, with the following differences:

Conversions Completed: 1963–67.
Engine: Paxman Ventura 12YJXL of 1010 kW (1350 hp).
Maximum Speed: 80 mph.

Latest Number Carried	Previous Number 1	Year Entered Service	Year Withdrawn	Current Status	Notes
D6100		1967	1971	Scrapped	
D6101		1965	1971	Scrapped	
D6102		1965	1971	Scrapped	
D6103		1965	1971	Scrapped	
D6106		1965	1971	Scrapped	
D6107		1967	1971	Scrapped	
D6108		1967	1969	Scrapped	
D6112		1966	1971	Scrapped	
D6113		1966	1971	Scrapped	
D6114		1966	1971	Scrapped	
D6116		1966	1971	Scrapped	
D6119		1967	1971	Scrapped	
D6121		1966	1971	Scrapped	
D6123		1963	1971	Scrapped	
D6124		1967	1971	Scrapped	
D6129		1967	1971	Scrapped	
D6130		1966	1971	Scrapped	
D6132		1966	1971	Scrapped	
D6133		1966	1971	Scrapped	
D6137		1967	1971	Scrapped	

CLASS 30 and CLASS 31   A1A-A1A

Classes 30 and 31 are the same locomotives. They were all introduced between 1957 and 1968 with a Mirrlees JVS12T engine but between 1965 and 1969 all were re-engined with English Electric 12SVT engines. Under the 1968 classification system, Mirrlees-engined locomotives were designated Class 30 and re-engined locomotives Class 31. By the time TOPS numbers came to be applied, the re-engining programme was complete and all locomotives thus received numbers as Class 31. The class was sub-divided, with 19 of the 20 pilot scheme locomotives (31001–31019 fitted with electro-magnetic control) being Class 31/0 and standard locomotives (with electro-pneumatic control) Class 31/1. The twentieth pilot scheme locomotive was substantially rebuilt with electro-pneumatic control following accident damage and thus became Class 31/1. Locomotives with electric train supply were Class 31/4. Sub-classes 31/5 and 31/6 were created later after further modifications.

Class 31/0
Built: 1957–62 by Brush Traction, Loughborough.
Engine: Re-engined with English Electric 12SVT of 1100 kW (1170 hp) at 850 rpm.
Transmission: Electric.
Maximum Speed: 75 mph.
Train Heating/Supply: Steam Heating.
Train Brakes: Built vacuum.

Latest Number Carried	Previous Number 1	Previous Number 2	Previous Number 3	Year Entered Service	Year Withdrawn	Current Status	Notes
31001	D5501			1957	1976	Scrapped	
ADB968014	31002	D5502		1957	1982	Scrapped	Locomotive was not self-propelled whilst in departmental use
31003	D5503			1958	1980	Scrapped	
31004	D5504			1958	1980	Scrapped	
31005	D5505			1958	1980	Scrapped	
31006	D5506			1958	1980	Scrapped	
31007	D5507			1958	1976	Scrapped	
ADB968016	31008	D5508		1958	1982	Scrapped	Locomotive was not self-propelled whilst in departmental use
31009	D5509			1958	1976	Scrapped	
31010	D5510			1958	1976	Scrapped	
31011	D5511			1958	1976	Scrapped	
31012	D5512			1958	1976	Scrapped	
ADB968013	31013	D5513		1958	1983	Scrapped	Locomotive was not self-propelled whilst in departmental use
ADB968015	31014	D5514		1958	1982	Scrapped	Locomotive was not self-propelled whilst in departmental use
31015	D5515			1958	1980	Scrapped	
31016	D5516			1958	1976	Scrapped	
31017	D5517			1958	1980	Scrapped	
31018	D5500			1957	1976	Preserved	
31019	D5519			1958	1980	Scrapped	

Class 31/1

Details as per Class 31/0 except:

Maximum Speed: 75–90 mph.

Train Heating/Supply: Steam heating, boilers subsequently isolated.

Train Brakes: Vacuum, most were later dual braked (air & vacuum).

Latest Number Carried	Previous Number 1	Previous Number 2	Previous Number 3	Year Entered Service	Year Withdrawn	Current Status	Notes
31101	D5518			1958	1993	Preserved	
31102	D5520			1959	1996	Scrapped	
31103	D5521			1959	1980	Scrapped	
31105	D5523			1959		Network Rail	
31106	D5524			1959		Preserved	
31107	D5525			1959	1995	Scrapped	
31108	D5526			1959	1991	Preserved	
31109	D5527			1959	1988	Scrapped	
31110	D5528			1959	2001	Scrapped	
31111	D5529			1959	1983	Scrapped	
31112	D5530			1959	1997	Scrapped	
31113	D5531			1959	1999	Scrapped	
31116	D5534			1959	1995	Scrapped	
31117	D5535			1959	1987	Scrapped	
31118	D5536			1959	1989	Scrapped	
31119	D5537			1959	1995	Preserved	
31120	D5538			1959	1991	Scrapped	
31121	D5539			1959	1988	Scrapped	
31122	D5540			1959	1988	Scrapped	
31123	D5541			1959	1992	Scrapped	
31124	D5542			1959	1990	Scrapped	
31125	D5543			1959	1994	Scrapped	
31126	D5544			1959	1999	Scrapped	
31127	D5545			1959	1989	Scrapped	
31128	D5546			1959		Nemesis Rail	
31130	D5548			1959	1997	Preserved	
31131	D5549			1959	1989	Scrapped	
31132	D5550			1959	1995	Scrapped	
31134	D5552			1959	1996	Scrapped	
31135	D5553			1959	1994	Scrapped	

31136	D5554	1959	1980	Scrapped	
31138	D5556	1959	1989	Scrapped	
31141	D5559	1959	1989	Scrapped	
31142	D5560	1959	1999	Scrapped	
31143	D5561	1959	1988	Scrapped	
31144	D5562	1959	1996	Scrapped	The cab remains
31145	D5563	1959	1997	Scrapped	
31146	D5564	1959	1998	Scrapped	
31147	D5565	1959	1996	Scrapped	
31149	D5567	1959	1996	Scrapped	
31150	D5568	1959	1975	Scrapped	
31152	D5570	1959	1989	Scrapped	
31154	D5572	1959	1999	Scrapped	
31155	D5573	1959	1995	Scrapped	
31156	D5574	1959	1992	Scrapped	
31158	D5576	1959	1994	Scrapped	
31159	D5577	1959	1996	Scrapped	
31160	D5578	1960	1996	Scrapped	
31162	D5580	1960	1992	Preserved	
31163	D5581	1960	1999	Preserved	
31164	D5582	1960	1995	Scrapped	
31165	D5583	1960	1996	Scrapped	
31166	D5584	1960	1999	Scrapped	
31167	D5585	1960	1988	Scrapped	
31168	D5586	1960	1991	Scrapped	
31170	D5588	1960	1990	Scrapped	
31171	D5590	1960	1993	Scrapped	
31173	D5593	1960	1989	Scrapped	
31174	D5594	1960	1994	Scrapped	
31175	D5595	1960	1987	Scrapped	
31176	D5597	1960	1987	Scrapped	
31178	D5599	1960	1995	Scrapped	
31180	D5601	1960	1995	Scrapped	
31181	D5602	1960	1995	Scrapped	
31183	D5604	1960	1988	Scrapped	
31184	D5607	1960	1994	Scrapped	
31185	D5608	1960	1996	Scrapped	
31187	D5610	1960	1995	Scrapped	
31188	D5611	1960	1999	Scrapped	
31189	D5612	1960	1989	Scrapped	
31190	D5613	1960		RMS Locotec	
31192	D5615	1960	1982	Scrapped	
31195	D5619	1960	1988	Scrapped	
31196	D5620	1960	1993	Scrapped	
31198	D5622	1960	1990	Scrapped	
31199	D5623	1960	1996	Scrapped	
31200	D5624	1960	1996	Scrapped	
31201	D5625	1960	1999	Scrapped	
31202	D5626	1960	1988	Scrapped	
31203	D5627	1960	2000	Preserved	
31205	D5629	1960	1995	Scrapped	
31206	D5630	1960	1999	Preserved	
31207	D5631	1960	2001	Preserved	
31208	D5632	1960	1990	Scrapped	
31209	D5633	1960	1995	Scrapped	
31210	D5634	1960	1992	Preserved	
31212	D5636	1960	1991	Scrapped	
31214	D5638	1960	1983	Scrapped	
31215	D5639	1960	1993	Scrapped	
31217	D5642	1960	1993	Scrapped	
31218	D5643	1960	1988	Scrapped	
31219	D5644	1960	1995	Scrapped	
31221	D5647	1960	1991	Scrapped	
31222	D5648	1960	1988	Scrapped	

31223	D5649		1960	1991	Scrapped
31224	D5650		1960	1995	Scrapped
31225	D5651		1960	1989	Scrapped
31226	D5652		1960	1989	Scrapped
31227	D5653		1960	1988	Scrapped
31229	D5655		1960	1998	Scrapped
31230	D5657		1960	1994	Scrapped
31231	D5658		1960	1990	Scrapped
31232	D5659		1960	1995	Scrapped
31233	D5660		1960		Network Rail
31234	D5661		1960	1993	Scrapped
31235	D5662		1960		Harry Needle Railroad Co HNRC locomotive stored on Mid Norfolk Railway
31237	D5664		1960	1995	Scrapped
31238	D5665		1960	1996	Scrapped
31240	D5667		1960	1990	Scrapped
31241	D5668		1960	1982	Scrapped
31242	D5670		1961	1998	Scrapped
31243	D5671		1961	1991	Scrapped
31244	D5672		1961	1983	Scrapped
31245	D5673		1961	1987	Scrapped
31247	D5675		1961	1995	Scrapped
31248	D5676		1961	1993	Scrapped
31249	D5677		1961	1991	Scrapped
31250	D5678		1961	2000	Scrapped
31252	D5680		1961	1995	Scrapped
31254	D5682		1961	1979	Scrapped
31255	D5683		1961	1999	Harry Needle Railroad Co
31257	D5685		1961	1990	Scrapped
31259	D5687		1961	1989	Scrapped
31260	D5688		1961	1990	Scrapped
31261	D5689		1961	1987	Scrapped
31262	D5690		1961	1983	Scrapped
31263	D5693		1961	1994	Scrapped
31264	D5694		1961	1991	Scrapped
31268	D5698		1961	1995	Scrapped
31270	D5800		1961	1995	Preserved
31271	D5801		1961	1997	Preserved
31272	D5802		1961	1995	Scrapped
31273	D5803		1961	1998	Scrapped
31275	D5805		1961	1997	Scrapped
31276	D5806		1961	1995	Scrapped
31278	D5808		1961	1989	Scrapped
31280	D5810		1961	1988	Scrapped
31281	D5811		1961	1989	Scrapped
31282	D5813		1961	1994	Scrapped
31283	D5815		1961	1989	Scrapped
31284	D5816		1961	1989	Scrapped
31285	D5817		1961		Harry Needle Railroad Co
31286	D5818		1961	1991	Scrapped
31287	D5819		1961	1987	Scrapped
31288	D5820		1961	1991	Scrapped
31289	D5821		1961	1992	Preserved
31290	D5822		1961	1995	Scrapped
31292	D5825		1961	1990	Scrapped
31293	D5826		1961	1990	Scrapped
31294	D5827		1961	1995	Scrapped
31296	D5829		1962	1993	Scrapped
97203	31298	D5831	1962	1987	Scrapped
31299	D5832		1962	1990	Scrapped
31301	D5834		1962	1999	Scrapped
31302	D5835		1962	1999	Scrapped
31304	D5837		1962	1996	Scrapped
31305	D5838		1962	1991	Scrapped

31306	D5839			1962	1999	Scrapped
31308	D5841			1962	1999	Scrapped
31309	D5843			1962	1991	Scrapped
31311	D5845			1962	1989	Scrapped
31312	D5846			1962	1996	Scrapped
31313	D5847			1962	1983	Scrapped
31314	D5848			1962	1982	Scrapped
31317	D5851			1962	1995	Scrapped
31319	D5853			1962	1997	Scrapped
31320	D5854			1962	1990	Scrapped
31322	D5857			1962	1989	Scrapped
31323	D5858			1962	1989	Scrapped
31324	D5859			1962	1993	Scrapped
31970	97204	31326	D5861	1962	1991	Scrapped
31327	D5862			1962	1995	Preserved

Class 31/4
Details as Class 31/1 except:
Maximum Speed: 90 mph.
Train Heating/Supply: Electric Train Supply. Some retained steam heating.

Latest Number Carried	Previous Number 1	Previous Number 2	Previous Number 3	Year Entered Service	Year Withdrawn	Current Status	Notes
31400	31161	D5579		1960	1991	Scrapped	
31401	D5589			1960	1988	Scrapped	
31402	D5592			1960	1992	Scrapped	
31403	D5596			1960	1995	Scrapped	
31404	D5605			1960	1991	Scrapped	
31405	D5606			1960	1999	Scrapped	
31406	D5616			1960	1991	Scrapped	
31407	31507	31407	D5640	1960	1998	Scrapped	
31408	D5646			1960	1994	Scrapped	
31409	D5656			1960	1991	Scrapped	
31410	D5669			1960	1997	Scrapped	
31411	31511	31411	D5691	1961	1995	Scrapped	
31412	31512	31412	D5692	1961	1998	Scrapped	
31413	D5812			1961	1997	Scrapped	
31415	D5824			1961	1995	Scrapped	
31417	D5856			1962	1995	Scrapped	
31418	D5522			1959	1995	Preserved	
31420	31172	D5591		1960	2001	Scrapped	
31421	31140	D5558		1959	1997	Scrapped	
31422	31522	31422	31310	1962	1999	Scrapped	Also carried previous number 4: D5844
31423	31197	D5621		1960	1996	Scrapped	
31425	31274	D5804		1961	1991	Scrapped	
31426	31526	31426	31193	1960	1995	Scrapped	Also carried previous number 4: D5617
31427	31194	D5618		1960	1999	Scrapped	
31428	31211	D5635		1960	1991	Scrapped	
31429	31269	D5699		1961	1991	Scrapped	
31432	31153	D5571		1959	1996	Scrapped	
31433	31533	31433	31236	1960	1995	Scrapped	Also carried previous number 4: D5663
31434	31258	D5686		1961	1998	Scrapped	
31435	31179	D5600		1960	1995	Preserved	
31436	31151	D5569		1959	1986	Scrapped	
31437	31537	31437	31182	1960	1999	Scrapped	Also carried previous number 4: D5603
31439	31239	D5666		1960	1999	Scrapped	
31440	31204	D5628		1960	1987	Scrapped	
31442	31251	D5679		1960	1993	Scrapped	
31443	31177	D5598		1960	1989	Scrapped	

Latest Number Carried	Previous Number 1	Previous Number 2	Previous Number 3	Year Entered Service	Year Withdrawn	Current Status	Notes
31444	31544	31444	31137	1959	1995	Scrapped	Also carried previous number 4: D5555
31450	31133	D5551		1959	1998	Scrapped	
31452	31552	31452	31279	1961		RMS Locotec	Also carried previous number 4: D5809
31454	31554	31454	31228	1960		RMS Locotec	Also carried previous number 4: D5654
31455	31555	31455	31246	1960	1996	Scrapped	Also carried previous number 4: D5674
31457	31169	D5587		1960	1994	Scrapped	
31459	31256	D5684		1961		Harry Needle Railroad Co	HNRC locomotive on loan to Weardale Railway
31460	31266	D5696		1961	1992	Scrapped	
31461	31129	D5547		1959		Nemesis Rail	
31462	31315	D5849		1962	1998	Scrapped	
31464	31325	D5860		1962	1991	Scrapped	
31465	31565	31465	31213	1960		Harry Needle Railroad Co	HNRC locomotive on loan to Weardale Railway. Also carried previous number 4: D5637
31466	31115	D5533		1959	2001	Preserved	
31467	31216	D5641		1960	1998	Scrapped	
31468	31568	31468	31321	1962		RMS Locotec	Also carried previous number 4: D5855

Class 31/5
Details as Class 31/4 except:
Train Heating/Supply: Electric Train Supply isolated.

Latest Number Carried	Previous Number 1	Previous Number 2	Previous Number 3	Year Entered Service	Year Withdrawn	Current Status	Notes
31514	31414	D5814		1961	1999	Preserved	
31516	31416	D5842		1962	1995	Scrapped	
31519	31419	D5697		1961	1995	Scrapped	
31524	31424	31157	D5575	1959	1996	Scrapped	
31530	31430	31265	D5695	1961	1999	Preserved	
31531	31431	31253	D5681	1961	1995	Scrapped	
31538	31438	31139	D5557	1959	1995	Preserved	
31541	31441	31220	D5645	1960	1996	Scrapped	
31545	31445	31300	D5833	1962	1997	Scrapped	
31546	31446	31316	D5850	1962	1995	Scrapped	
31547	31447	31295	D5828	1961	1996	Scrapped	
31548	31448	31148	D5566	1959	1995	Scrapped	
31549	31449	31307	D5840	1962	1996	Scrapped	
31551	31451	31318	D5852	1962	1996	Scrapped	
31553	31453	31114	D5532	1959	1995	Scrapped	
31556	31456	31556	31456	1961	1995	Scrapped	Also carried previous number 4: 31291 and previous number 5: D5823
31558	31458	31303	D5836	1962	1996	Scrapped	
31563	31463	31297	D5830	1962	1998	Preserved	
31569	31469	31277	D5807	1961	1995	Scrapped	

Class 31/6
Details as Class 31/4 except:
Train Heating/Supply: None. Through-wired for electric train supply.

Latest Number Carried	Previous Number 1	Previous Number 2	Previous Number 3	Year Entered Service	Year Withdrawn	Current Status	Notes
31601	31186	D5609		1960		Preserved	
31602	31191	D5614		1960		RMS Locotec	

CLASS 33 Bo-Bo

Built: 1960–62 by Birmingham Railway Carriage and Wagon Company.
Engine: Sulzer 8LDA28A of 1160 kW (1550 hp) at 750 rpm.
Transmission: Electric.
Maximum Speed: 85 mph.
Train Heating/Supply: Electric.
Train Brakes: Dual braked (air & vacuum).

Class 33/0

Latest Number Carried	Previous Number 1	Previous Number 2	Previous Number 3	Year Entered Service	Year Withdrawn	Current Status	Notes
33001	D6500			1960	1988	Scrapped	
33002	D6501			1960	1996	Preserved	
D6502	D6502			1960	1964	Scrapped	
33003	D6503			1960	1987	Scrapped	
33004	D6504			1960	1991	Scrapped	
33005	D6505			1960	1987	Scrapped	
33006	D6506			1960	1991	Scrapped	
33007	D6507			1960	1986	Scrapped	
33008	D6508			1960	1996	Preserved	
33009	D6509			1960	1992	Scrapped	
33010	D6510			1960	1988	Scrapped	
33011	D6512			1960	1989	Scrapped	
33012	D6515			1960	1997	Preserved	
33013	D6518			1960	1989	Scrapped	
33014	D6522			1960	1986	Scrapped	
33015	D6523			1960	1989	Scrapped	
33016	D6524			1960	1989	Scrapped	
33017	D6526			1960	1988	Scrapped	
33018	TDB968030	33018	D6530	1960	2000	Preserved	
33019	D6534			1960		Nemesis Rail	

▲ Direct Rail Services' 33025 and 33030 stand at Carlisle Citadel with a trial service of "Minimodal" containers on 28 August 2002. Both of these locomotives have subsequently passed into the custodianship of West Coast Railway Company. **Gordon Edgar/Rail Photoprints**

33020	D6537		1960	1993	Scrapped
33021	D6539		1961	2003	Preserved
33022	D6540		1961	1989	Scrapped
33023	D6541		1961	1997	Scrapped
33024	D6542		1961	1986	Scrapped
33025	D6543		1961		West Coast Railway Co
33026	D6544		1961	1998	Scrapped
33027	D6545		1961	1991	Scrapped
33028	D6546		1961	1988	Scrapped
33029	D6547		1961		West Coast Railway Co
33030	D6548		1961		West Coast Railway Co
33031	D6549		1961	1989	Scrapped
33032	D6550		1961	1987	Scrapped
33033	D6551		1961	1993	Scrapped
33034	D6552		1961	1988	Scrapped
33035	D6553		1961	1996	Preserved
33036	D6554		1961	1979	Scrapped
33037	D6555		1961	1987	Scrapped
33038	D6556		1961	1988	Scrapped
33039	D6557		1961	1989	Scrapped
33040	D6558		1961	1993	Scrapped
33041	D6559		1961	1975	Scrapped
33042	D6560		1961	1996	Scrapped
33043	D6561		1961	1987	Scrapped
33044	D6562		1961	1987	Scrapped
33045	D6563		1961	1987	Scrapped
33046	D6564		1961	1998	Preserved
33047	D6565		1961	1993	Scrapped
33048	D6566		1961	1997	Preserved
33049	D6567		1961	1988	Scrapped
33050	D6568		1961	1993	Scrapped
33051	D6569		1961	1998	Scrapped
33052	D6570		1961	1997	Preserved
33053	D6571		1961	1997	Preserved
33054	D6572		1961	1986	Scrapped
33055	D6573		1961	1989	Scrapped
33056	D6574		1961	1991	Scrapped
33057	D6575		1961	1997	Preserved
D6576	D6576		1961	1968	Scrapped
33058	D6577		1961	1991	Scrapped
33059	D6578		1961	1988	Scrapped
33060	D6579		1961	1990	Scrapped
33061	D6581		1961	1987	Scrapped
33062	D6582		1961	1987	Scrapped
33063	D6583		1962	1997	Preserved
33064	D6584		1962	1994	Scrapped
33065	D6585		1962	1997	Preserved

Class 33/1
Fitted with push-pull control system. Triple-braked (air, vacuum & electro-pneumatic).
Details as Class 33/0.

Latest Number Carried	Previous Number 1	Previous Number 2	Year Entered Service	Year Withdrawn	Current Status	Notes
33101	D6511		1960	1993	Scrapped	
33102	D6513		1960	1992	Preserved	
33103	D6514		1960	1997	Preserved	
33104	D6516		1960	1985	Scrapped	
33105	D6517		1960	1987	Scrapped	
33106	D6519		1960	1990	Scrapped	
33107	D6520		1960	1989	Scrapped	
33108	D6521		1960	2003	Preserved	
33109	D6525		1960	1997	Preserved	
33110	D6527		1960	1992	Preserved	

33111	D6528	1960	1991	Preserved
33112	D6529	1960	1988	Scrapped
33113	D6531	1960	1992	Scrapped
33114	D6532	1960	1993	Scrapped
33115	D6533	1960	1989	Scrapped
33116	D6535	1960	1998	Preserved
33117	D6536	1960	1997	Preserved
33118	D6538	1961	1993	Scrapped
33119	D6580	1961	1989	Scrapped

Class 33/2
Built to the former loading gauge of the Tonbridge–Battle line.
Details as Class 33/0.

Latest Number Carried	Previous Number 1	Previous Number 2	Previous Number 3	Year Entered Service	Year Withdrawn	Current Status	Notes
33201	D6586			1962	1993	Preserved	
33202	D6587			1962	2007	Preserved	
33203	D6588			1962	1991	Scrapped	
33204	D6589			1962	1997	Scrapped	
33205	33302	33205	D6590	1962	1992	Scrapped	
33206	D6591			1962	1996	Scrapped	
33207	D6592			1962		West Coast Railway Co	
33208	D6593			1962	1997	Preserved	
33209	D6594			1962	1988	Scrapped	
33210	D6595			1962	1987	Scrapped	
33211	D6596			1962	1993	Scrapped	
33212	D6597			1962	1987	Scrapped	

CLASS 35   B-B

Built: 1961–64 by Beyer Peacock & Co., Manchester.
Engine: Bristol Siddeley Maybach MD 870 of 1269 kW (1700 hp) at 1500 rpm.
Transmission: Hydraulic.
Maximum Speed: 90 mph.
Train Heating/Supply: Steam heating.
Train Brakes: Vacuum.

Latest Number Carried	Year Entered Service	Year Withdrawn	Current Status	Notes
D7000	1961	1973	Scrapped	
D7001	1961	1974	Scrapped	
D7002	1961	1971	Scrapped	
D7003	1961	1972	Scrapped	
D7004	1961	1972	Scrapped	
D7005	1961	1972	Scrapped	
D7006	1961	1971	Scrapped	
D7007	1961	1972	Scrapped	
D7008	1961	1972	Scrapped	
D7009	1961	1973	Scrapped	
D7010	1961	1972	Scrapped	
D7011	1961	1975	Scrapped	
D7012	1961	1972	Scrapped	
D7013	1961	1972	Scrapped	
D7014	1961	1972	Scrapped	
D7015	1961	1972	Scrapped	
D7016	1962	1974	Scrapped	
D7017	1962	1975	Preserved	
D7018	1962	1975	Preserved	
D7019	1962	1972	Scrapped	
D7020	1962	1972	Scrapped	
D7021	1962	1972	Scrapped	
D7022	1962	1975	Scrapped	
D7023	1962	1973	Scrapped	

D7024	1962	1972	Scrapped
D7025	1962	1972	Scrapped
D7026	1962	1974	Scrapped
D7027	1962	1971	Scrapped
D7028	1962	1975	Scrapped
D7029	1962	1975	Preserved
D7030	1962	1973	Scrapped
D7031	1962	1973	Scrapped
D7032	1962	1973	Scrapped
D7033	1962	1972	Scrapped
D7034	1962	1972	Scrapped
D7035	1962	1972	Scrapped
D7036	1962	1972	Scrapped
D7037	1962	1972	Scrapped
D7038	1962	1972	Scrapped
D7039	1962	1972	Scrapped
D7040	1962	1972	Scrapped
D7041	1962	1972	Scrapped
D7042	1962	1972	Scrapped
D7043	1962	1972	Scrapped
D7044	1962	1973	Scrapped
D7045	1962	1972	Scrapped
D7046	1962	1972	Scrapped
D7047	1962	1972	Scrapped
D7048	1962	1972	Scrapped
D7049	1962	1972	Scrapped
D7050	1962	1972	Scrapped
D7051	1962	1972	Scrapped
D7052	1962	1972	Scrapped
D7053	1962	1972	Scrapped
D7054	1962	1972	Scrapped
D7055	1962	1973	Scrapped
D7056	1962	1972	Scrapped
D7057	1962	1972	Scrapped
D7058	1962	1971	Scrapped
D7059	1962	1971	Scrapped
D7060	1962	1971	Scrapped
D7061	1962	1972	Scrapped
D7062	1963	1971	Scrapped
D7063	1962	1971	Scrapped
D7064	1963	1971	Scrapped
D7065	1963	1972	Scrapped
D7066	1963	1971	Scrapped
D7067	1963	1971	Scrapped
D7068	1963	1972	Scrapped
D7069	1963	1971	Scrapped
D7070	1963	1972	Scrapped
D7071	1963	1972	Scrapped
D7072	1963	1971	Scrapped
D7073	1963	1971	Scrapped
D7074	1963	1972	Scrapped
D7075	1963	1973	Scrapped
D7076	1963	1973	Preserved
D7077	1963	1972	Scrapped
D7078	1963	1971	Scrapped
D7079	1963	1971	Scrapped
D7080	1963	1972	Scrapped
D7081	1963	1971	Scrapped
D7082	1963	1972	Scrapped
D7083	1963	1971	Scrapped
D7084	1963	1972	Scrapped
D7085	1963	1972	Scrapped
D7086	1963	1972	Scrapped
D7087	1963	1972	Scrapped

D7088	1963	1972	Scrapped
D7089	1963	1973	Scrapped
D7090	1963	1972	Scrapped
D7091	1963	1972	Scrapped
D7092	1963	1972	Scrapped
D7093	1963	1974	Scrapped
D7094	1963	1972	Scrapped
D7095	1963	1972	Scrapped
D7096	1963	1972	Scrapped
D7097	1963	1972	Scrapped
D7098	1964	1972	Scrapped
D7099	1964	1972	Scrapped
D7100	1964	1972	Scrapped

CLASS 37   Co-Co

Built: 1960–65 by English Electric, Vulcan Foundry, Newton-le-Willows and Robert Stephenson & Hawthorns, Darlington.
Engine: English Electric 12CSVT of 1300 kW (1750 hp) at 850 rpm.
Transmission: Electric.
Maximum Speed: 90 mph.
Train Heating/Supply: D6700–D6938 were built with steam heating generators. Subsequently fitted to D6947/D6960–D6968 and later D6948 after preservation. Most were later isolated or removed. The remainder were built with through steam pipes.
Train Brakes: Built vacuum. All except D6983 were later converted to dual braked (air & vacuum).

Class 37/0

Includes Class 37/3 First Batch, which were renumbered 37310–37314 and 37320–37326.
Previous numbers were 37152, 37156, 37137, 37145, 37190, 37026, 37037, 37049, 37088, 37099, 37108 and 37111 respectively; unrefurbished Class 37/0s selected for exclusive use on Scottish Region air-braked steel traffic.
All reverted to 37/0 numbers in 1988–89 and are therefore listed with Class 37/0s.

Latest Number Carried	Previous Number 1	Previous Number 2	Previous Number 3	Year Entered Service	Year Withdrawn	Current Status	Notes
37003	D6703			1960	1998	Preserved	
37004	D6704			1961	1996	Scrapped	
37008	37352	37008	D6708	1961	1992	Scrapped	
37010	D6710			1961	2005	Scrapped	
37011	D6711			1961	1987	Scrapped	
37012	D6712			1961	1999	Scrapped	
37013	D6713			1961	1999	Scrapped	
37019	D6719			1961	1995	Scrapped	
37023	D6723			1961	1999	Preserved	
37025	D6725			1961		Colas Rail	Preserved locomotive on hire to Colas Rail
37026	37320	37026	D6726	1961	1996	Scrapped	
37029	D6729			1961	2006	Preserved	
37031	D6731			1961	1994	Scrapped	
37032	37353	37032	D6732	1962	1994	Preserved	
37035	D6735			1962	1996	Scrapped	
37037	37321	37037	D6737	1962	2003	Preserved	
37038	D6738			1962		Direct Rail Services	
37040	D6740			1962	2000	Scrapped	
37042	D6742			1962	2011	Preserved	
37043	37354	37043	D6743	1962	2000	Scrapped	
37046	D6746			1962	2000	Scrapped	
37047	D6747			1962	2007	Scrapped	
37048	D6748			1962	1996	Scrapped	
37051	D6751			1962	2005	Scrapped	
37054	D6754			1962	1999	Scrapped	
37055	D6755			1962	2002	Scrapped	
37057	D6757			1962		Colas Rail	
37058	D6758			1962	2000	Scrapped	

▲ Class 35 Hymek D7094 passes Netherhope Halt with a ballast train from Tintern Quarry on 5 May 1971. Despite being less than ten years old when this photo was taken, the locomotives was scrapped only a year later. **Dave Cobbe Collection/Rail Photoprints**

▼ 37294 in the newer Railfreight grey livery with petroleum sector decals, leads older Railfreight-liveried 37374 through Sonning Cutting with a Robeston–Langley oil service on 7 April 1990. **John Chalcraft/Rail Photoprints**

37059	D6759			1962		Direct Rail Services
37062	D6762			1962	1989	Scrapped
37063	D6763			1962	1994	Scrapped
37065	D6765			1962	2007	Scrapped
37066	D6766			1962	1997	Scrapped
37068	37356	37068	D6768	1962	1995	Scrapped
37069	D6769			1962		Direct Rail Services
37070	D6770			1962	1996	Scrapped
37071	D6771			1962	2000	Scrapped
37072	D6772			1962	1997	Scrapped
37073	D6773			1962	2000	Scrapped
37074	D6774			1962	2000	Scrapped
37075	D6775			1962	1999	Preserved
37077	D6777			1962	2000	Scrapped
37078	D6778			1962	1993	Scrapped
37079	37357	37079	D6779	1962	1998	Scrapped
37080	D6780			1962	1996	Scrapped
37083	D6783			1962	1994	Scrapped
37087	D6787			1962	2012	Scrapped
37088	37323	37088	D6788	1963	1996	Scrapped
37092	D6792			1963	1996	Scrapped
37095	D6795			1963	1999	Scrapped
37096	D6796			1962	1991	Scrapped
37097	D6797			1962	1998	Preserved
37098	D6798			1962	1998	Scrapped
37099	37324	37099	D6799	1962		Colas Rail
37104	D6804			1963	1997	Scrapped
37106	D6806			1963	1999	Scrapped
37107	D6807			1963	1999	Scrapped
37108	37325	37108	D6808	1963	1996	Preserved
37109	D6809			1963	2007	Preserved
37110	D6810			1963	1995	Scrapped
37111	37326	37111	D6811	1963	1996	Scrapped
37113	D6813			1963	1995	Scrapped
37114	D6814			1963	2007	Scrapped
37116	D6816			1963		Colas Rail
37131	D6831			1963	1999	Scrapped
37133	D6833			1963	2000	Scrapped
37137	37312	37137	D6837	1963	2006	Scrapped
37138	D6838			1963	1996	Scrapped
37139	D6839			1963	1994	Scrapped
37140	D6840			1963	1999	Scrapped
37141	D6841			1963	1997	Scrapped
37142	D6842			1963	1997	Preserved
37144	D6844			1963	1994	Scrapped
37146	D6846			1963		Colas Rail
37152	37310	37152	D6852	1963	1999	Preserved
37153	D6853			1963	1999	Scrapped
37154	D6854			1963	1999	Scrapped
37156	37311	37156	D6856	1963	1999	Scrapped
37158	D6858			1963	1999	Scrapped
37162	D6862			1963	2000	Scrapped
37165	37374	37165	D6865	1963		West Coast Railway Co
37174	D6874			1963	2005	Scrapped
37175	D6875			1963		Colas Rail
37184	D6884			1963	1996	Scrapped
37185	D6885			1963	1999	Scrapped
37188	D6888			1964		Colas Rail
37190	37314	37190	D6890	1964	1993	Preserved
37191	D6891			1964	1999	Scrapped
37194	D6894			1964	2015	Scrapped
37196	D6896			1964	2000	Scrapped
37197	D6897			1964	2007	Scrapped
37198	D6898			1964		Network Rail

Latest Number Carried	Previous Number 1	Previous Number 2	Previous Number 3	Year Entered Service	Year Withdrawn	Current Status	Notes
37201	D6901			1963	1996	Scrapped	
37203	D6903			1963	2009	Scrapped	
37207	D6907			1963		Colas Rail	
37209	D6909			1963	1992	Scrapped	
37211	D6911			1963	1999	Scrapped	
37212	D6912			1964	1999	Scrapped	
37213	D6913			1964	1996	Scrapped	
37214	D6914			1964		Preserved	
37215	D6915			1964	1993	Preserved	
37216	D6916			1964	2004	Preserved	
37218	D6918			1964		Direct Rail Services	
37219	D6919			1964		Colas Rail	
37220	D6920			1964	2000	Scrapped	
37221	D6921			1964	2000	Scrapped	
37222	D6922			1964	1997	Scrapped	
37223	D6923			1964	1995	Scrapped	
37225	D6925			1964	1999	Scrapped	
37227	D6927			1964	1997	Preserved	
37229	D6929			1964	2012	Scrapped	
37230	D6930			1964	2000	Scrapped	
37232	D6932			1964	1996	Scrapped	
37235	D6935			1964	1995	Scrapped	
37238	D6938			1964	2000	Scrapped	
37240	D6940			1964	1997	Preserved	
37241	D6941			1964	1996	Scrapped	
37242	D6942			1964	1999	Scrapped	
37244	D6944			1964	1999	Scrapped	
37245	D6945			1964	1999	Scrapped	
37248	D6948			1964		Preserved	
37250	D6950			1964	2000	Preserved	
37251	D6951			1964	1996	Scrapped	
37252	D6952			1965	1995	Scrapped	
37254	D6954			1965		Colas Rail	
37255	D6955			1965	1999	Preserved	
37259	37380	37259	D6959	1965		Direct Rail Services	
37260	D6960			1965	1989	Scrapped	
37261	D6961			1965	2014	Preserved	
37262	D6962			1965	1999	Scrapped	
37263	D6963			1965	1999	Preserved	
37264	D6964			1965	2001	Preserved	
37273[2]	37306	D6606		1965	1991	Scrapped	Second locomotive to be numbered 37273
37275	D6975			1965	1999	Preserved	
37278	D6978			1965	1994	Scrapped	
37280	D6980			1965	1994	Scrapped	
D6983				1965	1966	Scrapped	
37293	D6993			1965	2000	Scrapped	
37294	D6994			1965	2004	Preserved	
37298	D6998			1965	2000	Scrapped	
37308	37274[2]	37308	D6608	1965	2007	Preserved	Second locomotive to be numbered 37274

Class 37/3 Second Batch

Fitted with regeared CP7 Bogies. Locos 37352, 37353, 37354, 37355, 37356, 37357, 37374 & 37380 later reverted to their Class 37/0 numbers.
Details as Class 37/0 except:
Maximum Speed: 80 mph.

Latest Number Carried	Previous Number 1	Previous Number 2	Previous Number 3	Year Entered Service	Year Withdrawn	Current Status	Notes
37330	37128	D6828		1963	1997	Scrapped	
37331	37202	D6902		1963	1995	Scrapped	
37332	37239	D6939		1964	1998	Scrapped	

37333	37271[2]	37303	D6603	1965	1997	Scrapped	Second locomotive to be numbered 37271
37334	37272[2]	37304	D6604	1965	2005	Scrapped	Second locomotive to be numbered 37272
37335	37285	D6985		1965	1994	Scrapped	
37340	37009	D6709		1961	1995	Preserved	
37341	37015	D6715		1961	1994	Scrapped	
37343	37049	37322	37049	1962	1995	Scrapped	Also carried previous number 4: D6749
37344	37053	D6753		1962	1996	Scrapped	
37345	37101	D6801		1962	1994	Scrapped	
37350	37119	D6700		1960	1999	Preserved	
37351	37002	D6702		1960	1999	Scrapped	
37355	37045	D6745		1962	1998	Scrapped	
37358	37091	D6791		1963	2006	Scrapped	
37359	37118	D6818		1963	1994	Scrapped	
37370	37127	D6827		1963	2000	Scrapped	
37371	37147	D6847		1963	1999	Scrapped	
37372	37159	D6859		1963	2004	Converted	Being converted to D5910 (Class 23 Baby Deltic)
37373	37160	D6860		1963	1993	Scrapped	
37375	37193	D6893		1964	2007	Scrapped	
37376	37199	D6899		1963	2000	Scrapped	
37377	37200	D6900		1963	2001	Scrapped	The cab remains
37378	37204	D6904		1963	1996	Scrapped	
37379	37226	D6926		1964	2001	Scrapped	
37381	37284	D6984		1965	1993	Scrapped	
37382	37145	37313	37145	1963	1994	Scrapped	Also carried previous number 4: D6845
37383	37167	D6867		1963	1999	Scrapped	
37384	37258	D6958		1965	1999	Scrapped	

Class 37/4
Fitted with regeared CP7 Bogies.
Details as Class 37/0 except:
Maximum Speed: 80 mph.
Train Heating/Supply: Electric.

Latest Number Carried	Previous Number 1	Previous Number 2	Previous Number 3	Year Entered Service	Year Withdrawn	Current Status	Notes
37401	37268	D6968		1965		Direct Rail Services	
37402	37274	D6974		1965		Direct Rail Services	First of 2 locomotives to be numbered 37274
37403	37307	D6607		1965		Direct Rail Services	Preserved loco on hire to DRS
37404	37286	D6986		1965	1999	Scrapped	
37405	37282	D6982		1965		Direct Rail Services	
37406	37295	D6995		1965	2009	Scrapped	
37407	37305	D6605		1965		Direct Rail Services	
37408	37289	D6989		1965	2005	Scrapped	
37409	37270	D6970		1965		Direct Rail Services	
37410	37273	D6973		1965	2007	Scrapped	First of 2 locomotives to be numbered 37273
37411	37290	D6990		1965	2008	Scrapped	The cab remains
37412	37301	D6601		1965	2004	Scrapped	
37413	37276	D6976		1965	2000	Scrapped	
37414	37287	D6987		1965	2000	Scrapped	
37415	37277	D6977		1965	2003	Scrapped	
37416	37302	D6602		1965	2006	Scrapped	
37417	37269	D6969		1965	2008	Scrapped	
37418	37271	D6971		1965		Preserved	First of 2 locomotives to be numbered 37271.
37419	37291	D6991		1965		Direct Rail Services	
37420	37297	D6997		1965	2000	Scrapped	

37421	37267	D6967		1965		Colas Rail	
37422	37266	D6966		1965		Direct Rail Services	
37423	37296	D6996		1965		Direct Rail Services	
37424	37279	D6979		1965		Direct Rail Services	Temporarily carries number 37558
37425	37292	D6992		1965		Direct Rail Services	
37426	37299	D6999		1965	2003	Scrapped	
37427	37288	D6988		1965	2006	Scrapped	
37428	37281	D6981		1965	2004	Scrapped	
37429	37300	D6600		1965	2002	Scrapped	
37430	37265	D6965		1965	2000	Scrapped	
37431	37272	D6972		1965	1999	Scrapped	First of 2 locomotives to be numbered 37272

Class 37/5
Refurbished locomotives fitted with regeared CP7 Bogies.
Details as Class 37/0 except:
Maximum Speed: 80 mph.
Train Heating/Supply: None.

Latest Number Carried	Previous Number 1	Previous Number 2	Previous Number 3	Year Entered Service	Year Withdrawn	Current Status	Notes
37503	37017	D6717		1961		Europhoenix	
37505	37028	D6728		1961	2000	Scrapped	
37509	37093	D6793		1963	2001	Scrapped	
37510	37112	D6812		1963		Europhoenix	
37513	37056	D6756		1962	2000	Scrapped	
37515	37064	D6764		1962	2008	Scrapped	
37516	37086	D6786		1962		West Coast Railway Co	
37517	37018	D6718		1961		West Coast Railway Co	
37518	37076	D6776		1962		West Coast Railway Co	
37519	37027	D6727		1961	1999	Scrapped	
37520	37041	D6741		1962	2002	Scrapped	
37521	37117	D6817		1963		Colas Rail	Preserved locomotive on hire to Colas

Class 37/6
No train supply, but electric through-wired. All formerly Class 37/5.
Details as Class 37/0 except:
Maximum Speed: 90 mph.
Train Brakes: Air.

Latest Number Carried	Previous Number 1	Previous Number 2	Previous Number 3	Year Entered Service	Year Withdrawn	Current Status	Notes
37601	37501	37005	D6705	1961		Rail Operations Group	Europhoenix locomotive on hire to ROG
37602	37502	37082	D6782	1962		Direct Rail Services	
37603	37504	37039	D6739	1962		Direct Rail Services	
37604	37506	37007	D6707	1961		Direct Rail Services	
37605	37507	37036	D6736	1962		Direct Rail Services	
37606	37508	37090	D6790	1963		Direct Rail Services	
37607	37511	37103	D6803	1963		Colas Rail	HNRC locomotive on hire to Colas Rail
37608	37512	37022	D6722	1961		Rail Operations Group	Europhoenix locomotive on hire to ROG
37609	37514	37115	D6815	1963		Direct Rail Services	
37610	37687	37181	D6881	1963		Locomotive Services	
37611	37690	37171	D6871	1963		Rail Operations Group	Europhoenix locomotive on hire to ROG
37612	37691	37179	D6879	1963		Harry Needle Railroad Co	

Class 37/5 (continued)

Latest Number Carried	Previous Number 1	Previous Number 2	Previous Number 3	Year Entered Service	Year Withdrawn	Current Status	Notes
37667	37151	D6851		1963		Locomotive Services	
37668	37257	D6957		1965		West Coast Railway Co	
37669	37129	D6829		1963		West Coast Railway Co	
37670	37182	D6882		1963	2009	Scrapped	
37671	37247	D6947		1964	2000	Scrapped	
37672	37189	D6889		1964	2000	Scrapped	
37673	37132	D6832		1963	2000	Scrapped	
37674	37169	D6869		1963	2005	Preserved	
37675	37164	D6864		1963	2004	Scrapped	
37676	37126	D6826		1963		West Coast Railway Co	
37677	37121	D6821		1963	2002	Scrapped	
37678	37256	D6956		1965	2000	Scrapped	
37679	37123	D6823		1963		Preserved	
37680	37224	D6924		1964	2001	Scrapped	
37681	37130	D6830		1963	1992	Scrapped	
37682	37236	D6936		1964	2014	Scrapped	
37683	37187	D6887		1964	2000	Scrapped	
37684	37134	D6834		1963	2004	Scrapped	
37685	37234	D6934		1964		West Coast Railway Co	
37686	37172	D6872		1963	2000	Scrapped	
37688	37205	D6905		1963		Preserved	
37689	37195	D6895		1964	2005	Scrapped	
37692	37122	D6822		1963	2004	Scrapped	
37693	37210	D6910		1963	2000	Scrapped	
37694	37192	D6892		1964	2007	Scrapped	
37695	37157	D6857		1963	2004	Scrapped	
37696	37228	D6928		1964	2000	Scrapped	
37697	37243	D6943		1964	1999	Scrapped	
37698	37246	D6946		1964	2009	Scrapped	
37699	37253	D6953		1965	1997	Scrapped	

Class 37/7

Refurbished locomotives fitted with regeared CP7 Bogies and ballast weight added.
Details as Class 37/0 except:
Maximum Speed: 80 mph.
Train Heating/Supply: None.

Latest Number Carried	Previous Number 1	Previous Number 2	Previous Number 3	Year Entered Service	Year Withdrawn	Current Status	Notes
37701	37030	D6730		1961	1999	Scrapped	
37702	37020	D6720		1961	2007	Scrapped	
37703	37067	D6767		1962		Direct Rail Services	DRS locomotive on loan to Bo'ness & Kinneil Railway
37704	37034	D6734		1962	2003	Scrapped	
37705	37060	D6760		1962	1999	Scrapped	
37706	37016	D6716		1961		West Coast Railway Co	
37707	37001	D6701		1960	2007	Scrapped	
37708	37089	D6789		1963	2002	Scrapped	
37709	37014	D6714		1961	2007	Scrapped	
37710	37044	D6744		1962		West Coast Railway Co	
37711	37085	D6785		1962	1999	Scrapped	
37712	37102	D6802		1963		West Coast Railway Co	
37713	37052	D6752		1962	2000	Scrapped	
37714	37024	D6724		1961		Preserved	
37715	37021	D6721		1961	1999	Scrapped	
37716	37094	D6794		1963		Direct Rail Services	
37717	37050	D6750		1962	2004	Scrapped	
37718	37084	D6784		1962	2012	Scrapped	
37719	37033	D6733		1962	1999	Scrapped	
37796	37105	D6805		1963	2000	Scrapped	
37797	37081	D6781		1962	2005	Scrapped	

37798	37006	D6706		1961	2005	Scrapped	
37799	37061	D6761		1962	2008	Scrapped	
37800	37143	D6843		1963		Rail Operations Group	Europhoenix locomotive on hire to ROG
37801	37173	D6873		1963	2008	Scrapped	
37802	37163	D6863		1963	2003	Scrapped	
37803	37208	D6908		1963	2000	Scrapped	
37883	37176	D6876		1963	2011	Scrapped	
37884	37183	D6883		1963		Rail Operations Group	Europhoenix locomotive on hire to ROG
37885	37177	D6877		1963	2002	Scrapped	
37886	37180	D6880		1963	2005	Scrapped	
37887	37120	D6820		1963	1999	Scrapped	
37888	37135	D6835		1963	2007	Scrapped	
37889	37233	D6933		1964	1999	Scrapped	
37890	37168	D6868		1963	2009	Scrapped	
37891	37166	D6866		1963	2000	Scrapped	
37892	37149	D6849		1963	2000	Scrapped	
37893	37237	D6937		1964	2009	Scrapped	
37894	37124	D6824		1963	2000	Scrapped	
37895	37283	D6819		1963	2005	Scrapped	
37896	37231	D6931		1964	2009	Scrapped	
37897	37155	D6855		1963	2000	Scrapped	
37898	37186	D6886		1963	1999	Scrapped	
37899	37161	D6861		1963	2002	Scrapped	

Class 37/9
Locomotives fitted with regeared CP7 Bogies and ballast weight added.
Details as Class 37/0 except:
Engine: Mirrlees MB275T (37901–904); Ruston RK270T (37905/906).
Maximum Speed: 80 mph.

Latest Number Carried	Previous Number 1	Previous Number 2	Previous Number 3	Year Entered Service	Year Withdrawn	Current Status	Notes
37901	37150	D6850		1963		Colas Rail	
37902	37148	D6848		1963	1998	Scrapped	
37903	37249	D6949		1964	1998	Scrapped	
37904	37125	D6825		1963	1996	Scrapped	
37905	37136	D6836		1963		UK Rail Leasing	
37906	37206	D6906		1963		UK Rail Leasing	

Class 97 (Class 37)
Refurbished for Network Rail for use on Cambrian lines, fitted with ERTMS.
Details as Class 37/0.

Latest Number Carried	Previous Number 1	Previous Number 2	Previous Number 3	Year Entered Service	Year Withdrawn	Current Status	Notes
97301	37100	D6800		1962		Network Rail	
97302	37170	D6870		1963		Network Rail	
97303	37178	D6878		1963		Network Rail	
97304	37217	D6917		1964		Network Rail	

CLASS 40 1Co-Co1

Built: 1958–62 by English Electric, Vulcan Foundry, Newton-le-Willows and Robert Stephenson & Hawthorns, Darlington.
Engine: English Electric 16SVT MkII of 1492 kW (2000 hp) at 850 rpm.
Transmission: Electric.
Maximum Speed: 90 mph.
Train Heating/Supply: Steam heating, later removed or isolated on many locomotives.
Train Brakes: Built vacuum, many were later dual braked (air & vacuum).

Latest Number Carried	Previous Number 1	Previous Number 2	Previous Number 3	Year Entered Service	Year Withdrawn	Current Status	Notes
40001	D201			1958	1984	Scrapped	
40002	D202			1958	1984	Scrapped	
40003	D203			1958	1982	Scrapped	
40004	D204			1958	1984	Scrapped	
40005	D205			1958	1976	Scrapped	
40006	D206			1958	1983	Scrapped	
40007	D207			1958	1983	Scrapped	
40008	D208			1958	1982	Scrapped	
40009	D209			1958	1984	Scrapped	
40010	D210			1959	1981	Scrapped	
40011	D211			1959	1980	Scrapped	
40012	97407	40012	D212	1959	1986	Preserved	
40013	D213			1959		Locomotive Services	Preserved locomotive on hire to Locomotive Services
40014	D214			1959	1981	Scrapped	
40015	D215			1959	1984	Scrapped	
40016	D216			1959	1981	Scrapped	
40017	D217			1959	1981	Scrapped	
40018	D218			1959	1981	Scrapped	
40019	D219			1959	1981	Scrapped	
40020	D220			1959	1982	Scrapped	
40021	D221			1959	1976	Scrapped	
40022	D222			1959	1984	Scrapped	
40023	D223			1959	1981	Scrapped	
40024	D224			1959	1984	Scrapped	
40025	D225			1959	1982	Scrapped	
40026	D226			1959	1980	Scrapped	
40027	D227			1959	1983	Scrapped	
40028	D228			1959	1984	Scrapped	
40029	D229			1959	1984	Scrapped	
40030	D230			1959	1983	Scrapped	
40031	D231			1959	1981	Scrapped	
40032	D232			1959	1981	Scrapped	
40033	D233			1959	1984	Scrapped	
40034	D234			1959	1984	Scrapped	
40035	D235			1959	1984	Scrapped	
40036	D236			1959	1982	Scrapped	
40037	D237			1959	1981	Scrapped	
40038	D238			1959	1980	Scrapped	
40039	D239			1959	1976	Scrapped	
40040	D240			1959	1980	Scrapped	
40041	D241			1959	1976	Scrapped	
40042	D242			1959	1980	Scrapped	
40043	D243			1959	1976	Scrapped	
40044	D244			1959	1985	Scrapped	
40045	D245			1959	1976	Scrapped	
40046	D246			1959	1983	Scrapped	
40047	D247			1959	1984	Scrapped	
40048	D248			1959	1977	Scrapped	
40049	D249			1959	1983	Scrapped	
40050	D250			1959	1983	Scrapped	

40051	D251		1959	1978	Scrapped
40052	D252		1959	1983	Scrapped
40053	D253		1960	1976	Scrapped
40054	D254		1959	1977	Scrapped
40055	D255		1960	1982	Scrapped
40056	D256		1960	1984	Scrapped
40057	D257		1960	1984	Scrapped
40058	D258		1960	1984	Scrapped
40059	D259		1960	1977	Scrapped
97405	40060	D260	1960	1987	Scrapped
40061	D261		1960	1983	Scrapped
40062	D262		1960	1981	Scrapped
40063	D263		1960	1984	Scrapped
40064	D264		1960	1982	Scrapped
40065	D265		1960	1981	Scrapped
40066	D266		1960	1981	Scrapped
40067	D267		1960	1981	Scrapped
40068	D268		1960	1983	Scrapped
40069	D269		1960	1983	Scrapped
40070	D270		1960	1981	Scrapped
40071	D271		1960	1980	Scrapped
40072	D272		1960	1977	Scrapped
40073	D273		1960	1983	Scrapped
40074	D274		1960	1984	Scrapped

▲ Class 40 D202 with small yellow warning panel stands outside Stratford Depot in April 1967.
Mike Jefferies/Rail Photoprints

40075	D275			1960	1981	Scrapped	
40076	D276			1960	1983	Scrapped	
40077	D277			1960	1983	Scrapped	
40078	D278			1960	1981	Scrapped	
40079	D279			1960	1985	Scrapped	
40080	D280			1960	1983	Scrapped	
40081	D281			1960	1983	Scrapped	
40082	D282			1960	1984	Scrapped	
40083	D283			1960	1981	Scrapped	
40084	D284			1960	1983	Scrapped	
40085	D285			1960	1984	Scrapped	
40086	D286			1960	1985	Scrapped	
40087	D287			1960	1982	Scrapped	
40088	D288			1960	1982	Scrapped	Cab remains owned by Class 40 Preservation Society
40089	D289			1960	1976	Scrapped	
40090	D290			1960	1983	Scrapped	
40091	D291			1960	1984	Scrapped	
40092	D292			1960	1982	Scrapped	
40093	D293			1960	1983	Scrapped	
40094	D294			1960	1982	Scrapped	
40095	D295			1960	1981	Scrapped	
40096	D296			1960	1983	Scrapped	
40097	D297			1960	1983	Scrapped	
40098	D298			1960	1981	Scrapped	
40099	D299			1960	1984	Scrapped	
40100	D300			1960	1980	Scrapped	
40101	D301			1960	1982	Scrapped	
40102	D302			1960	1976	Scrapped	
40103	D303			1960	1982	Scrapped	
40104	D304			1960	1985	Scrapped	
40105	D305			1960	1980	Scrapped	
40106	D306			1960	1983	Preserved	
40107	D307			1960	1981	Scrapped	
40108	D308			1960	1980	Scrapped	
40109	D309			1960	1980	Scrapped	
40110	D310			1960	1980	Scrapped	
40111	D311			1960	1981	Scrapped	
40112	D312			1960	1980	Scrapped	
40113	D313			1960	1981	Scrapped	
40114	D314			1960	1980	Scrapped	
40115	D315			1961	1982	Scrapped	
40116	D316			1961	1981	Scrapped	
40117	D317			1961	1981	Scrapped	
40118	97408	40118	D318	1961	1986	Preserved	
40119	D319			1961	1980	Scrapped	
40120	D320			1961	1981	Scrapped	
40121	D321			1961	1983	Scrapped	
D322				1961	1967	Scrapped	
40122	D200			1958	1988	Preserved	
40123	D323			1961	1980	Scrapped	
40124	D324			1961	1984	Scrapped	
40125	D325			1960	1981	Scrapped	
40126	D326			1960	1984	Scrapped	
40127	D327			1960	1982	Scrapped	
40128	D328			1961	1982	Scrapped	
40129	D329			1961	1984	Scrapped	
40130	D330			1961	1982	Scrapped	
40131	D331			1961	1983	Scrapped	
40132	D332			1961	1982	Scrapped	
40133	D333			1961	1984	Scrapped	
40134	D334			1961	1981	Scrapped	
40135	97406	40135	D335	1961	1986	Preserved	
40136	D336			1961	1982	Scrapped	

40137	D337		1961	1981	Scrapped
40138	D338		1961	1982	Scrapped
40139	D339		1961	1982	Scrapped
40140	D340		1961	1982	Scrapped
40141	D341		1961	1983	Scrapped
40142	D342		1961	1980	Scrapped
40143	D343		1961	1985	Scrapped
40144	D344		1961	1981	Scrapped
40145	D345		1961	1983	Preserved
40146	D346		1961	1980	Scrapped
40147	D347		1961	1980	Scrapped
40148	D348		1961	1982	Scrapped
40149	D349		1961	1981	Scrapped
40150	D350		1961	1985	Scrapped
40151	D351		1961	1981	Scrapped
40152	D352		1961	1985	Scrapped
40153	D353		1961	1983	Scrapped
40154	D354		1961	1982	Scrapped
40155	D355		1961	1985	Scrapped
40156	D356		1961	1980	Scrapped
40157	D357		1961	1983	Scrapped
40158	D358		1961	1983	Scrapped
40159	D359		1961	1982	Scrapped
40160	D360		1961	1984	Scrapped
40161	D361		1961	1980	Scrapped
40162	D362		1961	1982	Scrapped
40163	D363		1961	1982	Scrapped
40164	D364		1961	1983	Scrapped
40165	D365		1961	1981	Scrapped
40166	D366		1961	1982	Scrapped
40167	D367		1961	1984	Scrapped
40168	D368		1961	1984	Scrapped
40169	D369		1961	1983	Scrapped
40170	D370		1961	1983	Scrapped
40171	D371		1961	1981	Scrapped
40172	D372		1962	1983	Scrapped
40173	D373		1962	1981	Scrapped
40174	D374		1962	1984	Scrapped
40175	D375		1962	1981	Scrapped
40176	D376		1962	1981	Scrapped
40177	D377		1962	1984	Scrapped
40178	D378		1962	1981	Scrapped
40179	D379		1962	1981	Scrapped
40180	D380		1962	1983	Scrapped
40181	D381		1962	1985	Scrapped
40182	D382		1962	1982	Scrapped
40183	D383		1962	1983	Scrapped
40184	D384		1962	1982	Scrapped
40185	D385		1962	1983	Scrapped
40186	D386		1962	1982	Scrapped
40187	D387		1962	1982	Scrapped
40188	D388		1962	1983	Scrapped
40189	D389		1962	1976	Scrapped
40190	D390		1962	1976	Scrapped
40191	D391		1962	1983	Scrapped
40192	D392		1962	1985	Scrapped
40193	D393		1962	1981	Scrapped
40194	D394		1962	1985	Scrapped
40195	D395		1962	1984	Scrapped
40196	D396		1962	1984	Scrapped
40197	D397		1962	1983	Scrapped
40198	D398		1962	1983	Scrapped
40199	D399		1962	1982	Scrapped

▲ North British Class 41 D604 "COSSACK" is seen at the head of an "up" parcels train at Truro on 23 August 1965. Although allocated Class 41, all five locomotives of this design were withdrawn from service as early as 1967.   **Richard Lewis/Rail Photoprints**

▼ The two prototype Class 41 HST power cars make an unusual sight without any of their trailers as they approach West Ealing, bound for Old Oak Common on 20 March 1976.
Dave Cobbe Collection/Rail Photoprints

CLASS 41 A1A-A1A

This class was designated Class 41 by BR at the end of 1967, however none carried TOPS numbers.

Built: 1958–59 by North British Locomotive Company, Glasgow.
Engine: Two NBL L12V18/21A of 746 kW (1000 hp) at 1445 rpm.
Transmission: Hydraulic.
Maximum Speed: 90 mph.
Train Heating/Supply: Steam heating.
Train Brakes: Vacuum.

Latest Number Carried	Previous Number 1	Year Entered Service	Year Withdrawn	Current Status	Notes
D600		1958	1967	Scrapped	
D601		1958	1967	Scrapped	
D602		1958	1967	Scrapped	
D603		1958	1967	Scrapped	
D604		1959	1967	Scrapped	

CLASS 41 HST POWER CAR Bo-Bo

Built: 1972 by BREL, Crewe.
Engine: Paxman Valenta 12RP200L of 1680 kW (2250 hp) at 1500 rpm.
Transmission: Electric.
Maximum Speed: 125 mph.
Train Heating/Supply: Electric.
Train Brakes: Air.

Latest Number Carried	Previous Number 1	Previous Number 2	Previous Number 3	Year Entered Service	Year Withdrawn	Current Status	Notes
41001	ADB975812	43000	41001	1972	1982	Preserved	
ADB975813	43001	41002		1972	1988	Scrapped	

CLASS 42 B-B

Built: 1958–61 by British Railways, Swindon
Engine: D800–D802: Two Bristol Siddeley Maybach MD650 of 796 kW (1000 hp) at 1400 rpm.
D830: Two Paxman 12YJXL 895 kW of (1200 hp) at 1500 rpm.
D803–D829, D831–D832 & D866–D870: Two Bristol Siddeley Maybach MD650 of 821 kW (1100 hp) at 1530 rpm.
Transmission: Hydraulic.
Maximum Speed: 90 mph.
Train Heating/Supply: Steam heating.
Train Brakes: Vacuum.

Latest Number Carried	Previous Number 1	Year Entered Service	Year Withdrawn	Current Status	Notes
D800		1958	1968	Scrapped	
D801		1958	1968	Scrapped	
D802		1958	1968	Scrapped	
D803		1959	1972	Scrapped	
D804		1959	1971	Scrapped	
D805		1959	1972	Scrapped	
D806		1959	1972	Scrapped	
D807		1959	1972	Scrapped	
D808		1959	1971	Scrapped	
D809		1959	1971	Scrapped	
D810		1959	1972	Scrapped	
D811		1959	1972	Scrapped	
D812		1959	1972	Scrapped	
D813		1959	1972	Scrapped	

D814	1960	1972	Scrapped
D815	1960	1971	Scrapped
D816	1960	1972	Scrapped
D817	1960	1971	Scrapped
D818	1960	1972	Scrapped
D819	1960	1972	Scrapped
D820	1960	1972	Scrapped
D821	1960	1972	Preserved
D822	1960	1971	Scrapped
D823	1960	1971	Scrapped
D824	1960	1972	Scrapped
D825	1960	1972	Scrapped
D826	1960	1971	Scrapped
D827	1960	1972	Scrapped
D828	1960	1971	Scrapped
D829	1960	1972	Scrapped
D830	1961	1969	Scrapped
D831	1961	1972	Scrapped
D832	1961	1972	Preserved
D866	1961	1972	Scrapped
D867	1961	1971	Scrapped
D868	1961	1971	Scrapped
D869	1961	1971	Scrapped
D870	1961	1971	Scrapped

CLASS 43   NORTH BRITISH TYPE 4   B-B

Built: 1960–62 by North British Locomotive Company, Glasgow.
Engine: Two MAN L12V18/21 of 820 kW (1100 hp) at 1530 rpm.
Transmission: Hydraulic.
Maximum Speed: 90 mph.
Train Heating/Supply: Steam heating.
Train Brakes: Vacuum.

Latest Number Carried	Previous Number 1	Year Entered Service	Year Withdrawn	Current Status	Notes
D833		1960	1971	Scrapped	
D834		1960	1971	Scrapped	
D835		1960	1971	Scrapped	
D836		1960	1971	Scrapped	
D837		1960	1971	Scrapped	
D838		1960	1971	Scrapped	
D839		1960	1971	Scrapped	
D840		1961	1969	Scrapped	
D841		1960	1971	Scrapped	
D842		1960	1971	Scrapped	
D843		1961	1971	Scrapped	
D844		1961	1971	Scrapped	
D845		1961	1971	Scrapped	
D846		1961	1971	Scrapped	
D847		1961	1971	Scrapped	
D848		1961	1969	Scrapped	
D849		1961	1971	Scrapped	
D850		1961	1971	Scrapped	
D851		1961	1971	Scrapped	
D852		1961	1971	Scrapped	
D853		1961	1971	Scrapped	
D854		1961	1971	Scrapped	
D855		1961	1971	Scrapped	
D856		1961	1971	Scrapped	
D857		1961	1971	Scrapped	
D858		1961	1971	Scrapped	
D859		1962	1971	Scrapped	

▲ Swindon-built Class 42 D866 "ZEBRA", in dire need of a repaint, stands at Woking with an Exeter St Davids–London Waterloo service in 1968. **Dave Cobbe/Rail Photoprints**

▼ North British Class 43 "Warship" 842 "ROYAL OAK" waits between duties at Exeter stabling point, adjacent to Exeter St Davids station in July 1969. **Mike Jefferies/Rail Photoprints**

D860	1962	1971	Scrapped
D861	1962	1971	Scrapped
D862	1962	1971	Scrapped
D863	1962	1969	Scrapped
D864	1962	1971	Scrapped
D865	1962	1971	Scrapped

CLASS 43   HST POWER CAR   Bo-Bo

Built: 1975–82 by BREL, Crewe.
Engine as Built: Paxman Valenta 12RP200L of 1680 kW (2250 hp) at 1500 rpm.
Subsequent Engines: Mirlees MB190 of 1680 kW (2250 hp) fitted to 43167–43170 between 1987 and 1996; Paxman Valenta engines were then reinstalled.
Paxman 12VP185 of 1565 kW (2100 hp) at 1500 rpm fitted to 43043–050, 052, 054–055, 058–061, 064, 066, 072–076, 081–083, 089, 165, 167–170, 173, 175, 177, 179 & 191.
MTU 16V4000 R41R of 1680 kW (2250 hp) at 1500rpm were fitted to the remaining power cars with original Paxman Valenta engines from 2005.
Transmission: Electric.
Maximum Speed: 125 mph.
Train Heating/Supply: Electric.
Train Brakes: Air.

Latest Number Carried	Previous Number 1	Year Entered Service	Year Withdrawn	Current Status	Notes
43002		1976		Great Western Railway	
43003		1976		Great Western Railway	Due to transfer to Scotrail during 2018
43004		1976		Great Western Railway	
43005		1976		Great Western Railway	
43009		1976		Great Western Railway	
43010		1976		Great Western Railway	
43011		1976	1999	Scrapped	
43012		1976		Scotrail	
43013		1976		Network Rail	
43014		1976		Network Rail	
43015		1976		Great Western Railway	Due to transfer to Scotrail during 2018
43016		1976		Great Western Railway	
43017		1976		Great Western Railway	
43018		1976		Great Western Railway	
43019		1976	2004	Scrapped	
43020		1976		Great Western Railway	
43021		1976		Scotrail	
43022		1976		Great Western Railway	
43023		1976		Great Western Railway	
43024		1976		Great Western Railway	
43025		1976		Great Western Railway	
43026		1976		Great Western Railway	Due to transfer to Scotrail during 2018
43027		1976		Great Western Railway	
43028		1976		Great Western Railway	Due to transfer to Scotrail during 2018
43029		1976		Great Western Railway	
43030		1976		Great Western Railway	Due to transfer to Scotrail during 2018
43031		1976		Great Western Railway	Due to transfer to Scotrail during 2018
43032		1976		Scotrail	
43033		1976		Scotrail	
43034		1976		Great Western Railway	Due to transfer to Scotrail during 2018
43035		1976		Great Western Railway	Due to transfer to Scotrail during 2018
43036		1976		Scotrail	
43037		1976		Scotrail	
43040		1976		Great Western Railway	
43041		1976		Great Western Railway	
43042		1977		Great Western Railway	
43043		1977		East Midlands Trains	
43044		1977		East Midlands Trains	

43045	1977	East Midlands Trains	
43046	1977	East Midlands Trains	
43047	1977	East Midlands Trains	
43048	1977	East Midlands Trains	
43049	1977	East Midlands Trains	
43050	1977	East Midlands Trains	
43052	1977	East Midlands Trains	
43053	1977	Great Western Railway	
43054	1977	East Midlands Trains	
43055	1977	East Midlands Trains	
43056	1977	Great Western Railway	
43058	1977	Virgin Trains East Coast	East Midlands Trains loco on hire to VTEC
43059	1977	East Midlands Trains	
43060	1977	East Midlands Trains	
43061	1977	Virgin Trains East Coast	East Midlands Trains loco on hire to VTEC
43062	1977	Network Rail	
43063	1977	Great Western Railway	
43064	1977	East Midlands Trains	
43066	1977	East Midlands Trains	
43069	1977	Great Western Railway	
43070	1977	Great Western Railway	
43071	1977	Great Western Railway	
43073	1977	East Midlands Trains	
43075	1977	East Midlands Trains	
43076	1977	East Midlands Trains	
43078	1978	Great Western Railway	
43079	1978	Great Western Railway	
43081	1978	East Midlands Trains	
43082	1978	East Midlands Trains	
43083	1978	East Midlands Trains	
43086	1978	Great Western Railway	
43087	1978	Great Western Railway	
43088	1978	Great Western Railway	
43089	1978	East Midlands Trains	
43091	1978	Great Western Railway	
43092	1978	Great Western Railway	
43093	1978	Great Western Railway	
43094	1978	Great Western Railway	
43097	1978	Great Western Railway	
43098	1978	Great Western Railway	
43122	1979	Great Western Railway	
43124	1981	Great Western Railway	Due to transfer to Scotrail during 2018
43125	1979	Great Western Railway	Due to transfer to Scotrail during 2018
43126	1979	Scotrail	
43127	1979	Scotrail	
43128	1979	Great Western Railway	Due to transfer to Scotrail during 2018
43129	1979	Great Western Railway	Due to transfer to Scotrail during 2018
43130	1979	Great Western Railway	Due to transfer to Scotrail during 2018
43131	1979	Great Western Railway	Due to transfer to Scotrail during 2018
43132	1979	Scotrail	
43133	1979	Great Western Railway	Due to transfer to Scotrail during 2018
43134	1979	Scotrail	
43135	1979	Scotrail	
43136	1979	Great Western Railway	Due to transfer to Scotrail during 2018
43137	1979	Great Western Railway	Due to transfer to Scotrail during 2018
43138	1979	Great Western Railway	Due to transfer to Scotrail during 2018
43139	1980	Great Western Railway	Due to transfer to Scotrail during 2018
43140	1980	Scotrail	
43141	1980	Great Western Railway	Due to transfer to Scotrail during 2018
43142	1980	Great Western Railway	Due to transfer to Scotrail during 2018
43143	1981	Scotrail	
43144	1981	Great Western Railway	Due to transfer to Scotrail during 2018
43145	1981	Scotrail	
43146	1981	Scotrail	

43147	1981		Great Western Railway	Due to transfer to Scotrail during 2018
43148	1981		Scotrail	
43149	1981		Scotrail	
43150	1981		Great Western Railway	Due to transfer to Scotrail during 2018
43151	1981		Great Western Railway	Due to transfer to Scotrail during 2018
43152	1981		Great Western Railway	Due to transfer to Scotrail during 2018
43153	1981		Great Western Railway	
43154	1981		Great Western Railway	
43155	1981		Great Western Railway	
43156	1981		Great Western Railway	
43158	1981		Great Western Railway	
43159	1981		Great Western Railway	
43160	1981		Great Western Railway	
43161	1981		Great Western Railway	
43162	1981		Great Western Railway	
43163	1981		Scotrail	
43164	1981		Great Western Railway	Due to transfer to Scotrail during 2018
43165	1981		Great Western Railway	
43168	1981		Scotrail	
43169	1981		Scotrail	
43170	1981		Great Western Railway	
43171	1981		Great Western Railway	
43172	1981		Great Western Railway	
43173	1981	1998	Scrapped	
43174	1981		Great Western Railway	
43175	1981		Great Western Railway	Due to transfer to Scotrail during 2018
43176	1981		Great Western Railway	Due to transfer to Scotrail during 2018
43177	1981		Great Western Railway	Due to transfer to Scotrail during 2018
43179	1981		Scotrail	
43180	1981		Great Western Railway	
43181	1981		Great Western Railway	Due to transfer to Scotrail during 2018

▲ HST 43129 leaves Plymouth with the 10.00 Penzance–London Paddington on 16 June 2017. This is one of the HST power cars due to transfer to Scotrail during 2018. **Robert Pritchard**

43182		1981	Great Western Railway	Due to transfer to Scotrail during 2018
43183		1982	Scotrail	
43185		1982	Great Western Railway	
43186		1982	Great Western Railway	
43187		1982	Great Western Railway	
43188		1982	Great Western Railway	
43189		1982	Great Western Railway	
43190		1982	Great Western Railway	
43191		1982	Great Western Railway	
43192		1982	Great Western Railway	
43193		1982	Great Western Railway	
43194		1982	Great Western Railway	
43195		1982	Great Western Railway	
43196		1982	Great Western Railway	
43197		1982	Great Western Railway	
43198		1982	Great Western Railway	
43206	43006	1976	Virgin Trains East Coast	
43207	43007	1976	Cross Country	
43208	43008	1976	Virgin Trains East Coast	
43238	43038	1976	Virgin Trains East Coast	
43239	43039	1976	Virgin Trains East Coast	
43251	43051	1977	Virgin Trains East Coast	
43257	43057	1977	Virgin Trains East Coast	
43272	43072	1977	Virgin Trains East Coast	
43274	43074	1977	Virgin Trains East Coast	
43277	43077	1977	Virgin Trains East Coast	
43285	43085	1978	Cross Country	
43290	43090	1978	Virgin Trains East Coast	
43295	43095	1978	Virgin Trains East Coast	
43296	43096	1978	Virgin Trains East Coast	
43299	43099	1978	Virgin Trains East Coast	
43300	43100	1978	Virgin Trains East Coast	
43301	43101	1978	Cross Country	
43302	43102	1978	Virgin Trains East Coast	
43303	43103	1978	Cross Country	
43304	43104	1978	Cross Country	
43305	43105	1978	Virgin Trains East Coast	
43306	43106	1978	Virgin Trains East Coast	
43307	43107	1978	Virgin Trains East Coast	
43308	43108	1978	Virgin Trains East Coast	
43309	43109	1979	Virgin Trains East Coast	
43310	43110	1979	Virgin Trains East Coast	
43311	43111	1979	Virgin Trains East Coast	
43312	43112	1979	Virgin Trains East Coast	
43313	43113	1979	Virgin Trains East Coast	
43314	43114	1979	Virgin Trains East Coast	
43315	43115	1979	Virgin Trains East Coast	
43316	43116	1979	Virgin Trains East Coast	
43317	43117	1979	Virgin Trains East Coast	
43318	43118	1979	Virgin Trains East Coast	
43319	43119	1979	Virgin Trains East Coast	
43320	43120	1977	Virgin Trains East Coast	
43321	43121	1977	Cross Country	
43357	43157	1981	Cross Country	
43366	43166	1981	Cross Country	
43367	43167	1981	Virgin Trains East Coast	
43378	43178	1981	Cross Country	
43384	43184	1982	Cross Country	
43423	43123	1979	East Midlands Trains	
43465	43065	1977	East Midlands Trains	
43467	43067	1977	East Midlands Trains	
43468	43068	1977	East Midlands Trains	
43480	43080	1978	East Midlands Trains	
43484	43084	1978	East Midlands Trains	

CLASS 44 1Co-Co1

Built: 1959–60 by British Railways, Derby.
Engine: Sulzer 12LDA28A of 1720 kW (2300 hp) at 750 rpm.
Transmission: Electric.
Maximum Speed: 90 mph.
Train Heating/Supply: Built with steam heating, subsequently removed.
Train Brakes: Vacuum.

Latest Number Carried	Previous Number 1	Year Entered Service	Year Withdrawn	Current Status	Notes
44001	D1	1959	1976	Scrapped	
44002	D2	1959	1979	Scrapped	
44003	D3	1959	1976	Scrapped	
44004	D4	1959	1980	Preserved	
44005	D5	1959	1978	Scrapped	
44006	D6	1959	1977	Scrapped	
44007	D7	1959	1980	Scrapped	
44008	D8	1959	1980	Preserved	
44009	D9	1959	1979	Scrapped	
44010	D10	1960	1977	Scrapped	

CLASS 45 1Co-Co1

Built: 1960–63 by British Railways, Crewe and Derby.
Engine: Sulzer 12LDA28B of 1860 kW (2500 hp) at 750 rpm.
Transmission: Electric.
Maximum Speed: 90 mph.
Train Heating/Supply: Built with steam heating, subsequently isolated on many.
Train Brakes: Built vacuum braked and later converted to dual braked (air & vacuum).

Class 45/0

Latest Number Carried	Previous Number 1	Previous Number 2	Year Entered Service	Year Withdrawn	Current Status	Notes
45001	D13		1960	1986	Scrapped	
45002	D29		1961	1984	Scrapped	
45003	D133		1961	1985	Scrapped	
45004	D77		1960	1985	Scrapped	
45005	D79		1960	1986	Scrapped	
45006	D89		1961	1986	Scrapped	
45007	D119		1961	1988	Scrapped	
45008	D90		1961	1980	Scrapped	
45009	D37		1961	1986	Scrapped	
45010	D112		1961	1985	Scrapped	
45011	D12		1960	1981	Scrapped	
45012	D108		1961	1988	Scrapped	
45013	D20		1961	1987	Scrapped	
45014	D137		1961	1986	Scrapped	
45015	D14		1960	1986	Preserved	
45016	D16		1960	1985	Scrapped	
ADB968024	45017	D23	1961	1988	Scrapped	
45018	D15		1960	1981	Scrapped	
45019	D33		1961	1985	Scrapped	
45020	D26		1961	1985	Scrapped	
45021	D25		1961	1980	Scrapped	
97409	45022	D60	1962	1988	Scrapped	
45023	D54		1962	1984	Scrapped	
45024	D17		1960	1980	Scrapped	
45025	D19		1960	1981	Scrapped	
45026	D21		1961	1986	Scrapped	
45027	D24		1961	1981	Scrapped	
45028	D27		1961	1981	Scrapped	

▲ A rather dilapidated 44007, bereft of its 'INGLEBOROUGH' nameplates, but with an enthusiastic Toton driver in the cab, prepares for departure from March Traction Maintenance Depot on 27 September 1979. **Gordon Edgar/Rail Photoprints**

▼ This image taken on 15 August 1979 clearly illustrates two of the different styles of headcode box applied to Class 45 "Peaks". 45120 approaches Gloucester with a North-East–South-West express, as 45149 waits in the siding on the right. A third style of headcode box can just be made out on 37198 in the left background. **Gordon Edgar/Rail Photoprints**

97410	45029	D30	1961	1988	Scrapped	
45030	D31		1961	1980	Scrapped	
45031	D36		1961	1981	Scrapped	
45032	D38		1961	1980	Scrapped	
45033	D39		1961	1988	Scrapped	
97411	45034	D42	1961	1988	Scrapped	
45035	D44		1961	1981	Scrapped	
45036	D45		1961	1986	Scrapped	
45037	D46		1961	1988	Scrapped	
45038	D48		1961	1985	Scrapped	
45039	D49		1961	1980	Scrapped	
97412	45040	D50	1962	1988	Scrapped	
45041	D53		1962	1988	Preserved	
45042	D57		1963	1985	Scrapped	
45043	D58		1962	1984	Scrapped	
45044	D63		1962	1987	Scrapped	
45045	D64		1962	1983	Scrapped	
45046	D68		1960	1988	Scrapped	
45047	D69		1960	1980	Scrapped	
45048	D70		1960	1985	Scrapped	
45049	D71		1960	1987	Scrapped	
45050	D72		1960	1984	Scrapped	
45051	D74		1960	1987	Scrapped	
45052	D75		1960	1988	Scrapped	
45053	D76		1960	1983	Scrapped	
45054[2]	D95		1960	1985	Scrapped	Second of 2 locomotives to be numbered 45054
45055	D84		1960	1985	Scrapped	
45056	D91		1961	1985	Scrapped	
45057	D93		1961	1985	Scrapped	
45058	D97		1961	1987	Scrapped	
45059	D98		1961	1986	Scrapped	
45060	D100		1961	1985	Preserved	
45061	D101		1961	1981	Scrapped	
45062	D103		1961	1987	Scrapped	
45063	D104		1961	1986	Scrapped	
45064	D105		1961	1985	Scrapped	
45065	D110		1961	1985	Scrapped	
97413	45066	D114	1961	1988	Scrapped	
45067	D115		1961	1977	Scrapped	
45068	D118		1961	1986	Scrapped	
45069	D121		1961	1986	Scrapped	
45070	D122		1961	1987	Scrapped	
45071	D125		1961	1981	Scrapped	
45072	D127		1961	1985	Scrapped	
45073	D129		1961	1981	Scrapped	
45074	D131		1961	1985	Scrapped	
45075	D132		1961	1985	Scrapped	
45076	D134		1961	1986	Scrapped	
45077	D136		1961	1986	Scrapped	

Class 45/1
Details as Class 45/0 except:
Train Heating/Supply: Electric.

Latest Number Carried	Previous Number 1	Previous Number 2	Year Entered Service	Year Withdrawn	Current Status	Notes
45101	D96		1961	1986	Scrapped	
45102	D51		1962	1986	Scrapped	
45103	D116		1961	1988	Scrapped	
45104	D59		1962	1988	Scrapped	
45105	D86		1961	1987	Preserved	
45106	D106		1961	1989	Scrapped	
45107	D43		1961	1988	Scrapped	

45108	D120		1961	1987	Preserved	
45109	D85		1961	1986	Scrapped	
45110	D73		1960	1988	Scrapped	
45111	D65		1962	1987	Scrapped	
45112	D61		1962	1987	Preserved	
45113	D80		1960	1988	Scrapped	
45114	D94		1961	1987	Scrapped	
45115	D81		1960	1988	Scrapped	
45116	D47		1961	1986	Scrapped	
45117	D35		1961	1986	Scrapped	
45118	D67		1962		Locomotive Services	
45119	D34		1961	1987	Scrapped	
45120	D107		1961	1987	Scrapped	
45121	D18		1960	1987	Scrapped	
45122	D11		1960	1987	Scrapped	
45123	D52		1962	1986	Scrapped	
45124	D28		1961	1988	Scrapped	
45125	D123		1961	1987	Preserved	
45126	D32		1961	1987	Scrapped	
45127	D87		1961	1987	Scrapped	
45128	D113		1961	1989	Scrapped	The cab remains
45129	D111		1961	1987	Scrapped	
45130	D117		1961	1987	Scrapped	
45131	D124		1961	1986	Scrapped	
45132	D22		1961	1987	Preserved	
45133	D40		1961	1987	Preserved	
45134	D126		1961	1987	Scrapped	
45135	D99		1961	1987	Preserved	
45136	D88		1961	1987	Scrapped	
45137	D56		1962	1987	Scrapped	
45138	D92		1961	1986	Scrapped	
45139	D109		1961	1987	Scrapped	
45140	D102		1961	1988	Scrapped	The cab remains
45141	D82		1960	1988	Scrapped	
45142	D83		1960	1987	Scrapped	
45143	D62		1962	1987	Scrapped	
45144	D55		1962	1987	Scrapped	
45145	D128		1961	1988	Scrapped	
45146	D66		1962	1987	Scrapped	
45147	D41		1961	1985	Scrapped	
45148	D130		1961	1987	Scrapped	
45149	D135		1961	1987	Preserved	
45150	45054	D78	1960	1988	Scrapped	First of 2 locomotives to be numbered 45054

CLASS 46   1Co-Co1

Built: 1961–63 by British Railways, Derby.
Engine: Sulzer 12LDA28B of 1860 kW (2500 hp) at 750 rpm.
Transmission: Electric.
Maximum Speed: 90 mph.
Train Heating/Supply: Steam Heating.
Train Brakes: Built vacuum braked and later converted to dual braked (air & vacuum).

Latest Number Carried	Previous Number 1	Previous Number 2	Previous Number 3	Year Entered Service	Year Withdrawn	Current Status	Notes
46001	D138			1961	1981	Scrapped	
46002	D139			1961	1981	Scrapped	
46003	D140			1961	1978	Scrapped	
46004	D141			1961	1983	Scrapped	
46005	D142			1961	1977	Scrapped	
46006	D143			1961	1982	Scrapped	

46007	D144			1961	1982	Scrapped
46008	D145			1961	1981	Scrapped
46009	D146			1961	1983	Scrapped
46010	D147			1961	1984	Preserved
46011	D148			1961	1984	Scrapped
46012	D149			1961	1980	Scrapped
46013	D150			1961	1980	Scrapped
46014	D151			1962	1984	Scrapped
46015	D152			1962	1980	Scrapped
46016	D153			1962	1983	Scrapped
46017	D154			1962	1984	Scrapped
46018	D155			1962	1983	Scrapped
46019	D156			1962	1980	Scrapped
46020	D157			1962	1980	Scrapped
46021	D158			1962	1983	Scrapped
46022	D159			1962	1982	Scrapped
46023	D160			1962	1983	Scrapped
46024	D161			1962	1978	Scrapped
46025	D162			1962	1984	Scrapped
46026	D163			1962	1984	Scrapped
46027	D164			1962	1984	Scrapped
46028	D165			1962	1984	Scrapped
46029	D166			1962	1983	Scrapped
46030	D167			1962	1980	Scrapped
46031	D168			1962	1983	Scrapped
46032	D169			1962	1984	Scrapped
46033	D170			1962	1983	Scrapped
46034	D171			1962	1980	Scrapped
D172	97403	46035	D172	1962	1991	Preserved
46036	D173			1962	1982	Scrapped
46037	D174			1962	1984	Scrapped
46038	D175			1962	1982	Scrapped
46039	D176			1962	1983	Scrapped
46040	D177			1962	1980	Scrapped
46041	D178			1962	1980	Scrapped
46042	D179			1962	1980	Scrapped
46043	D180			1962	1980	Scrapped
46044	D181			1962	1984	Scrapped
D182	97404	46045	D182	1962	1990	Preserved
46046	D183			1962	1984	Scrapped
46047	D184			1962	1984	Scrapped
46048	D185			1962	1981	Scrapped
46049	D186			1962	1982	Scrapped
46050	D187			1962	1982	Scrapped
46051	D188			1962	1983	Scrapped
46052	D189			1963	1984	Scrapped
46053	D190			1963	1981	Scrapped
46054	D191			1963	1982	Scrapped
46055	D192			1963	1982	Scrapped
46056	D193			1963	1982	Scrapped

CLASS 47 Co-Co

Built: 1962–68 by British Railways, Crewe and Brush Electrical Engineering Company, Loughborough.
Engine: Sulzer 12LDA28C of 1920 kW (2580 hp) at 750 rpm. D1702–D1706 were initially fitted with Sulzer 12LVA24 engines and classified as Class 48. They were subsequently fitted with standard 12LDA28C engines between 1969 and 1971 and converted to Class 47.
Transmission: Electric.
Maximum Speed: 95 mph.
Train Heating/Supply: Built with steam heating, except Class 47/3 (built D1782–D1836 & D1875–D1900) which had no heating and 47401–47420 (built D1500–D1519) 47803 (D1960) and 47515 (D1961) which were built with dual heating (electric & steam).
Train Brakes: Built vacuum braked, except D1100–D1111, D1631–D1681 and D1758–D1999 which were built dual braked (air & vacuum). Remaining locos were later converted to dual braked, except early withdrawals D1562 & D1734.

Class 47/0
Standard design built with steam heating generators, subsequently isolated or removed on most.

Latest Number Carried	Previous Number 1	Previous Number 2	Previous Number 3	Year Entered Service	Year Withdrawn	Current Status	Notes
47001	D1521			1963	1986	Scrapped	
47002	D1522			1963	1991	Scrapped	
47003	D1523			1963	1991	Scrapped	
47004	D1524			1963	1998	Preserved	
47005	D1526			1963	1991	Scrapped	
47006	D1528			1963	1991	Scrapped	
47007	D1529			1963	1991	Scrapped	
47008	D1530			1963	1989	Scrapped	
47009	D1532			1963	1991	Scrapped	
47010	D1537			1963	1992	Scrapped	
47011	D1538			1963	1987	Scrapped	
47012	D1539			1963	1989	Scrapped	
47013	D1540			1963	1987	Scrapped	
47014	D1543			1963	1991	Scrapped	
47015	D1544			1963	1987	Scrapped	
47016	D1546			1963	1998	Scrapped	
47017	D1570			1964	1991	Scrapped	
47018	D1572			1964	1991	Scrapped	
47019	D1573			1964	1997	Scrapped	
47033	D1613			1964	1999	Scrapped	
47049	D1631			1964	1998	Scrapped	
47050	D1632			1964	1994	Scrapped	
47051	D1633			1964	1998	Scrapped	
47052	D1634			1964	2000	Scrapped	
47053	D1635			1964	1998	Scrapped	
47054	D1638			1964	1992	Scrapped	
47060	D1644			1965	1999	Converted	Converted to 57008 in 1999
47063	D1647			1965	1995	Scrapped	
47079	D1664			1965	2000	Converted	Converted to 57009 in 2000
47085	D1670			1965	1998	Scrapped	
D1671				1965	1966	Scrapped	
47089	D1675			1965	1987	Scrapped	
47093	D1679			1965	1988	Scrapped	
47094	D1680			1965	1992	Scrapped	
47095	D1681			1965	1998	Scrapped	
47096	D1682			1963	1995	Scrapped	
47097	D1684			1963	1990	Scrapped	
47098	D1685			1963	1991	Scrapped	
47099	D1686			1963	1991	Scrapped	
47100	D1687			1963	1991	Scrapped	The cab remains
47101	D1688			1963	1989	Scrapped	
47102	D1690			1963	1995	Scrapped	
47103	D1691			1963	1987	Scrapped	

47104	D1692			1963	1988	Scrapped	
47105	D1693			1963	1993	Preserved	
47106	D1694			1963	1988	Scrapped	
47107	D1695			1963	1991	Scrapped	
47108	D1696			1963	1994	Scrapped	
47109	D1697			1963	1987	Scrapped	
47110	D1698			1964	1989	Scrapped	
47111	D1699			1963	1986	Scrapped	
47112	D1700			1964	1991	Scrapped	
47113	D1701			1964	1988	Scrapped	
47114	D1702			1965	2001	Scrapped	1 of 5 experimental Class 48s, converted back to Class 47 before TOPS renumbering
47115	D1703			1965	1991	Scrapped	1 of 5 experimental Class 48s, converted back to Class 47 before TOPS renumbering
47116	D1704			1966	1990	Scrapped	1 of 5 experimental Class 48s, converted back to Class 47 before TOPS renumbering
47117	D1705			1965	1991	Preserved	1 of 5 experimental Class 48s, converted back to Class 47 before TOPS renumbering
47118	D1706			1965	1991	Scrapped	1 of 5 experimental Class 48s, converted back to Class 47 before TOPS renumbering
47119	D1708			1964	1992	Scrapped	
47120	D1709			1964	1991	Scrapped	
47121	D1710			1964	1996	Scrapped	
47122	D1711			1964	1987	Scrapped	
47123	D1712			1964	1991	Scrapped	
47124	D1714			1964	1989	Scrapped	
47125	D1715			1964	1997	Scrapped	
47130	D1721			1964	1988	Scrapped	
47131	D1722			1964	1987	Scrapped	
47137	D1729			1964	1987	Scrapped	
47140	D1732			1964	1988	Scrapped	
D1734				1964	1965	Scrapped	
47142	D1735			1964	1998	Scrapped	
47143	D1736			1964	1989	Scrapped	
47144	D1737			1964	1998	Scrapped	
47145	D1738			1964	2007	Scrapped	
47146	D1739			1964	1998	Scrapped	
47147	D1740			1964	1998	Scrapped	
47148	D1741			1964	1987	Scrapped	
47150	47399	47150	D1743	1964	2007	Scrapped	
47152	47398	47152	D1745	1964	2001	Scrapped	
47156	D1749			1964	1996	Scrapped	
47157	D1750			1964	2001	Scrapped	
47159	D1752			1964	1988	Scrapped	
47162	D1756			1964	1987	Scrapped	
47186	D1781			1964	1998	Scrapped	
47187	D1837			1965	1999	Converted	Converted to 57006 in 1999
47188	D1838			1965	1998	Scrapped	
47189	D1839			1965	1989	Scrapped	
47190	D1840			1965	1994	Scrapped	
47191	D1841			1965	1987	Scrapped	
47192	D1842			1965	1988	Preserved	
47193	D1843			1965	2000	Scrapped	
47194	D1844			1965		West Coast Railway Co	
47195	D1845			1965	1991	Scrapped	
47196	D1846			1965	1994	Scrapped	
47197	D1847			1965	2005	Scrapped	
47198	D1848			1965	1989	Scrapped	
47199	D1849			1965	1987	Scrapped	

47200	D1850			1965	2006	Scrapped	
47201	D1851			1965	1998	Scrapped	
47202	D1852			1965	1987	Scrapped	
47203	D1853			1965	1989	Scrapped	
47204	47388	47204	D1854	1965	2000	Converted	Converted to 57012 in 2000
47205	47395	47205	D1855	1965	2001	Preserved	
47206	D1856			1965	2004	Converted	Converted to 57605 in 2004
47207	D1857			1965	2001	Scrapped	
47208	D1858			1965	1980	Scrapped	
47209	47393	47209	D1859	1965	004	Converted	Converted to 57604 in 2004
47210	D1860			1965	1998	Scrapped	
47211	47394	47211	D1861	1965	1998	Scrapped	
47212	D1862			1965	2003	Scrapped	
47213	D1863			1965	1999	Scrapped	
47214	D1864			1965	1994	Scrapped	
47215	D1865			1965	1991	Scrapped	
47217	D1867			1965	1999	Scrapped	
47218	D1868			1965	1999	Scrapped	
47219	D1869			1965	1999	Scrapped	
47220	D1870			1965	1993	Scrapped	
47221	D1871			1965	1996	Scrapped	
47222	D1872			1965	1998	Scrapped	
47223	D1873			1965	1995	Scrapped	
47224	D1874			1965	2003	Scrapped	
47225	D1901			1965	2003	Converted	Converted to 57307 in 2003
47226	47384	47226	D1902	1965	1999	Scrapped	
47227	D1903			1965	1993	Scrapped	
47228	D1904			1965	1999	Scrapped	
47229	D1905			1965	1998	Scrapped	
47230	D1906			1965	1987	Scrapped	
47231	D1907			1965	2000	Converted	Converted to 57010 in 2000
D1908				1965	1969	Scrapped	
47233	D1910			1965	1991	Scrapped	
47234	D1911			1965	2004	Converted	Converted to 57315 in 2004
47235	D1912			1965	1988	Scrapped	
47236	D1913			1965	1999	Scrapped	
47237	D1914			1965		West Coast Railway Co	
47238	D1915			1965	1995	Scrapped	
47241	D1918			1965	1999	Scrapped	
47245	D1922			1966		West Coast Railway Co	
47249	D1926			1966	1996	Scrapped	
47256	D1934			1966	1995	Scrapped	
47258	D1938			1966	2001	Scrapped	
47270	D1971			1965		West Coast Railway Co	
47275	D1977			1965	1986	Scrapped	
47276	D1978			1965	1999	Scrapped	
47277	D1979			1965	1994	Scrapped	
47278	D1980			1965	1999	Scrapped	
47279	D1981			1965	2003	Scrapped	
47280	D1982			1965	2002	Scrapped	
47281	D1983			1965	1998	Scrapped	
47282	D1984			1966	1986	Scrapped	
47283	D1985			1966	1999	Scrapped	
47284	D1986			1966	1999	Scrapped	
47285	D1987			1966	1999	Scrapped	
47286	D1988			1966	1999	Scrapped	
47287	D1989			1966	2002	Scrapped	
47288	D1990			1966	1995	Scrapped	
47289	D1991			1966	2003	Scrapped	
47290	D1992			1966	2004	Converted	Converted to 57316 in 2004
47291	D1993			1966	1998	Scrapped	
47292	D1994			1966	2003	Preserved	
47293	D1995			1966	1999	Scrapped	
47294	D1996			1966	1996	Scrapped	

47295	D1997			1966	2002	Scrapped
47296	D1998			1966	2001	Scrapped
47297	D1999			1966	1999	Scrapped
47298	D1100			1966	2006	Scrapped
47299	47216	D1866		1965	1999	Scrapped

Class 47/3

Locos built without train heating were designated Class 47/2 under 1968 classification, then later Class 47/3 under TOPS Classification.

Latest Number Carried	Previous Number 1	Previous Number 2	Previous Number 3	Year Entered Service	Year Withdrawn	Current Status	Notes
47300	47468	D1594		1964	1995	Scrapped	
47301	D1782			1964	2001	Scrapped	
47302	D1783			1964	2001	Scrapped	
47303	47397	47303	D1784	1964	2005	Scrapped	
47304	47392	47304	D1785	1964	1999	Scrapped	
47305	D1786			1964	1999	Scrapped	
47306	D1787			1964	2000	Preserved	
47307	D1788			1964	1999	Scrapped	
47308	D1789			1964	1999	Scrapped	
47309	47389	47309	D1790	1964	2006	Scrapped	
47310	D1791			1964	1999	Scrapped	
47311	D1792			1965	1991	Scrapped	
47312	D1793			1964	1999	Scrapped	
47313	D1794			1964	1999	Scrapped	
47314	47387	47314	D1795	1965	1999	Scrapped	
47315	D1796			1965	1999	Scrapped	
47316	D1797			1965	2006	Scrapped	

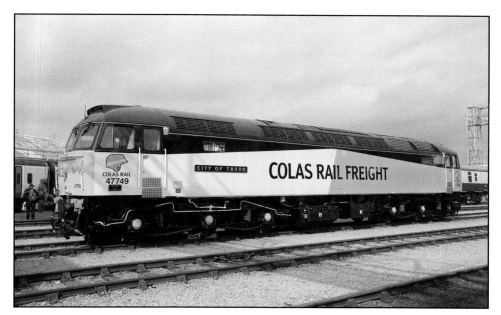

▲ 47749 "CITY OF TRURO" in Colas Rail livery is seen on display at Bristol St Philip's Marsh open day on 2 May 2016. "CITY OF TRURO" is the third name to be carried by this locomotive whilst numbered 47749, but is actually a reinstatement of a name previously carried when the same locomotive was numbered 47076 and later 47625. **Robert Pritchard**

47317	D1798			1965	1998	Converted	Converted to 57003 in 1998
47318	D1799			1965	1993	Scrapped	
47319	D1800			1965	1995	Scrapped	
47320	D1801			1965	1993	Scrapped	
47321	D1802			1965	1995	Scrapped	
47322	D1803			1965	1998	Converted	Converted to 57002 in 1998
47323	D1804			1965	2000	Scrapped	
47324	D1805			1965	1992	Scrapped	
47325	D1806			1965	1996	Scrapped	
47326	D1807			1965	1999	Scrapped	
47327	D1808			1965	1993	Scrapped	
47328	47396	47328	D1809	1965	1997	Scrapped	
47329	D1810			1965	2000	Converted	Converted to 57011 in 2000
47330	47390	47330	D1811	1965	2003	Converted	Converted to 57312 in 2003
47331	D1812			1965	1999	Scrapped	
47332	D1813			1965	1999	Converted	Converted to 57007 in 1999
47333	D1814			1965	1995	Scrapped	
47334	D1815			1965	2001	Scrapped	
47335	D1816			1965	1999	Scrapped	
47336	D1817			1965	1993	Scrapped	
47337	D1818			1965	2003	Converted	Converted to 57602 in 2003
47338	D1819			1965	1999	Scrapped	
47339	D1820			1965	2000	Scrapped	
47340	D1821			1965	1998	Scrapped	
47341	D1822			1965	1996	Scrapped	
47342	D1823			1965	1988	Scrapped	
47343	D1824			1965	1992	Scrapped	
47344	D1825			1965	1999	Scrapped	
47345	D1826			1965	2001	Scrapped	
47346	D1827			1965	1998	Scrapped	
47347	D1828			1965	1999	Converted	Converted to 57004 in 1999
47348	D1829			1965	2000	Scrapped	
47349	D1830			1965	2003	Converted	Converted to 57603 in 2003
47350	D1831			1965	1999	Converted	Converted to 57005 in 1999
47351	D1832			1965	1997	Scrapped	
47352	D1833			1965	1994	Scrapped	
47353	D1834			1965	1999	Scrapped	
47354	D1835			1965	2000	Scrapped	
47355	47391	47355	D1836	1965		West Coast Railway Co	
47356	D1875			1965	1998	Converted	Converted to 57001 in 1998
47357	D1876			1965	2001	Scrapped	
47358	D1877			1965	2005	Scrapped	
47359	D1878			1965	1998	Scrapped	
47360	D1879			1965	1999	Scrapped	
47361	D1880			1966	2001	Scrapped	
47362	D1881			1965	1999	Scrapped	
47363	47385	47363	D1882	1965	1999	Scrapped	
47365	D1884			1965	1998	Scrapped	
47366	D1885			1965	1999	Scrapped	
47367	D1886			1965	2001	Preserved	
47368	D1887			1965		West Coast Railway Co	
47369	D1888			1965	1996	Scrapped	
47370	D1889			1965	2003	Scrapped	
47371	D1890			1965	2004	Converted	Converted to 57313 in 2004
47372	D1891			1965	2004	Converted	Converted to 57314 in 2004
47373	D1892			1965	1992	Scrapped	
47374	D1893			1965	1992	Scrapped	
47375	D1894			1965	2009	Exported	
47376	D1895			1965	2001	Preserved	
47377	D1896			1965	2000	Scrapped	
47378	47386	47378	D1897	1965	1998	Scrapped	
47379	D1898			1965	1999	Scrapped	
47380	D1899			1965	1992	Scrapped	
47381	D1900			1965	1992	Scrapped	

Class 47/4

Locos fitted with electric heating. Class 47/4 includes 47798–47854, which were renumbered when fitted with additional fuel tanks for long range working; some later reverted to their previous numbers.

Latest Number Carried	Previous Number 1	Previous Number 2	Previous Number 3	Year Entered Service	Year Withdrawn	Current Status	Notes
47401	D1500			1962	1992	Preserved	
47402	D1501			1962	1992	Preserved	
47403	D1502			1962	1986	Scrapped	
47404	D1503			1962	1988	Scrapped	
47405	D1504			1963	1986	Scrapped	
47406	D1505			1963	1990	Scrapped	
47407	D1506			1963	1990	Scrapped	
47408	D1507			1963	1986	Scrapped	
47409	D1508			1963	1986	Scrapped	
47410	D1509			1963	1987	Scrapped	
47411	D1510			1963	1989	Scrapped	
47412	D1511			1963	1987	Scrapped	
47413	D1512			1963	1991	Scrapped	
47414	D1513			1963	1986	Scrapped	
47415	D1514			1963	1987	Scrapped	
47416	D1515			1963	1986	Scrapped	
47417	D1516			1963	1992	Preserved	
47418	D1517			1963	1991	Scrapped	
47419	D1518			1963	1987	Scrapped	
47420	D1519			1963	1987	Scrapped	
47421	D1520			1963	1991	Scrapped	
47422	D1525			1963	1991	Scrapped	
47423	D1527			1963	1992	Scrapped	
47424	D1531			1963	1991	Scrapped	
47425	D1533			1963	1992	Scrapped	
47426	D1534			1963	1992	Scrapped	
47427	D1535			1963	1990	Scrapped	
47428	D1536			1963	1989	Scrapped	
47429	D1541			1963	1987	Scrapped	
47430	D1542			1963	1992	Scrapped	
47431	D1545			1963	1992	Scrapped	
47432	D1547			1963	1992	Scrapped	
47433	D1548			1963	1993	Scrapped	
47434	D1549			1963	1991	Scrapped	
47435	D1550			1964	1990	Scrapped	
47436	D1552			1964	1991	Scrapped	
47437	D1553			1964	1987	Scrapped	
47438	D1554			1964	1992	Scrapped	
47439	D1555			1964	1993	Scrapped	
47440	D1556			1964	1991	Scrapped	
47441	D1557			1964	1992	Scrapped	
47442	D1558			1964	1993	Scrapped	
47443	D1559			1964	1993	Scrapped	
47444	D1560			1964	1990	Scrapped	
47445	D1561			1964	1991	Scrapped	
D1562				1964	1971	Scrapped	
47446	D1563			1964	1992	Scrapped	
47447	D1564			1964	1991	Scrapped	
47448	D1565			1964	1991	Scrapped	
47449	D1566			1964	1993	Preserved	
47450	D1567			1964	1991	Scrapped	
47451	D1568			1964	1991	Scrapped	
47452	D1569			1964	1991	Scrapped	
47453	D1571			1964	1992	Scrapped	
47454	D1574			1964	1991	Scrapped	
47455	D1575			1964	1990	Scrapped	
47456	D1576			1964	1991	Scrapped	

47457	D1577			1964	1992	Scrapped	
47458	D1578			1964	1993	Scrapped	
47459	D1579			1964	1992	Scrapped	
47460	D1580			1964	1992	Scrapped	
47461	D1581			1964	1991	Scrapped	
47462	D1582			1964	1995	Scrapped	
47463	D1586			1964	1995	Scrapped	
47464	D1587			1964	1986	Scrapped	
47465	D1589			1964	1991	Scrapped	
47466	D1590			1964	1991	Scrapped	
47467	D1593			1964	1998	Scrapped	
47469	D1595			1964	1989	Scrapped	
47470	D1596			1964	1991	Scrapped	
47471	D1598			1964	1996	Scrapped	
47472	97472	47472	D1600	1964	1991	Scrapped	
47473	D1601			1964	1998	Scrapped	
47474	D1602			1964	2000	Scrapped	
47475	D1603			1964	1999	Scrapped	
47476	D1604			1964	2000	Scrapped	
47477	D1607			1964	1992	Scrapped	
47478	D1608			1964	1995	Scrapped	
47479	D1612			1964	1992	Scrapped	
47481	D1627			1964	1996	Scrapped	
47482	D1636			1964	1993	Scrapped	
47483	D1637			1964	1993	Scrapped	
47484	D1662			1965	1998	Preserved	
47485	D1683			1963	1993	Scrapped	
47486	D1689			1963	1987	Scrapped	
47487	D1707			1964	1988	Scrapped	
47488	D1713			1964		Preserved	
47489	D1716			1964	1997	Scrapped	
47492	D1760			1964		West Coast Railway Co	
47500	47770	47500	D1943	1966		West Coast Railway Co	
47501	D1944			1966		Locomotive Services	Carries the number D1944
47508	D1952			1966	1993	Scrapped	
47509	D1953			1966	1992	Scrapped	
47512	D1958			1967	1991	Scrapped	
47513	D1959			1967	1997	Scrapped	
47515	D1961			1968	1991	Scrapped	
47518	D1101			1966	1991	Scrapped	
47519	D1102			1966	1999	Scrapped	
47520	D1103			1966	1998	Scrapped	
47521	D1104			1966	1995	Scrapped	
47522	D1105			1966	1998	Scrapped	
47523	D1106			1966	1999	Scrapped	
47524	D1107			1966	2002	Preserved	
47525	D1108			1967	1998	Scrapped	
47526	D1109			1967		West Coast Railway Co	
47527	D1110			1967	1992	Scrapped	
47528	D1111			1967	1998	Scrapped	
47529	D1551			1964	1987	Scrapped	
47530	D1930			1966	1996	Scrapped	
47532	D1641			1964	1996	Scrapped	
47533	D1651			1965	1991	Scrapped	
47534	D1678			1965	1991	Scrapped	
47535	D1649			1965	1999	Scrapped	
47536	D1655			1965	1996	Scrapped	
ADB968035	47538	D1669		1965	1990	Scrapped	
47539	D1718			1964	1996	Scrapped	
47540	47975	47540	D1723	1964	1998	Scrapped	
47542	D1585			1964	1989	Scrapped	
47543	D1588			1964	1998	Scrapped	
47544	D1592			1964	1990	Scrapped	
47547	D1642			1965	1996	Scrapped	

47549	D1724			1964	1991	Scrapped	
47550	D1731			1964	1996	Scrapped	
47555	47126	D1717		1964	1999	Scrapped	
47565	47039	D1620		1964	2000	Scrapped	
47566	47043	D1624		1964	1996	Scrapped	
47572	47168	D1763		1964	1999	Scrapped	
47574	47174	D1769		1964	1996	Scrapped	
47575	47175	D1770		1964	2001	Scrapped	
47576	47176	D1771		1964	1996	Scrapped	
47579	47793	47579	47183	1964	2004	Preserved	Also carried previous No 4: D1778
47580	47732	47580	47167	1964		West Coast Railway Co	Preserved loco on hire to WCRC. Also carried previous No 4: D1762
47584	47180	D1775		1964	2000	Scrapped	
47596	47255	D1933		1966	1999	Preserved	
47624	47087	D1673		1965	1998	Scrapped	
47627	47273	D1974		1965	2000	Scrapped	
47628	47078	D1663		1965	1997	Scrapped	
47633	47083	D1668		1965	1990	Scrapped	
47634	47158	D1751		1964	2001	Scrapped	
47635	47029	D1606		1964	2004	Preserved	
47640	47244	D1921		1966		Nemesis Rail	
47643	47269	D1970		1965	1991	Preserved	
47645	47075	D1659		1965	1990	Scrapped	
47676	47586	47042	D1623	1964	1994	Scrapped	
47677	47617	47149	D1742	1964	1998	Scrapped	

Class 47/7 (First Batch)
Fitted with push-pull equipment.
Details as Class 47/4 except:
Maximum Speed: 100 mph.

Latest Number Carried	Previous Number 1	Previous Number 2	Previous Number 3	Year Entered Service	Year Withdrawn	Current Status	Notes
47701	47493	D1932		1966		Nemesis Rail	
47702	47504	D1947		1966	2000	Scrapped	
47703	47514	D1960		1967		Harry Needle Railroad Co	
47704	47495	D1937		1966	1997	Scrapped	
47705	47554	D1957		1967	2003	Converted	Converted to 57303 in 2003
47706	47494	D1936		1966	1995	Scrapped	
47707	47506	D1949		1966	1996	Scrapped	
47708	47516	D1968		1965	1995	Scrapped	
47709	47499	D1942		1966	2007	Scrapped	
47710	47496	D1939		1966	1999	Scrapped	
47711	47498	D1941		1966	2000	Scrapped	
47712	47505	D1948		1966	2012	Preserved	
47713	47510	D1954		1966	1988	Scrapped	
47714	47511	D1955		1966		Harry Needle Railroad Co	
47715	47502	D1945		1966		Harry Needle Railroad Co	
47716	47507	D1951		1966	2007	Scrapped	
47717	47497	D1940		1966	1996	Scrapped	

Class 47/7 (Second Batch)
Fitted with additional fuel tanks for long range working. Some later reverted to their previous numbers.
Details as Class 47/4.

Latest Number Carried	Previous Number 1	Previous Number 2	Previous Number 3	Previous Number 4	Year Entered Service	Year Withdrawn	Current Status	Notes
47721	47557	47024	D1591		1964	2002	Scrapped	
47722	47558	47027	D1599		1964	2002	Scrapped	
47725	47567	47044	D1625		1964	2003	Scrapped	
47726	47568	47045	D1626		1964	2002	Scrapped	
47727	47569	47047	D1629		1964		GB Railfreight	

Latest Number Carried	Previous Number 1	Previous Number 2	Previous Number 3	Previous Number 4	Year Entered Service	Year Withdrawn	Current Status	Notes
47733	47582	47170	D1765		1964	2004	Scrapped	
47734	47583	47172	D1767		1964	2004	Scrapped	
47736	47587	47263	D1963		1965	2003	Scrapped	
47737	47588	47178	D1773		1964	2004	Scrapped	
47738	47592	47171	D1766		1964	2000	Scrapped	The cab remains
47739	47594	47035	D1615		1964		GB Railfreight	
47741	47597	47026	D1597		1964	2003	Scrapped	
47742	47598	47182	D1777		1964	2001	Scrapped	
47743	47599	47177	D1772		1964	1995	Scrapped	
47744	47600	47250	D1927		1966		Nemesis Rail	
47745	47603	47267	D1967		1965	2000	Scrapped	
47746	47605	47160	D1754		1964		West Coast Railway Co	
47747	47615	47252	D1929		1966	2004	Scrapped	
47749	47625	47076	D1660		1965		GB Railfreight	
47750	47626	47082	D1667		1965	2004	Scrapped	
47756	47644	47246	D1923		1966	2003	Scrapped	
47757	47585	47184	D1779		1964	2004	Scrapped	
47758	47517	D1975			1965	2003	Scrapped	
47759	47559	47028	D1605		1964	2003	Scrapped	
47760	47562	47672	47562	47036	1964		West Coast Railway Co	Also carried previous No 5: D1617
47761	47564	47038	D1619		1964		Preserved	
47762	47573	47173	D1768		1964	2001	Scrapped	
47763	47581	47169	D1764		1964	2000	Scrapped	
47764	47630	47041	D1622		1964	2001	Scrapped	
47765	47631	47059	D1643		1965		Preserved	
47766	47642	47040	D1621		1964	2000	Scrapped	
47767	47641	47086	D1672		1965	2003	Scrapped	The cab remains
47768	47490	D1725			1964		West Coast Railway Co	
47769	47491	D1753			1964		Harry Needle Railroad Co	
47771	47503	D1946			1966		Preserved	
47772	47537	D1657			1965		West Coast Railway Co	
47773	47541	D1755			1964		Vintage Trains	
47774	47551	47801	47551	47153	1964	2002	Scrapped	Also carried previous No 5: D1746
47775	47531	47974	47531	D1584	1964	2001	Scrapped	
47776	47578	47181	D1776		1964		West Coast Railway Co	
47777	47636	47243	D1920		1966	2000	Scrapped	
47778	47606	47842	47606	47081	1965	2004	Scrapped	Also carried previous No 5: D1666
47779	47612	47838	47612	47080	1965	1999	Scrapped	Also carried previous No 5: D1665
47780	47618	47836	47618	47030	1964	2003	Scrapped	Also carried previous No 5: D1609
47781	47653	47808	47653	47088	1965	2003	Scrapped	Also carried previous No 5: D1674
47782	47824	47602	47185	D1780	1964	2003	Scrapped	
47783	47809	47654	47056	D1640	1964	2002	Scrapped	
47784	47819	47664	47135	D1727	1964	2004	Scrapped	
47785	47820	47665	47232	D1909	1965		Preserved	
47786	47821	47607	47138	D1730	1964		West Coast Railway Co	
47787	47823	47610	47163	D1757	1964		West Coast Railway Co	
47788	47833	47608	47262	D1962	1965	2000	Scrapped	
47789	47616	47671	47616	47248	1966	2004	Scrapped	Also carried previous No 5: D1925
47790	47673	47593	47272	D1973	1965		Locomotive Services	
47791	47675	47595	47268	D1969	1965	2004	Scrapped	

Class 47/4 continued

Latest Number Carried	Previous Number 1	Previous Number 2	Previous Number 3	Year Entered Service	Year Withdrawn	Current Status	Notes
47798	47834	47609	47072	1965		Preserved	Also carried previous number 4: D1656

Latest Number Carried	Previous Number 1	Previous Number 2	Previous Number 3	Year Entered Service	Year Withdrawn	Current Status	Notes
47799	47835	47620	47070	1965	2004	Preserved	Also carried previous number 4: D1654
47802	47552	47259	D1950	1966		West Coast Railway Co	
47803	47553	47260	D1956	1966	1995	Scrapped	
47804	47792	47804	47591	1965		West Coast Railway Co	Also carried previous number 4: 47265 and previous number 5: D1965
47805	47650	47257	D1935	1966		Locomotive Services	Carries the number D1935
47806	47651	47254	D1931	1966	2003	Converted	Converted to 57309 in 2003
47807	47652	47055	D1639	1964	2003	Converted	Converted to 57304 in 2003
47810	47655	47247	D1924	1966		Locomotive Services	
47811	47656	47128	D1719	1964		Locomotive Services	
47812	47657	47239	D1916	1965		Rail Operations Group	
47813	47658	47129	D1720	1964		Rail Operations Group	
47814	47659	47242	D1919	1966	2003	Converted	Converted to 57306 in 2003
47815	47660	47155	D1748	1964		Rail Operations Group	
47816	47661	47066	D1650	1965		Locomotive Services	
47817	47662	47032	D1611	1964	2003	Converted	Converted to 57311 in 2003
47818	47663	47240	D1917	1965		Arlington Fleet Services	
47822	47571	47164	D1758	1964	2003	Converted	Converted to 57305 in 2003
47825	47590	47165	D1759	1964	2001	Converted	Converted to 57601 in 2001
47826	47637	47274	D1976	1965		West Coast Railway Co	
47827	47589	47251	D1928	1966	2002	Converted	Converted to 57302 in 2002
47828	47629	47266	D1966	1965	2015	Preserved	
47829	47619	47264	D1964	1965	2006	Scrapped	
47830	47649	47061	D1645	1965		Freightliner	
47831	47563	47037	D1618	1964	2003	Converted	Converted to 57310 in 2003
47832	47560	47031	D1610	1964		West Coast Railway Co	
47837	47611	47166	D1761	1964	1991	Scrapped	
47839	47621	47136	D1728	1964	2011	Scrapped	
47840	47613	47077	D1661	1965	2007	Preserved	
47841	47622	47134	D1726	1964		Locomotive Services	
47843	47623	47090	D1676	1965		Rail Operations Group	
47844	47556	47020	D1583	1964	2002	Scrapped	
47845	47638	47069	D1653	1965	2002	Converted	Converted to 57301 in 2002
47846	47647	47091	D1677	1965	2003	Converted	Converted to 57308 in 2003
47847	47577	47179	D1774	1964		Rail Operations Group	
47848	47632	47068	D1652	1965		Rail Operations Group	
47849	47570	47048	D1630	1964	2001	Scrapped	
47850	47648	47151	D1744	1964	1995	Scrapped	
47851	47639	47064	D1648	1965		West Coast Railway Co	
47852	47646	47074	D1658	1965	1991	Scrapped	
47853	47614	47141	D1733	1964		GB Railfreight	
47854	47674	47604	47271	1965		West Coast Railway Co	Also carried previous number 4: D1972
47971	97480	47480	D1616	1964	2000	Scrapped	
47972	97545	47545	D1646	1965	1998	Scrapped	
47973	97561	47561	47034	1964	1996	Scrapped	Also carried previous number 4: D1614. The cab remains
47976	47546	D1747		1964	1999	Scrapped	
47981	47364	D1883		1965	1998	Scrapped	

Class 47/9
47046 was re-engined as a testbed for the forthcoming Class 56 and renumbered 47601. In 1980 it was further converted to Class 47/9 as a testbed for the forthcoming Class 58 at BR Crewe works.

Details as Class 47/0 except:
Engine: Ruston Paxman RP12RK3CT of 2355 kW (3300 hp) at 900 rpm.

Latest Number Carried	Previous Number 1	Previous Number 2	Previous Number 3	Year Entered Service	Year Withdrawn	Current Status	Notes
47901	47601	47046	D1628	1964	1990	Scrapped	

CLASS 50   Co-Co

Built: 1967–68 by English Electric, Vulcan Foundry, Newton-le-Willows.
Engine: English Electric 16CVST of 2010 kW (2700 hp) at 850 rpm.
Transmission: Electric.
Maximum Speed: 100 mph.
Train Heating/Supply: Electric.
Train Brakes: Dual braked (air & vacuum).

Latest Number Carried	Previous Number 1	Previous Number 2	Previous Number 3	Year Entered Service	Year Withdrawn	Current Status	Notes
50001	D401			1967	1991	Scrapped	
50002	D402			1967	1991	Preserved	
50003	D403			1968	1991	Scrapped	
50004	D404			1967	1990	Scrapped	
50005	D405			1968	1990	Scrapped	
50006	D406			1968	1987	Scrapped	
50007	D407			1968	1994	Preserved	
50008	D408			1968	1992	Preserved	
50009	D409			1968	1991	Scrapped	
50010	D410			1968	1988	Scrapped	
50011	D411			1968	1987	Scrapped	
50012	D412			1968	1989	Scrapped	
50013	D413			1968	1988	Scrapped	
50014	D414			1968	1987	Scrapped	
50015	D415			1968	1992	Preserved	
50016	D416			1968	1990	Scrapped	
50017	D417			1968	1991	Preserved	
50018	D418			1968	1991	Scrapped	
50019	D419			1968	1990	Preserved	
50020	D420			1968	1990	Scrapped	
50021	D421			1968	1990	Preserved	
50022	D422			1968	1988	Scrapped	
50023	D423			1968	1990	Scrapped	
50024	D424			1968	1991	Scrapped	
50025	D425			1968	1989	Scrapped	
50026	D426			1968	1990	Preserved	
50027	D427			1968	1991	Preserved	
50028	D428			1968	1991	Scrapped	
50029	D429			1968	1992	Preserved	
50030	D430			1968	1992	Preserved	
50031	D431			1968	1991	Preserved	
50032	D432			1968	1990	Scrapped	
50033	D433			1968	1994	Preserved	
50034	D434			1968	1990	Scrapped	
50035	D435			1968	1990	Preserved	
50036	D436			1968	1991	Scrapped	
50037	D437			1968	1991	Scrapped	The cab remains
50038	D438			1968	1988	Scrapped	
50039	D439			1968	1989	Scrapped	
50040	D440			1968	1990	Scrapped	
50041	D441			1968	1990	Scrapped	
50042	D442			1968	1990	Preserved	
50043	D443			1968	1991	Scrapped	
50044	D444			1968	1991	Preserved	
50045	D445			1968	1990	Scrapped	
50046	D446			1968	1992	Scrapped	The cab remains
50047	D447			1968	1988	Scrapped	
50048	D448			1968	1991	Scrapped	
50049	50149	50049	D449	1968	1991	Preserved	
50050	D400			1967	1994	Preserved	

▲ 50021 "Rodney" stands in ex-works condition at Doncaster Works on 18 June 1978. The locomotive has only just emerged from the paint shop, hence its nameplates have not yet been re-attached. **Pete Berry/Rail Photoprints**

▼ Of the 74 Class 52 "Westerns" built by British Railways, seven have survived into preservation with a number of owning groups, across a variety of locations. D1023 "WESTERN FUSILIER" is part of the National Collection and is seen inside the National Railway Museum, York on 12 August 2014.
Andy Chard

CLASS 52 C-C

Built: 1961–64 by British Railways, Crewe & Swindon.
Engine: Two Bristol Siddeley Maybach MD655 of 1007 kW (1350 hp) at 1500 rpm.
Transmission: Hydraulic.
Maximum Speed: 90 mph.
Train Heating/Supply: Steam heating.
Train Brakes: Built vacuum braked and most were converted to dual braked (air & vacuum).

Latest Number Carried	Previous Number 1	Year Entered Service	Year Withdrawn	Current Status	Notes
D1000		1961	1974	Scrapped	
D1001		1962	1976	Scrapped	
D1002		1962	1974	Scrapped	
D1003		1962	1975	Scrapped	
D1004		1962	1973	Scrapped	
D1005		1962	1976	Scrapped	
D1006		1962	1975	Scrapped	
D1007		1962	1974	Scrapped	
D1008		1962	1974	Scrapped	
D1009		1962	1976	Scrapped	
D1010		1962	1977	Preserved	
D1011		1962	1975	Scrapped	
D1012		1962	1975	Scrapped	
D1013		1962	1977	Preserved	
D1014		1962	1974	Scrapped	
D1015		1963	1976	Preserved	
D1016		1963	1975	Scrapped	
D1017		1963	1973	Scrapped	
D1018		1963	1973	Scrapped	
D1019		1963	1973	Scrapped	
D1020		1963	1973	Scrapped	
D1021		1963	1976	Scrapped	
D1022		1963	1977	Scrapped	
D1023		1963	1977	Preserved	
D1024		1963	1973	Scrapped	
D1025		1963	1975	Scrapped	
D1026		1963	1975	Scrapped	
D1027		1964	1975	Scrapped	
D1028		1964	1976	Scrapped	
D1029		1964	1974	Scrapped	
D1030		1963	1976	Scrapped	
D1031		1963	1975	Scrapped	
D1032		1963	1973	Scrapped	
D1033		1964	1976	Scrapped	
D1034		1964	1975	Scrapped	
D1035		1962	1975	Scrapped	
D1036		1962	1976	Scrapped	
D1037		1962	1976	Scrapped	
D1038		1962	1973	Scrapped	
D1039		1962	1973	Scrapped	
D1040		1962	1976	Scrapped	
D1041		1962	1977	Preserved	
D1042		1962	1973	Scrapped	
D1043		1962	1976	Scrapped	
D1044		1962	1975	Scrapped	
D1045		1962	1974	Scrapped	
D1046		1962	1975	Scrapped	
D1047		1963	1976	Scrapped	
D1048		1962	1977	Preserved	
D1049		1962	1976	Scrapped	
D1050		1963	1975	Scrapped	
D1051		1963	1976	Scrapped	

D1052	1963	1975	Scrapped
D1053	1963	1976	Scrapped
D1054	1963	1976	Scrapped
D1055	1963	1976	Scrapped
D1056	1963	1976	Scrapped
D1057	1963	1976	Scrapped
D1058	1963	1977	Scrapped
D1059	1963	1975	Scrapped
D1060	1963	1973	Scrapped
D1061	1963	1974	Scrapped
D1062	1963	1974	Preserved
D1063	1963	1976	Scrapped
D1064	1963	1975	Scrapped
D1065	1963	1976	Scrapped
D1066	1963	1974	Scrapped
D1067	1963	1976	Scrapped
D1068	1963	1976	Scrapped
D1069	1963	1975	Scrapped
D1070	1963	1976	Scrapped
D1071	1963	1976	Scrapped
D1072	1963	1976	Scrapped
D1073	1963	1974	Scrapped

CLASS 55   Co-Co

Built: 1961–62 by English Electric, Vulcan Foundry, Newton-le-Willows.
Engine: Two Napier Deltic T18-25 of 1230 kW (1650 hp) at 1500 rpm.
Transmission: Electric.
Maximum Speed: 100 mph.
Train Heating/Supply: Built with steam heating, all later converted to dual heating.
Train Brakes: Built vacuum braked, all later converted to dual braked (air & vacuum).

Latest Number Carried	Previous Number 1	Year Entered Service	Year Withdrawn	Current Status	Notes
55001	D9001	1961	1980	Scrapped	
55002	D9002	1961	1982	Preserved	
55003	D9003	1961	1980	Scrapped	
55004	D9004	1961	1981	Scrapped	
55005	D9005	1961	1981	Scrapped	
55006	D9006	1961	1981	Scrapped	
55007	D9007	1961	1981	Scrapped	
55008	D9008	1961	1981	Scrapped	The cab remains
55009	D9009	1961	1982	Preserved	
55010	D9010	1961	1981	Scrapped	
55011	D9011	1961	1981	Scrapped	
55012	D9012	1961	1981	Scrapped	
55013	D9013	1961	1981	Scrapped	
55014	D9014	1961	1981	Scrapped	
55015	D9015	1961	1982	Preserved	
55016	D9016	1961		Locomotive Services	
55017	D9017	1961	1981	Scrapped	
55018	D9018	1961	1981	Scrapped	
55019	D9019	1961	1981	Preserved	
55020	D9020	1962	1980	Scrapped	
55021	D9021	1962	1981	Scrapped	The cab remains
55022	D9000	1961		Locomotive Services	

▲ Class 55 duo D9016 and D9009 pass Burrs Country Park with the 1355 Heywood to Rawtenstall, as part of the Deltic Gathering weekend at the East Lancashire Railway on 22 September 2012.
Paul Gerrard

▼ Almost 100 of the 135 Class 56s built have now been scrapped and the remaining locomotives are spread across a number of operators. Colas pair 56078 and 56113 power off the Forth Bridge through Dalmeny with a Moy to Millerhill engineers train on 21 June 2015. **Paul Gerrard**

CLASS 56   Co-Co

Built: 1976–84 by Electroputere, Craiova, Romania and BREL, Crewe & Doncaster
Engine: Ruston Paxman 16RK3CT of 2460 kW (3250 hp) at 900 rpm.
Transmission: Electric.
Maximum Speed: 80 mph.
Train Heating/Supply: None.
Train Brakes: Air.

Latest Number Carried	Previous Number 1	Year Entered Service	Year Withdrawn	Current Status	Notes
56001		1977	1996	Scrapped	
56002		1977	1992	Scrapped	
56004		1977	1999	Scrapped	
56005		1977	1996	Scrapped	
56006		1977	2003	Preserved	
56007		1977		UK Rail Leasing	
56008		1977	1992	Scrapped	
56009	56201	1977		UK Rail Leasing	
56010		1977	1999	Scrapped	
56011		1977	2001	Scrapped	
56012		1977	1992	Scrapped	
56013		1977	1993	Scrapped	
56014		1977	1993	Scrapped	
56015		1977	1993	Scrapped	
56016		1977	1996	Scrapped	
56017		1977	1992	Scrapped	
56018		1977		UK Rail Leasing	
56019		1977	1999	Scrapped	
56020		1977	1997	Scrapped	
56021		1977	1999	Scrapped	
56022		1977	1999	Scrapped	
56023		1977	1993	Scrapped	
56024		1977	1996	Scrapped	
56025		1977	2002	Scrapped	
56026		1977	1996	Scrapped	
56027		1977	2003	Scrapped	
56028		1977	1993	Scrapped	
56029		1977	1999	Scrapped	
56030		1977	1993	Scrapped	
56031		1977		UK Rail Leasing	
56032		1977		UK Rail Leasing	
56033		1977	2003	Scrapped	
56034		1977	1999	Scrapped	
56035		1977	1999	Scrapped	
56036		1978	2000	Scrapped	
56037		1978		UK Rail Leasing	
56038		1978		UK Rail Leasing	
56039		1978	1999	Scrapped	
56040		1978	2000	Scrapped	
56041		1978	2003	Scrapped	
56042		1978	1991	Scrapped	
56043		1978	2000	Scrapped	
56044		1978	2000	Scrapped	
56046		1978	2002	Scrapped	
56047		1978	1999	Scrapped	
56048		1978	2002	Scrapped	
56049		1978		Colas Rail	
56050		1978	1999	Scrapped	
56051		1978		Colas Rail	
56052		1978	1999	Scrapped	
56053		1978	1999	Scrapped	
56054		1979	2003	Scrapped	

56055	1979	2003	Scrapped	
56056	1979	2004	Scrapped	
56058	1979	2006	Scrapped	
56059	1979	2006	Scrapped	
56060	1979		UK Rail Leasing	
56061	1979	1999	Scrapped	
56062	1979	2004	Scrapped	
56063	1979	2002	Scrapped	
56064	1979	2000	Scrapped	
56065	1979		UK Rail Leasing	
56066	1979	1999	Scrapped	
56067	1979	2003	Scrapped	
56068	1979	2003	Scrapped	
56069	1979		UK Rail Leasing	
56070	1979	2004	Scrapped	
56071	1979	2006	Scrapped	
56072	1980	2004	Scrapped	
56073	1980	2002	Scrapped	
56074	1980	2006	Scrapped	
56075	1980	1999	Scrapped	
56076	1980	2000	Scrapped	
56077	1980		UK Rail Leasing	
56078	1980		Colas Rail	
56079	1980	1999	Scrapped	
56080	1980	2002	Scrapped	
56081	1980		UK Rail Leasing	
56082	1980	1999	Scrapped	
56083	1980	2003	Scrapped	
56084	1980	2000	Scrapped	
56085	1981	2002	Scrapped	
56086	1980	1999	Scrapped	
56087	1980		Colas Rail	
56088	1981	2004	Scrapped	
56089	1981	2002	Scrapped	
56090	1981		Colas Rail	
56091	1981		RMS Locotec	
56092	1981	1999	Scrapped	
56093	1981	1999	Scrapped	
56094	1981		Colas Rail	
56095	1981	2006	Scrapped	
56096	1981		Colas Rail	
56097	1981	1999	Preserved	
56098	1981		UK Rail Leasing	
56099	1981	2003	Scrapped	
56100	1981	2003	Scrapped	
56101	1981	2000	Exported	
56102	1981	2003	Scrapped	
56103	1981		RMS Locotec	
56104	1982		UK Rail Leasing	
56105	1982		Colas Rail	
56106	1982		UK Rail Leasing	1 x cab removed 2017
56107	1982	2004	Scrapped	
56108	1982	1999	Scrapped	
56109	1982	2003	Scrapped	
56110	1982	2002	Scrapped	
56111	1982	2003	Scrapped	
56112	1982	2003	Scrapped	
56113	1982		Colas Rail	
56114	1983	2003	Scrapped	
56115	1983	2006	Exported	Involved in serious collision abroad Nov 2016
56116	1983	2002	Scrapped	
56117	1983	2006	Exported	
56118	1983	2006	Scrapped	
56119	1983	2004	Scrapped	

56120		1983	2003	Scrapped
56121		1983	1999	Scrapped
56122		1983	1992	Scrapped
56123		1983	1999	Scrapped
56126		1983	1999	Scrapped
56127		1983	2002	Scrapped
56128		1983		Awaiting Disposal	At CF Booth, Rotherham
56129		1984	2003	Scrapped
56130		1984	1999	Scrapped
56131		1984	2002	Scrapped
56132		1984	2000	Scrapped
56133		1984	2004	Scrapped
56134		1984	2002	Scrapped
56135		1984	1999	Scrapped
56301	56045	1978		UK Rail Leasing	Preserved locomotive on hire to UK Rail Leasing
56302	56124	1983		Colas Rail
56303	56125	1983		Rail Operations Group	DCR locomotive on hire to ROG
56311	56057	1979		Preserved
56312	56003	1977		Preserved

CLASS 57   Co-Co

Built: 1964–67 as Class 47 (see Class 47) and converted to Class 57 1998–2004 by Brush Traction, Loughborough.
Transmission: Electric.
Train Brakes: Air.

Class 57/0
Engine: General Motors 12 645 E3 of 1860 kW (2500 hp) at 904 rpm.
Maximum Speed: 75 mph.
Train Heating/Supply: None.

Latest Number Carried	Previous Number 1	Year Entered Service	Year Withdrawn	Current Status	Notes
57001	47356	1998		West Coast Railway Co	
57002	47322	1998		Direct Rail Services	
57003	47317	1999		Direct Rail Services	
57004	47347	1999		Direct Rail Services	
57005	47350	1999		West Coast Railway Co	
57006	47187	1999		West Coast Railway Co	
57007	47332	1999		Direct Rail Services	
57008	47060	1999		Direct Rail Services	
57009	47079	1999		Direct Rail Services	
57010	47231	2000		Direct Rail Services	
57011	47329	2000		Direct Rail Services	
57012	47204	2000		Direct Rail Services	

Class 57/3
Engine: General Motors 12 645 F3B of 2050 kW (2750 hp) at 954 rpm.
Maximum Speed: 95 mph.
Train Heating/Supply: Electric.

Latest Number Carried	Previous Number 1	Year Entered Service	Year Withdrawn	Current Status	Notes
57301	47845	2002		Direct Rail Services	
57302	47827	2002		Direct Rail Services	
57303	47705	2003		Direct Rail Services	
57304	47807	2003		Direct Rail Services	
57305	47822	2003		Rail Operations Group	DRS Locomotive on hire to ROG
57306	47814	2003		Direct Rail Services	
57307	47225	2003		Direct Rail Services	
57308	47846	2003		Direct Rail Services	
57309	47806	2003		Direct Rail Services	
57310	47831	2003		Direct Rail Services	

57311	47817	2003	Direct Rail Services
57312	47330	2003	Direct Rail Services
57313	47371	2004	West Coast Railway Co
57314	47372	2004	West Coast Railway Co
57315	47234	2004	West Coast Railway Co
57316	47290	2004	West Coast Railway Co

Class 57/6
Engine: General Motors 12 645 E3 of 1860 kW (2500 hp) at 904 rpm.
Maximum Speed: 95 mph.
Train Heating/Supply: Electric.

Latest Number Carried	Previous Number 1	Year Entered Service	Year Withdrawn	Current Status	Notes
57601	47825	2001		West Coast Railway Co	
57602	47337	2003		Great Western Railway	
57603	47349	2003		Great Western Railway	
57604	47209	2004		Great Western Railway	
57605	47206	2004		Great Western Railway	

▲ 57311 "PARKER" passes Lunds, near Garsdale, hauling a Pendolino EMU with a diverted Glasgow Central–London Euston train on 14 April 2007. **Robert Pritchard**

CLASS 58

Co-Co

Built: 1983–87 by BREL, Doncaster.
Engine: Ruston Paxman 12RK3ACT of 2460 kW (3300 hp) at 1000 rpm.
Transmission: Electric.
Maximum Speed: 80 mph.
Train Heating/Supply: None.
Train Brakes: Air.

Latest Number Carried	Previous Number 1	Year Entered Service	Year Withdrawn	Current Status	Notes
58001		1983	1999	Exported	
58002		1983	2000	Scrapped	
58003		1983	1999	Scrapped	
58004		1983	2006	Exported	
58005		1983	2000	Exported	
58006		1983	2000	Exported	
58007		1983	2000	Exported	
58008		1983	1999	Scrapped	The cab remains
58009		1984	2002	Exported	
58010		1984	1999	Exported	
58011		1984	2000	Exported	
58012		1984	1999	Preserved	
58013		1984	2001	Exported	
58014		1984	2000	Scrapped	
58015		1984	2011	Exported	
58016		1984	2006	Preserved	
58017		1984	1999	Scrapped	
58018		1984	1999	Exported	
58019		1984	2001	Scrapped	
58020		1984	2011	Exported	
58021		1984	2002	Exported	
58022		1984	1999	Preserved	Frame of 58022 to be used for LMS10000 build
58023		1984	1999	Preserved	
58024		1984	2011	Exported	
58025		1985	2004	Exported	
58026		1985	2002	Exported	
58027		1985	1999	Exported	
58028		1985	1999	Scrapped	
58029		1985	2011	Exported	
58030		1985	2011	Exported	
58031		1985	2011	Exported	
58032		1985	1999	Exported	
58033		1985	2002	Exported	
58034		1985	1999	Exported	
58035		1986	1999	Exported	
58036		1986	2000	Exported	
58037		1986	2002	Scrapped	
58038		1986	1999	Exported	
58039		1986	2003	Exported	
58040		1986	1999	Exported	
58041		1986	2011	Exported	
58042		1986	2002	Exported	
58043		1986	2011	Exported	
58044		1986	2003	Exported	
58045		1986	2002	Scrapped	
58046		1986	2000	Exported	
58047		1986	2011	Exported	
58048		1986	2000	Preserved	
58049		1986	2002	Exported	
58050		1987	2002	Exported	

▲ Class 58 58014 "Didcot Power Station" passes Culham with empty MGR hoppers returning to the Midlands Coalfield from Didcot Power Station on 11 April 1992. Most Class 58s were later exported but this locomotives was one of the few examples to end up in the scrapyard.

John Chalcraft/Rail Photoprints

▼ In its new "Aggregate Industries" livery, Class 59/0 59004 heads west past Great Cheverell with 6V18, the 11.20 Allington ARC Sidings–Whatley Quarry on 6 May 2016. Note the large plaque commemorating "30 Years of Class 59" positioned just behind the driver's window.

John Chalcraft/Rail Photoprints

CLASS 59

Co-Co

Built: 1985 (59001–59004) and 1989 (59005) by General Motors, La Grange, Illinois, USA.
1990 (59101–59104), 1994 (59201) and 1995 (59202–59206) by General Motors, London, Canada.
Engine: General Motors 16-645E3C two stroke of 2460 kW (3300 hp) at 904 rpm.
Transmission: Electric.
Maximum Speed: 60 mph.
Train Heating/Supply: None.
Train Brakes: Air.

Class 59/0

Latest Number Carried	Previous Number 1	Year Entered Service	Year Withdrawn	Current Status	Notes
59001		1986		Aggregate Industries	
59002		1986		Aggregate Industries	
59003		1986		GB Railfreight	
59004		1986		Aggregate Industries	
59005		1989		Aggregate Industries	

Class 59/1
Details as Class 59/0.

Latest Number Carried	Previous Number 1	Year Entered Service	Year Withdrawn	Current Status	Notes
59101		1990		Hanson UK	
59102		1990		Hanson UK	
59103		1990		Hanson UK	
59104		1990		Hanson UK	

Class 59/2
Details as Class 59/0 except:
Maximum Speed: 75 mph.

Latest Number Carried	Previous Number 1	Year Entered Service	Year Withdrawn	Current Status	Notes
59201		1994		DB Cargo	
59202		1995		DB Cargo	
59203		1995		DB Cargo	
59204		1995		DB Cargo	
59205		1995		DB Cargo	
59206		1995		DB Cargo	

CLASS 60

Co-Co

Built: 1989–93 by Brush Traction, Loughborough.
Engine: Mirlees 8MB275T of 2310 kW (3100 hp) at 1000 rpm.
Transmission: Electric.
Maximum Speed: 62 mph.
Train Heating/Supply: None.
Train Brakes: Air.

Latest Number Carried	Previous Number 1	Year Entered Service	Year Withdrawn	Current Status	Notes
60001		1991		DB Cargo	
60002		1992		Colas Rail	
60003		1992		DB Cargo	
60004		1991		DB Cargo	
60005		1991		DB Cargo	
60006		1991		DB Cargo	
60007		1993		DB Cargo	
60008		1992		DB Cargo	
60009		1993		DB Cargo	
60010		1991		DB Cargo	
60011		1991		DB Cargo	

60012	1991	DB Cargo
60013	1993	DB Cargo
60014	1993	DB Cargo
60015	1993	DB Cargo
60017	1990	DB Cargo
60018	1990	DB Cargo
60019	1990	DB Cargo
60020	1991	DB Cargo
60021	1990	Colas Rail
60022	1991	DB Cargo
60023	1990	DB Cargo
60024	1990	DB Cargo
60025	1990	DB Cargo
60026	1990	Colas Rail
60027	1991	DB Cargo
60028	1990	DB Cargo
60029	1990	DB Cargo
60030	1990	DB Cargo
60031	1991	DB Cargo
60032	1990	DB Cargo
60033	1991	DB Cargo
60034	1990	DB Cargo
60035	1991	DB Cargo
60036	1991	DB Cargo
60037	1991	DB Cargo

▲ Steel Blue-liveried 60033 climbs past Brentry on 29 October 1997 with 6A65, the 09.03 Avonmouth–Didcot Power Station coal service, formed of a rake of HAA hopper wagons.
John Chalcraft/Rail Photoprints

60038		1991	DB Cargo
60039		1991	DB Cargo
60040		1992	DB Cargo
60041		1991	DB Cargo
60042		1991	DB Cargo
60043		1991	DB Cargo
60044		1991	DB Cargo
60045		1991	DB Cargo
60046		1991	DB Cargo
60047		1991	Colas Rail
60048		1991	DB Cargo
60049		1991	DB Cargo
60050		1991	DB Cargo
60051		1991	DB Cargo
60052		1991	DB Cargo
60053		1991	DB Cargo
60054		1991	DB Cargo
60055		1991	DB Cargo
60056		1991	Colas Rail
60057		1991	DB Cargo
60058		1991	DB Cargo
60059		1991	DB Cargo
60060		1991	DB Cargo
60061		1991	DB Cargo
60062		1991	DB Cargo
60063		1991	DB Cargo
60064		1991	DB Cargo
60065		1991	DB Cargo
60066		1991	DB Cargo
60067		1991	DB Cargo
60068		1991	DB Cargo
60069		1991	DB Cargo
60070		1991	DB Cargo
60071		1991	DB Cargo
60072		1991	DB Cargo
60073		1991	DB Cargo
60074		1991	DB Cargo
60075		1991	DB Cargo
60076		1991	Colas Rail
60077		1991	DB Cargo
60078		1991	DB Cargo
60079		1992	DB Cargo
60080		1991	DB Cargo
60081		1991	DB Cargo
60082		1991	DB Cargo
60083		1992	DB Cargo
60084		1993	DB Cargo
60085		1991	Colas Rail
60086		1992	DB Cargo
60087		1991	Colas Rail
60088		1992	DB Cargo
60089		1992	DB Cargo
60090		1992	DB Cargo
60091		1992	DB Cargo
60092		1992	DB Cargo
60093		1992	DB Cargo
60094		1992	DB Cargo
60095		1992	Colas Rail
60096		1992	Colas Rail
60097		1992	DB Cargo
60098		1992	DB Cargo
60099		1992	DB Cargo
60100		1992	DB Cargo
60500	60016	1993	DB Cargo

CLASS 66 Co-Co

Built: 1998–2016 by General Motors, London, Canada.
Engine: General Motors 12N-710G3B-EC two stroke of 2385 kW (3200 hp) at 904 rpm (Class 66/0, 66501–66572, 66/6, 66701–66717, 66733–66746, 66750–66751 and 66/8).
General Motors EMD 12N-710G3B-T2 two stroke of 2420 kW (3245 hp) at 904 rpm (Class 66/3, 66/4, 66585–66599, 66718–66732, 66747–66749, 66752–66779, 66/9 and 66953–66957 which are 66/5s).
Transmission: Electric.
Maximum Speed: 65 mph (Class 66/6) and 75 mph (others).
Train Heating/Supply: None.
Train Brakes: Air.

Latest Number Carried	Previous Number 1	Previous Number 2	Year Entered Service	Year Withdrawn	Current Status	Notes
66001			1998		DB Cargo	
66002			1998		DB Cargo	
66003			1998		DB Cargo	
66004			1998		DB Cargo	
66005			1998		DB Cargo	
66006			1998		DB Cargo	
66007			1998		DB Cargo	
66009			1998		DB Cargo	
66010			1998		Exported	
66011			1998		DB Cargo	
66012			1998		DB Cargo	
66013			1998		DB Cargo	
66014			1998		DB Cargo	
66015			1998		DB Cargo	
66017			1998		DB Cargo	
66018			1998		DB Cargo	
66019			1998		DB Cargo	
66020			1998		DB Cargo	
66021			1998		DB Cargo	
66022			1998		Exported	
66023			1998		DB Cargo	
66024			1998		DB Cargo	
66025			1998		DB Cargo	
66026			1998		Exported	
66027			1998		DB Cargo	
66028			1998		Exported	
66029			1998		Exported	
66030			1998		DB Cargo	
66031			1998		DB Cargo	
66032			1998		Exported	
66033			1998		Exported	
66034			1998		DB Cargo	
66035			1998		DB Cargo	
66036			1998		Exported	
66037			1998		DB Cargo	
66038			1998		Exported	
66039			1998		DB Cargo	
66040			1998		DB Cargo	
66041			1998		DB Cargo	
66042			1998		Exported	
66043			1998		DB Cargo	
66044			1998		DB Cargo	
66045			1999		Exported	
66047			1999		DB Cargo	
66048			1999		DB Cargo	Stored at Longport after derailment accident
66049			1999		Exported	
66050			1999		DB Cargo	
66051			1999		DB Cargo	

66052	1999	Exported
66053	1999	DB Cargo
66054	1999	DB Cargo
66055	1999	DB Cargo
66056	1999	DB Cargo
66057	1999	DB Cargo
66059	1999	DB Cargo
66060	1999	DB Cargo
66061	1999	DB Cargo
66062	1999	Exported
66063	1999	DB Cargo
66064	1999	Exported
66065	1999	DB Cargo
66066	1999	DB Cargo
66067	1999	DB Cargo
66068	1999	DB Cargo
66069	1999	DB Cargo
66070	1999	DB Cargo
66071	1999	Exported
66072	1999	Exported
66073	1999	Exported
66074	1999	DB Cargo
66075	1999	DB Cargo
66076	1999	DB Cargo
66077	1999	DB Cargo
66078	1999	DB Cargo
66079	1999	DB Cargo
66080	1999	DB Cargo
66082	1999	DB Cargo
66083	1999	DB Cargo
66084	1999	DB Cargo
66085	1999	DB Cargo
66086	1999	DB Cargo
66087	1999	DB Cargo
66088	1999	DB Cargo
66089	1999	DB Cargo
66090	1999	DB Cargo
66091	1999	DB Cargo
66092	1999	DB Cargo
66093	1999	DB Cargo
66094	1999	DB Cargo
66095	1999	DB Cargo
66096	1999	DB Cargo
66097	1999	DB Cargo
66098	1999	DB Cargo
66099	1999	DB Cargo
66100	1999	DB Cargo
66101	1999	DB Cargo
66102	1999	DB Cargo
66103	1999	DB Cargo
66104	1999	DB Cargo
66105	1999	DB Cargo
66106	1999	DB Cargo
66107	1999	DB Cargo
66108	1999	DB Cargo
66109	1999	DB Cargo
66110	1999	DB Cargo
66111	1999	DB Cargo
66112	1999	DB Cargo
66113	1999	DB Cargo
66114	1999	DB Cargo
66115	1999	DB Cargo
66116	1999	DB Cargo
66117	1999	DB Cargo

66118	1999	DB Cargo
66119	1999	DB Cargo
66120	1999	DB Cargo
66121	1999	DB Cargo
66122	1999	DB Cargo
66123	1999	Exported
66124	1999	DB Cargo
66125	1999	DB Cargo
66126	1999	DB Cargo
66127	1999	DB Cargo
66128	1999	DB Cargo
66129	1999	DB Cargo
66130	1999	DB Cargo
66131	1999	DB Cargo
66133	1999	DB Cargo
66134	1999	DB Cargo
66135	1999	DB Cargo
66136	1999	DB Cargo
66137	1999	DB Cargo
66138	1999	DB Cargo
66139	1999	DB Cargo
66140	1999	DB Cargo
66142	1999	DB Cargo
66143	1999	DB Cargo
66144	1999	DB Cargo
66145	1999	DB Cargo
66146	1999	Exported
66147	1999	DB Cargo
66148	1999	DB Cargo
66149	1999	DB Cargo
66150	1999	DB Cargo
66151	1999	DB Cargo
66152	1999	DB Cargo
66153	1999	Exported
66154	2000	DB Cargo
66155	2000	DB Cargo
66156	1999	DB Cargo
66157	1999	Exported
66158	1999	DB Cargo
66159	1999	Exported
66160	1999	DB Cargo
66161	1999	DB Cargo
66162	1999	DB Cargo
66163	1999	Exported
66164	1999	DB Cargo
66165	1999	DB Cargo
66166	1999	Exported
66167	1999	DB Cargo
66168	1999	DB Cargo
66169	1999	DB Cargo
66170	1999	DB Cargo
66171	1999	DB Cargo
66172	1999	DB Cargo
66173	1999	Exported
66174	1999	DB Cargo
66175	1999	DB Cargo
66176	1999	DB Cargo
66177	1999	DB Cargo
66178	1999	Exported
66179	1999	Exported
66180	1999	Exported
66181	1999	DB Cargo
66182	1999	DB Cargo
66183	1999	DB Cargo

66185	1999	DB Cargo
66186	1999	DB Cargo
66187	1999	DB Cargo
66188	1999	DB Cargo
66189	1999	Exported
66190	2000	Exported
66191	2000	Exported
66192	2000	DB Cargo
66193	2000	Exported
66194	2000	DB Cargo
66195	2000	Exported
66196	2000	Exported
66197	2000	DB Cargo
66198	2000	DB Cargo
66199	2000	DB Cargo
66200	2000	DB Cargo
66201	2000	Exported
66202	2000	Exported
66203	2000	Exported
66204	2000	Exported
66205	2000	Exported
66206	2000	DB Cargo
66207	2000	DB Cargo
66208	2000	Exported
66209	2000	Exported
66210	2000	Exported
66211	2000	Exported
66212	2000	Exported
66213	2000	Exported
66214	2000	Exported
66215	2000	Exported
66216	2000	Exported
66217	2000	Exported
66218	2000	Exported
66219	2000	Exported
66220	2000	Exported
66221	2000	DB Cargo
66222	2000	Exported
66223	2000	Exported
66224	2000	Exported
66225	2000	Exported
66226	2000	Exported
66227	2000	Exported
66228	2000	Exported
66229	2000	Exported
66230	2000	DB Cargo
66231	2000	Exported
66232	2000	Exported
66233	2000	Exported
66234	2000	Exported
66235	2000	Exported
66236	2000	Exported
66237	2000	Exported
66239	2000	Exported
66240	2000	Exported
66241	2000	Exported
66242	2000	Exported
66243	2000	Exported
66244	2000	Exported
66245	2000	Exported
66246	2000	Exported
66247	2000	Exported
66248	2000	Exported
66249	2000	Exported

66301	2008	Direct Rail Services
66302	2008	Direct Rail Services
66303	2008	Direct Rail Services
66304	2008	Direct Rail Services
66305	2008	Direct Rail Services
66411	2006	Exported
66412	2006	Exported
66413	2006	Freightliner
66414	2006	Freightliner
66415	2006	Freightliner
66416	2006	Freightliner
66417	2006	Exported
66418	2006	Freightliner
66419	2006	Freightliner
66420	2006	Freightliner
66421	2007	Direct Rail Services
66422	2007	Direct Rail Services
66423	2007	Direct Rail Services
66424	2007	Direct Rail Services
66425	2007	Direct Rail Services
66426	2007	Direct Rail Services
66427	2007	Direct Rail Services
66428	2007	Direct Rail Services
66429	2007	Direct Rail Services
66430	2007	Direct Rail Services
66431	2008	Direct Rail Services
66432	2008	Direct Rail Services
66433	2008	Direct Rail Services
66434	2008	Direct Rail Services
66501	1999	Freightliner
66502	1999	Freightliner

▲ The final Class 66 to be built entered service in 2016 and was named "EVENING STAR", in keeping with the final steam locomotive built for British Railways which carried the same name. 66779 pauses at Darlington on a southbound light engine movement on 6 July 2017. It is hoped 66779 will spend considerably more years in main line service than its steam namesake! **Andy Chard**

66503	1999		Freightliner
66504	1999		Freightliner
66505	1999		Freightliner
66506	2000		Freightliner
66507	2000		Freightliner
66508	2000		Freightliner
66509	2000		Freightliner
66510	2000		Freightliner
66511	2000		Freightliner
66512	2000		Freightliner
66513	2000		Freightliner
66514	2000		Freightliner
66515	2000		Freightliner
66516	2000		Freightliner
66517	2000		Freightliner
66518	2000		Freightliner
66519	2000		Freightliner
66520	2000		Freightliner
66521	2000	2001	Scrapped
66522	2000		Freightliner
66523	2000		Freightliner
66524	2000		Freightliner
66525	2000		Freightliner
66526	2001		Freightliner
66527	2001		Exported
66528	2001		Freightliner
66529	2001		Freightliner
66530	2001		Exported
66531	2001		Freightliner
66532	2001		Freightliner
66533	2001		Freightliner
66534	2001		Freightliner
66535	2001		Exported
66536	2001		Freightliner
66537	2001		Freightliner
66538	2001		Freightliner
66539	2001		Freightliner
66540	2001		Freightliner
66541	2001		Freightliner
66542	2001		Freightliner
66543	2001		Freightliner
66544	2001		Freightliner
66545	2001		Freightliner
66546	2001		Freightliner
66547	2001		Freightliner
66548	2001		Freightliner
66549	2001		Freightliner
66550	2001		Freightliner
66551	2001		Freightliner
66552	2001		Freightliner
66553	2001		Freightliner
66554	2002		Freightliner
66555	2002		Freightliner
66556	2002		Freightliner
66557	2002		Freightliner
66558	2002		Freightliner
66559	2002		Freightliner
66560	2002		Freightliner
66561	2002		Freightliner
66562	2002		Freightliner
66563	2003		Freightliner
66564	2003		Freightliner
66565	2003		Freightliner
66566	2003		Freightliner

66567	2003	Freightliner
66568	2003	Freightliner
66569	2003	Freightliner
66570	2003	Freightliner
66571	2003	Freightliner
66572	2003	Freightliner
66582	2007	Exported
66583	2007	Exported
66584	2007	Exported
66585	2007	Freightliner
66586	2007	Exported
66587	2007	Freightliner
66588	2007	Freightliner
66589	2007	Freightliner
66590	2007	Freightliner
66591	2007	Freightliner
66592	2007	Freightliner
66593	2007	Freightliner
66594	2007	Freightliner
66595	2008	Freightliner
66596	2008	Freightliner
66597	2008	Freightliner
66598	2008	Freightliner
66599	2008	Freightliner
66601	2000	Freightliner
66602	2000	Freightliner
66603	2000	Freightliner
66604	2000	Freightliner
66605	2000	Freightliner
66606	2000	Freightliner
66607	2002	Freightliner
66608	2002	Exported
66609	2002	Exported
66610	2002	Freightliner
66611	2002	Exported
66612	2002	Exported
66613	2003	Freightliner
66614	2003	Freightliner
66615	2003	Freightliner
66616	2003	Freightliner
66617	2003	Freightliner
66618	2003	Freightliner
66619	2005	Freightliner
66620	2005	Freightliner
66621	2005	Freightliner
66622	2005	Freightliner
66623	2007	Freightliner
66624	2007	Exported
66625	2007	Exported
66701	2001	GB Railfreight
66702	2001	GB Railfreight
66703	2001	GB Railfreight
66704	2001	GB Railfreight
66705	2001	GB Railfreight
66706	2001	GB Railfreight
66707	2001	GB Railfreight
66708	2002	GB Railfreight
66709	2002	GB Railfreight
66710	2002	GB Railfreight
66711	2002	GB Railfreight
66712	2002	GB Railfreight
66713	2003	GB Railfreight
66714	2003	GB Railfreight
66715	2003	GB Railfreight

66716			2003		GB Railfreight
66717			2003		GB Railfreight
66718			2006		GB Railfreight
66719			2006		GB Railfreight
66720			2006		GB Railfreight
66721			2006		GB Railfreight
66722			2006		GB Railfreight
66723			2006		GB Railfreight
66724			2006		GB Railfreight
66725			2006		GB Railfreight
66726			2006		GB Railfreight
66727			2006		GB Railfreight
66728			2008		GB Railfreight
66729			2008		GB Railfreight
66730			2008		GB Railfreight
66731			2008		GB Railfreight
66732			2008		GB Railfreight
66733	66401		2003		GB Railfreight
66734	66402		2003	2012	Scrapped
66735	66403		2003		GB Railfreight
66736	66404		2003		GB Railfreight
66737	66405		2003		GB Railfreight
66738	66578		2005		GB Railfreight
66739	66579		2005		GB Railfreight
66740	66580		2005		GB Railfreight
66741	66581		2005		GB Railfreight
66742	66841	66406	2003		GB Railfreight
66743	66842	66407	2003		GB Railfreight
66744	66843	66408	2003		GB Railfreight
66745	66844	66409	2003		GB Railfreight
66746	66845	66410	2003		GB Railfreight
66747			2012		GB Railfreight
66748			2012		GB Railfreight
66749			2012		GB Railfreight
66750			2013		GB Railfreight
66751			2013		GB Railfreight
66752			2014		GB Railfreight
66753			2014		GB Railfreight
66754			2014		GB Railfreight
66755			2014		GB Railfreight
66756			2014		GB Railfreight
66757			2014		GB Railfreight
66758			2014		GB Railfreight
66759			2014		GB Railfreight
66760			2014		GB Railfreight
66761			2014		GB Railfreight
66762			2014		GB Railfreight
66763			2014		GB Railfreight
66764			2014		GB Railfreight
66765			2014		GB Railfreight
66766			2014		GB Railfreight
66767			2014		GB Railfreight
66768			2014		GB Railfreight
66769			2014		GB Railfreight
66770			2014		GB Railfreight
66771			2014		GB Railfreight
66772			2014		GB Railfreight
66773			2016		GB Railfreight
66774			2016		GB Railfreight
66775			2016		GB Railfreight
66776			2016		GB Railfreight
66777			2016		GB Railfreight
66778			2016		GB Railfreight
66779			2016		GB Railfreight

66780	66008	1998	GB Railfreight	
66781	66016	1998	GB Railfreight	
66782	66046	1999	GB Railfreight	
66783	66058	1999	GB Railfreight	
66784	66081	1999	GB Railfreight	
66784	66081	1999	GB Railfreight	
66786	66141	1999	GB Railfreight	
66787	66184	1999	GB Railfreight	
66788	66238	2000	GB Railfreight	
66789	66250	2000	GB Railfreight	
66846	66573	2003	Colas Rail	
66847	66574	2003	Colas Rail	
66848	66575	2004	Colas Rail	
66849	66576	2004	Colas Rail	
66850	66577	2004	Colas Rail	
66951		2004	Freightliner	
66952		2004	Freightliner	
66953		2008	Freightliner	
66954		2008	Exported	
66955		2008	Freightliner	
66956		2008	Freightliner	
66957		2008	Freightliner	

CLASS 67   Bo-Bo

Built: 1999–2000 by Alstom, Valencia, Spain.
Engine: GM 12N-710G3B-EC two stroke of 2460 kW (3300 hp) at 904 rpm.
Transmission: Electric.
Maximum Speed: 125 mph.
Train Heating/Supply: Electric.
Train Brakes: Air.

Latest Number Carried	Previous Number 1	Year Entered Service	Year Withdrawn	Current Status	Notes
67001		2000		DB Cargo	
67002		2000		DB Cargo	
67003		1999		DB Cargo	
67004		2000		DB Cargo	
67005		2000		DB Cargo	
67006		2000		DB Cargo	
67007		2000		DB Cargo	
67008		2000		DB Cargo	
67009		2000		DB Cargo	
67010		2000		DB Cargo	
67011		2000		DB Cargo	
67012		2000		DB Cargo	
67013		2000		DB Cargo	
67014		2000		DB Cargo	
67015		2000		DB Cargo	
67016		2000		DB Cargo	
67017		2000		DB Cargo	
67018		2000		DB Cargo	
67019		2000		DB Cargo	
67020		2000		DB Cargo	
67021		2000		DB Cargo	
67022		2000		DB Cargo	
67023		2000		Colas Rail	
67024		2000		DB Cargo	
67025		2000		DB Cargo	
67026		2000		DB Cargo	
67027		2000		Colas Rail	
67028		2000		DB Cargo	
67029		2000		DB Cargo	
67030		2000		DB Cargo	

▲ 67005 "Queen's Messenger" brings up the rear of the 11.12 Taunton–Cardiff Central First Great Western service as it passes Parsons Street, Bristol on 23 July 2009. 67025 is at the head of the train. **John Chalcraft/Rail Photoprints**

▼ At the beginning of its life and only a matter of days after entering service, 68025 "Superb" makes a guest appearance at the Severn Valley Railway Diesel Festival and is seen approaching Bewdley with the empty coaching stock prior to working the 1244 service to Kidderminster on 21 May 2016. **Andy Chard**

CLASS 68   Bo-Bo

Built: 2012–17 by Vossloh, Valencia, Spain.
Engine: Caterpillar C175-16 of 2800 kW (3750 hp) at 1740 rpm.
Transmission: Electric.
Maximum Speed: 100 mph.
Train Heating/Supply: Electric.
Train Brakes: Air.

Latest Number Carried	Previous Number 1	Year Entered Service	Year Withdrawn	Current Status	Notes
68001		2014		Direct Rail Services	
68002		2014		Direct Rail Services	
68003		2014		Direct Rail Services	
68004		2014		Direct Rail Services	
68005		2014		Direct Rail Services	
68006		2014		Direct Rail Services	
68007		2014		Direct Rail Services	
68008		2014		Direct Rail Services	
68009		2014		Direct Rail Services	
68010		2014		Direct Rail Services	
68011		2014		Direct Rail Services	
68012		2014		Direct Rail Services	
68013		2014		Direct Rail Services	
68014		2014		Direct Rail Services	
68015		2014		Direct Rail Services	
68016		2015		Direct Rail Services	
68017		2015		Direct Rail Services	
68018		2015		Direct Rail Services	
68019		2015		Direct Rail Services	
68020		2016		Direct Rail Services	
68021		2016		Direct Rail Services	
68022		2016		Direct Rail Services	
68023		2016		Direct Rail Services	
68024		2016		Direct Rail Services	
68025		2016		Direct Rail Services	
68026		2017		Direct Rail Services	
68027		2017		Direct Rail Services	
68028		2017		Direct Rail Services	
68029		2017		Direct Rail Services	
68030		2017		Direct Rail Services	
68031		2017		Direct Rail Services	
68032		2017		Direct Rail Services	
68033		2017		Direct Rail Services	
68034		2017		Direct Rail Services	

CLASS 70   DIESEL   Co-Co

Built: 2009–17 by General Electric, Erie, Pennsylvania, USA and TULOMSAS, Eskisehir, Turkey (70801).
Engine: General Electric Powerhaul P616LDA1 of 2848 kW (3820 hp) at 1500 rpm.
Transmission: Electric.
Maximum Speed: 75mph.
Train Heating / Supply: None.
Train Brakes: Air.

Latest Number Carried	Previous Number 1	Year Entered Service	Year Withdrawn	Current Status	Notes
70001		2009		Freightliner	
70002		2009		Freightliner	
70003		2009		Freightliner	
70004		2009		Freightliner	
70005		2009		Freightliner	

70006		2009	Freightliner
70007		2011	Freightliner
70008		2011	Freightliner
70009		2011	Freightliner
70010		2011	Freightliner
70011		2011	Freightliner
70012		n/a	Exported	Damaged during unloading in 2011 and returned to USA
70013		2011	Freightliner
70014		2011	Freightliner
70015		2011	Freightliner
70016		2011	Freightliner
70017		2012	Freightliner
70018		2012	Freightliner
70019		2012	Freightliner
70020		2012	Freightliner
70801	70099	2012	Colas Rail
70802		2014	Colas Rail
70803		2014	Colas Rail
70804		2014	Colas Rail
70805		2014	Colas Rail
70806		2014	Colas Rail
70807		2014	Colas Rail
70808		2014	Colas Rail
70809		2014	Colas Rail
70810		2014	Colas Rail
70811		2017	Colas Rail
70812		2017	Colas Rail
70813		2017	Colas Rail
70814		2017	Colas Rail
70815		2017	Colas Rail
70816		2017	Colas Rail
70817		2017	Colas Rail

▲ Freightliner 70002 receives a wash and brush up at Ipswich stabling point on 13 November 2012.   **John Chalcraft/Rail Photoprints**

3. ELECTRIC LOCOMOTIVES

3.1. ELECTRIC LOCOMOTIVES WITH PRE-TOPS CLASSIFICATION

CLASS ES1   Bo-Bo

Built: 1903 by North Eastern Railway.
Electric Supply System: 600 V DC overhead or third rail.
Power Output: 477 kW (640 hp).
Maximum Speed: 25 mph.
Train Heating/Supply: None.

Latest Number Carried	Previous Number 1	Previous Number 2	Year Entered Service	Year Withdrawn	Current Status	Notes
26500	6480	1	1903	1964	Preserved	
26501	6481	2	1903	1964	Scrapped	

CLASS EB1   Bo-Bo

Built: 1915–20 by North Eastern Railway.
Electric Supply System: 1500 V DC overhead.
Power Output: 205 kW (1100 hp).
Maximum Speed: 45 mph.
Train Heating/Supply: None.

Latest Number Carried	Previous Number 1	Previous Number 2	Year Entered Service	Year Withdrawn	Current Status	Notes
26502	6490		1915	1950	Scrapped	
26503	6491		1915	1950	Scrapped	
26504	6492		1915	1950	Scrapped	
26505	6493		1915	1950	Scrapped	
26506	6494		1915	1950	Scrapped	
26507	6495		1915	1950	Scrapped	
26508	6496		1915	1950	Scrapped	
26509	6497		1915	1950	Scrapped	
100	26510	6498	1915	1950	Scrapped	
26511	6499		1920	1950	Scrapped	
26600	26999	6999	1922	1950	Scrapped	

▲ 1903 vintage North Eastern Railway 600 V DC electric Class ES1 26500 is seen in the company of a pair of steam locomotives at Heaton depot on 15 April 1957. **Rail Photoprints Collection**

▼ A rather grainy image but quite possibly the last ever taken of North Eastern Railway Class EB1 locomotives 26509, 26507 and 26502. They are seen awaiting their fate in Wanty & Co's scrapyard at Catcliffe, Sheffield on 24 March 1951. **Rail Photoprints Collection**

3.2. ELECTRIC LOCOMOTIVES WITH TOPS CLASSIFICATION

CLASS 70   ELECTRIC   Co-Co

Built: 1941–48 by Southern Railway, Ashford and British Railways, Brighton.
Electric Supply System: 660–750 V DC third rail or overhead.
Power Output: 1097 kW (1470 hp).
Maximum Speed: 75 mph.
Train Heating/Supply: Steam heating.
Train Brakes: Vacuum.

Latest Number Carried	Previous Number 1	Year Entered Service	Year Withdrawn	Current Status	Notes
20001	CC1	1941	1969	Scrapped	
20002	CC2	1945	1968	Scrapped	
20003		1948	1968	Scrapped	

CLASS 71   Bo-Bo

Built: 1958–60 by British Railways, Doncaster Works.
Electric Supply System: 660–750 V DC third rail or overhead.
Power Output: 1715 kW (2300 hp).
Maximum Speed: 90 mph.
Train Heating/Supply: Electric.
Train Brakes: Dual braked (air & vacuum).

Latest Number Carried	Previous Number 1	Year Entered Service	Year Withdrawn	Current Status	Notes
E5024	E5000	1958	1968	Converted	Converted to Class 74 E6104 in 1968
71001	E5001	1959	1977	Preserved	
71002	E5002	1959	1977	Scrapped	
E5003		1959	1968	Converted	Converted to Class 74 E6107 in 1968
71004	E5004	1959	1977	Scrapped	
E5005		1959	1968	Converted	Converted to Class 74 E6108 in 1968
E5006		1959	1967	Converted	Converted to Class 74 E6103 in 1967
71007	E5007	1959	1977	Scrapped	
71008	E5008	1959	1977	Scrapped	
71009	E5009	1959	1977	Scrapped	
71010	E5010	1959	1977	Scrapped	
71011	E5011	1959	1977	Scrapped	
71012	E5012	1959	1977	Scrapped	
71013	E5013	1959	1977	Scrapped	
71014	E5014	1960	1977	Scrapped	
E5015		1960	1968	Converted	Converted to Class 74 E6101 in 1968
E5016		1960	1967	Converted	Converted to Class 74 E6102 in 1967
E5017		1960	1968	Converted	Converted to Class 74 E6109 in 1968
71003	E5018	1960	1977	Scrapped	
E5019		1960	1968	Converted	Converted to Class 74 E6105 in 1968
71005	E5020	1960	1977	Scrapped	
E5021		1960	1968	Converted	Converted to Class 74 E6110 in 1968
71006	E5022	1960	1977	Scrapped	
E5023		1960	1968	Converted	Converted to Class 74 E6106 in 1968

▲ Class 70 electric 20003 stands at London Victoria on 15 May 1949 at the head of a boat train bound for Newhaven. **Rail Photoprints Collection**

▼ Class 71 E5017 passes Aylesford, Kent with an "up" freight in August 1963. This locomotive was subsequently converted to Class 74 electro-diesel E6109 in 1968.

Dave Cobbe Collection/Rail Photoprints

CLASS 73   Bo-Bo

Built: 1962–67 by British Railways, Eastleigh Works (73001–73006) and English Electric, Vulcan Foundry, Newton-le-Willows (all except 73001–73006).
Diesel Engine: English Electric 4SRKT of 447 kW (600 hp) at 850 rpm.
Electric Supply System: 660–750 V DC third rail.
Power Output: Electric 1060 kW (1420 hp).
Maximum Speed: 80 mph.
Train Heating/Supply: Electric.
Train Brakes: Triple braked (air, vacuum and electro-pneumatic).

Class 73/0

Latest Number Carried	Previous Number 1	Previous Number 2	Previous Number 3	Year Entered Service	Year Withdrawn	Current Status	Notes
73001	73901	73001	E6001	1962	2000	Preserved	
73002	E6002			1962	1995	Preserved	
73003	E6003			1962	1996	Preserved	
73004	E6004			1962	1991	Scrapped	
73005	E6005			1962	2015	Converted	Converted to 73966 in 2015

Class 73/1
Details as Class 73/0 except:
Maximum Speed: 90 mph.

Latest Number Carried	Previous Number 1	Previous Number 2	Previous Number 3	Year Entered Service	Year Withdrawn	Current Status	Notes
73101	73100	73101	E6007	1965		Loram UK	
73103	E6009			1965	2016	Converted	Converted to 73970 in 2016
73104	E6010			1965	2015	Converted	Converted to 73951 in 2015
73105	E6011			1965	2016	Converted	Converted to 73969 in 2016
73106	E6012			1965	2000	Scrapped	
73107	E6013			1965		GB Railfreight	
73108	E6014			1966	2002	Scrapped	
73109	E6015			1966		GB Railfreight	
73110	E6016			1966		GB Railfreight	
73111	E6017			1966	1991	Scrapped	
73114	E6020			1966		Nemesis Rail	
73115	E6021			1966	1982	Scrapped	
73117	E6023			1966	2015	Converted	Converted to 73968 in 2015
73118	E6024			1966		Preserved	
73119	E6025			1966		GB Railfreight	
E6027				1966	1972	Scrapped	
73126	E6033			1966	1999	Scrapped	
73128	E6035			1966		GB Railfreight	
73129	E6036			1966	2002	Preserved	
73130	E6037			1966		Preserved	
73131	E6038			1966	2003	Scrapped	
73132	E6039			1966	2003	Scrapped	
73133	E6040			1966		Transmart Trains	
73134	E6041			1966		GB Railfreight	
73136	E6043			1966		GB Railfreight	
73138	E6045			1966		Network Rail	
73139	E6046			1966		Loram UK	
73140	E6047			1966	1998	Preserved	
73141	E6048			1966		GB Railfreight	
73201	73142	E6049		1967		GB Railfreight	
73202	73137	E6044		1966		Southern	
73203	73127	E6034		1966	2001	Scrapped	
73204	73125	E6032		1966	2014	Converted	Converted to 73962 in 2014
73205	73124	E6031		1966	2015	Converted	Converted to 73964 in 2015
73206	73123	E6030		1966	2014	Converted	Converted to 73963 in 2014
73207	73122	E6029		1966	2016	Converted	Converted to 73971 in 2016
73208	73121	E6028		1966	2015	Converted	Converted to 73965 in 2015
73209	73120	E6026		1966	2014	Converted	Converted to 73961 in 2014

▲ In distinctive Network Rail yellow livery, 73138 approaches Clapham Junction, while working a Derby RTC to London Waterloo test train on 11 February 2016. 73107 is bringing up the rear.

Paul Gerrard

▼ Large electro-diesel E6101 (later 74001) is seen at Clapham Junction in September 1969.

Dave Cobbe Collection/Rail Photoprints

73210	73116	E6022	1966	2002	Preserved	
73211	73113	E6019	1966	2014	Converted	Converted to 73952 in 2014
73212	73102	E6008	1965		GB Railfreight	
73213	73112	E6018	1966		GB Railfreight	
73235	73135	E6042	1966		South Western Railway	
73906	73006	E6006	1962	2015	Converted	Converted to 73967 in 2015

Class 73/9 (RVEL)

Rebuilt: 2013–15 by RVEL Derby.
Diesel Engine: Two Cummins QSK19 of 560 kW (750 hp) at 1800 rpm (total 1120 kW, 1500 hp).
Electric Supply System: 750 V DC Third Rail.
Power Output: Electric 1060 kW (1420 hp).
Train Heating/Supply: Not fitted.
Train Brakes: Air.

Latest Number Carried	Previous Number 1	Year Entered Service	Year Withdrawn	Current Status	Notes
73951	73104	2015		Network Rail	
73952	73211	2014		Network Rail	

Class 73/9 (GBRf)

Rebuilt: 2014–16 by Brush, Loughborough.
Diesel Engine: MTU 8V4000 R43L of 1195 kW (1600 hp) at 1800 rpm.
Electric Supply System: 750 V DC Third Rail.
Power Output: Electric 1060 kW (1420 hp).
Train Heating/Supply: Electric.
Train Brakes: Air.

Latest Number Carried	Previous Number 1	Year Entered Service	Year Withdrawn	Current Status	Notes
73961	73209	2014		GB Railfreight	
73962	73204	2014		GB Railfreight	
73963	73206	2014		GB Railfreight	
73964	73205	2015		GB Railfreight	
73965	73208	2015		GB Railfreight	
73966	73005	2015		GB Railfreight	
73967	73906	2015		GB Railfreight	
73968	73117	2015		GB Railfreight	
73969	73105	2016		GB Railfreight	
73970	73103	2016		GB Railfreight	
73971	73207	2016		GB Railfreight	

CLASS 74

10 Locomotives were converted from Class 71 locomotives to Class 74 electro-diesel locomotives. Overhead supply equipment removed.

Technical details as Class 71 except:
Conversions Completed: 1967–68
Engine: Paxman 6YJXL of 485 kW (650 hp).

Latest Number Carried	Previous Number 1	Year Entered Service	Year Withdrawn	Current Status	Notes
74001	E6101	1968	1977	Scrapped	
74002	E6102	1967	1977	Scrapped	
74003	E6103	1967	1977	Scrapped	
74004	E6104	1968	1977	Scrapped	
74005	E6105	1968	1977	Scrapped	
74006	E6106	1968	1976	Scrapped	
74007	E6107	1968	1977	Scrapped	
74008	E6108	1968	1977	Scrapped	
74009	E6109	1968	1977	Scrapped	
74010	E6110	1968	1977	Scrapped	

CLASS 76

Bo+Bo

Built: 1941–53 by LNER at Doncaster Works and British Railways, Gorton Works.
Electric Supply System: 1500V DC overhead.
Power Output: 970 kW (1300 hp).
Maximum Speed: 65 mph.
Train Heating/Supply: E26000/E26050–057 were built with steam heating. It was also later fitted to E26020/E26046–049.
Train Brakes: Built vacuum braked some were later converted to air or dual (air & vacuum).

Latest Number Carried	Previous Number 1	Previous Number 2	Year Entered Service	Year Withdrawn	Current Status	Notes
26000	6000	6701	1941	1970	Scrapped	
76001	26001		1950	1980	Scrapped	
76002	26002		1950	1978	Scrapped	
76003[2]	76036	26036	1952	1981	Scrapped	Second of 2 locomotives to be numbered 76003. First of 2 locomotives to be numbered 76036
76004	26004		1951	1978	Scrapped	
26005			1951	1970	Scrapped	
76006	26006		1951	1981	Scrapped	
76007	26007		1951	1981	Scrapped	
76008	26008		1951	1981	Scrapped	
76009	26009		1951	1981	Scrapped	
76010	26010		1951	1981	Scrapped	
76011	26011		1951	1981	Scrapped	
76012	26012		1951	1981	Scrapped	
76013	26013		1951	1981	Scrapped	
76014	26014		1951	1981	Scrapped	
76015	26015		1951	1981	Scrapped	
76016	26016		1951	1981	Scrapped	
26017			1951	1970	Scrapped	
26019			1951	1971	Scrapped	
76020	26020		1951	1977	Preserved	
76021	26021		1951	1981	Scrapped	
76022	26022		1951	1981	Scrapped	
76023	26023		1951	1981	Scrapped	
76024	26024		1951	1981	Scrapped	
76025	26025		1952	1981	Scrapped	
76026	26026		1952	1981	Scrapped	
76027	26027		1952	1981	Scrapped	
76028	26028		1952	1981	Scrapped	
76029	26029		1951	1981	Scrapped	
76030	26030		1951	1971	Scrapped	
26031			1952	1981	Scrapped	
76031	76044	26044	1952	1981	Scrapped	
76032	26032		1952	1981	Scrapped	
76033	26033		1952	1981	Scrapped	
76034	26034		1952	1981	Scrapped	
26035			1952	1970	Scrapped	
76035	76018	26018	1951	1981	Scrapped	
76036[2]	76003	26003	1950	1981	Scrapped	Second of 2 locomotives to be numbered 76036 First of 2 locomotives to be numbered 76003
76037	26037		1952	1981	Scrapped	
76038[2]	76050	26050	1952	1981	Scrapped	Second of 2 locomotives to be numbered 76038
76039[2]	76048	26048	1952	1981	Scrapped	Second of 2 locomotives to be numbered 76039 First of 2 locomotives to be numbered 76048 The cab remains
76040	26040		1952	1981	Scrapped	
76041	26041		1952	1980	Scrapped	
26042			1952	1970	Scrapped	
76043	26043		1952	1978	Scrapped	
26045			1952	1971	Scrapped	
76046	26046		1952	1980	Scrapped	

76047	26047		1952	1980	Scrapped	
76048[2]	76039	26039	1952	1977	Scrapped	Second of 2 locomotives to be numbered 76048. First of 2 locomotives to be numbered 76039. The cab remains
76049	26049		1952	1980	Scrapped	
76050	76038	26038	1952	1977	Scrapped	First of 2 locomotives to be numbered 76038
76051	26051		1953	1981	Scrapped	
76052	26052		1953	1978	Scrapped	
76053	26053		1953	1980	Scrapped	
76054	26054		1953	1981	Scrapped	
76055	26055		1953	1977	Scrapped	
76056	26056		1953	1978	Scrapped	
76057	26057		1953	1977	Scrapped	

CLASS 77 (EM2)   Co-Co

Built: 1953–54 by British Railways, Gorton Works.
Electric Supply System: 1500V DC overhead.
Power Output: 1716 kW (2300 hp).
Maximum Speed: 90 mph.
Train Heating/Supply: Steam.
Train Brakes: Vacuum.

After withdrawal from BR in 1968, all seven locos were exported to the Netherlands where four were subsequently scrapped. Two later returned to the UK, where they are now preserved.

Latest Number Carried	Previous Number 1	Previous Number 2	Year Entered Service	Year Withdrawn	Current Status	Notes
1502	E27000	27000	1953	1968	Preserved	
1505	E27001	27001	1954	1968	Preserved	
1506	E27002	27002	1954	1968	Scrapped	
1501	E27003	27003	1954	1968	Exported	
1503	E27004	27004	1954	1968	Scrapped	
E27005	27005		1954	1968	Scrapped	
1504	E27006	27006	1954	1968	Scrapped	

CLASS 81   Bo-Bo

Built: 1959–64 by Birmingham Railway Carriage and Wagon Company.
Electric Supply System: 25 kV AC overhead.
Power Output: 2390 kW (3200 hp).
Maximum Speed: 100 mph.
Train Heating/Supply: Electric.
Train Brakes: Built vacuum braked, most converted to dual braked (air & vacuum brakes).

Latest Number Carried	Previous Number 1	Previous Number 2	Year Entered Service	Year Withdrawn	Current Status	Notes
81001	E3001		1959	1984	Scrapped	
E3002			1960	1968	Scrapped	
81002	E3003		1960	1990	Preserved	
81003	E3004		1960	1988	Scrapped	
81004	E3005		1960	1990	Scrapped	
81005	E3006		1960	1989	Scrapped	
81006	E3007		1960	1988	Scrapped	
81007	E3008		1960	1989	Scrapped	
E3009			1960	1968	Scrapped	
81008	E3010		1960	1988	Scrapped	
81009	E3011		1960	1990	Scrapped	
81010	E3012		1960	1990	Scrapped	
81011	E3013		1960	1989	Scrapped	
81012	E3014		1960	1991	Scrapped	
81013	E3015		1960	1989	Scrapped	
81014	E3016		1961	1988	Scrapped	

▲ Class 77 (EM2) 27000 "ELECTRA" basks in the sun at Sheffield Victoria circa 1968. Built to operate from 1500 V DC overhead supply, all seven EM2 locomotives were sold to Netherlands Railways not long after this photograph was taken. 27000 was subsequently secured for Preservation and repatriated to the UK. **Colin Whitfield/Rail Photoprints**

▼ E3017 (later 81015) climbs Camden Bank as it accelerates away from London Euston at the head of an express service to the North-West. **Dave Cobbe Collection/Rail Photoprints**

81015	E3017		1961	1984	Scrapped
81016	E3018		1961	1983	Scrapped
E3019			1961	1971	Scrapped
81017	E3020		1961	1991	Scrapped
81018	E3021		1961	1986	Scrapped
81019	E3022		1961	1989	Scrapped
81020	E3023		1961	1987	Scrapped
81021	E3096	E3301	1962	1987	Scrapped
81022	E3097		1964	1987	Scrapped

CLASS 82 Bo-Bo

Built: 1960–62 by Beyer Peacock & Co., Manchester
Electric Supply System: 25 kV AC overhead.
Power Output: 2460 kW (3300 hp).
Maximum Speed: 100 mph.
Train Heating/Supply: Electric.
Train Brakes: Built vacuum braked, most converted to dual braked (air & vacuum).

Latest Number Carried	Previous Number 1	Year Entered Service	Year Withdrawn	Current Status	Notes
E3046		1960	1971	Scrapped	
82001	E3047	1960	1983	Scrapped	
82002	E3048	1960	1983	Scrapped	
82003	E3049	1960	1983	Scrapped	
82004	E3050	1960	1983	Scrapped	
82005	E3051	1960	1987	Scrapped	
82006	E3052	1960	1983	Scrapped	
82007	E3053	1962	1983	Scrapped	
82008	E3054	1961	1987	Preserved	
E3055		1962	1969	Scrapped	

CLASS 83 Bo-Bo

Built: 1960–62 by English Electric, Vulcan Foundry, Newton-le-Willows.
Electric Supply System: 25 kV AC overhead.
Power Output: 2200 kW (2950 hp).
Maximum Speed: 100 mph.
Train Heating/Supply: Electric.
Train Brakes: Built vacuum braked, all converted to dual braked (air & vacuum).

Latest Number Carried	Previous Number 1	Previous Number 2	Year Entered Service	Year Withdrawn	Current Status	Notes
83001	E3024		1960	1983	Scrapped	
83002	E3025		1960	1983	Scrapped	
83003	E3026		1960	1975	Scrapped	
83004	E3027		1960	1978	Scrapped	
83005	E3028		1960	1983	Scrapped	
83006	E3029		1960	1983	Scrapped	
83007	E3030		1960	1983	Scrapped	
83008	E3031		1960	1983	Scrapped	
83009	E3032		1960	1989	Scrapped	
83010	E3033		1960	1983	Scrapped	
83011	E3034		1961	1983	Scrapped	
83012	E3035		1961	1989	Preserved	
83013	E3098	E3303	1961	1983	Scrapped	
83014	E3099	E3304	1961	1983	Scrapped	
83015	E3100		1962	1988	Scrapped	

▲ With Its bodywork tarnished due to constant visits to the Euston carriage washing plant, 83012 awaits its next duty at the London terminus in March 1989. **Colin Whitfield/Rail Photoprints**

▼ A pair of nearly new AC electric locomotives, E3040 (later 84005) and E3024 (later 83001) stand at the south end of Crewe station in September 1960. **Colin Whitfield/Rail Photoprints**

CLASS 84 — Bo-Bo

Built: 1960–61 by North British Locomotive Company, Glasgow.
Electric Supply System: 25 kV AC overhead.
Power Output: 2312 kW (3100 hp).
Maximum Speed: 100 mph.
Train Heating/Supply: Electric.
Train Brakes: Built vacuum braked, all converted to dual braked (air & vacuum).

Latest Number Carried	Previous Number 1	Previous Number 2	Year Entered Service	Year Withdrawn	Current Status	Notes
84001	E3036		1960	1979	Preserved	
84002	E3037		1960	1980	Scrapped	
84003	E3038		1960	1980	Scrapped	
84004	E3039		1960	1977	Scrapped	
84005	E3040		1960	1977	Scrapped	
84006	E3041		1960	1978	Scrapped	
84007	E3042		1960	1977	Scrapped	
84008	E3043		1960	1979	Scrapped	
ADB968021	84009	E3044	1960	1995	Scrapped	Locomotive was not self-propelled whilst in departmental use. The cab remains
84010	E3045		1961	1980	Scrapped	

CLASS 85 — Bo-Bo

Built: 1961–64 by British Railways, Doncaster Works.
Electric Supply System: 25 kV AC overhead.
Power Output: 2390 kW (3200 hp).
Maximum Speed: 100 mph.
Train Heating/Supply: Electric.
Train Brakes: Built vacuum braked, all converted to dual braked (air & vacuum).

Latest Number Carried	Previous Number 1	Previous Number 2	Previous Number 3	Year Entered Service	Year Withdrawn	Current Status	Notes
85001	E3056			1961	1985	Scrapped	
85002	E3057			1961	1989	Scrapped	
85005	E3060			1961	1990	Scrapped	
85006	85101	85006	E3061	1961	1992	Preserved	
85008	E3063			1961	1990	Scrapped	
85013	E3068			1962	1990	Scrapped	
85014	E3069			1962	1989	Scrapped	
85015	E3070			1962	1990	Scrapped	
85017	E3072			1962	1987	Scrapped	
85018	E3073			1963	1991	Scrapped	
85019	E3074			1962	1989	Scrapped	
85020	E3075			1963	1990	Scrapped	
85022	E3077			1963	1989	Scrapped	
85023	E3078			1963	1990	Scrapped	
85025	E3080			1963	1990	Scrapped	
85026	E3081			1963	1990	Scrapped	
85027	E3082			1963	1983	Scrapped	
85028	E3083			1963	1990	Scrapped	
85029	E3084			1964	1988	Scrapped	
85030	E3085			1964	1990	Scrapped	
85031	E3086			1962	1990	Scrapped	
85033	E3088			1963	1984	Scrapped	
85034	E3089			1963	1990	Scrapped	
85037	E3092			1964	1990	Scrapped	
85038	E3093			1963	1990	Scrapped	
85039	E3094			1964	1987	Scrapped	

85040	E3095		1964	1991	Scrapped
85102	85009	E3064	1961	1991	Scrapped
85103	85010	E3065	1961	1991	Scrapped
85104	85012	E3067	1962	1991	Scrapped
85105	85016	E3071	1962	1991	Scrapped
85106	85021	E3076	1963	1990	Scrapped
85107	85024	E3079	1963	1990	Scrapped
85108	85032	E3087	1962	1991	Scrapped
85109	85035	E3090	1963	1991	Scrapped
85110	85036	E3091	1963	1991	Scrapped
85111	85004	E3059	1961	1990	Scrapped
85112	85007	E3062	1961	1991	Scrapped
85113	85003	E3058	1961	1991	Scrapped
85114	85011	E3066	1962	1991	Scrapped

▲ In the twilight years of their lives, Class 85 85021 and Class 81 81007 are seen stabled at Carlisle Citadel on 23 April 1989. Both locomotives would be withdrawn within two years.

John Chalcraft/Rail Photoprints

CLASS 86 Bo-Bo

Built: 1965–66 by British Railways, Doncaster Works and English Electric, Vulcan Foundry, Newton-le-Willows.
Electric Supply System: 25 kV AC overhead.
Power Output: 2680 kW (3600 hp).
Maximum Speed: 100 mph.
Train Heating/Supply: Electric.
Train Brakes: Dual braked (vacuum and air).

Class 86/0
Locos as built to technical specification above. All locos subsequently modified and renumbered - see below.

Class 86/1
Fitted with new bogies.
Details as Class 86/0 except:
Power Output: 5860 kW (5000 hp).
Maximum Speed: 110 mph.

Latest Number Carried	Previous Number 1	Previous Number 2	Previous Number 3	Year Entered Service	Year Withdrawn	Current Status	Notes
86101	86201	E3191		1965		GB Railfreight	Preserved locomotive on hire to GBRf
86102	86202	E3150		1966	2002	Scrapped	
86103	86203	E3143		1966	1995	Scrapped	

Class 86/2
Fitted with flexicoil suspension.
Details as Class 86/0 except:
Power Output: 3010 kW (4040 hp).

Latest Number Carried	Previous Number 1	Previous Number 2	Previous Number 3	Year Entered Service	Year Withdrawn	Current Status	Notes
86204	E3173			1965	1998	Scrapped	
86206	E3184			1965	2002	Scrapped	
86207	E3179			1965	2002	Scrapped	
86208	E3141			1966	2000	Scrapped	
86209	E3125			1965	2004	Scrapped	
86211	E3147			1966	1986	Scrapped	
86212	E3151			1966	2003	Scrapped	
86213	E3193			1965	1998	Exported	
86214	E3106			1965	2002	Scrapped	
86215	E3165			1965	2004	Exported	
86216	E3166			1965	1998	Scrapped	
86217	86504	86217	E3177	1965	2004	Exported	
86218	E3175			1965	2004	Exported	
86219	E3196			1965	1996	Scrapped	
86220	E3156			1966	2002	Scrapped	
86221	E3132			1965	2003	Scrapped	
86222	86502	86222	E3131	1966	2002	Scrapped	
86223	E3158			1966	2004	Scrapped	
86224	E3134			1965	2002	Scrapped	
86225	E3164			1965	2002	Scrapped	
86226	E3162			1965	2002	Scrapped	
86227	E3117			1965	2004	Scrapped	
86228	E3167			1965	2003	Exported	
86229	E3119			1965	2003	Europhoenix	
86230	E3168			1965	2004	Scrapped	
86231	E3126			1965	2002	Exported	
86232	E3113			1965	2005	Exported	
86233	86506	86233	E3172	1965	2003	Exported	
86234	E3155			1966	2005	Exported	
86235	E3194			1966	2005	Exported	
86236	E3133			1965	2002	Scrapped	

86237	E3197			1966	2004	Scrapped	
86238	E3116			1965	2004	Scrapped	
86239	86507	86239	E3169	1965	1996	Scrapped	
86240	E3127			1965	2002	Scrapped	
86241	86508	86241	E3121	1965	2000	Scrapped	
86242	E3138			1966	2004	Exported	
86243	E3181			1965	2002	Scrapped	
86244	E3178			1965	2002	Scrapped	
86245	E3182			1965	2003	Scrapped	
86246	86505	86246	E3149	1966	2004	Scrapped	
86247	E3192			1965	2003	Scrapped	The cab remains
86248	E3107			1965	2002	Exported	
86249	E3161			1965	2003	Scrapped	
86250	E3189			1965	2004	Exported	
86251	E3183			1965	2002	Europhoenix	
86252	E3101			1965	2002	Scrapped	
86254	86047	E3142		1966	2002	Scrapped	
86255	86042	E3154		1966	1998	Scrapped	
86256	86040	E3135		1966	2002	Scrapped	
86257	86043	E3139		1966	2002	Scrapped	
86258	86501	86258	86046	1966	2002	Scrapped	First of 2 locomotives to be numbered 86501. Also carried previous number 4: E3140
86259	86045	E3137		1966		Rail Operations Group	Preserved locomotive on hire to ROG
86261	86041	E3118		1965	2002	Scrapped	

▲ 86242 in its distinctive Anglia Railways livery, awaits departure from Norwich with the 15.00 service to Ipswich on 18 August 2004. Services were terminating at Ipswich that day rather than running through to London Liverpool Street because of engineering work in Ipswich Tunnel.

John Chalcraft/Rail Photoprints

Class 86/4
Details as Class 86/2 except:
Power Output: 2680 kW (3600 hp).

Latest Number Carried	Previous Number 1	Previous Number 2	Previous Number 3	Year Entered Service	Year Withdrawn	Current Status	Notes
86401	86001	E3199		1966		GB Railfreight	Preserved locomotive on hire to GBRf
86416	86616	86416	86316	1965	2002	Scrapped	Also carried previous number 4: 86016 and previous number 5: E3109
86417	86317	86017	E3146	1966	2001	Scrapped	
86419	86319	86019	E3120	1965	1999	Scrapped	
86424	86324	86024	E3111	1965	2002	Exported	
86425	86325	86025	E3186	1965	2002	Scrapped	
86426	86326	86026	E3195	1965	2004	Scrapped	
86429	86329	86029	E3200	1966	1986	Scrapped	
86430	86030		E3105	1965	2004	Scrapped	

Class 86/6
Electric Train Supply isolated.
Details as Class 86/2 except:
Maximum Speed: 75 mph.

Latest Number Carried	Previous Number 1	Previous Number 2	Previous Number 3	Previous Number 4	Year Entered Service	Year Withdrawn	Current Status	Notes
86602	86402	86002	E3170		1965	2005	Scrapped	
86603	86403	86003	E3115		1965	1999	Scrapped	
86604	86404	86004	E3103		1965		Freightliner	
86605	86405	86605	86405	86005	1965		Freightliner	Also carried previous number 5: E3185
86606	86406	86006	E3112		1965	2003	Scrapped	
86607	86407	86007	E3176		1965		Freightliner	
86608	86501[2]	86408	86002	E3180	1965		Freightliner	Second of 2 locomotives to be numbered 86501
86609	86409	86009	E3102		1965		Freightliner	
86610	86410	86010	E3104		1965		Freightliner	
86611	86411	86611	86411	86311	1965	2003	Scrapped	Also carried previous number 5: 86011 and previous number 6: E3171
86612	86412	86312	86012	E3122	1965		Freightliner	
86613	86413	86313	86013	E3128	1965		Freightliner	
86614	86414	86614	86414	86314	1966		Freightliner	Also carried previous number 5: 86014 and previous number 6: E3145
86615	86415	86615	86415	86315	1965	2005	Scrapped	Also carried previous number 5: 86015 and previous number 6: E3123
86618	86418	86318	86018	E3163	1965	2001	Scrapped	
86620	86420	86320	86020	E3114	1965	2005	Scrapped	
86621	86421	86321	86021	E3157	1966	2011	Scrapped	
86622	86422	86322	86022	E3174	1965		Freightliner	
86623	86423	86323	86023	E3152	1966	2003	Scrapped	
86627	86427	86327	86027	E3110	1965		Freightliner	
86628	86428	86628	86428	86328	1966		Freightliner	Also carried previous number 5: 86028 and previous number 6: E3159
86631	86431	86631	86431	86031	1965	2003	Scrapped	Also carried previous number 5: E3188
86632	86432	86032	E3148		1966		Freightliner	

86633	86433	86033	E3198		1966	2004	Scrapped
86634	86434	86004	E3187		1965	2002	Scrapped
86635	86435	86035	E3124		1965	2004	Scrapped
86636	86436	86036	E3160		1966	2000	Scrapped
86637	86437	86037	E3130		1965		Freightliner
86638	86438	86038	E3108		1965		Freightliner
86639	86439	86039	E3153		1966		Freightliner

Class 86/7
Refurbished locos.
Details as Class 86/2 except:
Maximum Speed: 110 mph.

Latest Number Carried	Previous Number 1	Previous Number 2	Previous Number 3	Year Entered Service	Year Withdrawn	Current Status	Notes
86701	86503	86205	E3129	1965	2016	Exported	
86702	86260	86048	E3144	1966	2016	Exported	

Class 86/9
Rebuilt locos. Electric Train Supply isolated.
Details as Class 86/2 except:
Maximum Speed: 60 mph.

Latest Number Carried	Previous Number 1	Previous Number 2	Previous Number 3	Year Entered Service	Year Withdrawn	Current Status	Notes
86901	86253	86044	E3136	1965	2011	Freightliner	
86902	86210	E3190		1965	2011	Scrapped	

CLASS 87   Bo-Bo

Built: 1973–75 by BREL, Crewe Works.
Electric Supply System: 25 kV AC overhead.
Power Output: 3730 kW (5000 hp).
Maximum Speed: 110 mph.
Train Heating/Supply: Electric.
Train Brakes: Air.

Class 87/0

Latest Number Carried	Previous Number 1	Year Entered Service	Year Withdrawn	Current Status	Notes
87001		1973	2005	Preserved	
87002		1973		GB Railfreight	Preserved locomotive on hire to GBRf
87003		1973	2005	Exported	
87004		1973	2005	Exported	
87005		1973	2003	Scrapped	
87006		1973	2006	Exported	
87007		1973	2007	Exported	
87008		1973	2006	Exported	
87009		1973	2004	Exported	
87010		1973	2005	Exported	
87011		1974	2003	Scrapped	
87012		1974	2006	Exported	
87013		1974	2005	Exported	
87014		1974	2005	Exported	
87015		1974	2004	Scrapped	
87016		1974	2004	Scrapped	
87017		1974	2003	Exported	
87018		1974	2004	Scrapped	
87019		1974	2006	Exported	
87020		1974	2003	Exported	
87021		1974	2005	Scrapped	
87022		1974	2008	Exported	

▲ Class 87 87006 "City of Glasgow" received a unique variation of British Rail's large logo livery in 1984. It is seen on display at Crewe Works wearing its rather grubby "new" livery on 2 June 1984. The variation didn't catch on and no other locomotives were painted in this livery.

Brian Robbins/Rail Photoprints

▼ 88002 "Prometheus" and 68025 "Superb" pass Tebay in charge of 1Z39, the "Settle and Carlisle Pioneer" railtour from Didcot Parkway to Appleby on 27 May 2017. The locos were attached at Crewe and this was the first time a Class 88 had worked a passenger train. **Paul Gerrard**

87023	1974	2005	Exported	
87024	1974	2004	Scrapped	
87025	1974	2004	Exported	
87026	1974	2006	Exported	
87027	1974	2004	Scrapped	
87028	1974	2007	Exported	
87029	1974	2004	Exported	
87030	1974	2005	Scrapped	
87031	1974	2005	Scrapped	
87032	1974	2004	Scrapped	
87033	1974	2005	Exported	
87034	1974	2003	Exported	
87035	1974	2005	Preserved	

Class 87/1
Fitted with thyristor power control system.
Details as Class 87/0.

Latest Number Carried	Previous Number 1	Year Entered Service	Year Withdrawn	Current Status	Notes
87101		1975	1999	Scrapped	

CLASS 88   Bo-Bo

Built: 2015–16 by Stadler, Valencia, Spain.
Diesel Engine: Caterpillar C27 of 708 kW (950 hp) at 1750 rpm.
Electric Supply System: 25 kV AC overhead.
Power Output: 4000 kW (5360 hp).
Maximum Speed: 100 mph.
Train Heating/Supply: Electric.
Train Brakes: Air.

Latest Number Carried	Previous Number 1	Year Entered Service	Year Withdrawn	Current Status	Notes
88001		2017		Direct Rail Services	
88002		2017		Direct Rail Services	
88003		2017		Direct Rail Services	
88004		2017		Direct Rail Services	
88005		2017		Direct Rail Services	
88006		2017		Direct Rail Services	
88007		2017		Direct Rail Services	
88008		2017		Direct Rail Services	
88009		2017		Direct Rail Services	
88010		2017		Direct Rail Services	

CLASS 89   Co-Co

Built: 1987 by BREL, Crewe Works.
Electric Supply System: 25 kV AC overhead.
Power Output: 4350 kW (5850 hp).
Maximum Speed: 125 mph.
Train Heating/Supply: Electric.
Train Brakes: Air.

Latest Number Carried	Previous Number 1	Year Entered Service	Year Withdrawn	Current Status	Notes
89001		1986	2002	Preserved	

▲ Fresh out of Brush Works at Loughborough, the unique Class 89, 89001, awaits departure from London King's Cross with a service to Leeds on 30 March 1997. **Rail Photoprints Collection**

▼ Brush built Class 92s are currently scattered across a number of UK and European operators. GB Railfreight locomotive 92018 stands at London Euston on 21 August 2015 having arrived with the overnight Caledonian Sleeper from Glasgow and Edinburgh. **Paul Gerrard**

CLASS 90

Bo-Bo

Built: 1987–90 by BREL, Crewe Works.
Electric Supply System: 25 kV AC overhead.
Power Output: 3730 kW (5000 hp).
Maximum Speed: 110 mph.
Train Heating/Supply: Electric.
Train Brakes: Air.

Latest Number Carried	Previous Number 1	Previous Number 2	Previous Number 3	Year Entered Service	Year Withdrawn	Current Status	Notes
90001				1988		Greater Anglia	
90002				1988		Greater Anglia	
90003				1988		Greater Anglia	
90004				1988		Greater Anglia	
90005				1988		Greater Anglia	
90006				1988		Greater Anglia	
90007				1988		Greater Anglia	
90008				1988		Greater Anglia	
90009				1988		Greater Anglia	
90010				1988		Greater Anglia	
90011				1988		Greater Anglia	
90012				1988		Greater Anglia	
90013				1988		Greater Anglia	
90014				1988		Greater Anglia	
90015				1988		Greater Anglia	
90016				1988		Freightliner	
90017				1988		DB Cargo	
90018				1988		DB Cargo	
90019				1989		DB Cargo	
90020				1989		DB Cargo	
90021	90221	90021		1989		DB Cargo	
90022	90222	90022		1989		DB Cargo	
90023	90223	90023		1989		DB Cargo	
90024	90224	90024		1989		DB Cargo	
90025	90225	90125	90025	1989		DB Cargo	
90026	90126	90026		1989		DB Cargo	
90027	90227	90127	90027	1989		DB Cargo	
90028	90128	90028		1989		DB Cargo	
90029	90129	90029		1989		DB Cargo	
90030	90130	90030		1989		DB Cargo	
90031	90131	90031		1989		DB Cargo	
90032	90132	90032		1989		DB Cargo	
90033	90233	90133	90033	1989		DB Cargo	
90034	90134	90034		1989		DB Cargo	
90035	90135	90035		1989		DB Cargo	
90036	90136	90036		1990		DB Cargo	
90037	90137	90037		1990		DB Cargo	
90038	90238	90138	90038	1990		DB Cargo	
90039	90239	90139	90039	1990		DB Cargo	
90040	90140	90040		1990		DB Cargo	
90041	90141	90041		1990		Freightliner	
90042	90142	90042		1990		Freightliner	
90043	90143	90043		1990		Freightliner	
90044	90144	90044		1990		Freightliner	
90045	90145	90045		1990		Freightliner	
90046	90146	90046		1990		Freightliner	
90047	90147	90047		1990		Freightliner	
90048	90148	90048		1990		Freightliner	
90049	90149	90049		1990		Freightliner	
90050	90150	90050		1990		Freightliner	

CLASS 91

Bo-Bo

Built: 1988–91 by BREL, Crewe Works.
Electric Supply System: 25 kV AC overhead.
Power Output: 4540 kW (6090 hp).
Maximum Speed: 140 mph, restricted to 125 mph or 110 mph when running blunt end first.
Train Heating/Supply: Electric.
Train Brakes: Air.

Latest Number Carried	Previous Number 1	Year Entered Service	Year Withdrawn	Current Status	Notes
91101	91001	1988		Virgin Trains East Coast	
91102	91002	1988		Virgin Trains East Coast	
91103	91003	1988		Virgin Trains East Coast	
91104	91004	1988		Virgin Trains East Coast	
91105	91005	1988		Virgin Trains East Coast	
91106	91006	1988		Virgin Trains East Coast	
91107	91007	1988		Virgin Trains East Coast	
91108	91008	1988		Virgin Trains East Coast	
91109	91009	1988		Virgin Trains East Coast	
91110	91010	1989		Virgin Trains East Coast	
91111	91011	1990		Virgin Trains East Coast	
91112	91012	1990		Virgin Trains East Coast	
91113	91013	1990		Virgin Trains East Coast	
91114	91014	1990		Virgin Trains East Coast	
91115	91015	1990		Virgin Trains East Coast	
91116	91016	1990		Virgin Trains East Coast	
91117	91017	1990		Virgin Trains East Coast	
91118	91018	1990		Virgin Trains East Coast	
91119	91019	1990		Virgin Trains East Coast	
91120	91020	1990		Virgin Trains East Coast	
91121	91021	1990		Virgin Trains East Coast	
91122	91022	1990		Virgin Trains East Coast	
91124	91024	1990		Virgin Trains East Coast	
91125	91025	1990		Virgin Trains East Coast	
91126	91026	1990		Virgin Trains East Coast	
91127	91027	1990		Virgin Trains East Coast	
91128	91028	1990		Virgin Trains East Coast	
91129	91029	1991		Virgin Trains East Coast	
91130	91030	1991		Virgin Trains East Coast	
91131	91031	1991		Virgin Trains East Coast	
91132	91023	1990		Virgin Trains East Coast	

CLASS 92

Co-Co

Built: 1993–96 by Brush Traction, Loughborough.
Electric Supply System: 25 kV AC overhead or 750 V DC third rail.
Power Output: 5040 kW (6760 hp) on AC overhead and 4000 kW (5360 hp) on DC third rail.
Maximum Speed: 140 mph.
Train Heating/Supply: Electric.
Train Brakes: Air.

Latest Number Carried	Previous Number 1	Year Entered Service	Year Withdrawn	Current Status	Notes
92001		1994		Exported	
92002		1993		Exported	
92003		1994		Exported	
92004		1994		DB Cargo	
92005		1994		Exported	
92006		1994		GB Railfreight	
92007		1994		DB Cargo	
92008		1994		DB Cargo	

92009	1994	DB Cargo
92010	1994	GB Railfreight
92011	1994	DB Cargo
92012	1994	Exported
92013	1994	DB Cargo
92014	1994	GB Railfreight
92015	1994	DB Cargo
92016	1994	DB Cargo
92017	1994	DB Cargo
92018	1994	GB Railfreight
92019	1994	DB Cargo
92020	1994	GB Railfreight
92021	1995	GB Railfreight
92022	1995	Exported
92023	1995	GB Railfreight
92024	1995	Exported
92025	1995	Exported
92026	1995	Exported
92027	1995	Exported
92028	1995	GB Railfreight
92029	1995	DB Cargo
92030	1995	Exported
92031	1995	DB Cargo
92032	1995	GB Railfreight
92033	1995	GB Railfreight
92034	1995	Exported
92035	1995	DB Cargo
92036	1995	DB Cargo
92037	1995	DB Cargo
92038	1995	GB Railfreight
92039	1995	Exported
92040	1995	GB Railfreight
92041	1995	DB Cargo
92042	1995	DB Cargo
92043	1995	GB Railfreight
92044	1995	GB Railfreight
92045	1995	GB Railfreight
92046	1996	GB Railfreight

APPENDIX I: LOCOMOTIVE SUMMARY AND CLASSIFICATION INDEX

The following is a list of all locomotives by classification, in the order that they are listed in this book. It shows the total number produced and the number ranges for each loco classification.

Class Category	No. of Locos	TOPS Number Range (see Appx 1 for all)	1957 Numbers	1948 Numbers	Notes
Experimental Shunters	7		D0226–D0227, D9998 & 4 with names only		
Experimental Diesel Mainline Locos	13		D0260, Deltic, D1200, DP2, DHP1, HS4000	10000–10800	
Experimental Gas Turbine Locos	3		GT3	18000 & 18100	
Experimental Electric Mainline Locos	1		E2001		
Purpose Built Departmental Locos (with TOPS No.)	21	97020–97654	20, 56, 82–87, DS1169, ED1–ED7 & PWM650– PWM654		
Standard Locos–Unclassified Shunters	23			11001, 11104 & 15107	Also LMS Numbers 1831–7068
Standard Locs with no TOPS class					
Class D1/1 (0-4-0 Hunslet Shunter)	3		D2950–D2952	11500–11502	
Class D1/3 (0-4-0 Ruston & Hornsby Shunter)	2		D2957–D2958	11507–11508	
Class D2/1 (0-4-0 North British Shunter)	8		D2700–D2707	11700–11707	
Class D2/5 (0-6-0 Andrew Barclay Shunter, differs to Class 05)	10		D2400–D2409	11177–11186	
Class D2/7 (0-6-0 Hudswell Clarke Shunter)	10		D2500–D2509	11116–11148	
Class D2/10 (0-4-0 North British Shunter)	73		D2708–D2780	11709–11719	Not all were given 1948 Numbers
Class D2/11 (0-4-0 Beyer Peacock / Brush Shunter)	1		D2999		
Class D2/12 (0-4-0 Huswell Clarke Shunter)	10		D2510–D2519		
Class D3/1 (0-4-0 North British Shunter)	14		D2900–D2913		
Class D3/3 (0-6-0 British Rail Shunter)	10		D3117–D3126	13117–13126	
Class D3/5 (0-6-0 British Rail Shunter)	15		D3152–D3166	13152–13166	
Class D3/6 (0-6-0 LMS Shunter)	11			12000–12002	Also LMS Numbers 7069–7079
Class D3/7 (0-6-0 LMS Shunter)	40			12003–12032	Also LMS Numbers 7080–7119
Class D3/9 (0-6-0 LNER Shunter)	4			15000–15003	Also LNER Numbers 8000–8003
Class D3/10 (0-6-0 Great Western Shunter)	1			15100	
Class D3/11 (0-6-0 English Electric Shunter)	6			15101–15106	
Class D3/12 (0-6-0 Southern Railway Shunter)	3			15201–15203	
Class D3/14 (0-6-0 LNER / Brush Shunter)	1			15004	
Standard Locos with TOPS Class					
Class 01	5		D2953–D2956 (2)	81 & 11503– 11506	
Class 02	20	02001–02004	D2850–D2869		Not all were given TOPS numbers

Class	Qty	TOPS range	D range	Extra range	Notes
Class 03	230	03004–03399	D2000–D2399	11187–11211	Not all were given TOPS numbers
Class 04	142	04110	D2200–D2341	11100–11229	
Class 05	69	05001	D2550–D2618	11136–11176	
Class 06	35	06001–06010	D2411–D2444		Not all were given TOPS numbers
Class 07	14	07001–07013	D2985–D2998		Not all were given TOPS numbers
Class 08	996	08001–08995	D2400–D4192	11116–15206	
Class 09	38	09001–09205	D3536–D4114		
Class 10	146		D3137–D4094	13137–13151	
Class 11	106			12033–12138	
Class 12	26			15211–15236	
Class 13	3		D4500–D4502	13001–13002	
Class 14	56		D9500–D9555		
Class 15	44		D8200–D8243		
Class 16	10		D8400–D8409		
Class 17	117		D8500–D8616		
Class 20	228	20001–20906	D8000–D8327		
Class 21 (& 29)	58		D6100–D6157		
Class 22	58		D6300–D6357		
Class 23	11		D5900–D5910		
Class 24	151	24001–24150	D5000–D5150		Not all were given TOPS numbers
Class 25	327	25001–25912	D5151–D5299 & D7500–D7677		Not all were given TOPS numbers
Class 26	47		D5300–D5346		
Class 27	69	27001–27212	D5347–D5414		Not all were given TOPS numbers
Class 28	20		D5700–D5719		
Class 31 (& 30)	263	31001–31970	D5500–D5862		
Class 33	98	33001–33212	D6500–D6597		Not all were given TOPS numbers
Class 35	101		D7000–D7100		
Class 37	309	37001–97304	D6600–D6999		Not all were given TOPS numbers
Class 40	200	40001–40199	D200–D399		Not all were given TOPS numbers
Class 41	5		D600–D604		
Class 41 HST	2	41001–41002			
Class 42	38		D800–D870		
Class 43	33		D833–D865		
Class 43 HST	197	43002–43484			
Class 44	10	44001–44010	D1–D10		
Class 45	127	45001–45150	D11–D137		
Class 46	56	46001–46056	D138–D193		
Class 47	512	47001–47981	D1100–D1999		
Class 50	50	50001–50149	D400–D449		
Class 52	74		D1000–D1073		
Class 55	22		D9000–D9021		
Class 56	135	56001–56312			
Class 57	33	57001–57605			
Class 58	50	58001–58050			
Class 59	15	59001–59206			

Class	Qty	Number range			Notes
Class 60	100	60001–60500			
Class 66	485	66001–66957			
Class 67	30	67001–67030			
Class 68	34	68001–68034			
Class 70 (Diesel)	37	70001–80817			
Class 70 (Electric)	3			20001–20003	
Class 71	24	71001–71014	E5000–E5023		Not all were given TOPS numbers
Class 73	49	73001–73901	E6001–E6049		
Class 73/9	13	73951–73971			
Class 74	10	74001–74010	E6101–E6110		
Class 76	58	76001–76057		26000–26057	
Class ES1 (NER Bo-Bo Electric)	2			26500–26501	
Class EB1 (NER Bo-Bo Electric)	10			26502–26511	
Class EE1 (NER Bo-Bo Electric)	1			26600	
Class 77 (EM2)	7		E27000–E27006	27000–27006	
Class 81	25	81001–81022	E3001–E3097		Not all were given TOPS numbers
Class 82	10	82001–82008	E3046–E3055		Not all were given TOPS numbers
Class 83	15	83001–83015	E3024–E3100		
Class 84	10	84001–84010	E3036–E3045		
Class 85	40	85001–85114	E3056–E3095		
Class 86	100	86001–86902	E3101–E3200		
Class 87	36	87001–87101			
Class 88	10	88001–88010			
Class 89	1	89001–89001			
Class 90	50	90001–90239			
Class 91	31	91001–91132			
Class 92	46	92001–92046			

▲ Asymmetric Class 91 91124 "Reverend W Awdry" is seen leaving York with the 07.30 London King's Cross–Newcastle on 21 May 2003. **Rail Photoprints Collection**

APPENDIX II: MULTIPLE TOPS NUMBERS

This Appendix lists all previously carried TOPS numbers and shows the latest TOPS number under which the loco is listed in this book. Where a loco has two or more previously carried TOPS numbers, there are multiple entries for such locos. For example, 47780 has previously carried three different TOPS numbers (47030, 47618 and 47836), therefore each of these three previously carried numbers are listed, each entry referring to 47780 where the loco can be found in this book. Locos that have only carried one TOPS number are not included in Appendix 2.

Previous TOPS No.	TOPS No. Listed Under	Class
03901	03128	03
08111	ADB968012	08
08117	ADB968010	08
08119	ADB968011	08
08203	08991	08
08259	08992	08
08267	97801	08
08421	09201	09
08462	08994	08
08592	08993	08
08620	09205	09
08687	08995	08
08717	09204	09
08732	09202	09
08749	09104	09
08759	09106	09
08766	09103	09
08781	09203	09
08832	09102	09
08833	09101	09
08835	09105	09
08845	09107	09
20041	20904	20
20042	20312	20
20047	20301 (2)	20
20060	20902	20
20075	20309	20
20083	20903	20
20084	20302 (2)	20
20095	20305 (2)	20
20101	20901	20
20102	20311	20
20104	20315	20
20117	20314	20
20120	20304 (2)	20
20127	20303 (2)	20
20128	20307 (2)	20
20131	20306 (2)	20
20187	20308	20
20190	20310	20
20194	20313	20
20219	20906	20
20225	20905	20
20301	20023	20
20302	20059	20
20303	20134	20
20304	20168	20
20305	20172	20
20306	20173	20
20307	20313	20
20308	20196	20
24054	ADB968008	24
24061	RDB968007	24
24142	ADB968009	24
25131	97202	25
25262	25901	25
25268	25902	25
25276	25903	25
25283	25904	25
25286	25905	25
25296	25906	25
25297	25907	25
25305	97251	25
25307	25908	25
25309	25909	25
25310	97250	25
25314	97252	25
25315	25910	25
25316	25911	25
25322	25912	25
26001	76001	76
26002	76002	76
26004	76004	76
26006	76006	76
26007	76007	76
26008	76008	76
26009	76009	76
26010	76010	76
26011	76011	76
26012	76012	76
26013	76013	76
26014	76014	76
26015	76015	76
26016	76016	76
26020	76020	76
26021	76021	76
26022	76022	76
26023	76023	76
26024	76024	76
26025	76025	76
26026	76026	76
26027	76027	76
26028	76028	76
26029	76029	76
26030	76030	76
26032	76032	76
26033	76033	76
26034	76034	76
26037	76037	76
26040	76040	76
26041	76041	76
26043	76043	76
26046	76046	76
26047	76047	76
26049	76049	76
26051	76051	76
26052	76052	76
26053	76053	76
26054	76054	76
26055	76055	76
26056	76056	76
26057	76057	76
27024	ADB968028	27
27045	27101	27
27046	27102	27
27048	27104	27
27049	27105	27
27103	27066	27
27103 (2)	27047	27
27106	27050	27
27107	27051	27
27108	27052	27
27109	27053	27
27110	27054	27
27111	27055	27
27112	27056	27
27113	ADB968025	27
27114	27208	27
27115	27063	27
27116	27064	27
27117	27065	27
27118	27047	27
27119	27201	27
27120	27202	27
27121	27203	27
27122	27058	27
27123	27059	27
27124	27206	27
27204	27058	27
27205	27059	27
27207	ADB968025	27
27209	27063	27
27210	27064	27
27211	27065	27
27212	27066	27
31002	ADB968014	31
31008	ADB968016	31
31013	ADB968013	31
31014	ADB968015	31
31114	31553	31
31115	31466	31
31129	31461	31
31133	31450	31
31137	31444	31
31139	31538	31
31140	31421	31
31148	31548	31
31151	31436	31
31153	31432	31
31157	31524	31
31161	31400	31
31169	31457	31
31172	31420	31
31177	31443	31
31179	31435	31
31182	31437	31
31186	31601	31
31191	31602	31
31193	31426	31
31194	31427	31
31197	31423	31
31204	31440	31
31211	31428	31
31213	31465	31
31216	31467	31
31220	31541	31
31228	31454	31
31236	31433	31
31239	31439	31
31246	31455	31
31251	31442	31
31253	31531	31
31256	31459	31
31258	31434	31
31265	31530	31
31266	31460	31
31269	31429	31
31274	31425	31
31277	31569	31
31279	31452	31
31291	31556	31
31295	31547	31
31297	31563	31
31298	97203	31
31300	31545	31
31303	31558	31
31307	31549	31
31310	31422	31
31315	31462	31
31316	31546	31
31318	31551	31
31321	31468	31
31325	31464	31
31326	31970	31
31414	31514	31
31416	31516	31
31419	31519	31
31424	31524	31
31430	31530	31
31431	31531	31
31438	31538	31
31441	31541	31
31445	31545	31
31446	31546	31
31447	31547	31
31448	31548	31
31449	31549	31
31451	31551	31
31453	31553	31
31456	31556	31
31458	31558	31
31463	31563	31
31469	31569	31
31507	31407	31
31511	31411	31
31512	31412	31
31522	31422	31
31526	31426	31
31533	31433	31
31537	31437	31
31544	31444	31
31552	31452	31
31554	31454	31
31555	31455	31
31565	31465	31
31568	31468	31
33302	33205	33
37001	37707	37
37002	37351	37
37005	37601	37
37006	37798	37
37007	37604	37

37008	37352	37	37149	37892	37	37279	37424	37	47034	47973	47
37009	37340	37	37150	37901	37	37281	37428	37	47035	47739	47
37014	37709	37	37151	37667	37	37282	37405	37	47036	47760	47
37015	37341	37	37155	37897	37	37283	37895	37	47037	47831	47
37016	37706	37	37157	37695	37	37284	37381	37	47038	47761	47
37017	37503	37	37159	37372	37	37285	37335	37	47039	47565	47
37018	37517	37	37160	37373	37	37286	37404	37	47040	47766	47
37020	37702	37	37161	37899	37	37287	37414	37	47041	47764	47
37021	37715	37	37163	37802	37	37288	37427	37	47042	47676	47
37022	37608	37	37164	37675	37	37289	37408	37	47043	47566	47
37024	37714	37	37166	37891	37	37290	37411	37	47044	47725	47
37027	37519	37	37167	37383	37	37291	37419	37	47045	47726	47
37028	37505	37	37168	37890	37	37292	37425	37	47046	47901	47
37030	37701	37	37169	37674	37	37295	37406	37	47047	47727	47
37033	37719	37	37170	97302	37	37296	37423	37	47048	47849	47
37034	37704	37	37171	37611	37	37297	37420	37	47055	47807	47
37036	37605	37	37172	37686	37	37299	37426	37	47056	47783	47
37039	37603	37	37173	37801	37	37300	37429	37	47059	47765	47
37041	37520	37	37176	37883	37	37301	37412	37	47060	57008	57
37043	37354	37	37177	37885	37	37302	37416	37	47061	47830	47
37044	37710	37	37178	97303	37	37303	37333	37	47064	47851	47
37045	37355	37	37179	37612	37	37304	37334	37	47066	47816	47
37049	37343	37	37180	37886	37	37305	37407	37	47068	47848	47
37050	37717	37	37181	37610	37	37306	37273 (2)	37	47069	47845	47
37052	37713	37	37182	37670	37	37307	37403	37	47070	47799	47
37053	37344	37	37183	37884	37	37310	37152	37	47072	47798	47
37056	37513	37	37186	37898	37	37311	37156	37	47074	47852	47
37060	37705	37	37187	37683	37	37312	37137	37	47075	47645	47
37061	37799	37	37189	37672	37	37313	37382	37	47076	47749	47
37064	37515	37	37192	37694	37	37314	37190	37	47077	47840	47
37067	37703	37	37193	37375	37	37320	37026	37	47078	47628	47
37068	37356	37	37195	37689	37	37321	37037	37	47079	57009	57
37076	37518	37	37199	37376	37	37322	37343	37	47080	47779	47
37079	37357	37	37200	37377	37	37323	37088	37	47081	47778	47
37081	37797	37	37202	37331	37	37324	37099	37	47082	47750	47
37082	37602	37	37204	37378	37	37325	37108	37	47083	47633	47
37084	37718	37	37205	37688	37	37326	37111	37	47086	47767	47
37085	37711	37	37206	37906	37	37353	37032	37	47087	47624	47
37086	37516	37	37208	37803	37	37374	37165	37	47088	47781	47
37089	37708	37	37210	37693	37	37380	37259	37	47090	47843	47
37090	37606	37	37217	97304	37	37501	37601	37	47091	47846	47
37091	37358	37	37224	37680	37	37502	37602	37	47126	47555	47
37093	37509	37	37226	37379	37	37504	37603	37	47128	47811	47
37094	37716	37	37228	37696	37	37506	37604	37	47129	47813	47
37100	97301	37	37231	37896	37	37507	37605	37	47134	47841	47
37101	37345	37	37233	37889	37	37508	37606	37	47135	47784	47
37102	37712	37	37234	37685	37	37511	37607	37	47136	47839	47
37103	37607	37	37236	37682	37	37512	37608	37	47138	47786	47
37105	37796	37	37237	37893	37	37514	37609	37	47141	47853	47
37112	37510	37	37239	37332	37	37687	37610	37	47149	47677	47
37115	37609	37	37243	37697	37	37690	37611	37	47151	47850	47
37117	37521	37	37246	37698	37	37691	37612	37	47153	47774	47
37118	37359	37	37247	37671	37	40060	97405	40	47155	47815	47
37119	37350	37	37249	37903	37	41001	43000	41	47158	47634	47
37120	37887	37	37253	37699	37	41002	ADB975813	41	47160	47746	47
37121	37677	37	37256	37678	37	45017	ADB968024	45	47163	47787	47
37122	37692	37	37257	37668	37	45022	97409	45	47164	47822	47
37123	37679	37	37258	37384	37	45029	97410	45	47165	47825	47
37124	37894	37	37265	37430	37	45034	97411	45	47166	47837	47
37125	37904	37	37266	37422	37	45040	97412	45	47167	47580	47
37126	37676	37	37267	37421	37	45054	45150	45	47168	47572	47
37127	37370	37	37268	37401	37	45066	97413	45	47169	47763	47
37128	37330	37	37269	37417	37	46035	97403	46	47170	47733	47
37129	37669	37	37270	37409	37	46045	97404	46	47171	47738	47
37130	37681	37	37271	37418	37	47020	47844	47	47172	47734	47
37132	37673	37	37271 (2)	37333	37	47024	47721	47	47173	47762	47
37134	37684	37	37272	37431	37	47026	47741	47	47174	47574	47
37135	37888	37	37272 (2)	37334	37	47027	47722	47	47175	47575	47
37136	37905	37	37273	37410	37	47028	47759	47	47176	47576	47
37143	37800	37	37274	37402	37	47029	47635	47	47177	47743	47
37145	37382	37	37274 (2)	37308	37	47030	47780	47	47178	47737	47
37147	37371	37	37276	37413	37	47031	47832	47	47179	47847	47
37148	37902	37	37277	37415	37	47032	47817	47	47180	47584	47

47181	47776	47	47490	47768	47	47609	47798	47	47831	57310	57
47182	47742	47	47491	47769	47	47610	47787	47	47833	47788	47
47183	47579	47	47493	47701	47	47611	47837	47	47834	47798	47
47184	47757	47	47494	47706	47	47612	47779	47	47835	47799	47
47185	47782	47	47495	47704	47	47613	47840	47	47836	47780	47
47187	57006	57	47496	47710	47	47614	47853	47	47838	47779	47
47204	57012	57	47497	47717	47	47615	47747	47	47842	47778	47
47206	57605	57	47498	47711	47	47616	47789	47	47845	57301	57
47209	57604	57	47499	47709	47	47617	47677	47	47846	57308	57
47216	47299	47	47502	47715	47	47618	47780	47	47974	47775	47
47225	57307	57	47503	47771	47	47619	47829	47	47975	47540	47
47231	57010	57	47504	47702	47	47620	47799	47	50149	50049	50
47232	47785	47	47505	47712	47	47621	47839	47	56003	56312	56
47234	57315	57	47506	47707	47	47622	47841	47	56045	56301	56
47239	47812	47	47507	47716	47	47623	47843	47	56057	56311	56
47240	47818	47	47510	47713	47	47625	47749	47	56124	56302	56
47242	47814	47	47511	47714	47	47626	47750	47	56125	56303	56
47243	47777	47	47514	47703	47	47629	47828	47	56201	56009	56
47244	47640	47	47516	47708	47	47630	47764	47	60016	60500	60
47246	47756	47	47517	47758	47	47631	47765	47	66008	66780	66
47247	47810	47	47531	47775	47	47632	47848	47	66016	66781	66
47248	47789	47	47537	47772	47	47636	47777	47	66046	66782	66
47250	47744	47	47538	ADB968035	47	47637	47826	47	66058	66783	66
47251	47827	47	47541	47773	47	47638	47845	47	66081	66784	66
47252	47747	47	47545	47972	47	47639	47851	47	66081	66784	66
47254	47806	47	47546	47976	47	47641	47767	47	66141	66786	66
47255	47596	47	47551	47774	47	47642	47766	47	66184	66787	66
47257	47805	47	47552	47802	47	47644	47756	47	66238	66788	66
47259	47802	47	47553	47803	47	47646	47852	47	66250	66789	66
47260	47803	47	47554	47705	47	47647	47846	47	66401	66733	66
47262	47788	47	47556	47844	47	47648	47850	47	66402	66734	66
47263	47736	47	47557	47721	47	47649	47830	47	66403	66735	66
47264	47829	47	47558	47722	47	47650	47805	47	66404	66736	66
47265	47804	47	47559	47759	47	47651	47806	47	66405	66737	66
47266	47828	47	47560	47832	47	47652	47807	47	66406	66742	66
47267	47745	47	47561	47973	47	47653	47781	47	66407	66743	66
47268	47791	47	47562	47760	47	47654	47783	47	66408	66744	66
47269	47643	47	47563	47831	47	47655	47810	47	66409	66745	66
47271	47854	47	47564	47761	47	47656	47811	47	66410	66746	66
47272	47790	47	47567	47725	47	47657	47812	47	66573	66846	66
47273	47627	47	47568	47726	47	47658	47813	47	66574	66847	66
47274	47826	47	47569	47727	47	47659	47814	47	66575	66848	66
47290	57316	57	47570	47849	47	47660	47815	47	66576	66849	66
47317	57003	57	47571	47822	47	47661	47816	47	66577	66850	66
47322	57002	57	47573	47762	47	47662	47817	47	66578	66738	66
47329	57011	57	47577	47847	47	47663	47818	47	66579	66739	66
47330	57312	57	47578	47776	47	47664	47784	47	66580	66740	66
47332	57007	57	47581	47763	47	47665	47785	47	66581	66741	66
47337	57602	57	47582	47733	47	47671	47789	47	66841	66742	66
47347	57004	57	47583	47734	47	47672	47760	47	66842	66743	66
47349	57603	57	47585	47757	47	47673	47790	47	66843	66744	66
47350	57005	57	47586	47676	47	47674	47854	47	66844	66745	66
47356	57001	57	47587	47736	47	47675	47791	47	66845	66746	66
47364	47981	47	47588	47737	47	47705	57303	57	70099	70801	70
47371	57313	57	47589	47827	47	47732	47580	47	73005	73966	73/9
47372	57314	57	47590	47825	47	47770	47500	47	73006	73906	73
47384	47226	47	47591	47804	47	47792	47804	47	73100	73101	73
47385	47363	47	47592	47738	47	47793	47579	47	73102	73212	73
47386	47378	47	47593	47790	47	47801	47774	47	73103	73970	73/9
47387	47314	47	47594	47739	47	47806	57309	57	73104	73951	73/9
47388	47204	47	47595	47791	47	47807	57304	57	73105	73969	73/9
47389	47309	47	47597	47741	47	47808	47781	47	73112	73213	73
47390	47330	47	47598	47742	47	47809	47783	47	73113	73211	73
47391	47355	47	47599	47743	47	47814	57306	57	73116	73210	73
47393	47209	47	47600	47744	47	47817	57311	57	73117	73968	73/9
47394	47211	47	47601	47901	47	47819	47784	47	73120	73209	73
47395	47205	47	47602	47782	47	47820	47785	47	73120	73209	73
47396	47328	47	47603	47745	47	47821	47786	47	73121	73208	73
47397	47303	47	47604	47854	47	47822	57305	57	73122	73207	73
47398	47152	47	47605	47746	47	47823	47787	47	73123	73206	73
47399	47150	47	47606	47778	47	47824	47782	47	73124	73205	73
47468	47300	47	47607	47786	47	47825	57601	57	73125	73204	73
47480	47971	47	47608	47788	47	47827	57302	57	73127	73203	73

73135	73235	73	86024	86424	86	86411	86611	86	90222	90022	90
73137	73202	73	86025	86425	86	86412	86612	86	90223	90023	90
73142	73201	73	86026	86426	86	86413	86613	86	90224	90024	90
73204	73962	73/9	86027	86627	86	86414	86614	86	90227	90027	90
73205	73964	73/9	86028	86628	86	86415	86615	86	90233	90033	90
73206	73963	73/9	86029	86429	86	86418	86618	86	90238	90038	90
73207	73971	73/9	86030	86430	86	86420	86620	86	90239	90039	90
73208	73965	73/9	86031	86631	86	86421	86621	86	91001	91101	91
73209	73961	73/9	86032	86632	86	86422	86622	86	91002	91102	91
73211	73952	73/9	86033	86633	86	86423	86623	86	91003	91103	91
73901	73001	73	86035	86635	86	86427	86627	86	91004	91104	91
73906	73967	73/9	86036	86636	86	86428	86628	86	91005	91105	91
76003	76036 (2)	76	86037	86637	86	86431	86631	86	91006	91106	91
76018	76035	76	86038	86638	86	86432	86632	86	91007	91107	91
76036	76003 (2)	76	86039	86639	86	86433	86633	86	91008	91108	91
76038	76050	76	86040	86256	86	86434	86634	86	91009	91109	91
76039	76048 (2)	76	86041	86261	86	86435	86635	86	91010	91110	91
76044	76031	76	86042	86255	86	86436	86636	86	91011	91111	91
76048	76039 (2)	76	86043	86257	86	86437	86637	86	91012	91112	91
76050	76038 (2)	76	86044	86901	86	86438	86638	86	91013	91113	91
84009	ADB968021	84	86045	86259	86	86439	86639	86	91014	91114	91
85003	85113	85	86046	86258	86	86501	86258	86	91015	91115	91
85004	85111	85	86047	86254	86	86501 (2)	86608	86	91016	91116	91
85007	85112	85	86048	86702	86	86502	86222	86	91017	91117	91
85009	85102	85	86201	86101	86	86503	86701	86	91018	91118	91
85010	85103	85	86202	86102	86	86504	86217	86	91019	91119	91
85011	85114	85	86203	86103	86	86505	86246	86	91020	91120	91
85012	85104	85	86205	86701	86	86506	86233	86	91021	91121	91
85016	85105	85	86210	86902	86	86507	86239	86	91022	91122	91
85021	85106	85	86253	86901	86	86508	86241	86	91023	91132	91
85024	85107	85	86260	86702	86	86616	86416	86	91024	91124	91
85032	85108	85	86311	86611	86	90125	90025	90	91025	91125	91
85035	85109	85	86312	86612	86	90126	90026	90	91026	91126	91
85036	85110	85	86313	86613	86	90127	90027	90	91027	91127	91
85101	85006	85	86314	86614	86	90128	90028	90	91028	91128	91
86001	86401	86	86315	86615	86	90129	90029	90	91029	91129	91
86002	86602	86	86316	86416	86	90130	90030	90	91030	91130	91
86002	86608	86	86317	86417	86	90131	90031	90	91031	91131	91
86003	86603	86	86318	86618	86	90132	90032	90	97201	RDB968007	24
86004	86604	86	86319	86419	86	90133	90032	90	97204	31970	31
86004	86634	86	86320	86620	86	90133	90033	90	97406	40135	40
86005	86605	86	86321	86621	86	90134	90034	90	97407	40012	40
86006	86606	86	86322	86622	86	90135	90035	90	97408	40118	40
86007	86607	86	86323	86623	86	90136	90036	90	97472	47472	47
86009	86609	86	86324	86424	86	90137	90037	90	97480	47971	47
86010	86610	86	86325	86425	86	90138	90038	90	97545	47972	47
86011	86611	86	86326	86426	86	90139	90039	90	97561	47973	47
86012	86612	86	86327	86627	86	90140	90040	90	97800	08600	08
86013	86613	86	86328	86628	86	90141	90041	90	97803	05001	05
86014	86614	86	86329	86429	86	90142	90042	90	97804	06003	06
86015	86615	86	86402	86602	86	90143	90043	90	97806	09017	09
86016	86416	86	86403	86603	86	90144	90044	90	PWM650	97650	97
86017	86417	86	86404	86604	86	90145	90045	90	PWM651	97651	97
86018	86618	86	86405	86605	86	90146	90046	90	PWM652	97652	97
86019	86419	86	86406	86606	86	90147	90047	90	PWM653	97653	97
86020	86620	86	86407	86607	86	90148	90048	90	PWM654	97654	97
86021	86621	86	86408	86608	86	90149	90049	90	RDB968020	97801	08
86022	86622	86	86409	86609	86	90150	90050	90	TDB968030	33018	33
86023	86623	86	86410	86610	86	90221	90021	90			

APPENDIX III: 1948 BR NUMBER & 1957 BR NUMBER SERIES INDEX

This appendix lists all locomotives that carried a 1948 BR Number or 1957 BR Number and were subsequently given a different number, under which they are listed in this book. The 1948 numbers show the subsequently-carried 1957 number (where the loco was not given a TOPS number) or TOPS number, under which it can be found in this book; the 1957 numbers show the TOPS number under which it can be found in this book. Locos that only carried one 1948 or one 1957 number throughout their lives are not listed in this Appendix, as they are listed under that one number.

There are a small number of locos where the "Number Loco is listed by" is not the latest number carried, but a previously carried number, to which it is more logical to refer, such as for some industrial or departmental renumberings. For example, for D8066 it refers to 20066 rather than the last carried number 82. Locomotives renumbered into the departmental 97xxx series have their service TOPS number shown in parentheses to indicate the class of locomotive under which the locomotives' entries can be found. Such locomotives are listed under their 97xxx departmental series number.

Previously carried 1948 No.	Loco is listed by								
11100	D2200	11147	D2508	11196	03009	11706	D2706	13034	D3034
11101	D2201	11148	D2509	11197	03010	11707	D2707	13035	D3035
11102	D2202	11149	D2230	11198	D2011	11708	D2708	13036	08026
11103	D2203	11150	D2231	11199	03012	11709	D2709	13037	D3035
11105	D2204	11151	D2232	11200	03013	11710	D2710	13038	D3038
11106	D2205	11152	D2233	11201	03014	11711	D2711	13039	08027
11107	D2206	11153	D2234	11202	D2015	11712	D2712	13040	08028
11108	D2207	11154	D2235	11203	03016	11713	D2713	13041	08029
11109	D2208	11155	D2236	11204	03017	11714	D2714	13042	08030
11110	D2209	11156	D2237	11205	03018	11715	D2715	13043	08031
11111	D2210	11157	D2238	11206	D2019	11716	D2716	13044	08032
11112	D2211	11158	D2239	11207	03020	11717	D2717	13045	D3045
11113	D2212	11159	D2240	11208	03021	11718	D2718	13046	08033
11114	D2213	11160	D2241	11209	03022	11719	D2719	13047	08034
11115	D2214	11161	D2558	11210	D2023	12082	12049 (2)	13048	08035
11116	D2500	11162	D2559	11211	D2024	13000	D3000	13049	08036
11117	D2501	11163	D2560	11212	D2242	13001	D3001	13050	08037
11118	D2502	11164	D2561	11213	D2243	13002	D3002	13051	08038
11119	D2503	11165	D2562	11214	D2244	13003	D3003	13052	08039
11120	D2504	11166	D2563	11215	D2245	13004	08001	13053	08040
11121	D2215	11167	D2564	11216	D2246	13005	08002	13054	08041
11122	D2216	11168	D2565	11217	D2247	13006	D3006	13055	08042
11123	D2217	11169	D2566	11218	D2248	13007	08003	13056	08043
11124	D2218	11170	D2567	11219	D2249	13008	08004	13057	08044
11125	D2219	11171	D2568	11220	D2250	13009	08005	13058	08045
11126	D2220	11172	D2569	11221	D2251	13010	08006	13059	08046
11127	D2221	11173	D2570	11222	D2252	13011	D3011	13060	08047
11128	D2222	11174	D2571	11223	D2253	13012	08007	13061	08048
11129	D2223	11175	D2572	11224	D2254	13013	D3013	13062	08049
11130	D2224	11176	D2573	11225	D2255	13014	D3014	13063	08050
11131	D2225	11177	D2400	11226	D2256	13015	08008	13064	08051
11132	D2226	11178	D2401	11227	D2257	13016	08009	13065	08052
11133	D2227	11179	D2402	11228	D2258	13017	08010	13066	08053
11134	D2228	11180	D2403	11229	D2259	13018	08011	13067	08054
11135	D2229	11181	D2404	11500	D2950	13019	08012	13068	08055
11136	D2550	11182	D2405	11501	D2951	13020	08013	13069	D3069
11137	D2551	11183	D2406	11502	D2952	13021	08014	13070	08056
11138	D2552	11184	D2407	11503	D2953	13022	08015	13071	08057
11139	D2553	11185	D2408	11504	01001	13023	08016	13072	08058
11140	05001	11186	D2409	11505	01002	13024	08017	13073	08059
11141	D2555	11187	D2000	11506	D2956	13025	08018	13074	08060
11142	D2556	11188	D2001	11507	D2957	13026	D3026	13075	08061
11143	D2557	11189	D2002	11508	D2958	13027	08019	13076	08062
11144	D2505	11190	D2003	11700	D2700	13028	08020	13077	08063
11145	D2506	11191	03004	11701	D2701	13029	08021	13078	D3078
11146	D2507	11192	03005	11702	D2702	13030	08022	13079	08064
		11193	D2006	11703	D2703	13031	08023	13080	08065
		11194	03007	11704	D2704	13032	08024	13081	08066
		11195	03008	11705	D2705	13033	08025	13082	08067

13083	08068	13151	D3151	13219	08151	13286	08216	13353	08283
13084	08069	13152	D3152	13220	08152	13287	08217	13354	08284
13085	08070	13153	D3153	13221	08153	13288	08218	13355	08285
13086	08071	13154	D3154	13222	08154	13289	08219	13356	08286
13087	08072	13155	D3155	13223	08155	13290	08220	13357	08287
13088	08073	13156	D3156	13224	08156	13291	08221	13363	08293
13089	08074	13157	D3157	13225	08157	13292	08222	13364	08294
13090	08075	13158	D3158	13226	08158	13293	08223	13365	08295
13091	08076	13159	D3159	13227	08159	13294	08224	13366	08296
13092	D3092	13160	D3160	13228	08160	13295	08225	26001	76001
13093	D3093	13161	D3161	13229	08161	13296	08226	26002	76002
13094	D3094	13162	D3162	13230	08162	13297	08227	26003	76036 (2)
13095	D3095	13163	D3163	13231	08163	13298	08228	26004	76004
13096	D3096	13164	D3164	13232	08164	13299	08229	26006	76006
13097	D3097	13165	D3165	13233	08165	13300	08230	26007	76007
13098	D3098	13166	D3166	13234	08166	13301	08231	26008	76008
13099	D3099	13167	08102	13235	08167	13302	08232	26009	76009
13100	D3100	13168	08103	13236	08168	13303	08233	26010	76010
13101	D3101	13169	08104	13237	08169	13304	08234	26011	76011
13102	08077	13170	08105	13238	08170	13305	08235	26012	76012
13103	08078	13171	08106	13239	08171	13306	08236	26013	76013
13104	08079	13172	D3172	13240	08172	13307	08237	26014	76014
13105	08080	13173	08107	13241	08173	13308	08238	26015	76015
13106	08081	13174	08108	13242	08174	13309	08239	26016	76016
13107	08082	13175	08109	13243	08175	13310	08240	26018	76035
13108	08083	13176	08110	13244	08176	13311	08241	26020	76020
13109	08084	13177	08111	13245	08177	13312	08242	26021	76021
13110	08085	13178	08112	13246	08178	13313	08243	26022	76022
13111	08086	13179	08113	13247	08179	13314	08244	26023	76023
13112	08087	13180	08114	13248	08180	13315	08245	26024	76024
13113	08088	13181	08115	13249	08181	13316	08246	26025	76025
13114	08089	13182	08116	13250	08182	13317	08247	26026	76026
13115	08090	13183	D3183	13251	08183	13318	08248	26027	76027
13116	08091	13184	08117	13252	08184	13319	08249	26028	76028
13117	D3117	13185	08118	13253	08185	13320	08250	26029	76029
13118	D3118	13186	08119	13254	08186	13321	08251	26030	76030
13119	D3119	13187	08120	13255	D3255	13322	08252	26032	76032
13120	D3120	13188	08121	13256	08187	13323	08253	26033	76033
13121	D3121	13189	08122	13257	08188	13324	08254	26034	76034
13122	D3122	13190	08123	13258	08189	13325	08255	26036	76003 (2)
13123	D3123	13191	08124	13259	08190	13326	08256	26037	76037
13124	D3124	13192	08125	13260	08191	13327	08257	26038	76050
13125	D3125	13193	D3193	13261	D3261	13328	08258	26039	76048 (2)
13126	D3126	13194	08126	13262	08192	13329	08992	26040	76040
13127	08092	13195	08127	13263	08193	13330	08260	26041	76041
13128	08093	13196	08128	13264	08194	13331	08261	26043	76043
13129	08094	13197	08129	13265	08195	13332	08262	26044	76031
13130	08095	13198	08130	13266	08196	13333	08263	26046	76046
13131	08096	13199	08131	13267	08197	13334	08264	26047	76047
13132	08097	13200	08132	13268	08198	13335	08265	26048	76039 (2)
13133	08098	13201	08133	13269	08199	13336	08266	26049	76049
13134	08099	13202	08134	13270	08200	13337	8267	26050	76038 (2)
13135	08100	13203	08135	13271	08201	13338	08268	26051	76051
13136	08101	13204	08136	13272	08202	13339	08269	26052	76052
13137	D3137	13205	08137	13273	08991	13340	08270	26053	76053
13138	D3138	13206	08138	13274	08204	13341	08271	26054	76054
13139	D3139	13207	08139	13275	08205	13342	08272	26055	76055
13140	D3140	13208	08140	13276	08206	13343	08273	26056	76056
13141	D3141	13209	08141	13277	08207	13344	08274	26057	76057
13142	D3142	13210	08142	13278	08208	13345	08275	27000	E27000
13143	D3143	13211	08143	13279	08209	13346	08276	27001	E27001
13144	D3144	13212	08144	13280	08210	13347	08277	27002	E27002
13145	D3145	13213	08145	13281	08211	13348	08278	27003	E27003
13146	D3146	13214	08146	13282	08212	13349	08279	27004	E27004
13147	D3147	13215	08147	13283	08213	13350	08280	27005	E27005
13148	D3148	13216	08148	13284	08214	13351	08281	27006	E27006
13149	D3149	13217	08149	13285	08215	13352	08282	81	D2956 (2)
13150	D3150	13218	08150						

Previous Number 1957 Number	Loco is listed by								
D1	44001	D33	45019	D68	45046	D103	45062	D138	46001
D2	44002	D34	45119	D69	45047	D104	45063	D139	46002
D3	44003	D35	45117	D70	45048	D105	45064	D140	46003
D4	44004	D36	45031	D71	45049	D106	45106	D141	46004
D5	44005	D37	45009	D72	45050	D107	45120	D142	46005
D6	44006	D38	45032	D73	45110	D108	45012	D143	46006
D7	44007	D39	45033	D74	45051	D109	45139	D144	46007
D8	44008	D40	45133	D75	45052	D110	45065	D145	46008
D9	44009	D41	45147	D76	45053	D111	45129	D146	46009
D10	44010	D42	97411 (45034)	D77	45004	D112	45010	D147	46010
D11	45122	D43	45107	D78	45150	D113	45128	D148	46011
D12	45011	D44	45035	D79	45005	D114	97413 (45066)	D149	46012
D13	45001	D45	45036	D80	45113	D115	45067	D150	46013
D14	45015	D46	45037	D81	45115	D116	45103	D151	46014
D15	45018	D47	45116	D82	45141	D117	45130	D152	46015
D16	45016	D48	45038	D83	45142	D118	45068	D153	46016
D17	45024	D49	45039	D84	45055	D119	45007	D154	46017
D18	45121	D50	97412 (45040)	D85	45109	D120	45108	D155	46018
D19	45025	D51	45102	D86	45105	D121	45069	D156	46019
D20	45013	D52	45123	D87	45127	D122	45070	D157	46020
D21	45026	D53	45041	D88	45136	D123	45125	D158	46021
D22	45132	D54	45023	D89	45006	D124	45131	D159	46022
D23	968024 (45017)	D55	45144	D90	45008	D125	45071	D160	46023
D24	45027	D56	45137	D91	45056	D126	45134	D161	46024
D25	45021	D57	45042	D92	45138	D127	45072	D162	46025
D26	45020	D58	45043	D93	45057	D128	45145	D163	46026
D27	45028	D59	45104	D94	45114	D129	45073	D164	46027
D28	45124	D60	97409 (45022)	D95	45054	D130	45148	D165	46028
D29	45002	D61	45112	D96	45101	D131	45074	D166	46029
D30	97410 (45029)	D62	45143	D97	45058	D132	45075	D167	46030
D31	45030	D63	45044	D98	45059	D133	45003	D168	46031
D32	45126	D64	45045	D99	45135	D134	45076	D169	46032
		D65	45111	D100	45060	D135	45149	D170	46033
		D66	45146	D101	45061	D136	45077	D171	46034
		D67	45118	D102	45140	D137	45014	D172	97403 (46035)

▲ Class 46 "Peak" 46015 pulls away from Bristol Parkway with a northbound service on 3 June 1975.
Graham Smith/Rail Photoprints

D173 46036	D252 40052	D326 40126	D399 40199	D1510 47411
D174 46037	D253 40053	D327 40127	D400 50050	D1511 47412
D175 46038	D254 40054	D328 40128	D401 50001	D1512 47413
D176 46039	D255 40055	D329 40129	D402 50002	D1513 47414
D177 46040	D256 40056	D330 40130	D403 50003	D1514 47415
D178 46041	D257 40057	D331 40131	D404 50004	D1515 47416
D179 46042	D258 40058	D332 40132	D405 50005	D1516 47417
D180 46043	D259 40059	D333 40133	D406 50006	D1517 47418
D181 46044	D260 97405 (40060)	D334 40134	D407 50007	D1518 47419
D182 97404 (46045)	D261 40061	D335 40135	D408 50008	D1519 47420
D183 46046	D262 40062	D336 40136	D409 50009	D1520 47421
D184 46047	D263 40063	D337 40137	D410 50010	D1521 47001
D185 46048	D264 40064	D338 40138	D411 50011	D1522 47002
D186 46049	D265 40065	D339 40139	D412 50012	D1523 47003
D187 46050	D266 40066	D340 40140	D413 50013	D1524 47004
D188 46051	D267 40067	D341 40141	D414 50014	D1525 47422
D189 46052	D268 40068	D342 40142	D415 50015	D1526 47005
D190 46053	D269 40069	D343 40143	D416 50016	D1527 47423
D191 46054	D270 40070	D344 40144	D417 50017	D1528 47006
D192 46055	D271 40071	D345 40145	D418 50018	D1529 47007
D193 46056	D272 40072	D346 40146	D419 50019	D1530 47008
D200 40122	D273 40073	D347 40147	D420 50020	D1531 47424
D201 40001	D274 40074	D348 40148	D421 50021	D1532 47009
D202 40002	D275 40075	D349 40149	D422 50022	D1533 47425
D203 40003	D276 40076	D350 40150	D423 50023	D1534 47426
D204 40004	D277 40077	D351 40151	D424 50024	D1535 47427
D205 40005	D278 40078	D352 40152	D425 50025	D1536 47428
D206 40006	D279 40079	D353 40153	D426 50026	D1537 47010
D207 40007	D280 40080	D354 40154	D427 50027	D1538 47011
D208 40008	D281 40081	D355 40155	D428 50028	D1539 47012
D209 40009	D282 40082	D356 40156	D429 50029	D1540 47013
D210 40010	D283 40083	D357 40157	D430 50030	D1541 47429
D211 40011	D284 40084	D358 40158	D431 50031	D1542 47430
D212 40012	D285 40085	D359 40159	D432 50032	D1543 47014
D213 40013	D286 40086	D360 40160	D433 50033	D1544 47015
D214 40014	D287 40087	D361 40161	D434 50034	D1545 47431
D215 40015	D288 40088	D362 40162	D435 50035	D1546 47016
D216 40016	D289 40089	D363 40163	D436 50036	D1547 47432
D217 40017	D290 40090	D364 40164	D437 50037	D1548 47433
D218 40018	D291 40091	D365 40165	D438 50038	D1549 47434
D219 40019	D292 40092	D366 40166	D439 50039	D1550 47435
D220 40020	D293 40093	D367 40167	D440 50040	D1551 47529
D221 40021	D294 40094	D368 40168	D441 50041	D1552 47436
D222 40022	D295 40095	D369 40169	D442 50042	D1553 47437
D223 40023	D296 40096	D370 40170	D443 50043	D1554 47438
D224 40024	D297 40097	D371 40171	D444 50044	D1555 47439
D225 40025	D298 40098	D372 40172	D445 50045	D1556 47440
D226 40026	D299 40099	D373 40173	D446 50046	D1557 47441
D227 40027	D300 40100	D374 40174	D447 50047	D1558 47442
D228 40028	D301 40101	D375 40175	D448 50048	D1559 47443
D229 40029	D302 40102	D376 40176	D449 50049	D1560 47444
D230 40030	D303 40103	D377 40177	D1100 47298	D1561 47445
D231 40031	D304 40104	D378 40178	D1101 47518	D1563 47446
D232 40032	D305 40105	D379 40179	D1102 47519	D1564 47447
D233 40033	D306 40106	D380 40180	D1103 47520	D1565 47448
D234 40034	D307 40107	D381 40181	D1104 47521	D1566 47449
D235 40035	D308 40108	D382 40182	D1105 47522	D1567 47450
D236 40036	D309 40109	D383 40183	D1106 47523	D1568 47451
D237 40037	D310 40110	D384 40184	D1107 47524	D1569 47452
D238 40038	D311 40111	D385 40185	D1108 47525	D1570 47017
D239 40039	D312 40112	D386 40186	D1109 47526	D1571 47453
D240 40040	D313 40113	D387 40187	D1110 47527	D1572 47018
D241 40041	D314 40114	D388 40188	D1111 47528	D1573 47019
D242 40042	D315 40115	D389 40189	D1500 47401	D1574 47454
D243 40043	D316 40116	D390 40190	D1501 47402	D1575 47455
D244 40044	D317 40117	D391 40191	D1502 47403	D1576 47456
D245 40045	D318 40118	D392 40192	D1503 47404	D1577 47457
D246 40046	D319 40119	D393 40193	D1504 47405	D1578 47458
D247 40047	D320 40120	D394 40194	D1505 47406	D1579 47459
D248 40048	D321 40121	D395 40195	D1506 47407	D1580 47460
D249 40049	D323 40123	D396 40196	D1507 47408	D1581 47461
D250 40050	D324 40124	D397 40197	D1508 47409	D1582 47462
D251 40051	D325 40125	D398 40198	D1509 47410	D1583 47844

D1584 47775	D1657 47772	D1731 47550	D1805 47324	D1878 47359
D1585 47542	D1658 47852	D1732 47140	D1806 47325	D1879 47360
D1586 47463	D1659 47645	D1733 47853	D1807 47326	D1880 47361
D1587 47464	D1660 47749	D1735 47142	D1808 47327	D1881 47362
D1588 47543	D1661 47840	D1736 47143	D1809 47328	D1882 47363
D1589 47465	D1662 47484	D1737 47144	D1810 47329	D1883 47981
D1590 47466	D1663 47628	D1738 47145	D1811 47330	D1884 47365
D1591 47721	D1664 47079	D1739 47146	D1812 47331	D1885 47366
D1592 47544	D1665 47779	D1740 47147	D1813 47332	D1886 47367
D1593 47467	D1666 47778	D1741 47148	D1814 47333	D1887 47368
D1594 47300	D1667 47750	D1742 47677	D1815 47334	D1888 47369
D1595 47469	D1668 47633	D1743 47150	D1816 47335	D1889 47370
D1596 47470	D1669 968035 (47538)	D1744 47850	D1817 47336	D1890 47371
D1597 47741	D1670 47085	D1745 47152	D1818 47337	D1891 47372
D1598 47471	D1672 47767	D1746 47774	D1819 47338	D1892 47373
D1599 47722	D1673 47624	D1747 47976	D1820 47339	D1893 47374
D1600 47472	D1674 47781	D1748 47815	D1821 47340	D1894 47375
D1601 47473	D1675 47089	D1749 47156	D1822 47341	D1895 47376
D1602 47474	D1676 47843	D1750 47157	D1823 47342	D1896 47377
D1603 47475	D1677 47846	D1751 47634	D1824 47343	D1897 47378
D1604 47476	D1678 47534	D1752 47159	D1825 47344	D1898 47379
D1605 47759	D1679 47093	D1753 47769	D1826 47345	D1899 47380
D1606 47635	D1680 47094	D1754 47746	D1827 47346	D1900 47381
D1607 47477	D1681 47095	D1755 47773	D1828 47347	D1901 47225
D1608 47478	D1682 47096	D1756 47162	D1829 47348	D1902 47226
D1609 47780	D1683 47485	D1757 47787	D1830 47349	D1903 47227
D1610 47832	D1684 47097	D1758 47822	D1831 47350	D1904 47228
D1611 47817	D1685 47098	D1759 47825	D1832 47351	D1905 47229
D1612 47479	D1686 47099	D1760 47492	D1833 47352	D1906 47230
D1613 47033	D1687 47100	D1761 47837	D1834 47353	D1907 47231
D1614 47973	D1688 47101	D1762 47580	D1835 47354	D1909 47785
D1615 47739	D1689 47486	D1763 47572	D1836 47355	D1910 47233
D1616 47971	D1690 47102	D1764 47763	D1837 47187	D1911 47234
D1617 47760	D1691 47103	D1765 47733	D1838 47188	D1912 47235
D1618 47831	D1692 47104	D1766 47738	D1839 47189	D1913 47236
D1619 47761	D1693 47105	D1767 47734	D1840 47190	D1914 47237
D1620 47565	D1694 47106	D1768 47762	D1841 47191	D1915 47238
D1621 47766	D1695 47107	D1769 47574	D1842 47192	D1916 47812
D1622 47764	D1696 47108	D1770 47575	D1843 47193	D1917 47818
D1623 47676	D1697 47109	D1771 47576	D1844 47194	D1918 47241
D1624 47566	D1698 47110	D1772 47743	D1845 47195	D1919 47814
D1625 47725	D1699 47111	D1773 47737	D1846 47196	D1920 47777
D1626 47726	D1700 47112	D1774 47847	D1847 47197	D1921 47640
D1627 47481	D1701 47113	D1775 47584	D1848 47198	D1922 47245
D1628 47901	D1702 47114	D1776 47776	D1849 47199	D1923 47756
D1629 47727	D1703 47115	D1777 47742	D1850 47200	D1924 47810
D1630 47849	D1704 47116	D1778 47579	D1851 47201	D1925 47789
D1631 47049	D1705 47117	D1779 47757	D1852 47202	D1926 47249
D1632 47050	D1706 47118	D1780 47782	D1853 47203	D1927 47744
D1633 47051	D1707 47487	D1781 47186	D1854 47204	D1928 47827
D1634 47052	D1708 47119	D1782 47301	D1855 47205	D1929 47747
D1635 47053	D1709 47120	D1783 47302	D1856 47206	D1930 47530
D1636 47482	D1710 47121	D1784 47303	D1857 47207	D1931 47806
D1637 47483	D1711 47122	D1785 47304	D1858 47208	D1932 47701
D1638 47054	D1712 47123	D1786 47305	D1859 47209	D1933 47596
D1639 47807	D1713 47488	D1787 47306	D1860 47210	D1934 47256
D1640 47783	D1714 47124	D1788 47307	D1861 47211	D1935 47805
D1641 47532	D1715 47125	D1789 47308	D1862 47212	D1936 47706
D1642 47547	D1716 47489	D1790 47309	D1863 47213	D1937 47704
D1643 47765	D1717 47555	D1791 47310	D1864 47214	D1938 47258
D1644 47060	D1718 47539	D1792 47311	D1865 47215	D1939 47710
D1645 47830	D1719 47811	D1793 47312	D1866 47299	D1940 47717
D1646 47972	D1720 47813	D1794 47313	D1867 47217	D1941 47711
D1647 47063	D1721 47130	D1795 47314	D1868 47218	D1942 47709
D1648 47851	D1722 47131	D1796 47315	D1869 47219	D1943 47500
D1649 47535	D1723 47540	D1797 47316	D1870 47220	D1944 47501
D1650 47816	D1724 47549	D1798 47317	D1871 47221	D1945 47715
D1651 47533	D1725 47841	D1799 47318	D1872 47222	D1946 47771
D1652 47848	D1726 47841	D1800 47319	D1873 47223	D1947 47702
D1653 47845	D1727 47784	D1801 47320	D1874 47224	D1948 47712
D1654 47799	D1728 47839	D1802 47321	D1875 47356	D1949 47707
D1655 47536	D1729 47137	D1803 47322	D1876 47357	D1950 47802
D1656 47798	D1730 47786	D1804 47323	D1877 47358	D1951 47716

D1952 47508	D2050 03050	D2163 03163	D3029 08021	D3129 08094
D1953 47509	D2055 03055	D2164 03164	D3030 08022	D3130 08095
D1954 47713	D2056 03056	D2165 03165	D3031 08023	D3131 08096
D1955 47714	D2058 03058	D2166 03166	D3032 08024	D3132 08097
D1956 47803	D2059 03059	D2167 03167	D3033 08025	D3133 08098
D1957 47705	D2060 03060	D2168 03168	D3036 08026	D3134 08099
D1958 47512	D2061 03061	D2169 03169	D3039 08027	D3135 08100
D1959 47513	D2062 03062	D2170 03170	D3040 08028	D3136 08101
D1960 47703	D2063 03063	D2171 03171	D3041 08029	D3167 08102
D1961 47515	D2064 03064	D2172 03172	D3042 08030	D3168 08103
D1962 47788	D2066 03066	D2174 03174	D3043 08031	D3169 08104
D1963 47736	D2067 03067	D2175 03175	D3044 08032	D3170 08105
D1964 47829	D2068 03068	D2179 03179	D3046 08033	D3171 08106
D1965 47804	D2069 03069	D2180 03180	D3047 08034	D3173 08107
D1966 47828	D2072 03072	D2189 03189	D3048 08035	D3174 08108
D1967 47745	D2073 03073	D2196 03196	D3049 08036	D3175 08109
D1968 47708	D2075 03075	D2197 03197	D3050 08037	D3176 08110
D1969 47791	D2076 03076	D2310 04110	D3051 08038	D3177 08111
D1970 47643	D2078 03078	D2370 03370	D3052 08039	D3178 08112
D1971 47270	D2079 03079	D2371 03371	D3053 08040	D3179 08113
D1972 47854	D2080 03080	D2382 03382	D3054 08041	D3180 08114
D1973 47790	D2081 03081	D2386 03386	D3055 08042	D3181 08115
D1974 47627	D2084 03084	D2389 03389	D3056 08043	D3182 08116
D1975 47758	D2086 03086	D2397 03397	D3057 08044	D3184 08117
D1976 47826	D2089 03089	D2399 03399	D3058 08045	D3185 08118
D1977 47275	D2090 03090	D2413 06001	D3059 08046	D3186 08119
D1978 47276	D2091 03091	D2414 06002	D3060 08047	D3187 08120
D1979 47277	D2092 03092	D2420 06003	D3061 08048	D3188 08121
D1980 47278	D2094 03094	D2421 06004	D3062 08049	D3189 08122
D1981 47279	D2095 03095	D2422 06005	D3063 08050	D3190 08123
D1982 47280	D2096 03096	D2423 06006	D3064 08051	D3191 08124
D1983 47281	D2097 03097	D2426 06007	D3065 08052	D3192 08125
D1984 47282	D2098 03098	D2437 06008	D3066 08053	D3194 08126
D1985 47283	D2099 03099	D2440 06009	D3067 08054	D3195 08127
D1986 47284	D2102 03102	D2444 06010	D3068 08055	D3196 08128
D1987 47285	D2103 03103	D2554 05001	D3070 08056	D3197 08129
D1988 47286	D2104 03104	D2851 02001	D3071 08057	D3198 08130
D1989 47287	D2105 03105	D2852 02002	D3072 08058	D3199 08131
D1990 47288	D2106 03106	D2853 02003	D3073 08059	D3200 08132
D1991 47289	D2107 03107	D2856 02004	D3074 08060	D3201 08133
D1992 47290	D2108 03108	D2954 01001	D3075 08061	D3202 08134
D1993 47291	D2109 03109	D2955 01002	D3076 08062	D3203 08135
D1994 47292	D2110 03110	D2985 07001	D3077 08063	D3204 08136
D1995 47293	D2111 03111	D2986 07002	D3079 08064	D3205 08137
D1996 47294	D2112 03112	D2987 07003	D3080 08065	D3206 08138
D1997 47295	D2113 03113	D2989 07005	D3081 08066	D3207 08139
D1998 47296	D2118 03118	D2990 07006	D3082 08067	D3208 08140
D1999 47297	D2119 03119	D2991 07007	D3083 08068	D3209 08141
D2004 03004	D2120 03120	D2993 07009	D3084 08069	D3210 08142
D2005 03005	D2121 03121	D2994 07010	D3085 08070	D3211 08143
D2007 03007	D2128 03128	D2995 07011	D3086 08071	D3212 08144
D2008 03008	D2129 03129	D2996 07012	D3087 08072	D3213 08145
D2009 03009	D2134 03134	D2997 07013	D3088 08073	D3214 08146
D2010 03010	D2135 03135	D3004 08001	D3089 08074	D3215 08147
D2012 03012	D2137 03137	D3005 08002	D3090 08075	D3216 08148
D2013 03013	D2141 03141	D3007 08003	D3091 08076	D3217 08149
D2014 03014	D2142 03142	D3008 08004	D3102 08077	D3218 08150
D2016 03016	D2144 03144	D3009 08005	D3103 08078	D3219 08151
D2017 03017	D2145 03145	D3010 08006	D3104 08079	D3220 08152
D2018 03018	D2147 03147	D3012 08007	D3105 08080	D3221 08153
D2020 03020	D2149 03149	D3015 08008	D3106 08081	D3222 08154
D2021 03021	D2151 03151	D3016 08009	D3107 08082	D3223 08155
D2022 03022	D2152 03152	D3017 08010	D3108 08083	D3224 08156
D2025 03025	D2153 03153	D3018 08011	D3109 08084	D3225 08157
D2026 03026	D2154 03154	D3019 08012	D3110 08085	D3226 08158
D2027 03027	D2155 03155	D3020 08013	D3111 08086	D3227 08159
D2029 03029	D2156 03156	D3021 08014	D3112 08087	D3228 08160
D2034 03034	D2157 03157	D3022 08015	D3113 08088	D3229 08161
D2035 03035	D2158 03158	D3023 08016	D3114 08089	D3230 08162
D2037 03037	D2159 03159	D3024 08017	D3115 08090	D3231 08163
D2044 03044	D2160 03160	D3025 08018	D3116 08091	D3232 08164
D2045 03045	D2161 03161	D3027 08019	D3127 08092	D3233 08165
D2047 03047	D2162 03162	D3028 08020	D3128 08093	D3234 08166

D3235 08167	D3310 08240	D3383 08313	D3471 08386	D3573 08458
D3236 08168	D3311 08241	D3384 08314	D3472 08387	D3574 08459
D3237 08169	D3312 08242	D3385 08315	D3503 08388	D3575 08460
D3238 08170	D3313 08243	D3386 08316	D3504 08389	D3576 08461
D3239 08171	D3314 08244	D3387 08317	D3505 08390	D3577 08994
D3240 08172	D3315 08245	D3388 08318	D3506 08391	D3578 08463
D3241 08173	D3316 08246	D3389 08319	D3507 08392	D3579 08464
D3242 08174	D3317 08247	D3390 08320	D3508 08393	D3580 08465
D3243 08175	D3318 08248	D3391 08321	D3509 08394	D3581 08466
D3244 08176	D3319 08249	D3392 08322	D3510 08395	D3582 08467
D3245 08177	D3320 08250	D3393 08323	D3511 08396	D3583 08468
D3246 08178	D3321 08251	D3394 08324	D3512 08397	D3584 08469
D3247 08179	D3322 08252	D3395 08325	D3513 08398	D3585 08470
D3248 08180	D3323 08253	D3396 08326	D3514 08399	D3586 08471
D3249 08181	D3324 08254	D3397 08327	D3515 08400	D3587 08472
D3250 08182	D3325 08255	D3398 08328	D3516 08401	D3588 08473
D3251 08183	D3326 08256	D3399 08329	D3517 08402	D3589 08474
D3252 08184	D3327 08257	D3400 08330	D3518 08403	D3590 08475
D3253 08185	D3328 08258	D3401 08331	D3519 08404	D3591 08476
D3254 08186	D3329 08992	D3402 08332	D3520 08405	D3592 08477
D3256 08187	D3330 08260	D3403 08333	D3521 08406	D3593 08478
D3257 08188	D3331 08261	D3404 08334	D3522 08407	D3594 08479
D3258 08189	D3332 08262	D3405 08335	D3523 08408	D3595 08480
D3259 08190	D3333 08263	D3406 08336	D3524 08409	D3596 08481
D3260 08191	D3334 08264	D3407 08337	D3525 08410	D3597 08482
D3262 08192	D3335 08265	D3408 08338	D3526 08411	D3598 08483
D3263 08193	D3336 08266	D3409 08339	D3527 08412	D3599 08484
D3264 08194	D3337 97801 (08267)	D3410 08340	D3528 08413	D3600 08485
D3265 08195	D3338 08268	D3411 08341	D3529 08414	D3601 08486
D3266 08196	D3339 08269	D3412 08342	D3530 08415	D3602 08487
D3267 08197	D3340 08270	D3413 08343	D3531 08416	D3603 08488
D3268 08198	D3341 08271	D3414 08344	D3532 08417	D3604 08489
D3269 08199	D3342 08272	D3415 08345	D3533 08418	D3605 08490
D3270 08200	D3343 08273	D3416 08346	D3534 08419	D3606 08491
D3271 08201	D3344 08274	D3417 08347	D3535 08420	D3607 08492
D3272 08202	D3345 08275	D3418 08348	D3536 08421	D3608 08493
D3273 08991	D3346 08276	D3419 08349	D3536 09201	D3609 08494
D3274 08204	D3347 08277	D3420 08350	D3537 08422	D3610 08495
D3275 08205	D3348 08278	D3421 08351	D3538 08423	D3611 08496
D3276 08206	D3349 08279	D3422 08352	D3539 08424	D3652 08497
D3277 08207	D3350 08280	D3423 08353	D3540 08425	D3653 08498
D3278 08208	D3351 08281	D3424 08354	D3541 08426	D3654 08499
D3279 08209	D3352 08282	D3425 08355	D3542 08427	D3655 08500
D3280 08210	D3353 08283	D3426 08356	D3543 08428	D3656 08501
D3281 08211	D3354 08284	D3427 08357	D3544 08429	D3657 08502
D3282 08212	D3355 08285	D3428 08358	D3545 08430	D3658 08503
D3283 08213	D3356 08286	D3429 08359	D3546 08431	D3659 08504
D3284 08214	D3357 08287	D3430 08360	D3547 08432	D3660 08505
D3285 08215	D3358 08288	D3431 08361	D3548 08433	D3661 08506
D3286 08216	D3359 08289	D3432 08362	D3549 08434	D3662 08507
D3287 08217	D3360 08290	D3433 08363	D3550 08435	D3663 08508
D3288 08218	D3361 08291	D3434 08364	D3551 08436	D3664 08509
D3289 08219	D3362 08292	D3435 08365	D3552 08437	D3665 09001
D3290 08220	D3363 08293	D3436 08366	D3553 08438	D3666 09002
D3291 08221	D3364 08294	D3437 08367	D3554 08439	D3667 09003
D3292 08222	D3365 08295	D3438 08368	D3555 08440	D3668 09004
D3293 08223	D3366 08296	D3454 08369	D3556 08441	D3669 09005
D3294 08224	D3367 08297	D3455 08370	D3557 08442	D3670 09006
D3295 08225	D3368 08298	D3456 08371	D3558 08443	D3671 09007
D3296 08226	D3369 08299	D3457 08372	D3559 08444	D3672 08510
D3297 08227	D3370 08300	D3458 08373	D3560 08445	D3673 08511
D3298 08228	D3371 08301	D3459 08374	D3561 08446	D3674 08512
D3299 08229	D3372 08302	D3460 08375	D3562 08447	D3675 08513
D3300 08230	D3373 08303	D3461 08376	D3563 08448	D3676 08514
D3301 08231	D3374 08304	D3462 08377	D3564 08449	D3677 08515
D3302 08232	D3375 08305	D3463 08378	D3565 08450	D3678 08516
D3303 08233	D3376 08306	D3464 08379	D3566 08451	D3679 08517
D3304 08234	D3377 08307	D3465 08380	D3567 08452	D3680 08518
D3305 08235	D3378 08308	D3466 08381	D3568 08453	D3681 08519
D3306 08236	D3379 08309	D3467 08382	D3569 08454	D3682 08520
D3307 08237	D3380 08310	D3468 08383	D3570 08455	D3683 08521
D3308 08238	D3381 08311	D3469 08384	D3571 08456	D3684 08522
D3309 08239	D3382 08312	D3470 08385	D3572 08457	D3685 08523

D3686 08524	D3761 08594	D3833 08666	D3905 08737	D3974 08806
D3687 08525	D3762 08595	D3834 08667	D3906 08738	D3975 08807
D3688 08526	D3763 08596	D3835 08668	D3907 08739	D3976 08808
D3689 08527	D3764 08597	D3836 08669	D3908 08740	D3977 08809
D3690 08528	D3765 08598	D3837 08670	D3909 08741	D3978 08810
D3691 08529	D3766 08599	D3838 08671	D3910 08742	D3979 08811
D3692 08530	D3767 08600	D3839 08672	D3911 08743	D3980 08812
D3693 08531	D3768 08601	D3840 08673	D3912 08744	D3981 08813
D3694 08532	D3769 08602	D3841 08674	D3913 08745	D3982 08814
D3695 08533	D3770 08603	D3842 08675	D3914 08746	D3983 08815
D3696 08534	D3771 08604	D3843 08676	D3915 08747	D3984 08816
D3699 08535	D3772 08605	D3844 08677	D3916 08748	D3985 08817
D3700 08536	D3773 08606	D3845 08678	D3917 08749	D3986 08818
D3701 08537	D3774 08607	D3846 08679	D3917 09104	D3987 08819
D3702 08538	D3775 08608	D3847 08680	D3918 08750	D3988 08820
D3703 08539	D3776 08609	D3848 08681	D3919 08751	D3989 08821
D3704 08540	D3777 08610	D3849 08682	D3920 08752	D3990 08822
D3705 08541	D3778 08611	D3850 08683	D3921 08753	D3991 08823
D3706 08542	D3779 08612	D3851 08684	D3922 08754	D3992 08824
D3707 08543	D3780 08613	D3852 08685	D3923 08755	D3993 08825
D3708 08544	D3781 08614	D3853 08686	D3924 08756	D3994 08826
D3709 08545	D3782 08615	D3854 08995	D3925 08757	D3995 08827
D3710 08546	D3783 08616	D3855 08688	D3926 08758	D3996 08828
D3711 08547	D3784 08617	D3856 08689	D3927 08759	D3997 08829
D3712 08548	D3785 08618	D3857 08690	D3927 09106	D3998 08830
D3713 08549	D3786 08619	D3858 08691	D3928 08760	D3999 08831
D3714 08550	D3787 08620	D3859 08692	D3929 08761	D4000 08832
D3715 08551	D3787 09205	D3860 08693	D3930 08762	D4001 08833
D3716 08552	D3788 08621	D3861 08694	D3931 08763	D4002 08834
D3717 08553	D3789 08622	D3862 08695	D3932 08764	D4003 08835
D3718 08554	D3790 08623	D3863 08696	D3933 08765	D4004 08836
D3719 09008	D3791 08624	D3864 08697	D3934 08766	D4005 08837
D3720 09009	D3792 08625	D3865 08698	D3934 09103	D4006 08838
D3721 09010	D3793 08626	D3866 08699	D3935 08767	D4007 08839
D3722 08555	D3794 08627	D3867 08700	D3936 08768	D4008 08840
D3723 08556	D3795 08628	D3868 08701	D3937 08769	D4009 08841
D3724 08557	D3796 08629	D3869 08702	D3938 08770	D4010 08842
D3725 08558	D3797 08630	D3870 08703	D3939 08771	D4011 08843
D3726 08559	D3798 08631	D3871 08704	D3940 08772	D4012 08844
D3727 08560	D3799 08632	D3872 08705	D3941 08773	D4013 08845
D3728 08561	D3800 08633	D3873 08706	D3942 08774	D4014 08846
D3729 08562	D3801 08634	D3874 08707	D3943 08775	D4015 08847
D3730 08563	D3802 08635	D3875 08708	D3944 08776	D4016 08848
D3731 08564	D3803 08636	D3876 08709	D3945 08777	D4017 08849
D3732 08565	D3804 08637	D3877 08710	D3946 08778	D4018 08850
D3733 08566	D3805 08638	D3878 08711	D3947 08779	D4019 08851
D3734 08567	D3806 08639	D3879 08712	D3948 08780	D4020 08852
D3735 08568	D3807 08640	D3880 08713	D3949 08781	D4021 08853
D3736 08569	D3808 08641	D3881 08714	D3949 09203	D4022 08854
D3737 08570	D3809 08642	D3882 08715	D3950 08782	D4023 08855
D3738 08571	D3810 08643	D3884 08717	D3951 08783	D4024 08856
D3739 08572	D3811 08644	D3884 09204	D3952 08784	D4025 08857
D3740 08573	D3812 08645	D3886 08718	D3953 08785	D4026 08858
D3741 08574	D3813 08646	D3887 08719	D3954 08786	D4027 08859
D3742 08575	D3814 08647	D3888 08720	D3955 08787	D4028 08860
D3743 08576	D3815 08648	D3889 08721	D3956 08788	D4029 08861
D3744 08577	D3816 08649	D3890 08722	D3957 08789	D4030 08862
D3745 08578	D3817 08650	D3891 08723	D3958 08790	D4031 08863
D3746 08579	D3818 08651	D3892 08724	D3959 08791	D4032 08864
D3747 08580	D3819 08652	D3893 08725	D3960 08792	D4033 08865
D3748 08581	D3820 08653	D3894 08726	D3961 08793	D4034 08866
D3749 08582	D3821 08654	D3895 08727	D3962 08794	D4035 08867
D3750 08583	D3822 08655	D3896 08728	D3963 08795	D4036 08868
D3751 08584	D3823 08656	D3897 08729	D3964 08796	D4037 08869
D3752 08585	D3824 08657	D3898 08730	D3965 08797	D4038 08870
D3753 08586	D3825 08658	D3899 08731	D3966 08798	D4039 08871
D3754 08587	D3826 08659	D3900 08732	D3967 08799	D4040 08872
D3755 08588	D3827 08660	D3900 09202	D3968 08800	D4041 08873
D3756 08589	D3828 08661	D3901 08733	D3969 08801	D4042 08874
D3757 08590	D3829 08662	D3902 08734	D3970 08802	D4043 08875
D3758 08591	D3830 08663	D3903 08735	D3971 08803	D4044 08876
D3759 08993	D3831 08664	D3904 08736	D3972 08804	D4045 08877
D3760 08593	D3832 08665		D3973 08805	D4046 08878

D4047	08879	D4182	08952	D5046	24046	D5126	24126	D5203	25053
D4048	08880	D4183	08953	D5047	24047	D5127	24127	D5204	25054
D4095	08881	D4184	08954	D5048	24048	D5128	24128	D5205	25055
D4096	08882	D4185	08955	D5049	24049	D5129	24129	D5206	25056
D4097	08883	D4186	08956	D5050	24050	D5130	24130	D5207	25057
D4098	08884	D4191	08957	D5052	24052	D5132	24132	D5208	25058
D4115	08885	D4192	08958	D5053	24053	D5133	24133	D5209	25059
D4116	08886	D4099	09011	D5054	968008 (24054)	D5134	24134	D5210	25060
D4117	08887	D4100	09012	D5055	24055	D5135	24135	D5211	25061
D4118	08888	D4101	09013	D5056	24056	D5136	24136	D5212	25062
D4119	08889	D4102	09014	D5057	24057	D5137	24137	D5213	25063
D4120	08890	D4103	09015	D5058	24058	D5140	24140	D5214	25064
D4121	08891	D4104	09016	D5059	24059	D5141	24141	D5215	25065
D4122	08892	D4105	09017	D5060	24060	D5142	968009 (24142)	D5216	25066
D4123	08893	D4106	09018	D5061	968007 (24061)	D5143	24143	D5217	25067
D4124	08894	D4107	09019	D5062	24062	D5144	24144	D5218	25068
D4125	08895	D4108	09020	D5063	24063	D5145	24145	D5219	25069
D4126	08896	D4109	09021	D5064	24064	D5146	24146	D5220	25070
D4127	08897	D4110	09022	D5065	24065	D5147	24147	D5221	25071
D4128	08898	D4111	09023	D5066	24066	D5148	24148	D5222	25072
D4129	08899	D4112	09024	D5069	24069	D5150	24150	D5223	25073
D4130	08900	D4113	09025	D5070	24070	D5151	25001	D5224	25074
D4131	08901	D4114	09026	D5071	24071	D5152	25002	D5225	25075
D4132	08902	D4001	09101	D5072	24072	D5153	25003	D5226	25076
D4133	08903	D4000	09102	D5073	24073	D5154	25004	D5227	25077
D4134	08904	D4003	09105	D5074	24074	D5155	25005	D5228	25078
D4135	08905	D4013	09107	D5075	24075	D5156	25006	D5229	25079
D4136	08906	D4501	13001	D5076	24076	D5157	25007	D5230	25080
D4137	08907	D4502	13002	D5077	24077	D5158	25008	D5231	25081
D4138	08908	D4500	13003	D5078	24078	D5159	25009	D5232	25082
D4139	08909	D5000	24005	D5079	24079	D5160	25010	D5233	25083
D4140	08910	D5001	24001	D5080	24080	D5161	25011	D5234	25084
D4141	08911	D5002	24002	D5081	24081	D5162	25012	D5235	25085
D4142	08912	D5003	24003	D5082	24082	D5163	25013	D5236	25086
D4143	08913	D5004	24004	D5083	24083	D5164	25014	D5237	25087
D4144	08914	D5006	24006	D5084	24084	D5165	25015	D5238	25088
D4145	08915	D5007	24007	D5085	24085	D5166	25016	D5239	25089
D4146	08916	D5008	24008	D5086	24086	D5167	25017	D5240	25090
D4147	08917	D5009	24009	D5087	24087	D5168	25018	D5241	25091
D4148	08918	D5010	24010	D5089	24089	D5169	25019	D5242	25092
D4149	08919	D5011	24011	D5090	24090	D5170	25020	D5243	25093
D4150	08920	D5012	24012	D5091	24091	D5171	25021	D5244	25094
D4151	08921	D5013	24013	D5092	24092	D5172	25022	D5245	25095
D4152	08922	D5014	24014	D5094	24094	D5173	25023	D5246	25096
D4153	08923	D5015	24015	D5095	24095	D5174	25024	D5247	25097
D4154	08924	D5016	24016	D5096	24096	D5175	25025	D5248	25098
D4155	08925	D5017	24017	D5097	24097	D5176	25026	D5249	25099
D4156	08926	D5018	24018	D5098	24098	D5177	25027	D5250	25100
D4157	08927	D5019	24019	D5099	24099	D5178	25028	D5251	25101
D4158	08928	D5020	24020	D5100	24100	D5179	25029	D5252	25102
D4159	08929	D5021	24021	D5101	24101	D5180	25030	D5253	25103
D4160	08930	D5022	24022	D5102	24102	D5181	25031	D5254	25104
D4161	08931	D5023	24023	D5103	24103	D5182	25032	D5255	25105
D4162	08932	D5024	24024	D5104	24104	D5183	25033	D5256	25106
D4163	08933	D5025	24025	D5105	24105	D5184	25034	D5257	25107
D4164	08934	D5026	24026	D5106	24106	D5185	25035	D5258	25108
D4165	08935	D5027	24027	D5107	24107	D5186	25036	D5259	25109
D4166	08936	D5029	24029	D5108	24108	D5187	25037	D5260	25110
D4167	08937	D5030	24030	D5109	24109	D5188	25038	D5261	25111
D4168	08938	D5031	24031	D5110	24110	D5189	25039	D5262	25112
D4169	08939	D5032	24032	D5111	24111	D5190	25040	D5263	25113
D4170	08940	D5033	24033	D5112	24112	D5191	25041	D5264	25114
D4171	08941	D5034	24034	D5113	24113	D5192	25042	D5265	25115
D4172	08942	D5035	24035	D5115	24115	D5193	25043	D5266	25116
D4173	08943	D5036	24036	D5116	24116	D5194	25044	D5267	25117
D4174	08944	D5037	24037	D5117	24117	D5195	25045	D5268	25118
D4175	08945	D5038	24038	D5118	24118	D5196	25046	D5269	25119
D4176	08946	D5039	24039	D5119	24119	D5197	25047	D5270	25120
D4177	08947	D5040	24040	D5120	24120	D5198	25048	D5271	25121
D4178	08948	D5041	24041	D5121	24121	D5199	25049	D5272	25122
D4179	08949	D5042	24042	D5123	24123	D5200	25050	D5273	25123
D4180	08950	D5044	24044	D5124	24124	D5201	25051	D5274	25124
D4181	08951	D5045	24045	D5125	24125	D5202	25052	D5275	25125

D5276 25126	D5351 27005	D5508 968016 (31008)	D5581 31163	D5654 31454
D5277 25127	D5352 27006	D5509 31009	D5582 31164	D5655 31229
D5279 25129	D5353 27007	D5510 31010	D5583 31165	D5656 31409
D5280 25130	D5354 27008	D5511 31011	D5584 31166	D5657 31230
D5281 97202 (25131)	D5355 27009	D5512 31012	D5585 31167	D5658 31231
D5282 25132	D5356 27010	D5513 968013 (31013)	D5586 31168	D5659 31232
D5283 25133	D5357 27011	D5514 968015 (31014)	D5587 31457	D5660 31233
D5284 25134	D5358 27012	D5515 31015	D5588 31170	D5661 31234
D5285 25135	D5359 27013	D5516 31016	D5589 31401	D5662 31235
D5286 25136	D5360 27014	D5517 31017	D5590 31171	D5663 31433
D5287 25137	D5361 27015	D5518 31101	D5591 31420	D5664 31237
D5288 25138	D5362 27016	D5519 31019	D5592 31402	D5665 31238
D5289 25139	D5363 27017	D5520 31102	D5593 31173	D5666 31439
D5290 25140	D5364 27018	D5521 31103	D5594 31174	D5667 31240
D5291 25141	D5365 27019	D5522 31418	D5595 31175	D5668 31241
D5292 25142	D5366 27020	D5523 31105	D5596 31403	D5669 31410
D5293 25143	D5367 27021	D5524 31106	D5597 31176	D5670 31242
D5294 25144	D5368 27022	D5525 31107	D5598 31443	D5671 31243
D5295 25145	D5369 27023	D5526 31108	D5599 31178	D5672 31244
D5296 25146	D5370 968028 (27024)	D5527 31109	D5600 31435	D5673 31245
D5297 25147	D5371 27025	D5528 31110	D5601 31180	D5674 31455
D5298 25148	D5372 27026	D5529 31111	D5602 31181	D5675 31247
D5299 25149	D5373 27027	D5530 31112	D5603 31437	D5676 31248
D5300 26007	D5374 27101	D5531 31113	D5604 31183	D5677 31249
D5301 26001	D5375 27028	D5532 31553	D5605 31404	D5678 31250
D5302 26002	D5376 27029	D5533 31466	D5606 31405	D5679 31442
D5303 26003	D5377 27030	D5534 31116	D5607 31184	D5680 31252
D5304 26004	D5378 27031	D5535 31117	D5608 31185	D5681 31531
D5305 26005	D5379 27032	D5536 31118	D5609 31601	D5682 31254
D5306 26006	D5380 27102	D5537 31119	D5610 31187	D5683 31255
D5307 26020	D5381 27033	D5538 31120	D5611 31188	D5684 31459
D5308 26008	D5382 27034	D5539 31121	D5612 31189	D5685 31257
D5309 26009	D5383 27124	D5540 31122	D5613 31190	D5686 31434
D5310 26010	D5384 27035	D5541 31123	D5614 31602	D5687 31259
D5311 26011	D5385 27036	D5542 31124	D5615 31192	D5688 31260
D5312 26012	D5386 27066	D5543 31125	D5616 31406	D5689 31261
D5313 26013	D5387 27104	D5544 31126	D5617 31426	D5690 31262
D5314 26014	D5388 27105	D5545 31127	D5618 31427	D5691 31411
D5315 26015	D5389 27037	D5546 31128	D5619 31195	D5692 31412
D5316 26016	D5390 27038	D5547 31461	D5620 31196	D5693 31263
D5317 26017	D5391 27201	D5548 31130	D5621 31423	D5694 31264
D5318 26018	D5392 27202	D5549 31131	D5622 31198	D5695 31530
D5319 26019	D5393 27203	D5550 31132	D5623 31199	D5696 31460
D5320 26028	D5394 27050	D5551 31450	D5624 31200	D5697 31519
D5321 26021	D5395 27051	D5552 31134	D5625 31201	D5698 31268
D5322 26022	D5396 27052	D5553 31135	D5626 31202	D5699 31429
D5323 26023	D5397 27053	D5554 31136	D5627 31203	D5800 31270
D5324 26024	D5398 27039	D5555 31444	D5628 31440	D5801 31271
D5325 26025	D5399 27054	D5556 31138	D5629 31205	D5802 31272
D5326 26026	D5400 27055	D5557 31538	D5630 31206	D5803 31273
D5327 26027	D5401 27056	D5558 31421	D5631 31207	D5804 31425
D5329 26029	D5402 27057	D5559 31141	D5632 31208	D5805 31275
D5330 26030	D5403 27058	D5560 31142	D5633 31209	D5806 31276
D5331 26031	D5404 968025 (27207)	D5561 31143	D5634 31210	D5807 31569
D5332 26032	D5405 27041	D5562 31144	D5635 31428	D5808 31278
D5333 26033	D5406 27042	D5563 31145	D5636 31212	D5809 31452
D5334 26034	D5407 27208	D5564 31146	D5637 31465	D5810 31280
D5335 26035	D5408 27063	D5565 31147	D5638 31214	D5811 31281
D5336 26036	D5409 27064	D5566 31548	D5639 31215	D5812 31413
D5337 26037	D5410 27059	D5567 31149	D5640 31407	D5813 31282
D5338 26038	D5411 27065	D5568 31150	D5641 31467	D5814 31514
D5339 26039	D5412 27206	D5569 31436	D5642 31217	D5815 31283
D5340 26040	D5413 27047	D5570 31152	D5643 31218	D5816 31284
D5341 26041	D5414 27043	D5571 31432	D5644 31219	D5817 31285
D5342 26042	D5415 27044	D5572 31154	D5645 31541	D5818 31286
D5343 26043	D5500 31018	D5573 31155	D5646 31408	D5819 31287
D5344 26044	D5501 31001	D5574 31156	D5647 31221	D5820 31288
D5345 26045	D5502 968014 (31002)	D5575 31524	D5648 31222	D5821 31289
D5346 26046	D5503 31003	D5576 31158	D5649 31223	D5822 31290
D5347 27001	D5504 31004	D5577 31159	D5650 31224	D5823 31556
D5348 27002	D5505 31005	D5578 31160	D5651 31225	D5824 31415
D5349 27003	D5506 31006	D5579 31400	D5652 31226	D5825 31292
D5350 27004	D5507 31007	D5580 31162	D5653 31227	D5826 31293

D5827 31294	D6538 33118	D6705 37601	D6778 37078	D6851 37667
D5828 31547	D6539 33021	D6706 37798	D6779 37357	D6852 37152
D5829 31296	D6540 33022	D6707 37604	D6780 37080	D6853 37153
D5830 31563	D6541 33023	D6708 37352	D6781 37797	D6854 37154
D5831 97203 (31298)	D6542 33024	D6709 37340	D6782 37602	D6855 37897
D5832 31299	D6543 33025	D6710 37010	D6783 37083	D6856 37156
D5833 31545	D6544 33026	D6711 37011	D6784 37718	D6857 37695
D5834 31301	D6545 33027	D6712 37012	D6785 37711	D6858 37158
D5835 31302	D6546 33028	D6713 37013	D6786 37516	D6859 37372
D5836 31558	D6547 33029	D6714 37709	D6787 37087	D6860 37373
D5837 31304	D6548 33030	D6715 37341	D6788 37088	D6861 37899
D5838 31305	D6549 33031	D6716 37706	D6789 37708	D6862 37162
D5839 31306	D6550 33032	D6717 37503	D6790 37606	D6863 37802
D5840 31549	D6551 33033	D6718 37517	D6791 37358	D6864 37675
D5841 31308	D6552 33034	D6719 37519	D6792 37092	D6865 37165
D5842 31516	D6553 33035	D6720 37702	D6793 37509	D6866 37891
D5843 31309	D6554 33036	D6721 37715	D6794 37716	D6867 37383
D5844 31422	D6555 33037	D6722 37608	D6795 37095	D6868 37890
D5845 31311	D6556 33038	D6723 37023	D6796 37096	D6869 37674
D5846 31312	D6557 33039	D6724 37714	D6797 37097	D6870 97302 (37170)
D5847 31313	D6558 33040	D6725 37025	D6798 37098	D6871 37611
D5848 31314	D6559 33041	D6726 37026	D6799 37099	D6872 37686
D5849 31462	D6560 33042	D6727 37519	D6800 97301 (37100)	D6873 37801
D5850 31546	D6561 33043	D6728 37505	D6801 37345	D6874 37174
D5851 31317	D6562 33044	D6729 37029	D6802 37712	D6875 37175
D5852 31551	D6563 33045	D6730 37701	D6803 37607	D6876 37883
D5853 31319	D6564 33046	D6731 37031	D6804 37104	D6877 37885
D5854 31320	D6565 33047	D6732 37032	D6805 37796	D6878 97303 (37178)
D5855 31468	D6566 33048	D6733 37719	D6806 37106	D6879 37612
D5856 31417	D6567 33049	D6734 37704	D6807 37107	D6880 37886
D5857 31322	D6568 33050	D6735 37035	D6808 37108	D6881 37610
D5858 31323	D6569 33051	D6736 37605	D6809 37109	D6882 37670
D5859 31324	D6570 33052	D6737 37037	D6810 37110	D6883 37884
D5860 31464	D6571 33053	D6738 37038	D6811 37111	D6884 37184
D5861 31970 (31326)	D6572 33054	D6739 37603	D6812 37510	D6885 37185
D5862 31327	D6573 33055	D6740 37040	D6813 37113	D6886 37898
D6500 33001	D6574 33056	D6741 37520	D6814 37114	D6887 37683
D6501 33002	D6575 33057	D6742 37042	D6815 37609	D6888 37188
D6503 33003	D6577 33058	D6743 37354	D6816 37116	D6889 37672
D6504 33004	D6578 33059	D6744 37710	D6817 37521	D6890 37190
D6505 33005	D6579 33060	D6745 37355	D6818 37359	D6891 37191
D6506 33006	D6580 33119	D6746 37046	D6819 37895	D6892 37694
D6507 33007	D6581 33061	D6747 37047	D6820 37883	D6893 37375
D6508 33008	D6582 33062	D6748 37048	D6821 37677	D6894 37194
D6509 33009	D6583 33063	D6749 37343	D6822 37692	D6895 37689
D6510 33010	D6584 33064	D6750 37717	D6823 37679	D6896 37196
D6511 33101	D6585 33065	D6751 37051	D6824 37894	D6897 37197
D6512 33011	D6586 33201	D6752 37713	D6825 37904	D6898 37198
D6513 33102	D6587 33202	D6753 37344	D6826 37676	D6899 37376
D6514 33103	D6588 33203	D6754 37054	D6827 37370	D6900 37377
D6515 33012	D6589 33204	D6755 37055	D6828 37330	D6901 37201
D6516 33104	D6590 33205	D6756 37513	D6829 37669	D6902 37331
D6517 33105	D6591 33206	D6757 37057	D6830 37681	D6903 37203
D6518 33013	D6592 33207	D6758 37058	D6831 37131	D6904 37378
D6519 33106	D6593 33208	D6759 37059	D6832 37673	D6905 37688
D6520 33107	D6594 33209	D6760 37705	D6833 37133	D6906 37906
D6521 33108	D6595 33210	D6761 37799	D6834 37684	D6907 37207
D6522 33014	D6596 33211	D6762 37062	D6835 37888	D6908 37803
D6523 33015	D6597 33212	D6763 37063	D6836 37905	D6909 37209
D6524 33016	D6600 37429	D6764 37515	D6837 37137	D6910 37693
D6525 33109	D6601 37412	D6765 37065	D6838 37138	D6911 37211
D6526 33017	D6602 37416	D6766 37066	D6839 37139	D6912 37212
D6527 33110	D6603 37333	D6767 37703	D6840 37140	D6913 37213
D6528 33111	D6604 37334	D6768 37356	D6841 37141	D6914 37214
D6529 33112	D6605 37407	D6769 37069	D6842 37142	D6915 37215
D6530 33018	D6606 37273 (2)	D6770 37070	D6843 37800	D6916 37216
D6531 33113	D6607 37403	D6771 37071	D6844 37144	D6917 97304 (37217)
D6532 33114	D6608 37308	D6772 37072	D6845 37382	D6918 37218
D6533 33115	D6700 37350	D6773 37073	D6846 37146	D6919 37219
D6534 33019	D6701 37707	D6774 37074	D6847 37371	D6920 37220
D6535 33116	D6702 37351	D6775 37075	D6848 37902	D6921 37221
D6536 33117	D6703 37003	D6776 37518	D6849 37892	D6922 37222
D6537 33020	D6704 37004	D6777 37077	D6850 37901	D6923 37223

D6924 37680	D6998 37298	D7571 25221	D7645 25295	D8040 20040
D6925 37225	D6999 37426	D7572 25222	D7646 25906	D8041 20904
D6926 37379	D7500 25150	D7573 25223	D7647 25907	D8042 20312
D6927 37227	D7501 25151	D7574 25224	D7648 25298	D8043 20043
D6928 37696	D7502 25152	D7575 25225	D7649 25299	D8044 20044
D6929 37229	D7503 25153	D7576 25226	D7650 25300	D8045 20045
D6930 37230	D7504 25154	D7577 25227	D7651 25301	D8046 20046
D6931 37896	D7505 25155	D7578 25228	D7652 25302	D8047 20301 (2)
D6932 37232	D7506 25156	D7579 25229	D7653 25303	D8048 20048
D6933 37889	D7507 25157	D7580 25230	D7654 25304	D8049 20049
D6934 37685	D7508 25158	D7581 25231	D7655 97251 (25305)	D8050 20307 (2)
D6935 37235	D7509 25159	D7582 25232	D7656 25306	D8051 20051
D6936 37682	D7510 25160	D7583 25233	D7657 25908	D8052 20052
D6937 37893	D7511 25161	D7584 25234	D7658 25308	D8053 20053
D6938 37238	D7512 25162	D7585 25235	D7659 25909	D8054 20054
D6939 37332	D7513 25163	D7586 25236	D7660 97250 (25310)	D8055 20055
D6940 37240	D7514 25164	D7587 25237	D7661 25311	D8056 20056
D6941 37241	D7515 25165	D7588 25238	D7662 25312	D8057 20057
D6942 37242	D7516 25166	D7589 25239	D7663 25313	D8058 20058
D6943 37697	D7517 25167	D7590 25240	D7664 97252 (25314)	D8059 20059
D6944 37244	D7518 25168	D7591 25241	D7665 25910	D8060 20902
D6945 37245	D7519 25169	D7592 25242	D7666 25911	D8061 20061
D6946 37698	D7520 25170	D7593 25243	D7667 25317	D8062 20062
D6947 37671	D7521 25171	D7594 25244	D7668 25318	D8063 20063
D6948 37248	D7522 25172	D7595 25245	D7669 25319	D8064 20064
D6949 37903	D7523 25173	D7596 25246	D7670 25320	D8065 20065
D6950 37250	D7524 25174	D7597 25247	D7671 25321	D8066 20066
D6951 37251	D7525 25175	D7598 25248	D7672 25912	D8067 20067
D6952 37252	D7526 25176	D7599 25249	D7673 25323	D8068 20068
D6953 37699	D7527 25177	D7600 25250	D7674 25324	D8069 20069
D6954 37254	D7528 25178	D7601 25251	D7675 25325	D8070 20070
D6955 37255	D7529 25179	D7602 25252	D7676 25326	D8071 20071
D6956 37678	D7530 25180	D7603 25253	D7677 25327	D8072 20072
D6957 37668	D7531 25181	D7604 25254	D8000 20050	D8073 20073
D6958 37384	D7532 25182	D7606 25256	D8001 20001	D8074 20074
D6959 37259	D7533 25183	D7607 25257	D8002 20002	D8075 20309
D6960 37260	D7534 25184	D7608 25258	D8003 20003	D8076 20076
D6961 37261	D7535 25185	D7609 25259	D8004 20004	D8077 20077
D6962 37262	D7536 25186	D7610 25260	D8005 20005	D8078 20078
D6963 37263	D7537 25187	D7611 25261	D8006 20006	D8079 20079
D6964 37264	D7538 25188	D7612 25901	D8007 20007	D8080 20080
D6965 37430	D7539 25189	D7613 25263	D8008 20008	D8081 20081
D6966 37422	D7540 25190	D7614 25264	D8009 20009	D8082 20082
D6967 37421	D7541 25191	D7615 25265	D8010 20010	D8083 20903
D6968 37401	D7542 25192	D7616 25266	D8011 20011	D8084 20302 (2)
D6969 37417	D7543 25193	D7617 25267	D8012 20012	D8085 20085
D6970 37409	D7544 25194	D7618 25902	D8013 20013	D8086 20086
D6971 37418	D7545 25195	D7619 25269	D8014 20014	D8087 20087
D6972 37431	D7546 25196	D7620 25270	D8015 20015	D8088 20088
D6973 37410	D7547 25197	D7621 25271	D8016 20016	D8089 20089
D6974 37402	D7548 25198	D7622 25272	D8017 20017	D8090 20090
D6975 37275	D7549 25199	D7623 25273	D8018 20018	D8091 20091
D6976 37413	D7550 25200	D7624 25274	D8019 20019	D8092 20092
D6977 37415	D7551 25201	D7625 25275	D8020 20020	D8093 20093
D6978 37278	D7552 25202	D7626 25903	D8021 20021	D8094 20094
D6979 37424	D7553 25203	D7627 25277	D8022 20022	D8095 20305 (2)
D6980 37280	D7554 25204	D7628 25278	D8023 20023	D8096 20096
D6981 37428	D7555 25205	D7629 25279	D8024 20024	D8097 20097
D6982 37405	D7556 25206	D7630 25280	D8025 20025	D8098 20098
D6984 37381	D7557 25207	D7631 25281	D8026 20026	D8099 20099
D6985 37335	D7558 25208	D7632 25282	D8027 20027	D8100 20100
D6986 37404	D7559 25209	D7633 25904	D8028 20028	D8101 20901
D6987 37414	D7560 25210	D7634 25284	D8029 20029	D8102 20311
D6988 37427	D7561 25211	D7635 25285	D8030 20030	D8103 20103
D6989 37408	D7562 25212	D7636 25905	D8031 20031	D8104 20315
D6990 37411	D7563 25213	D7637 25287	D8032 20032	D8105 20105
D6991 37419	D7564 25214	D7638 25288	D8033 20033	D8106 20106
D6992 37425	D7565 25215	D7639 25289	D8034 20034	D8107 20107
D6993 37293	D7566 25216	D7640 25290	D8035 20035	D8108 20108
D6994 37294	D7567 25217	D7641 25291	D8036 20036	D8109 20109
D6995 37406	D7568 25218	D7642 25292	D8037 20037	D8110 20110
D6996 37423	D7569 25219	D7643 25293	D8038 20038	D8111 20111
D6997 37420	D7570 25220	D7644 25294	D8039 20039	D8112 20112

D8113 20113	D8149 20149	D8185 20185	D8321 20221	E3008 81007
D8114 20114	D8150 20150	D8186 20186	D8322 20222	E3010 81008
D8115 20115	D8151 20151	D8187 20308	D8323 20223	E3011 81009
D8116 20116	D8152 20152	D8188 20188	D8324 20224	E3012 81010
D8117 20314	D8153 20153	D8189 20189	D8325 20905	E3013 81011
D8118 20118	D8154 20154	D8190 20310	D8326 20226	E3014 81012
D8119 20119	D8155 20155	D8191 20191	D8327 20227	E3015 81013
D8120 20304 (2)	D8156 20156	D8192 20192	D9000 55022	E3016 81014
D8121 20121	D8157 20157	D8193 20193	D9001 55001	E3017 81015
D8122 20122	D8158 20158	D8194 20313	D9002 55002	E3018 81016
D8123 20123	D8159 20159	D8195 20195	D9003 55003	E3020 81017
D8124 20124	D8160 20160	D8196 20196	D9004 55004	E3021 81018
D8125 20125	D8161 20161	D8197 20197	D9005 55005	E3022 81019
D8126 20126	D8162 20162	D8198 20198	D9006 55006	E3023 81020
D8127 20303 (2)	D8163 20163	D8199 20199	D9007 55007	E3024 83001
D8128 20228	D8164 20164	D8300 20200	D9008 55008	E3025 83002
D8129 20129	D8165 20165	D8301 20201	D9009 55009	E3026 83003
D8130 20130	D8166 20166	D8302 20202	D9010 55010	E3027 83004
D8131 20306 (2)	D8167 20167	D8303 20203	D9011 55011	E3028 83005
D8132 20132	D8168 20168	D8304 20204	D9012 55012	E3029 83006
D8133 20133	D8169 20169	D8305 20205	D9013 55013	E3030 83007
D8134 20134	D8170 20170	D8306 20206	D9014 55014	E3031 83008
D8135 20135	D8171 20171	D8307 20207	D9015 55015	E3032 83009
D8136 20136	D8172 20172	D8308 20208	D9016 55016	E3033 83010
D8137 20137	D8173 20173	D8309 20209	D9017 55017	E3034 83011
D8138 20138	D8174 20174	D8310 20210	D9018 55018	E3035 83012
D8139 20139	D8175 20175	D8311 20211	D9019 55019	E3036 84001
D8140 20140	D8176 20176	D8312 20212	D9020 55020	E3037 84002
D8141 20141	D8177 20177	D8313 20213	D9021 55021	E3038 84003
D8142 20142	D8178 20178	D8314 20214	D9524 14901	E3039 84004
D8143 20143	D8179 20179	D8315 20215	E3001 81001	E3040 84005
D8144 20144	D8180 20180	D8316 20216	E3003 81002	E3041 84006
D8145 20145	D8181 20181	D8317 20217	E3004 81003	E3042 84007
D8146 20146	D8182 20182	D8318 20218	E3005 81004	E3043 84008
D8147 20147	D8183 20183	D8319 20906 (3)	E3006 81005	E3044 968021 (84009)
D8148 20148	D8184 20184	D8320 20220	E3007 81006	E3045 84010

▲ Class 82 E3048 passes northbound through Crewe on the centre road with an unscheduled additional service circa 1961.
R. Whitfield/Rail Photoprints

E3047	82001	E3095	85040	E3142	86254	E3188	86631	E6019	73211
E3048	82002	E3096	81021	E3143	86103	E3189	86250	E6020	73114
E3049	82003	E3097	81022	E3144	86702	E3190	86902	E6021	73115
E3050	82004	E3098	83013	E3145	86614	E3191	86101	E6022	73210
E3051	82005	E3099	83014	E3146	86417	E3192	86247	E6023	73117
E3052	82006	E3100	83015	E3147	86211	E3193	86213	E6024	73118
E3053	82007	E3101	86252	E3148	86632	E3194	86235	E6025	73119
E3054	82008	E3102	86609	E3149	86246	E3195	86426	E6026	73209
E3056	85001	E3103	86604	E3150	86102	E3196	86219	E6028	73208
E3057	85002	E3104	86610	E3151	86212	E3197	86237	E6029	73207
E3058	85113	E3105	86430	E3152	86623	E3198	86633	E6030	73206
E3059	85111	E3106	86214	E3153	86639	E3199	86401	E6031	73205
E3060	85005	E3107	86248	E3154	86255	E3200	86429	E6032	73204
E3061	85006	E3108	86638	E3155	86234	E5000	E5024	E6033	73126
E3062	85112	E3109	86416	E3156	86220	E5001	71001	E6034	73203
E3063	85008	E3110	86627	E3157	86621	E5002	71002	E6035	73128
E3064	85102	E3111	86424	E3158	86223	E5004	71004	E6036	73129
E3065	85103	E3112	86606	E3159	86628	E5007	71007	E6037	73130
E3066	85114	E3113	86232	E3160	86636	E5008	71008	E6038	73131
E3067	85104	E3114	86620	E3161	86249	E5009	71009	E6039	73132
E3068	85013	E3115	86603	E3162	86226	E5010	71010	E6040	73133
E3069	85014	E3116	86238	E3163	86618	E5011	71011	E6041	73134
E3070	85015	E3117	86227	E3164	86225	E5012	71012	E6042	73235
E3071	85105	E3118	86261	E3165	86215	E5013	71013	E6043	73136
E3072	85017	E3119	86229	E3166	86216	E5014	71014	E6044	73202
E3073	85018	E3120	86419	E3167	86228	E5018	71003	E6045	73138
E3074	85019	E3121	86241	E3168	86230	E5020	71005	E6046	73139
E3075	85020	E3122	86612	E3169	86239	E5022	71006	E6047	73140
E3076	85106	E3123	86615	E3170	86602	E6001	73001	E6048	73141
E3077	85022	E3124	86635	E3171	86611	E6002	73002	E6049	73201
E3078	85023	E3125	86209	E3172	86233	E6003	73003	E6101	74001
E3079	85107	E3126	86231	E3173	86204	E6004	73004	E6102	74002
E3080	85025	E3127	86240	E3174	86622	E6005	73005	E6103	74003
E3081	85026	E3128	86613	E3175	86218	E6006	73906	E6104	74004
E3082	85027	E3129	86701	E3176	86607	E6007	73101	E6105	74005
E3083	85028	E3130	86637	E3177	86217	E6008	73212	E6106	74006
E3084	85029	E3131	86222	E3178	86244	E6009	73103	E6107	74007
E3085	85030	E3132	86221	E3179	86207	E6010	73104	E6108	74008
E3086	85031	E3133	86236	E3180	86608	E6011	73105	E6109	74009
E3087	85108	E3134	86224	E3181	86243	E6012	73106	E6110	74010
E3088	85033	E3135	86256	E3182	86245	E6013	73107		
E3089	85034	E3136	86901	E3183	86251	E6014	73108	PWM650	97650
E3090	85109	E3137	86259	E3184	86206	E6015	73109	PWM651	97651
E3091	85110	E3138	86242	E3185	86605	E6016	73110	PWM652	97652
E3092	85037	E3139	86257	E3186	86425	E6017	73111	PWM653	97653
E3093	85038	E3140	86258	E3187	86634	E6018	73213	PWM654	97654
E3094	85039	E3141	86208						

APPENDIX IV: DEPARTMENTAL NUMBERS

This appendix lists all locomotives that were renumbered for departmental use. It does not include locos that were assigned a departmental number which was not actually carried, or departmental locos that were not given a separate departmental number, such as the Network Rail HSTs (43013, 43014 and 43062). In each case, the departmental number is shown, along with the corresponding loco class and the number by which it is listed in this book.

Departmental No.	Class the loco is listed under	Number listed by	Notes
20	Purpose built departmental	97020	
56	Purpose built departmental	56	
82	Purpose built departmental	82	
83	Purpose built departmental	83	
84	Purpose built departmental	84	
85	Purpose built departmental	85	
86	Purpose built departmental	86	
87	Purpose built departmental	87	
88	05	D2612	
89	05	D2615	
100	EB1	26510	
31970	31	31970	Second of two departmental numbers carried by 31326
47971	47	47971	Second of two departmental numbers carried by 47480
47972	47	47972	Second of two departmental numbers carried by 47545
47973	47	47973	Second of two departmental numbers carried by 47561
47974	47	47775	
47975	47	47540	
47976	47	47976	
47981	47	47981	
73951	73/9	73951	
73952	73/9	73952	
86901	86	86901	
86902	86	86902	
97201	24	24061	First of two departmental numbers carried by 24061
97202	25	25131	
97203	31	31298	
97204	31	31970	First of two departmental numbers carried by 31326
97250	25	25310	
97251	25	25305	
97252	25	25314	
97301	37	97301	
97302	37	97302	
97303	37	97303	
97304	37	97304	
97403	46	46035	
97404	46	46045	
97405	40	40060	
97406	40	40135	
97407	40	40012	
97408	40	40118	
97409	45	45022	
97410	45	45029	
97411	45	45034	
97412	45	45040	
97413	45	45066	
97472	47	47472	
97480	47	47971	First of two departmental numbers carried by 47480
97545	47	47972	First of two departmental numbers carried by 47545
97561	47	47973	First of two departmental numbers carried by 47561
97650	Purpose built departmental	97650	
97651	Purpose built departmental	97651	
97652	Purpose built departmental	97652	
97653	Purpose built departmental	97653	
97654	Purpose built departmental	97654	

97800	08	08600	
97801	08	08267	Second of two departmental numbers carried by 08267
97803	05	05001	
97804	06	06003	
97806	09	09017	
ADB966506	08	D3078	
ADB966507	08	D3006	
ADB966508	08	D3035	
ADB966509	08	D3069	
ADB966510	08	D3037	
ADB966511	08	08119	First of two departmental numbers carried by 08119
ADB966512	08	08111	First of two departmental numbers carried by 08111
ADB966513	08	08117	First of three departmental numbers carried by 08117
ADB968000	15	D8243	
ADB968001	15	D8233	
ADB968002	15	D8237	
ADB968003	15	D8203	
ADB968008	24	24054	
ADB968009	24	24142	
ADB968010	08	08117	Third of three departmental numbers carried by 08117
ADB968011	08	08119	Second of two departmental numbers carried by 08119
ADB968012	08	08111	Second of two departmental numbers carried by 08111
ADB968013	08	08117	Second of three departmental numbers carried by 08117
ADB968013[2]	31	31013	
ADB968014	31	31002	
ADB968015	31	31014	
ADB968016	31	31008	
ADB968021	84	84009	
ADB968024	45	45017	
ADB968025	27	27207	
ADB968028	27	27024	
ADB968035	47	47538	
ADB975812	41	41001	
ADB975813	41	41002	
DS1169	Purpose built departmental	DS1169	
ED1	Purpose built departmental	ED1	
ED2	Purpose built departmental	ED2	
ED3	Purpose built departmental	ED3	
ED4	Purpose built departmental	ED4	
ED5	Purpose built departmental	ED5	
ED6	Purpose built departmental	ED6	
ED7	Purpose built departmental	ED7	
PO1	08	08247	
PO1[2]	08	08173	
PWM650	Purpose built departmental	97650	
PWM651	Purpose built departmental	97651	
PWM652	Purpose built departmental	97652	
PWM653	Purpose built departmental	97653	
PWM654	Purpose built departmental	97654	
RDB968007	24	24061	Second of two departmental numbers carried by 24061
RDB968020	08	08267	First of two departmental numbers carried by 08267
S18521	17	D8521	
TDB968006	28	D5705	Formerly carried departmental number S15705
TDB968030	33	33018	

APPENDIX V: LOCOMOTIVE NAMES

This appendix contains a list of all official locomotive names carried during main line service with BR or its successors. Names given during preservation are not included. The name listings are case sensitive as carried on locos and where a loco has carried more than one name, they are listed chronologically, in the order they were carried.

Names are listed adjacent to the locomotive number carried in the period when the name was also carried. In the case of subsequently renumbered locomotives, this is not the number under which the locomotive's entry can be found in this book. Please refer to appendices 2 and 3 as necessary to locate where the locomotive's details can be found in this book.

Unofficial names are not included and in cases where it is not clear whether a name is official, names on cast nameplates are included and names painted on to the sides of locos have been excluded. Where a crest or plaque is mounted separately, and this also includes text, this is not listed. For example, 31602 had a separate "19B" plaque under the "DRIVER DAVE GREEN" nameplate and only the text on the nameplate is included.

Number	Name/Names
03179	CLIVE
08389	NOEL KIRTON OBE
08442	RICHARD J. WENHAM EASTLEIGH DEPOT DECEMBER 1989 – JULY 1999
08451	M.A. SMITH
	LONGSIGHT TMD
08460	SPIRIT OF THE OAK
08482	DON GATES 1952–2000
08483	DUSTY Driver David Miller
	NEIL/SCOUSEY Neil Morgan 1964–2014
	Team Leader O.O.C.
08484	CAPTAIN NATHANIEL DARELL
08495	NOEL KIRTON OBE
08499	REDLIGHT
08502	Lybert Dickinson
08516	RORY
08525	Percy The Pilot
	DUNCAN BEDFORD
08562	The Doncaster Postman
08575	The Doncaster Postman
08578	Lybert Dickinson
08585	Vicky
08598	HERCULES
08604	PHANTOM
08611	DOWNHILL C.S. M.A. SMITH LONGSIGHT TMD
08616	COOKIE
	TYSELEY 100
08617	Steve Purser
08624	Rambo PAUL RAMSEY
08629	BRML WOLVERTON LEVEL 5
	Bradwell
	Wolverton
08630	BOB BROWN
	Celsa Endeavour
08631	EAGLE C.U.R.C.
08633	The Sorter
08644	Laira Diesel Depot 50 Years 1962–2012
08645	Mike Baggott
08647	CRIMPSALL
08648	Amanda
08649	G.H. Stratton
	Wolverton
	Bradwell
08661	Europa
08663	Jack
	St. Silas
08664	DON GATES 1952–2000
08669	Bob Machin
08682	Lionheart
08690	DAVID THIRKHILL
08691	Terri

Number	Name/Names
08694	PAT BARR
08696	LONGSIGHT TMD
08701	GATESHEAD TMD 1852–1991
	The Sorter
08709	MOLLY'S DAY
08711	EAGLE C.U.R.C.
08714	Cambridge
08721	STARLET
	M.A. Smith
	DOWNHILL C.S.
	LONGSIGHT TMD
08730	The Caley
08738	SILVER FOX
08743	ANGIE
	Bryan Turner
08757	EAGLE C.U.R.C.
08772	CAMULODUNUM
08774	ARTHUR VERNON DAWSON
08780	FRED
08782	CASTLETON WORKS
08790	M.A. Smith
	STARLET
	Steve Purser
08799	ANDY BOWER
	FRED
08804	RICHARD J. WENHAM EASTLEIGH DEPOT DECEMBER 1989 – JULY 1999
08805	CONCORDE
08810	RICHARD J. WENHAM EASTLEIGH DEPOT DECEMBER 1989 – JULY 1999
08818	MOLLY
08822	John
	Dave Mills
08823	LIBBIE
08844	CHRIS WREN 1955–2002
08869	THE CANARY
08872	TONY LONG STRATFORD DEPOT 1971–2002
08874	Catherine
08879	Sheffield Childrens Hospital
08888	Postman's Pride
08891	J.R. 1951 – 2005
08896	STEPHEN DENT
08899	Midland Counties Railway 175 1839 – 2014
08903	John W Antill
08905	DANNY DANIELS
08907	MOLLY'S DAY
08908	IVAN STEPHENSON
08911	MATEY
08919	Steep Holm
08950	Neville Hill 1st
	DAVID LIGHTFOOT
08951	FRED

08991	KIDWELLY
08992	GWENDRAETH
08993	ASHBURNHAM
08994	GWENDRAETH
	SPIRIT OF INNOVATION
08995	KIDWELLY
09008	Sheffield Childrens Hospital
09009	Three Bridges C.E.D.
09012	Dick Hardy
09026	William Pearson Cedric Wares
20075	Sir William Cooke
20096	Ian Goddard 1938 – 2016
20118	Saltburn-by-the Sea
20122	Cleveland Potash
20128	Guglielmo Marconi
20131	Almon B. Strowger
20132	Barrow Hill Depot
20137	Murray B. Hofmeyr
20142	SIR JOHN BETJEMAN
20165	Henry Pease
20168	SIR GEORGE EARLE
20187	Sir Charles Wheatstone
20301	FURNESS RAILWAY 150
	Max Joule 1958–1999
20303	Max Joule 1958–1999
20305	Gresty Bridge
20310	Gresty Bridge
20311	Class 20 'Fifty'
20901	NANCY
20902	NANCY
20902	LORNA
20903	ALISON
20904	JANIS
20905	IONA
20906	GEORGINA
	KILMARNOCK 400
25912	TAMWORTH CASTLE
26001	Eastfield
31102	Cricklewood
31105	Bescot TMD
	Bescot TMD Bescot & Saltley Quality Assured
31106	The Blackcountryman
	SPALDING TOWN
31107	John H Carless V.C.
31110	TRACTION magazine
31116	RAIL 1981 – 1991
	RAIL Celebrity
31128	CHARYBDIS
31130	Calder Hall Power Station
31146	Brush Veteran
31147	Floreat Salopia
31165	Stratford Major Depot
31190	GRYPHON
31201	Fina Energy
31233	Phillips Imperial
	Severn Valley Railway
31276	Calder Hall Power Station
31296	Amlwch Freighter/Trên Nwyddau Amlwch
31309	Cricklewood
31327	Phillips Imperial
31405	Mappa Mundi
31410	Granada Telethon
31413	Severn Valley Railway
31421	Wigan Pier
31423	Jerome K. Jerome
31428	North Yorkshire Moors Railway
31430	Sister Dora
31439	North Yorkshire Moors Railway
31444	Keighley and Worth Valley Railway
31452	MINOTAUR
31454	THE HEART OF WESSEX
31455	Our Eli
31459	CERBERUS

31468	The Enginemen's Fund
	HYDRA
31530	Sister Dora
31544	Keighley and Worth Valley Railway
31558	Nene Valley Railway
31568	The Enginemen's Fund
31601	BLETCHLEY PARK 'STATION X'
	THE MAYOR OF CASTERBRIDGE
	GAUGE 'O' GUILD 1956–2006
	Devon Diesel Society
31602	CHIMAERA
	DRIVER DAVE GREEN
33002	Sea King
33008	Eastleigh
33009	Walrus
33012	Lt Jenny Lewis RN
33019	Griffon
33021	Eastleigh
33025	Sultan
	Glen Falloch
33026	Seafire
33027	Earl Mountbatten of Burma
33029	Glen Loy
33035	Spitfire
33046	Merlin
33047	Spitfire
33050	Isle of Grain
33051	Shakespeare Cliff
33052	Ashford
33056	The Burma Star
33057	Seagull
33065	Sealion
33103	SWORDFISH
33108	VAMPIRE
33109	Captain Bill Smith RNR
33112	Templecombe
33114	Sultan
	Ashford 150
33116	Hertfordshire Rail Tours
33202	The Burma Star
	METEOR
33207	Earl Mountbatten of Burma
	Jim Martin
37012	Loch Rannoch
37023	Stratford
	Stratford TMD Quality Approved
37025	Inverness TMD
37026	Loch Awe
	Shapfell
37027	Loch Eli
37037	Gartcosh
37043	Loch Lomond
37049	Imperial
37051	Merehead
37055	RAIL Celebrity
37057	Viking
37059	Port of Tilbury
37062	British Steel Corby
37066	British Steel Workington
37068	Grainflow
37069	Thornaby T.M.D.
37071	British Steel Skinningrove
37073	Fort William An Gearasdan
37077	British Steel Shelton
37078	Teesside Steelmaster
37079	Medite
37081	Loch Long
37087	VULCAN AVRO B1 & B2
	Keighley & Worth Valley Railway 40th Anniversary
	1968–2008
37088	Clydesdale
37095	British Steel Teesside
37099	Clydebridge

	MERL EVANS 1947–2016
37108	Lanarkshire Steel
37111	Loch Eil Outward Bound
	Glengarnock
37113	Radio Highland
37114	Dunrobin Castle
	City of Worcester
37116	Sister Dora
37137	Clyde Iron
37152	British Steel Ravenscraig
37154	Johnson Stevens Agencies
37156	British Steel Hunterston
37180	Sir Dyfed County of Dyfed
37185	Lea & Perrins
37188	Jimmy Shand
37190	Dalzell
37191	International Youth Year 1985
37194	British International Freight Association
	NEIL WEBSTER 1957–2001
37196	Tre Pol and Pen
37197	Loch Laidon
37198	CHIEF ENGINEER
37201	Saint Margaret
37207	William Cookworthy
37214	Loch Laidon
37216	Great Eastern
37219	Jonty Jarvis 8-12-1998 to 18-3-2005
37220	Westerleigh
37229	The Cardiff Rod Mill
	Jonty Jarvis 8-12-1998 to 18-3-2005
37232	The Institution of Railway Signal Engineers
37235	The Coal Merchants' Association of Scotland
37239	The Coal Merchants' Association of Scotland
37248	Midland Railway Centre
	Loch Arkaig
37251	The Northern Lights
37254	Cardiff Canton
37260	Radio Highland
37261	Caithness
	Loch Arkaig
37262	Dounreay
37275	Stainless Pioneer
	Oor Wullie
37310	British Steel Ravenscraig
37311	British Steel Hunterston
37312	Clyde Iron
37314	Dalzell
37320	Shap Fell
37321	Gartcosh
37322	Imperial
37323	Clydesdale
37324	Clydebridge
37325	Lanarkshire Steel
37326	Glengarnock
37332	The Coal Merchants' Association of Scotland
37343	Imperial
37350	NATIONAL RAILWAY MUSEUM
37356	Grainflow
37358	P & O Containers
37379	Ipswich WRD Quality Approved
37401	Mary Queen of Scots
	The Royal Scotsman
	Mary Queen of Scots
37402	Oor Willie
	Bont Y Bermo
	Stephen Middlemore 23.12.1954 – 8.6.2013
37403	Isle of Mull
	Glendarroch
	Ben Cruachan
	Isle of Mull
37404	Ben Cruachan
	Loch Long
37405	Strathclyde Region

37406	The Saltire Society
37407	Loch Long
	Blackpool Tower
37408	Loch Rannoch
37409	Loch Awe
	Lord Hinton
37410	Aluminium 100
37411	The Institution of Railway Signal Engineers
	Ty Hafan
	The Scottish Railway Preservation Society
	CAERPHILLY CASTLE/CASTELL CAERFFILI
37412	Loch Lomond
	Driver John Elliot
37413	Loch Eil Outward Bound
	The Scottish Railway Preservation Society
37414	Cathays C&W Works 1846 – 1993
37416	Sir Robert McAlpine/Concrete Bob
37417	Highland Region
	RAIL MAGAZINE
	Richard Trevithick
37418	An Comunn Gaidhealach
	Pectinidae
	Gordon Graig
	Pectinidae
	East Lancashire Railway
37419	Carl Haviland 1954–2012
37420	The Scottish Hosteller
37421	Strombidae
	Star of The East
	The Kingsman
37422	Robert F. Fairlie Locomotive Engineer 1831–1885
	Cardiff Canton
37423	Sir Murray Morrison 1873–1948 Pioneer of the British Aluminium Industry
	Spirit of the Lakes
37424	Glendarroch
	Isle of Mull
	Avro Vulcan XH558
37425	Sir Robert McAlpine/Concrete Bob
	Pride of the Valleys/Balchder y Cymoedd
	Sir Robert McAlpine/Concrete Bob
37426	Y Lein Fach/Vale of Rheidol
37427	Bont Y Bermo
	Highland Enterprise
37428	David Lloyd George
	The Royal Scotsman
	Loch Long/Loch Awe
37429	Sir Dyfed/County of Dyfed
	Eisteddfod Genedlaethol
37430	Cwmbrân
37431	Sir Powys/County of Powys
	Bullidae
37501	Teesside Steelmaster
37502	British Steel Teesside
37503	British Steel Shelton
37504	British Steel Corby
37505	British Steel Workington
37506	British Steel Skinningrove
37507	Hartlepool Pipe Mill
37511	Stockton Haulage
37512	Thornaby Demon
37516	Loch Laidon
37517	St Aidan's CE Memorial School Hartlepool Railsafe Trophy Winners 1995
37518	Fort William/An Gearasdan
37521	English China Clays
37601	Class 37-'Fifty'
	Perseus
37608	Andromeda
37610	The MALCOLM Group
	T.S. (Ted) Cassady 14.5.61 – 6.4.08
37611	Pegasus
37667	Wensleydale

	Meldon Quarry Centenary
37668	Leyburn
37670	St. Blazey T&RS Depot
37671	Tre Pol and Pen
37672	Freight Transport Association
37674	Saint Blaise Church 1445 – 1995
37675	William Cookworthy
	Margam TMD
37676	Loch Rannoch
37682	Hartlepool Pipe Mill
37684	Peak National Park
37685	Loch Arkaig
37688	Great Rocks
	Kingmoor TMD
37692	The Lass O' Ballochmyle
	Didcot Depot
37693	Sir William Arrol
37694	The Lass O' Ballochmyle
37698	Coedbach
37702	Taff Merthyr
37706	Conidae
37711	Tremorfa Steel Works
37712	The Cardiff Rod Mill
	Teesside Steelmaster
37713	British Steel Workington
37714	Thornaby TMD
37715	British Steel Teesside
	British Petroleum
37716	British Steel Corby
37717	Stainless Pioneer
	Maltby Lilly Hall Junior School Rotherham Railsafe Trophy Winners 1996
	St Margaret's Church of England Primary School City of Durham Railsafe Trophy Winners 1997
	Berwick Middle School Railsafe Trophy Winners 1998
37718	Hartlepool Pipe Mill
37799	Sir Dyfed/County of Dyfed
37800	Glo Cymru
	Cassiopeia
37801	Aberthaw/Aberddawan
37884	Gartcosh
37886	Sir Dyfed/County of Dyfed
37887	Castell Caerffili/Caerphilly Castle
37888	Petrolea
37890	The Railway Observer
37892	Ripple Lane
37898	Cwmbargoed D.P.
37899	County of West Glamorgan/Sir Gorllewin Morgannwg
37901	Mirrlees Pioneer
37902	British Steel Llanwern
37905	Vulcan Enterprise
97304	John Tiley
40010	EMPRESS OF BRITAIN
40011	MAURETANIA
40012	AUREOL
40013	ANDANIA
40014	ANTONIA
40015	AQUITANIA
40016	CAMPANIA
40017	CARINTHIA
40018	CARMANIA
40019	CARONIA
40020	FRANCONIA
40021	IVERNIA
40022	LACONIA
40023	LANCASTRIA
40024	LUCANIA
40025	LUSITANIA
40027	PARTHIA
40028	SAMARIA
40029	SAXONIA
40030	SCYTHIA
40031	SYLVANIA

40032	EMPRESS OF CANADA
40033	EMPRESS OF ENGLAND
40034	ACCRA
40035	APAPA
40145	East Lancashire Railway
43002	Top of the Pops
	TECHNI?UEST
	Sir Kenneth Grange
43003	ISAMBARD KINGDOM BRUNEL
43004	Swan Hunter
	Borough of Swindon
	First for the Future/First ar gyfer y dyfodol
43006	Kingdom of Fife
43008	City of Aberdeen
43009	First transforming travel
43010	TSW Today
43011	Reader 125
43012	Exeter Panel Signal Box 21st Anniversary 2009
43013	University of Bristol
	CROSSCOUNTRY VOYAGER
43014	The Railway Observer
43016	Gwyl Gerddi Cymru 1992/Garden Festival Wales 1992
	Peninsular Medical School
43017	HTV West
	Hannahs discoverhannahs.org
43018	The Red Cross
43019	Dinas Abertawe/City of Swansea
43020	John Grooms
	MTU Power. Passion. Partnership
43021	David Austin – Cartoonist
43022	The Duke of Edinburgh's Award Diamond Anniversary 1956 – 2016
43023	County of Cornwall
	SQN LDR HAROLD STARR ONE OF THE FEW
43024	Great Western Society 1961 – 2011 Didcot Railway Centre
43025	Exeter
	IRO The Institution of Railway Operators 2000 – 2010 TEN YEARS PROMOTING OPERATIONAL EXCELLENCE
43026	City of Westminster
	Michael Eavis
43027	Westminster Abbey
	Glorious Devon
43030	Christian Lewis Trust
43032	The Royal Regiment of Wales
43033	Driver Brian Cooper 15 June 1947 – 5 October 1999
43034	The Black Horse
	TravelWatch SouthWest
43037	PENYDARREN
43038	National Railway Museum The First Ten Years 1975–1985
43039	The Royal Dragoon Guards
43040	Granite City
	Bristol St. Philip's Marsh
43041	City of Discovery
	Meningitis Trust Support for Life
43043	LEICESTERSHIRE COUNTY CRICKET CLUB
43044	Borough of Kettering
43045	The Grammer School Doncaster AD 1350
43046	Royal Philharmonic
43047	Rotherham Enterprise
43048	T.C.B. Miller MBE
43049	Neville Hill
43051	The Duke and Duchess of York
43052	City of Peterborough
43053	County of Humberside
	Leeds United
	University of Worcester
43055	Sheffield Star
	The Sheffield Star 125 Years
43056	University of Bradford
	The Royal British Legion
43058	MIDLAND PRIDE

43060	County of Leicestershire
	COUNTY OF LEICESTERSHIRE
43061	City of Lincoln
	The Fearless Foxes
43062	John Armitt
43063	Maiden Voyager
	Rio Challenger
43064	City of York
43065	City of Edinburgh
43066	Nottingham Playhouse
43068	The Red Nose
	The Red Arrows
43069	Rio Enterprise
43070	Rio Pathfinder
	The Corps of Royal Electrical and Mechanical Engineers
43071	Forward Birmingham
43072	Derby Etches Park
43074	BBC EAST MIDLANDS TODAY
43076	BBC East Midlands Today
	THE MASTER CUTLER 1947–1997
	IN SUPPORT OF HELP for HEROES
43077	County of Nottingham
43078	Shildon County Durham
	Golowan Festival Penzance
43079	Rio Venturer
43081	Midland Valenta
43082	DERBYSHIRE FIRST
	RAILWAY children THE VOICE FOR STREET CHILDREN
	WORLDWIDE
48084	County of Derbyshire
43085	City of Bradfod
43086	Rio Talisman
43087	Rio Invader
	11 Explosive Ordnance Disposal Regiment Royal
	Logistic Corps
43088	XIII Commonwealth Games Scotland 1986
43089	Rio Thunderer
	HAYABUSA
43091	Edinburgh Military Tattoo
43092	Highland Chieftain
	Highland Chieftain
	Highland Chieftain
	Institution of Mechanical Engineers 150th Anniversary
	1847 – 1997
43093	York Festival '88
	Lady in Red
	Old Oak Common HST Depot 1976–2018
43095	Heaton
	Perth
43096	The Queen's Own Hussars
	The Great Racer
	Stirling Castle
43097	The Light Infantry
	Environment Agency
43098	Tyne and Wear Metropolitan County
	railwaychildren
43099	Diocese of Newcastle
43100	Craigentinny
43101	Edinburgh International Festival
	The Irish Mail Trên Post Gwyddelig
43102	City of WakefieldHST Silver Jubilee
	Diocese of Newcastle
43103	John Wesley
	Helston Furry Dance
43104	County of Cleveland
	City of Edinburgh
43105	Hartlepool
	City of Inverness
43106	Songs of Praise
	Fountains Abbey
43107	City of Derby
	Tayside
43108	BBC Television Railwatch
	Old Course St Andrews
43109	Yorkshire Evening Press
	Scone Palace
	Leeds International Film Festival
43110	Darlington
	Stirlingshire
43111	Scone Palace
43112	Doncaster
43113	City of Newcastle upon Tyne
	The Highlands
43114	National Garden Festival Gateshead 1990
	East Riding of Yorkshire
43115	Yorkshire Cricket Academy
	Aberdeenshire
43116	City of Kingston upon Hull
	The Black Dyke Band
43117	Bonnie Prince Charlie
43118	Charles Wesley
	City of Kingston upon Hull
43119	Harrogate Spa
43120	National Galleries of Scotland
43121	West Yorkshire Metropolitan County
43122	South Yorkshire Metropolitan County
43123	VALENTA 1972 - 2010
43124	BBC Points West
43125	Merchant Venturer
43126	City of Bristol
43127	Sir Peter Parker 1924–2002 Cotswold Line 150
43130	Sulis Minerva
43131	Sir Felix Pole
43132	Worshipful Company of Carmen
	We Save the Children – Will You?
43134	County of Somerset
43135	Quaker Enterprise
43137	Newton Abbot 150
43139	Driver Stan Martin 25 June 1960–6 November 2004
43140	Landore Diesel Depot 1963 Celebrating 50 Years 2013/
	Depo Diesel Glandŵr 1963 Dathlu 50 Mlynedd 2013
43141	Cardiff Panel Signal Box 1966–2016/Blwch Signalau
	Panel Caerdydd 1966–2016
43142	St Mary's Hospital Paddington
	Reading Panel Signal Box 1965–2010
43143	Stroud 700
43147	Red Cross
	The Red Cross
	Royal Marines Celebrating 350 Years
43149	BBC Wales Today
	University of Plymouth
43150	Bristol Evening Post
43151	Blue Peter II
43152	St. Peter's School York AD 627
43153	University of Durham
	THE ENGLISH RIVIERA TORQUAY PAIGNTON BRIXHAM
43154	INTERCITY
43155	BBC Look North
	The Red Arrows
	City of Aberdeen
	The Red Arrows 50 Seasons of Excellence
43156	Dartington International Summer School
43157	Yorkshire Evening Post
	HMS Penzance
43158	Dartmoor The Pony Express
43159	Rio Warrior
43160	Storm Force
	PORTERBROOK
	Sir Moir Lockhead OBE
43161	Reading Evening Post
	Rio Monach
43162	Borough of Stevenage
	Project Rio
43163	Exeter Panel Signal Box 21st Anniversary 2009
43165	Prince Michael of Kent
43167	DELTIC 50 1955–2005

43169	THE NATIONAL TRUST
43170	Edward Paxman
43172	Harry Patch – The last survivor of the trenches
43173	Swansea University
43174	Bristol – Bordeaux
43175	GWR 175th ANNIVERSARY
43177	University of Exeter
43179	Pride of Laira
43180	City of Newcastle upon Tyne
	Rio Glory
43181	Devonport Royal Dockyard 1693–1993
43185	Great Western
43186	Sir Francis Drake
43188	City of Plymouth
43189	RAILWAY HERITAGE TRUST
43191	Seahawk
43192	City of Truro
43193	Yorkshire Post
	Plymouth SPIRIT OF DISCOVERY
	Rio Triumph
43194	Royal Signals
43195	British Red Cross 125th Birthday 1995
	Rio Swift
43196	The Newspaper Society
	The Newspaper Society Founded 1836
	Rio Prince
43197	The RAILWAY MAGAZINE Centenary 1897–1997
	Rio Princess
43198	HMS Penzance
	Rio Victorious
	Oxfordshire 2007
43206	Kingdom of Fife
43208	Lincolnshire Echo
43238	City of Dundee
	National Railway Museum 40 Years 1975–2015
43257	Bounds Green
43274	Spirit of Sunderland
43290	mtu fascination of power
43296	Stirling Castle
43300	Craigentinny
	Blackpool Rock
	Craigentinny
	Craigentinny 100 YEARS 1914–2014
43306	Fountains Abbey
43308	Old Course St Andrews
	HIGHLAND CHIEFTAIN
43309	Leeds International Film Festival
43313	The Highlands
43314	East Riding of Yorkshire
43316	The Black Dyke Band
43318	City of Kingston upon Hull
43320	National Galleries of Scotland
43367	DELTIC 50 1955 – 2005
43423	'VALENTA' 1972 – 2010
43467	British Transport Police Nottingham/Nottinghamshire Fire And Rescue Services
43484	PETER FOX 1942 – 2011 PLATFORM 5
44001	SCAFELL PIKE
44002	HELVELLYN
44003	SKIDDAW
44004	GREAT GABLE
44005	CROSS FELL
44006	WHERNSIDE
44007	INGLEBOROUGH
44008	PENYGHENT
44009	SNOWDON
44010	TRYFAN
45004	ROYAL IRISH FUSILIER
45006	HONOURABLE ARTILLERY COMPANY
45014	THE CHESHIRE REGIMENT
45022	LYTHAM ST ANNES
45023	THE ROYAL PIONEER CORPS
45039	THE MANCHESTER REGIMENT

45040	THE KING'S SHROPSHIRE LIGHT INFANTRY
45041	ROYAL TANK REGIMENT
45043	THE KING'S OWN ROYAL BORDER REGIMENT
45044	ROYAL INNISKILLING FUSILIER
45045	COLDSTREAM GUARDSMAN
45046	ROYAL FUSILIER
45048	THE ROYAL MARINES
45049	THE STAFFORDSHIRE REGIMENT (THE PRINCE OF WALES'S)
45055	ROYAL CORPS OF TRANSPORT
45059	ROYAL ENGINEER
45060	SHERWOOD FORESTER
45104	THE ROYAL WARWICKSHIRE FUSILIER
45111	GRENADIER GUARDSMAN
45112	THE ROYAL ARMY ORDNANCE CORPS
45118	THE ROYAL ARTILLERYMAN
45123	THE LANCASHIRE FUSILIER
45135	3RD CARABINIER
45137	THE BEDFORDSHIRE AND HERTFORDSHIRE REGIMENT (TA)
45143	5th ROYAL INNISKILLING DRAGOON GUARDS 5TH ROYAL INNISKILLING DRAGOON GUARDS 1685–1985
45144	ROYAL SIGNALS
46026	LEICESTERSHIRE AND DERBYSHIRE YEOMANRY
46035	Ixion
47004	Old Oak Common Traction & Rolling Stock Depot
47007	Stratford
47010	Xancidae
47016	The Toleman Group
	ATLAS
47033	The Royal Logistics Corps
47049	GEFCO
47053	Cory Brothers 1842–1992
	Dollands Moor International
47054	Xancidae
47060	Halewood Silver Jubilee 1988
47076	CITY OF TRURO
47077	NORTH STAR
47078	SIR DANIEL GOOCH
47079	GEORGE JACKSON CHURCHWARD G. J. CHURCHWARD
47080	TITAN
47081	ODIN
47082	ATLAS
47083	ORION
47085	MAMMOTH
	Conidae
	REPTA 1893–1993
47086	COLOSSUS
47087	CYCLOPS
47088	SAMSON
47089	AMAZON
	Amazon
47090	VULCAN
47091	THOR
47095	Southampton WRD Quality Approved
47114	Freightlinerbulk
47119	Arcidae
47120	R.A.F. Kinloss
47121	Pochard
47125	Tonnidae
47142	The Sapper
47145	MYRDDIN EMRYS
47146	Loughborough Grammar School
47157	Johnson Stevens Agencies
47158	Henry Ford
47167	County of Essex
47169	Great Eastern
47170	County of Norfolk
47172	County of Hertfordshire
47180	County of Suffolk
47184	County of Cambridgeshire

47186	Catcliffe Demon
47190	Pectinidae
47193	Lucinidae
47194	Bullidae
	Carlisle Currock Quality Approved
47195	Muricidae
47196	Haliotidae
47200	Herbert Austin
	The Fosse Way
47206	The Morris Dancer
47207	Bulmers of Hereford
	The Felixstowe Partnership
47209	Herbert Austin
47210	Blue Circle Cement
47211	Johnson Stevens Agencies
47213	Marchwood Military Port
47214	Tinsley Traction Depot
	Distillers MG
47218	United Transport Europe
47219	Arnold Kunzler
47222	Appleby-Frodingham
	W.A. Camwell
47223	British Petroleum
47224	Arcidae
47228	axial
47231	The Silcock Express
47233	Stombidae
	Strombidae
47236	ROVER GROUP QUALITY ASSURED
47238	Bescot Yard
47241	The Silcock Express
	Halewood Silver Jubilee 1988
47245	The Institute of Export
47258	Forth Ports Tilbury
47270	Cory Brothers 1842–1992
	SWIFT
47278	Vasidae
47280	Pedigree
47283	Johnnie Walker
47286	Port of Liverpool
47291	The Port of Felixstowe
47293	TRANSFESA
47297	Cobra RAILFREIGHT
47298	Pegasus
47301	Freightliner Birmingham
47303	Freightliner Cleveland
47306	The Sapper
47309	The Halewood Transmission
	European Rail Operator of the Year
47310	Henry Ford
47311	Warrington Yard
47312	Parsec of Europe
47314	Transmark
47315	Templecombe
47316	Cam Peak
47317	Willesden Yard
47319	Norsk Hydro
47323	ROVER GROUP QUALITY ASSURED
47324	Glossidae
47326	Saltley Depot Quality Approved
47330	Amlwch Freighter/Trên Nwyddau Amlwch
47333	Civil Link
47334	P&O Nedlloyd
47337	Herbert Austin
47338	Warrington Yard
47348	St Christopher's Railway Home
47350	British Petroleum
47355	AVOCET
47357	The Permanent Way Institution
47361	Wilton Endeavour
47363	Billingham Enterprise
47365	Diamond Jubilee
47366	The Institution of Civil Engineers

	Capital Radio's Help a London Child
47368	Neritidae
47370	Andrew A Hodgkinson
47374	Petrolea
47375	Tinsley Traction Depot Quality Approved
	TINSLEY TRACTION DEPOT
47376	Freightliner 1995
47379	Total Energy
47380	Immingham
47387	Transmark
47390	Amlwch Freighter/Trên Nwyddau Amlwch
47392	Cory Brothers 1842–1992
47394	Johnson Stevens Agencies
47401	North Eastern
	Star of The East
	North Eastern
47402	Gateshead
47403	The Geordie
47404	Hadrian
47405	Northumbria
47406	Rail Riders
47407	Aycliffe
47408	Finsbury Park
47409	David Lloyd George
47411	The Geordie
47421	The Brontës of Haworth
47424	The Brontës of Haworth
47425	Holbeck
47434	Pride in Huddersfield
47443	North Eastern
47444	University of Nottingham
47448	Gateshead
47452	Aycliffe
47457	Ben Line
47458	County of Cambridgeshire
47461	Charles Rennie Mackintosh
47462	Cambridge Traction & Rolling Stock Depot
47469	Glasgow Chamber of Commerce
47470	University of Edinburgh
47471	Norman Tunna G.C.
47474	Sir Rowland Hill
47475	Restive
47476	Night Mail
47479	Track 29
47484	ISAMBARD KINGDOM BRUNEL
47488	Rail Riders
	DAVIES THE OCEAN
47489	Crewe Diesel Depot
	Crewe Diesel Depot Quality Approved
47490	Bristol Bath Road
	Resonant
47491	Horwich Enterprise
	Resolve
47492	The Enterprising Scot
47500	GREAT WESTERN
47501	Craftsman
	CRAFTSMAN
47503	The Geordie
	Heaton Traincare Depot
47508	Great Britain
	S.S. Great Britain
47509	Albion
47510	Fair Rosamund
47511	Thames
	Grampian Region
47513	Severn
47515	Night Mail
47517	Andrew Carnegie
47520	Thunderbird
47522	Doncaster Enterprise
47524	Res Gestae
47526	Northumbria
47527	Kettering

47528	The Queen's Own Mercian Yeomanry
47531	Respite
47535	University of Leicester
	Saint Aidan
47537	Sir Gwynedd/County of Gwynedd
47538	PYTHON
47539	Rochdale Pioneers
47540	The Institution of Civil Engineers
47541	The Queen Mother
47546	Aviemore Centre
47547	University of Oxford
47549	Royal Mail
47550	University of Dundee
47551	Poste Restante
47555	The Commonwealth Spirit
47558	Mayflower
47559	Sir Joshua Reynolds
47560	Tamar
47562	Sir William Burrell
	Restless
47563	Woman's Guild
47564	COLOSSUS
47565	Responsive
47567	Red Star
	Red Star ISO 9002
47568	Royal Engineers Postal & Courier Services
	Royal Logistic Corps Postal & Courier Services
47569	The Gloucestershire Regiment
47572	Ely Cathedral
47573	THE LONDON STANDARD
47574	LLOYD'S LIST 250TH ANNIVERSARY
	Benjamin Gimbert G.C.
47575	City of Hereford
47576	King's Lynn
47577	Benjamin Gimbert G.C.
47578	The Royal Society of Edinburgh
	Respected
47579	James Nightall G.C.
47580	County of Essex Restormel
	County of Essex
47581	Great Eastern
47582	County of Norfolk
47583	County of Hertfordshire
47584	County of Suffolk
	THE LOCOMOTIVE & CARRIAGE INSTITUTION 1911
47585	County of Cambridgeshire
47586	Northamptonshire
47587	Ruskin College Oxford
47588	Carlisle Currock
	Resurgent
47590	Thomas Telford
47592	County of Avon
47593	Galloway Princess
47594	Resourceful
47595	Confederation of British Industry
47596	Aldeburgh Festival
47597	Resilient
47600	Dewi Saint/Saint David
47602	Glorious Devon
47603	County of Somerset
47604	Women's Royal Voluntary Service
47606	ODIN
	Irresistible
47607	Royal Worcester
47609	FIRE FLY
47611	Thames
47612	TITAN
47613	NORTH STAR
47615	Castell Caerffilli/Caerphilly Castle
47616	Y Ddraig Goch/The Red Dragon
47617	University of Stirling
47618	Fair Rosamund

47620	Windsor Castle
47621	Royal County of Berkshire
47622	The Institution of Civil Engineers
47623	VULCAN
47624	CYCLOPS
	Saint Andrew
47625	CITY OF TRURO
	Resplendent
47626	ATLAS
47627	City of Oxford
47628	SIR DANIEL GOOCH
47630	Resounding
47631	Ressalder
47633	ORION
47634	Henry Ford
	Holbeck
47635	Jimmy Milne
	The Lass O' Ballochmyle
47636	Sir John De Graeme
	Restored
47637	Springburn
47638	County of Kent
47639	Industry Year 1986
47640	University of Strathclyde
47641	COLOSSUS
	Fife Region
47642	Strathisla
	Resolute
47644	The Permanent Way Institution
47645	Robert F. Fairlie Locomotive Engineer 1831–1885
47647	THOR
47654	Finsbury Park
47671	Y Ddraig Goch/The Red Dragon
47672	Sir William Burrell
47673	Galloway Princess
	York InterCity Control
47674	Women's Royal Voluntary Service
47675	Confederation of British Industry
47676	Northamptonshire
47677	University of Stirling
47701	Saint Andrew
	Old Oak Common Traction & Rolling Stock Depot
	Waverley
47702	Saint Cuthbert
	County of Suffolk
47703	Saint Mungo
	The Queen Mother
	LEWIS CARROLL
	HERMES
47704	Dunedin
47705	Lothian
	GUY FAWKES
47706	Strathclyde
47707	Holyrood
47708	Waverley
	Templecombe
47709	The Lord Provost
	DIONYSOS
47710	Sir Walter Scott
	Capital Radio's Help a London Child
	LADY GODIVA
	QUASIMODO
47711	Greyfriars Bobby
	County of Hertfordshire
47712	Lady Diana Spencer
	DICK WHITTINGTON
	ARTEMIS
	Pride of Carlisle
47713	Fair Rosamund
	Tayside Region
47714	Thames
	Grampian Region
47715	Haymarket

	POSEIDON
47716	Duke of Edinburgh's Award
47717	Tayside Region
47721	Saint Bede
47722	The Queen Mother
47725	The Railway Mission
	Bristol Barton Hill
47726	Manchester Airport Progress
47727	Duke of Edinburgh's Award
	Castell Caerffilli/Caerphilly Castle
	Rebecca
47733	Eastern Star
47734	Crewe Diesel Depot Quality Approved
47736	Cambridge Traction & Rolling Stock Depot
47737	Resurgent
47738	Bristol Barton Hill
47739	Resourceful
	Robin of Templecombe
47741	Resilient
47742	The Enterprising Scot
47744	Saint Edwin
	The Cornish Experience
	Royal Mail Cheltenham
47745	Royal London Society for the Blind
47746	The Bobby
	Chris Fudge 29.7.70–22.6.10
47747	Res Publica
	Graham Farish
	Florence Nightingale
47749	Atlantic College
	Demelza
	CITY OF TRURO
47750	Royal Mail Cheltenham
	ATLAS
47756	The Permanent Way Institution
	Royal Mail Tyneside
47757	Restitution
	Capabilty Brown
47758	Regency Rail Cruises
47760	Restless
	Ribblehead Viaduct
47764	Resounding
47765	Ressalder
47766	Resolute
47767	Saint Columba
	Mappa Mundi
47768	Resonant
47769	Resolve
47770	Reserved
47771	Heaton Traincare Depot
47772	Carnforth TMD
47773	Reservist
	The Queen Mother
47774	Poste Restante
47775	Respite
47776	Respected
47777	Restored
47778	Irresistible
	Duke of Edinburgh's Award
47781	Isle of Iona
47783	Finsbury Park
	Saint Peter
47784	Condover Hall
47785	The Statesman
	Fiona Castle
47786	Roy Castle OBE
47787	Victim Support
	Windsor Castle
47788	Captain Peter Manisty RN
47789	Lindisfarne
47790	Dewi Saint/Saint David
	Galloway Princess
47791	VENICE SIMPLON ORIENT-EXPRESS

47792	Saint Cuthbert
	Robin Hood
47793	Saint Augustine
	Christopher Wren
47798	FIRE FLY
	Prince William
47799	Windsor Castle
	Prince Henry
47802	Pride of Cumbria
47803	Woman's Guild
47805	Bristol Bath Road
	Pride of Toton
	TALISMAN
	John Scott 12.5.45–22.5.12
47808	SAMSON
47809	Finsbury Park
47810	PORTERBROOK
	Captain Sensible
	Peter Bath MBE 1927–2006
47812	Pride of Eastleigh
47813	S.S. Great Britain
	John Peel
	Solent
47814	Totnes Castle
47815	Abertawe Landore
	GREAT WESTERN
47816	Bristol Bath Road Quality Approved
47817	The Institution of Mechanical Engineers
47818	Strathclyde
	Emily
47821	Royal Worcester
47822	Pride of Shrewsbury
47823	SS Great Britain
47824	Glorious Devon
47825	Thomas Telford
47826	Springburn
47828	Severn Valley Railway Kidderminster Bewdley
	Bridgnorth
	Joe Strummer
47830	BEECHING'S LEGACY
47831	Bolton Wanderer
47832	Tamar
	DRIVER TOM CLARK O.B.E.
	Solway Princess
47833	Captain Peter Manisty RN
47834	FIRE FLY
47835	Windsor Castle
47836	Fair Rosamund
47839	Royal County of Berkshire
	Pride of Saltley
	PEGASUS
47840	NORTH STAR
47841	The Institution of Mechanical Engineers
	Spirit of Chester
47843	VULCAN
47844	Derby & Derbyshire Chamber of Commerce & Industry
47845	County of Kent
47846	THOR
47847	Railway World Magazine/Brian Morrison
47848	Newton Abbot Festival of Transport
	TITAN STAR
47849	Cadeirlan Bangor Cathedral
47851	Traction Magazine
47853	RAIL EXPRESS
47854	Women's Royal Voluntary Service
	Diamond Jubilee
47971	Robin Hood
47972	The Royal Army Ordnance Corps
47973	Midland Counties Railway 150 1839–1989
	Derby Evening Telegraph
47974	The Permanent Way Institution
47975	The Institution of Civil Engineers
47976	Aviemore Centre

50001	Dreadnought
50002	Superb
50003	Temeraire
50004	St Vincent
50005	Collingwood
50006	Neptune
50007	Hercules
	SIR EDWARD ELGAR
	Hercules
50008	Thunderer
50009	Conqueror
50010	Monarch
50011	Centurion
50012	Benbow
50013	Agincourt
50014	Warspite
50015	Valiant
50016	Barham
50017	Royal Oak
50018	Resolution
50019	Ramillies
50020	Revenge
50021	Rodney
50022	Anson
50023	Howe
50024	Vanguard
50025	Invicible
50026	Indomitable
50027	Lion
50028	Tiger
50029	Renown
50030	Repulse
50031	Hood
50032	Courageous
50033	Glorious
50034	Furious
50035	Ark Royal
50036	Victorious
50037	Illustrious
50038	Formidable
50039	Implacable
50040	Leviathan
	Centurion
50041	Bulwark
50042	Triumph
50043	Eagle
50044	Exeter
	EXETER
	Exeter
50045	Achilles
50046	Ajax
50047	Swiftsure
50048	Dauntless
50049	Defiance
50050	Fearless
55001	ST. PADDY
55002	THE KING'S OWN YORKSHIRE LIGHT INFANTRY
55003	MELD
55004	QUEEN'S OWN HIGHLANDER
55005	THE PRINCE OF WALES'S OWN REGIMENT OF YORKSHIRE
55006	THE FIFE AND FORFAR YEOMANRY
55007	PINZA
55008	THE GREEN HOWARDS
55009	ALYCIDON
55010	THE KING'S OWN SCOTTISH BORDERER
55011	THE ROYAL NORTHUMBERLAND FUSILIERS
55012	CREPELLO
55013	THE BLACK WATCH
55014	THE DUKE OF WELLINGTON'S REGIMENT
55015	TULYAR
55016	GORDON HIGHLANDER
55017	THE DURHAM LIGHT INFANTRY

55018	BALLYMOSS
55019	ROYAL HIGHLAND FUSILIER
55020	NIMBUS
55021	ARGYLL AND SUTHERLAND HIGHLANDER
55022	ROYAL SCOTS GREY
56001	Whatley
56006	Ferrybridge 'C' Power Station
56012	Maltby Colliery
56028	West Burton Power Station
56030	Eggborough Power Station
56031	Merehead
56032	Sir De Morgannwg County of South Glamorgan
56033	Shotton Paper Mill
56034	Castell Ogwr Ogmore Castle
56035	Taff Merthyr
56037	Richard Trevithick
56038	Western Mail
	PATHFINDER TOURS 30 YEARS OF RAILTOURING 1973 – 2003
56039	ABP Port of Hull
56040	Oystermouth
56044	Cardiff Canton
	Cardiff Canton Quality Approved
56045	British Steel Shelton
56049	Robin of Templecombe 1938 – 2013
56050	British Steel Teeside
56051	Isle of Grain
56052	The Cardiff Rod Mill
56053	Sir Morgannwg Ganol County of Mid Glamorgan
56054	British Steel Llanwern
56057	British Fuels
56060	The Cardiff Rod Mill
56062	Mountsorrel
56063	Bardon Hill
56069	Thornaby TMD
	Wolverhampton Steel Terminal
56073	Tremorfa Steel Works
56074	Kellingley Colliery
56075	West Yorkshire Enterprise
56076	Blyth Power
	British Steel Trostre
56077	Thorpe Marsh Power Station
56078	Doncaster Enterprise
56080	Selby Coalfied
56086	The Magistrates' Association
56087	ABP Port of Hull
56089	Ferrybridge 'C' Power Station
56091	Castle Donington Power Station
	Stanton
56093	The Institution of Mining Engineers
56094	Eggborough Power Station
56095	Harworth Colliery
56098	Lost Boys 68 – 88
56099	Fiddlers Ferry Power Station
56101	Mutual Improvement
	Frank Hornby
56102	Scunthorpe Steel Centenary
56103	STORA
56110	Croft
56112	Stainless Pioneer
56114	Maltby Colliery
56115	Bassetlaw
	Barry Needham
56117	Wilton-Coalpower
56122	Wilton-Coalpower
56123	Drax Power Station
56124	Blue Circle Cement
56128	West Burton Power Station
56130	Wardley Opencast
56131	Ellington Colliery
56132	Fina Energy
56133	Crewe Locomotive Works
56134	Blyth Power

56135	Port of Tyne Authority
56302	Wilson Walshe
	PECO The Railway Modeller 2016 40 Years
56312	ARTEMIS
	Jermiah Dixon Son of County Durham Surveyor of the Mason-Dixon Line U.S.A.
57001	Freightliner Pioneer
57002	Freightliner Phoenix
	RAIL EXPRESS
57003	Freightliner Evolution
57004	Freightliner Quality
57005	Freightliner Excellence
57006	Freightliner Reliance
57007	Freightliner Bond
57008	Freightliner Explorer
	Telford International Railfreight Park June 2009
57009	Freightliner Venturer
57010	Freightliner Crusader
57011	Freightliner Challenger
57012	Freightliner Envoy
57301	SCOTT TRACY
	Goliath
57302	VIRGIL TRACY
	Chad Varah
57303	ALAN TRACY
	Pride of Carlisle
57304	GORDON TRACY
	Pride of Cheshire
57305	ALAN TRACY
	JOHN TRACY
	Northern Princess
57306	JEFF TRACY
	Her Majesty's Railway Inspectorate 175
57307	LADY PENELOPE
57308	TIN TIN
	County of Staffordshire
	Jamie Ferguson
57309	BRAINS
	Pride of Crewe
57310	KYRANO
	Pride of Cumbria
57311	PARKER
	Thunderbird
57312	THE HOOD
	Peter Henderson
	Solway Princess
57313	TRACY ISLAND
57314	FIREFLY
57315	THE MOLE
57316	FAB1
57601	Sheila
57602	Restormel Castle
57603	Tintagel Castle
57604	PENDENNIS CASTLE
57605	Totnes Castle
58002	Daw Mill Colliery
58003	Markham Colliery
58005	Ironbridge Power Station
58007	Drakelow Power Station
58011	Worksop Depot
58014	Didcot Power Station
58017	Eastleigh Depot
58018	High Marnham Power Station
58019	Shirebrook Colliery
58020	Doncaster Works BRE
	Doncaster Works
58021	Hither Green Depot
58023	Peterborough Depot
58032	Thoresby Colliery
58034	Bassetlaw
58037	Worksop Depot
58039	Rugeley Power Station
58040	Cottam Power Station

58041	Ratcliffe Power Station
58042	Ironbridge Power Station
	Petrolea
58043	Knottingley
58044	Oxcroft Opencast
58046	Thoresby Colliery
	Asfordby Mine
58047	Manton Colliery
58048	Coventry Colliery
58049	Littleton Colliery
58050	Toton Traction Depot
59001	YEOMAN ENDEAVOUR
59002	YEOMAN ENTERPRISE
	ALAN J DAY
59003	YEOMAN HIGHLANDER
59004	YEOMAN CHALLENGER
	PAUL A HAMMOND
59005	KENNETH J PAINTER
59101	Village of Whatley
59102	Village of Chantry
59103	Village of Mells
59104	Village of Great Elm
59201	Vale of York
59202	Vale of White Horse
	Alan Meddows Taylor MD. Mendip Rail Limited
59203	Vale of Pickering
59204	Vale of Glamorgan
59205	Vale of Evesham
	L. Keith McNair
59206	Pride of Ferrybridge
	John F. Yeoman Rail Pioneer
60001	Steadfast
	The Railway Observer
60002	Capability Brown
	High Peak
60003	Christopher Wren
	FREIGHT TRANSPORT ASSOCIATION
60004	Lochnagar
60005	Skiddaw
	BP Gas Avonmouth
60006	Great Gable
	Scunthorpe Ironmaster
60007	Robert Adam
	The Spirit of Tom Kendell
60008	Moel Fammau
	GYPSUM QUEEN II
	Sir William McAlpine
60009	Carnedd Dafydd
60010	Pumlumon Plynlimon
60011	Cader Idris
60012	Glyder Fawr
60013	Robert Boyle
60014	Alexander Fleming
60015	Bow Fell
60016	Langdale Pikes
	RAIL MAGAZINE
60017	Arenig Fawr
	Shotton Works Centenary Year 1996
60018	Moel Siabod
60019	Wild Boar Fell
	PATHFINDER TOURS 30 YEARS OF RAILTOURING 1973–2003
	Port of Grimsby & Immingham
60020	Great Whernside
	The Willows
60021	Pen-y-Ghent
	Star of the East
60022	Ingleborough
60023	The Cheviot
60024	Elizabeth Fry
	Clitheroe Castle
60025	Joseph Lister
	Caledonian Paper

60026	William Caxton
60027	Joseph Banks
60028	John Flamsteed
60029	Ben Nevis
	Clitheroe Castle
60030	Cir Mhor
60031	Ben Lui
	ABP Connect
60032	William Booth
60033	Anthony Ashley Cooper
	Tees Steel Express
60034	Carnedd Llewelyn
60035	Florence Nightingale
60036	Sgurr Na Ciche
	GEFC
60037	Helvellyn
	Aberddawan Aberthaw
60038	Bidean Nam Bian
	AvestaPolarit
60039	Glastonbury Tor
	Dove Holes
60040	Brecon Beacons
	The Territorial Army Centenary
60041	High Willhays
60042	Dunkery Beacon
	The Hundred of Hoo
60043	Yes Tor
60044	Ailsa Craig
	Dowlow
60045	Josephine Butler
	The Permanent Way Institution
60046	William Wilberforce
60047	Robert Owen
60048	Saddleback
	EASTERN
60049	Scafell
60050	Roseberry Topping
60051	Mary Somerville
60052	Goat Fell
	Glofa Twr The last deep mine in Wales Tower Colliery
60053	John Reith
	NORDIC TERMINAL
60054	Charles Babbage
60055	Thomas Barnardo
60056	William Beveridge
60057	Adam Smith
60058	John Howard
60059	Samuel Plimsoll
	Swinden Dalesman
60060	James Watt
60061	Alexander Graham Bell
60062	Samuel Johnson
	Stainless Pioneer
60063	James Murray
60064	Back Tor
60065	Kinder Low
	Spirit of JAGUAR
60066	John Logie Baird
60067	James Clerk-Maxwell
60068	Charles Darwin
60069	Humphry Davy
	Slioch
60070	John Loudon McAdam
60071	Dorothy Garrod
	Ribblehead Viaduct
60072	Cairn Toul
60073	Cairn Gorm
60074	Braeriach
	Teenage Spirit
60075	Liathach
60076	Suilven
	Dunbar
60077	Canisp
60078	Stac Pollaidh
60079	Foinaven
60080	Kinder Scout
	Cloudside Junior School, Saniacre EWS Rail Safety Competition Winners 2001
	Little Eaton Primary School Little Eaton EWS Railsafe Trophy Winners 2002
	Stanley Common C of E Primary School Ilkeston EWS Rail Safety Competition Winners 2003
	Bispham Drive Junior School, Toton EWS Rail Safety Competition Winners 2004
60081	Bleaklow Hill
	ISAMBARD KINGDOM BRUNEL
60082	Mam Tor
	Hillhead '93
	Mam Tor
60083	Shining Tor
	Mountsorrel
60084	Cross Fell
60085	Axe Edge
	MINI Pride of Oxford
60086	Schiehallion
60087	Slioch
	Barry Needham
	CLIC Sargent www.clicsargent.co.uk
60088	Buachaille Etive More
	Buachaille Etive Mor
60089	Arcuil
	THE RAILWAY HORSE
60090	Quinag
60091	An Teallach
	Barry Needham
60092	Reginald Munns
60093	Jack Stirk
	Adrian Harrington 1955–2003 Royal Navy/ Burges Salmon
60094	Tryfan
	Rugby Flyer
60095	Crib Goch
60096	Ben Macdui
60097	Pillar
	ABP Port of Grimsby & Immingham
60098	Charles Francis Brush
60099	Ben More Assynt
60100	Boar of Badenoch
	Pride of Acton
60500	RAIL Magazine
66002	Lafarge Buddon Wood
	Lafarge Quorn
66022	Lafarge Charnwood
66035	Resourceful
66042	Lafarge Buddon Wood
66048	James the Engine
66050	EWS Energy
66055	Alain Thauvette
66058	Derek Clark
66066	Geoff Spencer
66077	Benjamin Gimbert G.C.
66079	James Nightall G.C.
66152	Derek Holmes Railway Operator
66172	PAUL MELLENEY
66185	DP WORLD London Gateway
66200	RAILWAY HERITAGE COMMITTEE
66250	In Memory of Robert K Romak
66301	Kingmoor TMD
66411	Eddie the Engine
66414	James the Engine
66418	PATRIOT IN MEMORY OF FALLEN RAILWAY EMPLOYEES
66501	Japan 2001
66502	Basford Hall Centenary 2001
66503	The RAILWAY MAGAZINE
66506	Crewe Regeneration

66526	Driver Steve Dunn (George)
66527	Don Raider
66528	Madge Elliot MBE Borders Railway Opening 2015
66532	P&O Nedlloyd Atlas
66533	Hanjin Express / Senator Express
66534	OOCL Express
66540	Ruby
66552	Maltby Raider
66576	Hamburg Sud Advantage
66581	Sophie
66585	The Drax Flyer
66592	Johnson Stevens Agencies
66593	3MG MERSEY MULTIMODAL GATEWAY
66594	NYK Spirit of Kyoto
66597	Viridor
66601	The Hope Valley
66612	Forth Raider
66614	1916 POPPY 2016
66618	Railways Illustrated Annual Photographic Awards Ian Lothian
	Railways Illustrated Annual Photographic Awards David Gorton
	Railways Illustrated Annual Photographic Awards Alan Barnes
66619	Derek W. Johnson MBE
66623	Bill Bolsover
66701	Railtrack National Logistics
	Whitemoor
66702	Blue Lightning
66703	Doncaster PSB 1981–2002
66704	Colchester Power Signalbox
66705	Golden Jubilee
66706	Nene Valley
66707	Sir Sam Fay GREAT CENTRAL RAILWAY
66708	Jayne
66709	Joseph Arnold Davies
	Sorrento
66710	Phil Packer BRIT
66711	Sence
66712	Peterborough Power Signalbox
66713	Forest City
66714	Cromer Lifeboat
66715	VALOUR IN MEMORY OF ALL RAILWAY EMPLOYEES WHO GAVE THEIR LIVES FOR THEIR COUNTRY
66716	Willesden Traincare Centre
	LOCOMOTIVE & CARRIAGE INSTITUTION CENTENARY 1911–2011
66717	Good Old Boy
66718	Gwyneth Dunwoody
	Sir Peter Hendy CBE
66719	METRO-LAND
66720	Metronet Pathfinder
66721	Harry Beck
66722	Sir Edwards Watkin
66723	Chinook
66724	Drax Power Station
66725	SUNDERLAND
66726	SHEFFIELD WEDNESDAY
66727	Andrew Scott CBE
	Maritime One
66728	Institution of Railway Operators
66729	DERBY COUNTY
66730	Whitemoor
66731	interhubGB
66732	GBRf The First Decade 1999–2009 John Smith – MD
66733	Cambridge PSB
66734	The Eco Express
66736	WOLVERHAMPTON WANDERERS
66737	Lesia
66738	HUDDERSFIELD TOWN
66739	Bluebell Railwa
66740	Sarah
66741	Swanage Railway

66742	ABP Port of Immingham Centenary 1912–2012
66744	Crossrail
66745	Modern Railways The first 50 Years
66748	West Burton 50
66750	Bristol Panel Signal Box
66751	Inspirational Delivered Hitachi Rail Europe
66752	The Hoosier State
66753	EMD Roberts Road
66754	Northampton Saints
66756	Royal Corps of Signals
66757	West Somerset Railway
66759	Chippy
66760	David Gordon Harris
66761	Wensleydale Railway Association 25 Years 1990 – 2015
66763	Severn Valley Railway
66775	HMS Argyll
66776	Joanne
66777	Annette
66778	Darius Cheskin
66779	EVENING STAR
66789	British Rail 1948–1997
66849	Wylam Dilly
66850	David Maidment OBE www.railwaychildren.org.uk
66957	Stephenson Locomotive Society 1909–2009
67001	Night Mail
67002	Special Delivery
67004	Post Haste
	Cairn Gorm
67005	Queen's Messenger
67006	Royal Sovereign
67010	Unicorn
67012	A Shropshire Lad
67013	Dyfrbont Pontcysyllte
67014	Thomas Telford
67015	David J. Lloyd
67017	Arrow
67018	Rapid
	Keith Heller
67023	Stella
67025	Western Star
67026	Diamond Jubilee
67027	Rising Star
	Charlotte
67029	Royal Diamond
68001	Evolution
68002	Intrepid
68003	Astute
68004	Rapid
68005	Defiant
68006	Daring
68007	Valiant
68008	Avenger
68009	Titan
68010	Oxford Flyer
68016	Fearless
68017	Hornet
68018	Vigilant
68019	Brutus
68020	Reliance
68021	Tireless
68022	Resolution
68023	Achilles
68024	Centaur
68025	Superb
70001	PowerHaul
70004	The Coal Industry Society
73003	Sir Herbert Walker
73004	The Bluebell Railway
73005	Mid-Hants WATERCRESS LINE
73100	Brighton Evening Argus
73101	Brighton Evening Argus
	The Royal Alex'

73102	Airtour Suisse		86101	Sir William A Stanier FRS
73105	Quadrant		86102	Robert A Riddles
73107	Redhill 1844–1944		86103	André Chapelon
	SPITFIRE		86204	City of Carlisle
	Redhill 1844–1944		86205	City of Lancaster
	Tracy		86206	City of Stoke on Trent
73109	Battle of Britain 50th Anniversary		86207	City of Lichfield
	Force 'O' Weymouth		86208	City of Chester
	Battle of Britain 50th Anniversary		86209	City of Coventry
73112	University of Kent at Canterbury		86210	City of Edinburgh
73114	County of West Sussex			C.I.T. 75th Anniversary
73114	Stewarts Lane Traction Maintenance Depot		86211	City of Milton Keynes
73116	Selhurst		86212	Preston Guild
73117	University of Surrey			Preston Guild 1328–1992
73118	The Romney, Hythe and Dymchurch Railway		86213	Lancashire Witch
73119	Kentish Mercury Borough of Eastleigh		86214	Sans Pareil
73121	Croydon 1883–1983		86215	Joseph Chamberlain
73122	County of East Sussex			Norwich Cathedral
73123	Gatwick Express			Norwich and Norfolk Festival
73124	London Chamber of Commerce			The Round Tabler
73125	Stewarts Lane 1860–1985		86216	Meteor
73126	Kent & East Sussex Railway		86217	Comet
73128	O.V.S. BULLEID C.B.E.			Halley's Comet
73129	City of Winchester			City University
73130	City of Portsmouth		86218	Planet
73131	County of Surrey			Harold MacMillan
73133	The Bluebell Railway			YEAR OF OPERA & MUSICAL THEATRE 1997
73134	Woking Homes 1885–1985			NHS 50
73136	Kent Youth Music		86219	Phoenix
	Perseverance		86220	Goliath
	Mhairi			The Round Tabler
73137	Royal Observer Corps		86221	Vesta
73138	Post Haste 150 YEARS OF TRAVELLING POST OFFICES			BBC Look East
73141	David Gay / Ron Westwood		86222	Fury
	Charlotte			LLOYD'S LIST 250th ANNIVERSARY
73201	Broadlands			Clothes Show Live
73202	Royal Observer Corps		86223	Hector
	Dave Berry			Norwich Union
	Graham Stenning		86224	Caledonian
73204	Stewarts Lane 1860–1985		86225	Hardwicke
	Janice		86226	Mail
73205	London Chamber of Commerce			Royal Mail Midlands
	Jeanette			CHARLES RENNIE MACKINTOSH
73206	Gatwick Express		86227	Sir Henry Johnson
	Lisa			Golden Jubilee
73207	County of East Sussex		86228	Vulcan Heritage
73208	Croydon 1883–1983		86229	Sir John Betjeman
	Kirsten			Lions Clubs International
73209	Alison		86230	The Duke of Wellington
73210	Selhurst		86231	Starlight Express
73211	County of West Sussex		86232	Harold MacMillan
73212	Airtour Suisse			Norwich FestivalNorfolk and Norwich Festival
	Fiona		86233	Laurence Olivier
73213	University of Kent at Canterbury			ALSTOM Heritage
	Rhodalyn		86234	J B Priestley O.M.
73951	Malcolm Brinded			Suffolk Relax.Refresh.Return
73952	Janis Kong		86235	Novelty
73961	Alison			Harold MacMillan
73962	Dick Mabbutt			Crown Point
73963	Janice		86236	Josiah Wedgewood MASTER POTTER 1736–1795
73964	Jeanette		86237	Sir Charles Hallé
76038	STENTOR			University of East Anglia
76039	HECTOR		86238	European Community
76046	ARCHIMEDES		86239	L S Lowry
76047	DIOMEDES		86240	Bishop Eric Treacy
76049	JASON		86241	Glenfiddich
76051	MENTOR		86242	James Kennedy G.C.
76052	NESTOR			Colchester Castle
76053	PERSEUS		86243	The Boys' Brigade
76054	PLUTO		86244	The Royal British Legion
76055	PROMETHEUS		86245	Dudley Castle
76056	TRITON			Caledonian
76057	ULYSSES		86246	Royal Anglian Regiment

86247	Abraham Darby
86248	Sir Clwyd County of Clwyd
86249	County of Merseyside
86250	The Glasgow Herald
	Sheppard 100
86251	The Birmingham Post
86252	The Liverpool Daily Post
	Sheppard 100
86253	The Manchester Guardian
86254	William Webb Ellis
86255	Penrith Beacon
86256	Pebble Mill
86257	Snowdon
86258	Talyllyn The First Preserved Railway
	Talyllyn 50 Years of Railway Preservation 1951–2001
86259	Peter Pan
	GM! Greater MANCHESTER THE LIFE & SOUL OF BRITAIN
	Les Ross
86260	Driver Wallace Oakes G.C.
86261	Driver John Axon G.C.
	THE RAIL CHARTER PARTNERSHIP
86311	Airey Neave
86312	Elizabeth Garrett Anderson
86315	Rotary International
86316	Wigan Pier
86328	Aldaniti
86401	Northampton Town
	Hertfordshire Railtours
	Northampton Town
	Mons Meg
86405	Intercontainer
86407	The Institution of Electrical Engineers
86408	St. John Ambulance
86411	Airey Neave
86412	Elizabeth Garrett Anderson
86413	County of Lancashire
86414	Frank Hornby
86415	Rotary International
86416	Wigan Pier
86417	The Kingsman
86419	Post Haste 150 YEARS OF TRAVELLING POST OFFICES
86421	London School of Economics
86425	Saint Mungo
86426	Pride of the Nation
86427	The Industrial Society
86428	Aldaniti
86429	The Times
86430	Scottish National Orchestra
	Saint Edmund
86432	Brookside
86433	Wulfruna
86434	University of London
86501 (2)	Talyllyn The First Preserved Railway
	Crewe Basford Hall
86502	LLOYD'S LIST 250TH ANNIVERSARY
86503	City of Lancaster
86504	Halley's Comet
86505	Royal Anglian Regiment
86506	Laurence Olivier
86507	L S Lowry
86508	Glenfiddich
86605	Intercontainer
86607	The Institution of Electrical Engineers
86608	St. John Ambulance
86611	Airey Neave
86612	Elizabeth Garrett Anderson
86613	County of Lancashire
86614	Frank Hornby
86615	Rotary International
86620	Philip G Walton
86621	London School of Economics
86627	The Industrial Society

86628	Aldaniti
86632	Brookside
86633	Wulfruna
86634	University of London
86701	Orion
86702	Cassiopeia
86901	CHIEF ENGINEER
86902	RAIL VEHICLE ENGINEERING
87001	STEPHENSON
	Royal Scot
	STEPHENSON
87002	Royal Sovereign
	The AC Locomotive Group
	Royal Sovereign
87003	Patriot
87004	Britannia
87005	City of London
87006	City of Glasgow
	Glasgow Garden Festival
	City of Glasgow
	George Reynolds
87007	City of Manchester
87008	City of Liverpool
	Royal Scot
87009	City of Birmingham
87010	King Arthur
	Driver Tommy Farr
87011	The Black Prince
	City of Wolverhampton
87012	Coeur de Lion
	The Royal Bank of Scotland
	Coeur de Lion
	The Olympian
87013	John O' Gaunt
87014	Knight of the Thistle
87015	Howard of Effingham
87016	Sir Francis Drake
	Willesden Intercity Depot
87017	Iron Duke
87018	Lord Nelson
87019	Sir Winston Churchill
	ACoRP Association of Community Rail Partnerships
87020	North Briton
87021	Robert the Bruce
87022	Cock o' the North
	Lew Adams The Black Prince
	Cock o' the North
87023	Highland Chieftain
	Velocity
	Polmadie
	Velocity
87024	Lord of the Isles
87025	Borderer
	County of Cheshire
87026	Redgauntlet
	Sir Richard Arkwright
87027	Wolf of Badenoch
87028	Lord President
87029	Earl Marischal
87030	Black Douglas
87031	Hal o' the Wynd
	Keith Harper
87032	Kenilworth
	Richard Fearn
87033	Thane of Fife
87034	William Shakespeare
87035	Robert Burns
87101	STEPHENSON
88001	Revolution
88002	Prometheus
88003	Genesis
88004	Pandora
88005	Minerva

88006	Juno
88007	Electra
88008	Ariadne
88009	Diana
88010	Aurora
89001	Avocet
90001	BBC Midlands Today
	Crown Point
90002	The Girls' Brigade
	Mission: Impossible
	Eastern Daily Press 1870–2010 SERVING NORFOLK FOR 140 YEARS
90003	THE HERALD
	Rædwald of East Anglia
90004	The D'Oyly Carte Opera Company
	City of Glasgow
	Eastern Daily Press 1870–2010 SERVING NORFOLK FOR 140 YEARS
	City of Chelmsford
90005	Financial Times
	Vice-Admiral Lord Nelson
90006	High Sheriff
	Modern Railways Magazine / Roger Ford
90007	Lord Stamp
	Keith Harper
	Sir John Betjeman
90008	The Birmingham Royal Ballet
	The East Anglian
90009	Royal Show
	The Economist
	Diamond Jubilee
90010	275 Railway Squadron (Volunteers)
	BRESSINGHAM STEAM & GARDENS
90011	The Chartered Institute of Transport
	West Coast Rail 250
	Let's Go East of England
	East Anglian Daily Times Suffolk & Proud
90012	Glasgow 1990 Cultural Capital of Europe
	British Transport Police
	Royal Anglian Regiment
90013	The Law Society
	The Evening Star PRIDE OF IPSWICH 1885–2010 125 YEARS OF SERVING SUFFOLK
90014	'The Liverpool Phil'
	The Big Dish
	Driver Tom Clark O.B.E.
	Norfolk and Norwich Festival
90015	BBC North West
	The International Brigades SPAIN 1936–1939
	Colchester Castle
90017	Rail express systems Quality Assured
90018	The Pride of Bellshill
90019	Penny Black
	Multimodal
90020	Colonel Bill Cockburn CBE TD
	Sir Michael Heron
	Collingwood
90022	Freightconnection
90026	Crewe International Electric Maintenance Depot
90027	Allerton T&RS Depot Quality Approved
90028	Vrachtverbinding
	Hertfordshire Rail Tours
90029	Frachtverbindungen
	The Institution of Civil Engineers
90030	Fretconnection
	Crewe Locomotive Works
90031	Intercontainer
	The Railway Children Partnership Working For Street Children Worldwide
90032	Cerestar
90035	Crewe Basford Hall
90036	Driver Jack Mills
90037	Spirit of Dagenham

90040	The Railway Mission
90043	Freightliner Coatbridge
90126	Crewe International Electric Maintenance Depot
90127	Allerton T&RS Depot Quality Approved
90128	Vrachtverbinding
90129	Fratchverbindungen
90130	Fretconnection
90131	Intercontainer
90132	Cerestar
90135	Crewe Basford Hall
90143	Freightliner Coatbridge
90222	Freightconnection
90227	Allerton T&RS Depot Quality Approved
91001	Swallow
91002	Durham Cathedral
91003	THE SCOTSMAN
91004	The Red Arrows
	Grantham
91005	Royal Air Force Regiment
91007	Ian Allan
	SKYFALL
91008	Thomas Cook
91009	Saint Nicholas
	The Samaritans
91010	Northern Rock
91011	Terence Cuneo
91012	County of Cambridgeshire
91013	Michael Faraday
	County of North Yorkshire
91014	Northern Electric
	St. Mungo Cathedral
91015	Holyrood
91017	Commonwealth Institute
	City of Leeds
91018	Robert Louis Stevenson
	Bradford Film Festival
91019	Scottish Enterprise
	County of Tyne & Wear
91021	Royal Armouries
	Archbishop Thomas Cranmer
91022	Robert Adley
	Double Trigger
91024	Reverend W Awdry
91025	BBC Radio One FM
91026	Voice of the North
	York Minster
91027	Great North Run
91028	Guide Dog
91029	Queen Elizabeth II
91030	Palace of Holyroodhouse
91031	Sir Henry Royce
	County of Northumberland
91101	City of London
	FLYING SCOTSMAN
91102	Durham Cathedral
	City of York
91103	County of Lincolnshire
91104	Grantham
91105	County Durham
91106	East Lothian
91107	Newark on Trent
	SKYFALL
91108	City of Leeds
91109	The Samaritans
	Sir Bobby Robson
91110	David Livingstone
	BATTLE OF BRITAIN MEMORIAL FLIGHT
91111	Terence Cuneo
	For the Fallen
91112	County of Cambridgeshire
91113	County of North Yorkshire
91114	St. Mungo Cathedral
	Durham Cathedral